NORTH ATLANTIC COAST FISHERIES

PROCEEDINGS

IN THE

North Atlantic Coast Fisheries Arbitration

BEFORE

THE PERMANENT COURT OF ARBITRATION AT THE HAGUE

UNDER THE PROVISIONS OF THE GENERAL TREATY OF
ARBITRATION OF APRIL 4, 1908, AND THE SPECIAL
AGREEMENT OF JANUARY 27, 1909, BETWEEN
THE UNITED STATES OF AMERICA
AND GREAT BRITAIN

(IN TWELVE VOLUMES)

VOLUME I

WASHINGTON
GOVERNMENT PRINTING OFFICE
1912

[PUBLIC RESOLUTION—No. 58.]

[S. J. Res. 139.]

Joint Resolution Authorizing the printing of the message of the President, together with the report of the agent of the United States in the North Atlantic Coast Fisheries Arbitration at The Hague.

Resolved by the Senate and House of Representatives of the United States of America in Congress assembled, That the President's message of February first, nineteen hundred and eleven, together with the report of the agent of the United States in the North Atlantic Coast Fisheries Arbitration at The Hague, transmitted therewith, and the appendices to the report, be printed as a public document, together with an additional five hundred copies for the Department of State, the cost thereof to be defrayed out of the appropriation for printing and binding for Congress.

Approved, February 23, 1911.

II

CONTENTS OF PROCEEDINGS.

250426

NORTH ATLANTIC COAST FISHERIES

FINAL REPORT

OF

HON. CHANDLER P. ANDERSON,

AGENT OF THE UNITED STATES

CONTENTS.*

* This volume contains also the Case of the United States.

LETTER OF TRANSMITTAL.

To the Senate and the House of Representatives:

I transmit a communication from the Secretary of State submitting a report made by Chandler P. Anderson, Esq., the agent of the United States in the North Atlantic Coast Fisheries Arbitration before the Permanent Court at The Hague, and invite the attention of Congress to the request made by the Secretary of State that Congress may authorize the printing of the report and appendices at the cost of the appropriation for printing and binding for Congress.

WM. H. TAFT.

THE WHITE HOUSE,
Washington, February 2, 1911.

LETTER OF SUBMITTAL.

The PRESIDENT:

The undersigned, the Secretary of State, has the honor to submit, with a view to its transmission to Congress should you approve, the report of Chandler P. Anderson, Esq., the agent of the United States in the North Atlantic Coast Fisheries Arbitration before the Permanent Court at The Hague.

The agent has also filed in the department, as appendices to his report, copies of the cases and countercases and printed arguments of the United States and of Great Britain, and the printed record of the oral arguments and proceedings before the tribunal, and other documents pertaining to the arbitration. It is desirable that these documents should be printed; but this has not been undertaken by the department, because it would involve a larger expenditure than the department's allotment for printing permits. In this connection it should be stated that many communications have been received requesting copies of these documents, the interest manifested no doubt being due to the great amount of historical, diplomatic, and legal information which they contain. For this reason and because of the general public interest in a publication containing the complete record of a case of such great international importance, I express the hope that Congress, following its uniform practice in respect to printing in full the proceedings of international arbitrations, may see fit to authorize the printing of the report and appendices, the cost to be defrayed out of the appropriation for printing and binding for Congress.

Respectfully submitted.

P. C. KNOX.

DEPARTMENT OF STATE,
Washington, January 31, 1911.

LIST OF DOCUMENTS.

Final Report of Honorable Chandler P. Anderson, Agent of the United States.
Protocols of the arbitration.
United States Case and Appendix.
British Case and Appendix.
United States Counter Case and Appendix.
British Counter Case and Appendix.
United States Printed Argument.
British Printed Argument.
Oral Arguments before the Permanent Court.
Appendix to the Oral Arguments.

FINAL REPORT OF THE AGENT OF THE UNITED STATES.

WASHINGTON, *November 14, 1910.*

The undersigned, agent of the United States in the North Atlantic Coast Fisheries Arbitration recently held at The Hague, has the honor to submit his report as follows:

The general arbitration treaty of April 4, 1908, between the United States and Great Britain requires that in each case submitted to arbitration thereunder the parties shall conclude a special agreement defining clearly the matter in dispute, the scope and power of the arbitrators, and the periods to be fixed for the formation of the arbitration tribunal and the several stages of procedure.

In this case, such a special agreement was signed on the 27th day of January, 1909, confirmed by the Senate on the 18th of February following, and formally ratified by both Governments on the 4th of March, 1909. In compliance with the requirements of the general treaty of arbitration, the special agreement sets out, first, a series of seven questions to be answered by the tribunal relating to the interpretation of the true intent and meaning of Article I of the treaty of October 20, 1818, between the United States and Great Britain; and it provides that the tribunal of arbitration shall be chosen in accordance with the provisions of Article XLV of The Hague Convention of October 18, 1907, for the pacific settlement of international disputes; and provides further that when not inconsistent with any particular provision of the special agreement, the provisions of that convention shall govern the proceedings in the case. The special agreement also contains a series of provisions covering the presentation of the case and the procedure before the tribunal.

The article of The Hague Convention, in accordance with which the members of the tribunal were required to be chosen, provides that the tribunal shall be composed of five members selected from the list of the members of the Permanent Court at The Hague, and that their selection shall be made by direct agreement of the parties if possible, and in case of failure to agree other methods of selection are provided for. In this case, a direct agreement was reached, and the members of the tribunal selected were as follows:

Dr. H. Lammasch, doctor of law, professor of the University of Vienna, Aulic Councilor, Member of the Upper House of the Austrian Parliament;

His Excellency, Jonkheer A. F. de Savornin Lohman, doctor of law, Minister of State, former Minister of the Interior, member of the Second Chamber of the Netherlands;

The Hon. George Gray, judge of the United States Circuit Court of Appeals;

The Right Hon. Sir Charles Fitzpatrick, doctor of law, Chief Justice of Canada;

Mr. Luis Maria Drago, doctor of law, former Minister of Foreign Affairs of the Argentine Republic.

The names of the agents and of the counsel appearing before the tribunal on each side are set forth in the protocol of its first meeting, a copy of which is hereto annexed.

Pursuant to the provisions of the special agreement, the printed case of each Government, together with copies of the evidence upon which it relied, was served upon the other within the period of seven months after the exchange of ratifications confirming the agreement, such service being made on the 4th day of October, 1909, the last day of such period; and on each side a countercase in answer to the case was served upon the other side on the 21st day of February last, to which date the period for the service of such countercase was extended by mutual consent. So also a printed argument on each side was delivered to the other on the 16th day of May last, in accordance with an arrangement agreed upon for the mutual convenience of both parties, which slightly modified the terms of the special agreement in that respect. Copies of these cases, countercases and arguments were also delivered to the members of the tribunal in accordance with the requirements of the special agreement.

The determination of the true intent and meaning of Article I of the treaty of 1818 with reference to the questions submitted for the decision of the tribunal, required an examination not only of the language of the treaty, but also of the events leading up to its negotiation and signature and of the actions taken by either Government since the date of the treaty having a bearing upon its interpretation. The evidence presented in support of the contentions of the United States upon these questions, therefore, covered the entire period from the date of the special agreement submitting these questions to arbitration back to the treaty of peace of 1783, at the close of the Revolution, and some features of the controversy necessitated the introduction of a considerable amount of evidence even prior to that date.

The case of the United States, which was prepared by the agent, presented the contentions of the United States in the form of a brief on the facts, reviewing chronologically the course of events leading up to the treaty of 1818 and the subsequent governmental actions on each side having a bearing upon its interpretation, and was based upon documentary evidence presented in the appendix to the case of the United States, which comprised upwards of 1,300 printed pages and included all the pertinent and material diplomatic correspondence between the United States and Great Britain, and the correspondence between Great Britain and her colonies and her diplomatic representatives, in so far as it was available to the United States; also all legislative and executive acts on the part of the United States and of Great Britain and the British colonies, bearing upon the questions submitted, together with the available records of the negotiations leading up to the treaties of 1783, 1814, 1818, 1854, 1871 and the unratified treaty of 1888, and the *modus vivendi* entered into in 1885, in 1888, in 1906, in 1907 and in 1908 between Great Britain and the United States.

The countercase of the United States, which also was prepared by the agent, presented in the form of a brief on the facts the evidence on the part of the United States in support of its contentions in reply to the evidence presented in the British case, dealing separately with each of the seven questions submitted for decision, the documentary evidence relied upon being printed in an accompanying appendix covering about 700 printed pages.

The documentary evidence presented in the British case and countercase was similar in character to that presented on the part of the United States, and to a considerable extent identical with it, and about equally voluminous. The method of dealing with such evidence, however, in the British case and countercase was somewhat different from that followed in the case and countercase of the United States, a large part of the British pleadings being devoted to argument on the law and citations of authorities and precedents, in distinction from the mere argumentative presentation of the facts and evidence relied upon, which was the course adopted in the case and countercase of the United States.

The Hon. Robert Lansing acted as solicitor for the agency, and rendered valuable assistance to the agent throughout the period devoted to the preparation of the case and countercase, in connection with the preparation of the appendices of the case and countercase containing the documentary evidence relied on by the United States. Upon the completion of that work, Mr. Lansing was designated as one of the associate counsel for the United States in the arbitration proceedings.

The Hon. James Brown Scott, then Solicitor for the Department of State and one of the associate counsel for the United States in this case, compiled for the use of the agent and counsel a very complete and useful collection of extracts from the writings of all the leading authorities on international law dealing with the doctrine of international servitudes. A similar compilation of extracts from the leading international law publicists dealing with the subject of coastal waters was prepared by Edwin M. Borchardt, Esq., of the Library of

Congress, who was attached to the staff of the agency as international law expert. These compilations proved of great service in connection with the preparation both of the printed and of the oral arguments on the part of the United States.

The date originally fixed by the special agreement for the meeting of the tribunal having been found inconvenient on account of the extension of time agreed upon for the service of the countercases, it was subsequently agreed by the two Governments that it should be postponed until the 1st day of June, 1910, and on that date the first ment was taken by the tribunal from June 1st to June 6th, when the oral argument was commenced.

The protocols of the proceedings of the tribunal are hereto annexed as a part of this report, and from them it will appear that an adjournment was taken by the tribunal from June 1 to June 6, when the oral argument was commenced.

By agreement between the agents and senior counsel on both sides it was arranged that Great Britain should have the opening argument and the United States the closing argument, and that counsel on each side should speak alternately. Accordingly, Sir Robert Finlay opened for Great Britain and the Hon. George Turner opened for the United States, followed by Sir James Winter for Great Britain, Charles B. Warren, Esq., for the United States, Hon. John S. Ewart for Great Britain, Hon. Samuel J. Elder for the United States, Sir William Robson closing for Great Britain, and the Hon. Elihu Root making the closing argument for the United States.

Forty sessions in all were consumed in the oral argument, which ended on August 12, 1910, four days in each week having been devoted to such sessions, the daily sittings of the tribunal continuing for about four or four and one-half hours, the intervening time being required for the preparation of the arguments and for the other business involved in carrying through proceedings of such an extensive and voluminous character. By agreement of the parties the meetings of the tribunal were open to the public.

On the close of the oral argument the case was taken under consideration by the tribunal, and on Wednesday, September 7, 1910, the award of the tribunal was announced.

Before proceeding to a consideration of the provisions and effect of the award, it is desirable that the situation existing before resort was had to arbitration should be briefly reviewed.

Throughout the entire history of this controversy, which extends back almost to the time when the treaty of 1818 was entered into, there has been a wide divergence of view between the United States and Great Britain as to the meaning and effect of Article I of that treaty. With the exception of the first 20 years after the treaty was entered into there has hardly been a time throughout the entire existence of this treaty when the United States and Great Britain have not had under consideration some question arising out of their different views as to the meaning of its provisions, and these questions have involved not only the extent of the rights and obligations of American fishermen in the Canadian and Newfoundland waters affected by the treaty, but also the extent of the treaty waters themselves.

In all of these discussions the interpretation insisted upon by the colonial authorities has been such as to exclude the American fishermen from the enjoyment of the treaty liberties claimed for them by the United States, or to so limit and restrict such liberties as to render them worthless; and the admitted purpose of the colonial authorities throughout the controversy has been to compel the United States to grant trade concessions as the price of the uninterrupted enjoyment of privileges claimed by the United States as a matter of right under the treaty.

The reciprocal agreements entered into by the two Governments in 1854 and 1871, in which the fishery privileges of the treaty of 1818 were merged and more extensive fishery privileges were secured in exchange for trade concessions, proved unsatisfactory to the United States and were short lived.

The experience afforded by these treaties and by other unsuccessful attempts to dispose of this controversy by similar means, long since demonstrated to the satisfaction of both Governments that a permanent settlement of this dispute by such means was a practical impossibility.

The proposed Blaine-Bond treaty of 1892, adjusting the differences between the United States and Newfoundland, failed of ratification on account of opposition on the part of Canada, and the Hay-Bond treaty, negotiated in 1902, by which an adjustment with Newfoundland was again attempted, also failed of ratification.

During the period between the Blaine-Bond treaty and the rejection of the Hay-Bond treaty Newfoundland refrained from any attempts to enforce any objectionable local regulations against American fishermen exercising their treaty rights in Newfoundland waters. The friendly attitude of the Newfoundland Government during that period was publicly admitted by governmental authorities to be due to the fact that the United States having demonstrated its willingness to adjust the matters in dispute with Newfoundland by entering into the Blaine-Bond treaty, the American fishermen were entitled to the treatment which they would have received under that treaty if its ratification had not been defeated by the opposition of Canada.

In 1905, however, upon the failure of the United States to ratify the Hay-Bond treaty, the Newfoundland Government completely reversed its former attitude toward the American fishing interests and proceeded, as shown by the case of the United States in this arbitration, by legislative and executive action to terminate all commercial privileges, which for many years prior to that time had been extended to American fishing vessels both on the treaty coasts and on the other coasts of Newfoundland. This new policy of the Newfoundland Government, as was frankly admitted by leading officials of that Government, was intended to force the Government of the United States to open the American markets to Newfoundland fish and fishery products free of duty, in exchange for more extensive fishing and commercial privileges on the Newfoundland coasts.

Such, briefly, was the situation when Mr. Root became Secretary of State in 1905, and, as it soon became evident that the Newfoundland Government in carrying out its new policy would undertake to impose upon American fishermen in the exercise of their treaty liberties certain limitations and restraints which were regarded by the United States as in conflict with such liberties, the Secretary of State at once proceeded to take up with Great Britain the question of defining the rights of American fishermen under the treaty of 1818 and restraining the colonial governments from interfering with such rights.

In the diplomatic correspondence which ensued, the views of both Governments on these questions were fully and ably presented. It appeared, however, as stated by the British secretary of state for foreign affairs in his note of August 14, 1906, " that the wide divergence of view between the two Governments, which is disclosed by the correspondence, makes it hopeless to expect an immediate settlement of the various questions at issue." A *modus vivendi* for that year accordingly was entered into, but upon a renewal of the discussion the following year it became evident, on account of the conflict of views between the two Governments, that it would be impossible to find a basis for an agreement for the permanent adjustment of the question in dispute. It was accordingly recognized on both sides that recourse must be had to arbitration, and after the general arbitration treaty of April 4, 1908, was entered into, negotiations were undertaken for the arbitration of the questions at issue in this controversy with the result that the special agreement of January 27, 1909, was concluded, submitting seven questions to arbitration.

These questions covered all the unsettled matter of difference growing out of the fisheries provisions of the treaty of 1818, many of which had been under discussion almost continuously for more than half a century.

On one of the issues under discussion, which was ultimately presented as the first question submitted for decision, several points of agreement had been reached by the parties in the negotiations which led up to the special agreement under which the arbitration was held. This question related to the enforcement by Great Britain or her colonies of fisheries regulations against American fishermen exercising their treaty right of fishing in British territorial waters. Great Britain had originally contended that under the language of the treaty, which secured to American fishermen a "liberty in common with British fishermen to take fish," American fishermen were subject, when fishing under the treaty in British waters, to all fishing regulations and restrictions imposed by British law upon British fishermen. In formulating this question for submission to arbitration, however, the United States succeeded in securing from Great Britain a modification of this position, and it was admitted by Great Britain in presenting its contention in this question that no fishing regulations could be enforced against American fishermen in British waters under the treaty, unless they were appropriate and necessary for the protection and preservation of the fisheries, and reasonable in themselves, and not so framed as to give the local fishermen an unfair advantage over the American fishermen. To this extent the contentions of the two parties coincided. Great Britain further contended, however, that the United States was not entitled to be consulted with regard to the enforcement of any such regulations, and that Great Britain alone must be the sole judge as to their appropriateness, necessity, reasonableness and fairness; and this was the issue between the two Governments presented in the first question.

As a result of this arbitration, therefore, British regulations limiting the time, manner and implements of fishing can no longer be enforced against American fishermen exercising their fishing liberties on the treaty coasts, unless such regulations are reasonable, appropriate, necessary and fair, as defined in question 1. In the award on this question it was further decided that, in case the United States raises the question of the reasonableness, etc., of any regulation hereafter adopted, Great Britain can not be the judge of that question, which now must be decided by a special commission of experts constituting an impartial tribunal according to a mode of procedure established by the award, the enforcement of any such regulations being suspended pending the decision of such special commission. Furthermore, a series of legislative provisions of Newfoundland and Canada which the United States had objected to as unreasonable and under Article II of the special agreement had called to the attention of the tribunal, on the ground that they were inconsistent with the true interpretation of the treaty of 1818, were referred, at the request of the United States, in accordance with Article III of the special agreement, to a commission of experts for examination and report as to their reasonableness, appropriateness, necessity and fairness. This commission has not yet reported on the questions so referred to it.

It is evident, therefore, that as a result of the award no regulations limiting the time, manner and implements of fishing can hereafter be imposed upon American fishermen exercising their treaty liberties in Newfoundland and Canadian waters if any objection has been raised to them by the United States, unless their reasonableness, necessity and fairness has been approved by an impartial commission or tribunal.

The result thus obtained is one which the United States Government would have been willing to agree to at any time during the history of this controversy. Secretaries of State Marcy, Fish, Evarts, and Root have each in turn specifically stated that the United States was willing that the American fishermen on the treaty coasts should be subjected to just and reasonable regulations, but they all insisted that Great Britain and her colonies could not be permitted to be the sole judge of the justness and reasonableness of such regulations.

The only feature of the contention of the United States on question 1 which was not sustained by the tribunal was the extreme position taken in the argument of counsel that the treaty established an international servitude in favor of the United States, exempting American fishermen absolutely from obedience to British fishing regulations. This contention was based upon a principle of international law, supported by the great majority of international publicists, but which was regarded by the tribunal as antiquated and not suited to modern conditions, although the treaty under consideration was equally antiquated, having been entered into in the early part of the last century. Nevertheless, the decision in practical effect secures the same measure of protection against unfair and arbitrary regulation of the fisheries which this contention of the United States was designed to secure, and the strength of the contention of the United States on this point unquestionably had a very effective influence in obtaining for the United States the large measure of advantage which is secured to its fishermen by the award.

An alternative line of argument which was relied on by the United States, and which finally prevailed, was that under the obligations imposed by the treaty and by the interpretation of it adopted by both parties in their subsequent governmental actions and particularly by the limitations accepted under the special agreement submitting the question to arbitration, the exercise of British sovereignty had been limited with respect to the matters under consideration even if British sovereignty itself was not limited; and the award has sustained this contention of the United States.

Although British sovereign rights over the fisheries in British waters are affirmed in the decision, nevertheless the exercise of such rights is effectively limited by the award to the extent above indicated.

On question 2 the tribunal has decided in favor of the contention of the United States that the inhabitants of the United States while exercising their treaty liberties of fishing have a right to employ as members of the fishing crews of their vessels persons not inhabitants of the United States, thus overruling the British contention that the liberty of fishing, which the treaty secures " to inhabitants of the United States," gave them only the right to exercise themselves the manual act of taking fish and did not permit them to employ persons who were not inhabitants of the United States to assist them in exercising that right. It is pointed out in the award, however, that the persons so employed derive no benefit or immunity from the treaty in their own right.

The third and fourth questions deal with the contentions always maintained by Great Britain that American fishermen exercising their fishing liberties on the treaty coasts and the special privileges reserved to them on the nontreaty coasts, might be subjected to the same customhouse regulations which were imposed upon vessels enjoying trading privileges on those coasts, and also to the payment of light and harbor dues and other exactions of a similar character, although the local fishermen were exempt from such requirements.

The United States, on the other hand, although admitting that American fishing vessels exercising their treaty liberties or privileges in British waters might properly be called upon to notify the local authorities of their presence there and exhibit their credentials if convenient opportunity was afforded, has always contended that American fishing vessels could not be subjected to the customs regulations imposed upon other vessels, or required to pay light, harbor or other dues not imposed upon local fishing vessels. The contentions of the United States on these questions have been fully sustained by the award. It holds, under question 3, with reference to the treaty coasts that " the exercise of the fishing liberty by the inhabitants of the United States should not be subjected to the purely commercial formalities of report, entry, and clearance at a customhouse, nor to light, harbor, or other dues not imposed upon Newfoundland fishermen " and that American fishing vessels should not be required even to report their presence on the coast " unless there be reasonably convenient opportunity afforded to report in person or by telegraph, either at a customhouse or to a customs official."

So also, under question 4, with reference to the exercise of the treaty privilege of entering bays or harbors on the nontreaty coast for the four purposes specified in the treaty, the award decides that " to impose restrictions making the exercise of such privileges conditional upon the payment of light, harbor, or other dues, or entering and reporting at customhouses, or any similar conditions would be inconsistent with the grounds upon which such privileges rest, and therefore is not permissible." It declares, however, in the case of fishermen who remain more than 48 hours in such bays and harbors in the exercise of their treaty privileges, that it would not be unreasonable to require them "if thought necessary by Great Britain or the Colonial Government, to report either in person or by telegraph at a customhouse or to a customs official if reasonably convenient opportunity therefor is afforded."

Question 5, which was introduced into the arbitration by Great Britain, deals with the historic contention of the British Government that the renunciation by the United States in the treaty of 1818 of the liberty of fishing on or within 3 miles of any bays on the nontreaty coasts, must be interpreted as excluding American fishermen from fishing in any of the indentations of the coast which might properly be defined as bays, regardless of their size. The position of the United States on this question has always been that inasmuch as the language of the treaty is "bays of His Britannic Majesty's Dominions" the bays referred to were only such bays as were included within the usual 3-mile limit of territorial jurisdiction bordering the coast, and that the right to fish in the larger bays was, therefore, not renounced by the treaty.

As appears from the opinion, the tribunal determined that the renunciation of the right to fish "on or within 3 marine miles of any bays," etc., must be interpreted as applying only to geographical bays, the tribunal declaring that it is "unable to understand the term bays in the renunciatory clause in other than its geographical sense." The award on this question is as follows:

In case of bays the three marine miles are to be measured from a straight line drawn across the body of water at the place where it ceases to have the configuration and characteristics of a bay. At all other places the three marine miles are to be measured following the sinuosities of the coast.

Great Britain's contention did not rest upon the assertion of territorial jurisdiction over such bays, and the award does not go to the extent of holding that Great Britain has territorial jurisdiction over the large bays, although the United States has renounced for its fishermen the right to fish therein.

The award, therefore, still leaves American fishermen in such bays, subject to American and not British law, and confers upon Great Britain or the British colonies no right to seize or interfere with American fishing vessels beyond the 3-mile limit from shore in such bays, such vessels being in a similar situation to British vessels violating their obligation under the fur-seal award, which excludes them from fishing in certain portions of the high seas.

The award of the tribunal on this question does not define what is a bay, holding merely that the 3-mile limit of exclusion must be measured from a "line drawn across the body of water at the place where it ceases to have the configuration and characteristics of a bay." This answer leaves open the question of where such line is to be drawn in each particular case, and also the question of whether any particular body of water has the " configuration and characteristics of a bay." The tribunal recognized this difficulty, and in order to " render the decision more practicable and to remove the danger of future differences " the award contains a further provision recommending the adoption of the rule approved and accepted by Great Britain in many treaties that " only bays of 10-mile width should be considered as those where the fishing is reserved to nationals "— extending this rule, however, to include certain larger bays as exceptions to it. These recommendations are substantially in accordance with the agreement adopted by the unratified Bayard-Chamberlain treaty of 1888, with certain considerable modifications in favor of the United States.

The Bay of Fundy, which is the only large bay where the American fishermen now fish or have fished to any extent within recent years, is expressly excepted from the application of the award on this question.

The strength of the position of the United States on this question is shown by the very able argument presented in the dissenting opinion by Dr. Drago and by the fact that the British contention was not fully sustained, and that this was the only question of the seven submitted upon which the decision of the tribunal was not unanimous.

The sixth question deals with the contention of Great Britain, advanced for the first time in recent years, that the treaty did not secure to American fishermen the liberty of fishing in the bays on the southern and western coasts of Newfoundland and on the Magdalen Islands. This contention rested on the argument that the liberties secured by the treaty to fish on the southern and western coasts of Newfoundland and on the shores of the Magdalen Islands did not extend to the bays on those coasts, inasmuch as the treaty does not mention bays in connection with those coasts, and does expressly mention them in connection with the coast of Labrador, which forms part of the treaty coast. The United States, on the other hand, contended that the liberty secured by the treaty to fish on those coasts necessarily extended to the bays of such coasts, and that this interpretation must be adopted, not only because it was supported by the language of the treaty read in the light of the evident intention of the parties in entering into it, but also because usage and custom and the action of both Governments subsequent to the treaty had combined to give the treaty that interpretation in actual practice for the entire period since the treaty was entered into.

The award of the tribunal sustained fully and without qualification the contention of the United States on this question.

In many respects this was the most important question submitted for decision. The bait fish, which are procured in immense quantities in the bays of Newfoundland and of the Magdalen Islands, are a very important factor in the successful prosecution of the exceedingly valuable cod fishery on the Grand Bank and on the other banks in the North Atlantic; and this situation discloses the real importance of this question. If the contention of the Newfoundland Government had been sustained, and American fishermen deprived of the opportunity of taking bait for themselves in these bays, it was the admitted intention of the Newfoundland Government to threaten the entire cod-fishing industry on the banks by prohibiting the Newfoundland fishermen from selling bait to the American fishermen, in order to compel the United States to yield to Newfoundland's demand for the free entry of Newfoundland fish and fish products and for other commercial concessions in exchange for the privilege of procuring bait. Furthermore, the very important and profitable winter herring fishing was also dependent upon the decision of this question, inasmuch as it is carried on by the American fishermen wholly in the bays on the west coast of Newfoundland.

The decision of this question in favor of the United States also disposes of a claim for a very large amount of damages which the Newfoundland Government was preparing to present against the United States for the value of all the fish taken by American vessels in these bays during the 90 years since the treaty was entered into, on the ground that American fishermen under the treaty had no right to fish in such bays.

The seventh question called upon the tribunal to determine whether or not the inhabitants of the United States, whose vessels resorted to the treaty coasts for the purpose of exercising their treaty liberties of fishing, were entitled to use the same vessels, when duly authorized by the United States, in the exercise of such commercial privileges on the treaty coasts as were accorded by agreement or otherwise to American trading vessels generally. The position of the United States on this question was that fishing vessels exercising commercial privileges necessarily subjected themselves to all the requirements and conditions imposed upon commercial vessels generally, but that the use of a vessel by inhabitants of the United States in the exercise of their fishing rights did not disqualify such vessel from being used for commercial purposes after it had completed its fishing operations, and conversely, that a commercial vessel might be used for fishing purposes as soon as its use for commercial purposes ceased.

The award of the tribunal fully sustains the contentions of the United States on this question, holding that—

The inhabitants of the United States are so entitled, in so far as concerns this treaty, there being nothing in its provisions to disentitle them, provided the treaty liberty of fishing and the commercial privileges are not exercised concurrently.

The provisions of Articles II and III of the special agreement and the proceedings already taken and to be taken pursuant thereto, form an important part of the award on question 1, and require brief examination.

Pursuant to the provisions of Article II of the special agreement, the United States called the attention of the tribunal upon the oral argument to certain acts of Newfoundland and Canada which had already been specified by the United States to Great Britain within the period required for such specification, and called upon the tribunal " to express in its award its opinion upon such acts, and to point out in what respects, if any, they were inconsistent with the principles laid. down in the award." The objection of the United States to such acts was based on the grounds that in their application to American fishermen on the treaty coasts they were not appropriate, and necessary, and reasonable, and fair as defined in question 1.

The United States further requested that, in case the character of the award should require the determination of the reasonableness, etc., of the acts specified, the tribunal should refer to a commission of expert specialists for action thereon, in accordance with Article III of the special agreement, such of the acts specified as required an examination of the practical effect thereof in relation to the conditions surrounding the exercise of the liberty of fishing, or required expert information about the fisheries themselves. In reply to this application on the part of the United States, Great Britain filed an answer submitting that the acts referred to were reasonable in themselves and that the United States had not sufficiently stated the grounds of objection to the various acts referred to, and had laid no ground for the request that certain of these acts should be referred to a commission of expert specialists. The proceedings thus taken were set forth in a printed statement on behalf of the United States, and a printed answer on behalf of Great Britain, both of which were filed with the tribunal, and copies of which are included in the appendix to the printed record of the proceedings of the tribunal, which forms part of this repórt. The issues thus raised were discussed in written communications exchanged between the agents of both parties and the tribunal, copies of which also are included in the appendix to the printed record of the proceedings of the tribunal.

The position taken by the United States was sustained by the award of the tribunal under question 1, whereby it was held that—

The decision of the reasonableness of these regulations requires expert information about the fisheries themselves, and an examination of the practical effect of a great number of these provisions in relation to the conditions surrounding the exercise of the liberty of fishery enjoyed by the inhabitants of the United States as contemplated in Article III.

The tribunal accordingly referred the regulations objected to by the United States to a commission of experts, as provided for in Article III of the special agreement, for action in accordance therewith, and called upon the parties to designate, within one month from the date of the award, their respective representatives on such commission.   Dr. P. P. C. Hoek, scientific adviser for the fisheries of the Netherlands, was designated in the award as the nonnational member of this commission.   Dr. Hugh M. Smith, Deputy Fish Commissioner of the United States, was designated within the period fixed by the award as the commissioner on the part of the United States.   Hon. Donald Morison, minister of justice of Newfoundland, has been designated as the commissioner on the part of Great Britain.

In the course of the oral argument before the tribunal, the position was taken by counsel on both sides that in determining the rights of the parties under question 1, the tribunal should take into consideration the provisions of Article IV of the special agreement submitting this case to arbitration.   By this article it was agreed that unless the parties should adopt some alternative method of procedure, any differences arising in the future relating to the interpretation of the treaty of 1818, or to the effect or application of the award of the tribunal, should be referred informally to the Permanent Court at The Hague " for decision by the summary procedure provided for in chapter 4 of The Hague convention of the 18th of October, 1907." In view, however, of the fact that this special agreement was entered into under the general treaty of arbitration concluded between the United States and Great Britain on the 4th day of April, 1908, the duration of which, by its own terms, was limited to a period of five years, it seemed desirable to the agent and counsel on the part of the United States that the view which was entertained by both court and counsel and formed part of the basis upon which the case was considered should be declared beyond the possibility of future question to the effect that the provisions of Article IV of the special agreement continued with the fisheries provisions of the treaty of 1818, and did not terminate with the general arbitration treaty of 1908.   This subject was, therefore, brought up for consideration at the session of the tribunal on Friday, August 5th, 1910, and it was then stated by counsel on behalf of the United States and of Great Britain respectively, that the provisions of Article IV were regarded as constituting, in effect, a new treaty which would survive the termination of the general treaty of arbitration, and that Article IV of the special agreement was not limited by any term, but related to the future generally, and therefore was not a determinable article so far as affects its subject matter.   The same view was expressed on the part of the tribunal; and in the award on question 1, the tribunal held that—

Article IV of the agreement is, as stated by counsel of the respective parties at the argument, permanent in its effect and not determinable by the expiration of the general arbitration treaty of 1908 between Great Britain and the United States.

The foregoing examination of the award and of Articles II, III and IV of the special agreement makes it evident that the wise and farsighted provisions of that agreement entered very largely into the satisfactory outcome of this arbitration, and both countries are to be congratulated that a permanent and expeditious method is now provided for settling future differences, if any should arise, in regard to the fisheries under the treaty of 1818.

The duplicate original of the award, signed by the members of the tribunal, and also of the dissenting opinion of Dr. Drago on question 5, which were delivered to the agent of the United States when the award was announced, are transmitted herewith, and a copy of the award and of Dr. Drago's opinion are hereto annexed as part of this report.

The very important services rendered by counsel in the presentation of the oral arguments on behalf of the United States and otherwise in the course of the proceedings are too well understood and appreciated to require special mention in this report further than to say that Mr. Turner's opening of the case was a very strong and able argument and exhibited the results of great industry and research, and the same is true of the arguments of Mr. Elder and Mr. Warren on the particular questions dealt with by them, and that Mr. Root's argument in closing was a masterly presentation of the entire case of the United States. It is appropriate that the agent should express his obligation to the counsel of the United States for the very cordial and loyal support which they have given him throughout the entire course of these proceedings; also that mention should be made of the fact that the distinguished services rendered by Senator Root in this case as senior counsel have been rendered by him without compensation. Such services, in addition to the responsibilities attendant upon the duties of chief counsel in a case of such magnitude and importance, involved also the necessity of spending, at the expense of his summer vacation, more than three months away from home, and, from June 1st to August 12th, in almost daily attendance at the sessions of the tribunal, and the preparation and delivery of the closing argument, which consumed six sessions of the tribunal, summing up the entire case for the United States. The acceptance of the position of chief counsel was urged upon Mr. Root by the President and the Secretary of State, and the agent and the other counsel for the United States in this case; and he gave his services freely to the Government without the expectation of receiving compensation, and to him, as chief counsel, the United States is indebted in large measure for the successful outcome of the arbitration.

It is also appropriate that acknowledgment should be made of the obligation of the agent and counsel to the Department of State for the hearty and effective cooperation and assistance rendered to them by the department throughout the entire period covered by the arbitration proceedings. Valuable assistance was also rendered in these proceedings by Dr. Hugh M. Smith, Deputy Fish Commissioner of the United States , who acted as expert adviser on practical and technical questions relating to the regulations of the fisheries, and has now been designated as the member on the part of the United States of the special commission of experts; and by Messrs. Alvin B. Alexander, Carl C. Young and Arthur L. Millett, attached to the agency as fisheries experts; and by Mr. Otis T. Cartwright, secretary of the agency and special disbursing officer, Department of State; Mr. Edwin M. Borchardt, expert on international law; and Messrs. Wallace J. Young, James B. Davies, Charles Jenkinson, and John D. Johnson, who were attached to the Agency as members of the clerical staff.

I am, sir, very respectfully your obedient servant,

CHANDLER P. ANDERSON,
Agent of the United States in the
North Atlantic Coast Fisheries Arbitration.

The SECRETARY OF STATE,
Washington, D. C.

5   *Special agreement for the submission of questions relating to fisheries on the North Atlantic coast under the general treaty of arbitration concluded between the United States and Great Britain on the 4th day of April, 1908.*

ARTICLE I.

Whereas by Article I of the Convention signed at London on the 20th day of October, 1818, between Great Britain and the United States, it was agreed as follows:—

Whereas differences have arisen respecting the liberty claimed by the United States for the Inhabitants thereof, to take, dry and cure Fish on Certain Coasts, Bays, Harbours and Creeks of His Britannic Majesty's Dominions in America, it is agreed between the High Contracting Parties, that the Inhabitants of the said United States shall have forever, in common with the Subjects of His Britannic Majesty, the Liberty to take Fish of every kind on that part of the Southern Coast of Newfoundland which extends from Cape Ray to the Rameau Islands, on the Western and Northern Coast of Newfoundland, from the said Cape Ray to the Quirpon Islands, on the shores of the Magdalen Islands, and also on the Coasts, Bays, Harbours, and Creeks from Mount Joly on the Southern Coast of Labrador, to and through the Straits of Belleisle and thence Northwardly indefinitely along the Coast, without prejudice, however, to any of the exclusive Rights of the Hudson Bay Company; and that the American Fishermen shall also have liberty forever, to dry and cure Fish in any of the unsettled Bays, Harbours and Creeks of the Southern part of the Coast of Newfoundland hereabove described, and of the Coast of Labrador; but so soon as the same, or any Portion thereof, shall be settled, it shall not be lawful for the said Fishermen to dry or cure Fish at such Portion so settled, without previous agreement for such purpose with the Inhabitants, Proprietors, or Possessors of the ground.—And the United States hereby renounce forever, any Liberty heretofore enjoyed or claimed by the Inhabitants thereof, to take, dry, or cure Fish on, or within three marine Miles of any of the Coasts, Bays, Creeks, or Harbours of His Britannic Majesty's Dominions in America not included within the above-

---

* Protocols of The North Atlantic Coast Fisheries Arbitration, published by authority of the Permanent Court, The Hague, 1910.

mentioned limits provided, however, that the American Fishermen shall be admitted to enter such Bays or Harbours for the purpose of Shelter and of repairing Damages therein, of purchasing Wood, and of obtaining Water, and for no other purpose whatever. But they shall be under such Restrictions as may be necessary to prevent their taking, drying or curing Fish therein, or in any other manner whatever abusing the Privileges hereby reserved to them.

6   And, whereas, differences have arisen as to the scope and meaning of the said Article, and of the liberties therein referred to, and otherwise in respect of the rights and liberties which the inhabitants of the United States have or claim to have in the waters or on the shores therein referred to:

It is agreed that the following questions shall be submitted for decision to a tribunal of arbitration constituted as hereinafter provided:—

Question 1.—To what extent are the following contentions or either of them justified?

It is contended on the part of Great Britain that the exercise of the liberty to take fish referred to in the said Article, which the inhabitants of the United States have forever in common with the subjects of His Britannic Majesty, is subject, without the consent of the United States, to reasonable regulation by Great Britain, Canada, or Newfoundland in the form of municipal laws, ordinances, or rules, as, for example, to regulations in respect of (1) the hours, days, or seasons when fish may be taken on the treaty coasts; (2) the method, means, and implements to be used in the taking of fish or in the carrying on of fishing operations on such coasts; (3) any other matters of a similar character relating to fishing; such regulations being reasonable, as being, for instance—

(*a*) Appropriate or necessary for the protection and preservation of such fisheries and the exercise of the rights of British subjects therein and of the liberty which by the said Article I the inhabitants of the United States have therein in common with British subjects;

(*b*) Desirable on grounds of public order and morals;

(*c*) Equitable and fair as between local fishermen and the inhabitants of the United States exercising the said treaty liberty and not so framed as to give unfairly an advantage to the former over the latter class.

It is contended on the part of the United States that the exercise of such liberty is not subject to limitations or restraints by Great Britain, Canada, or Newfoundland in the form of municipal laws, ordinances, or regulations in respect of (1) the hours, days, or seasons when the inhabitants of the United States may take fish on the treaty coasts, or (2) the method, means, and implements used by them in taking fish or in carrying on fishing operations on such coasts, or (3) any other limitations or restraints of similar character—

(*a*) Unless they are appropriate and necessary for the protection and preservation of the common rights in such fisheries and the exercise thereof; and

7   (*b*) Unless they are reasonable in themselves and fair as between local fishermen and fishermen coming from the United States, and not so framed as to give an advantage to the former over the latter class; and

(*c*) Unless their appropriateness, necessity, reasonableness, and fairness be determined by the United States and Great Britain by common accord and the United States concurs in their enforcement.

Question 2. Have the inhabitants of the United States, while exercising the liberties referred to in said Article, a right to employ as members of the fishing crews of their vessels persons not inhabitants of the United States?

Question 3. Can the exercise by the inhabitants of the United States of the liberties referred to in the said Article be subjected, without the consent of the United States, to the requirements of entry or report at custom-houses or the payment of light or harbour or other dues, or to any other similar requirement or condition or exaction?

Question 4. Under the provision of the said Article that the American fishermen shall be admitted to enter certain bays or harbours for shelter, repairs, wood, or water, and for no other purpose whatever, but that they shall be under such restrictions as may be necessary to prevent their taking, drying, or curing fish therein or in any other manner whatever abusing the privileges thereby reserved to them, is it permissible to impose restrictions making the exercise of such privileges conditional upon the payment of light or harbour or other dues, or entering or reporting at custom-houses or any similar conditions?

Question 5. From where must be measured the "three marine miles of any of the coasts, bays, creeks, or harbours" refered to in the said Article?

Question 6. Have the inhabitants of the United States the liberty under the said Article or otherwise to take fish in the bays, harbours, and creeks on that part of the southern coast of Newfoundland which extends from Cape Ray to Rameau Islands, or on the western and northern coasts of Newfoundland from Cape Ray to Quirpon Islands, or on the Magdalen Islands?

Question 7. Are the inhabitants of the United States whose vessels resort to the treaty coasts for the purpose of exercising the liberties referred to in Article I of the treaty of 1818 entitled to have for those vessels, when duly authorized by the United States in that behalf, the commercial privileges on the treaty coasts accorded by agreement or otherwise to United States trading-vessels generally?

ARTICLE II.

Either Party may call the attention of the Tribunal to any legislative or executive act of the other Party, specified within
8   three months of the exchange of notes enforcing this agreement, and which is claimed to be inconsistent with the true interpretation of the Treaty of 1818; and may call upon the Tribunal to express in its award its opinion upon such acts, and to point out in what respects, if any, they are inconsistent with the principles laid down in the award in reply to the preceding questions; and each Party agrees to conform to such opinion.

ARTICLE III.

If any question arises in the arbitration regarding the reasonableness of any regulation or otherwise which requires an examination of the practical effect of any provisions in relation to the conditions surrounding the exercise of the liberty of fishery enjoyed by the inhabitants of the United States, or which requires expert information about the fisheries themselves, the Tribunal may, in that case, refer such question to a Commission of three expert specialists in such matters; one to be designated by each of the Parties hereto, and the third, who shall not be a national of either Party, to be designated by the Tribunal. This Commission shall examine into and report their conclusions on any question or questions so referred to it by the Tribunal and such report shall be considered by the Tribunal and shall, if incorporated by them in the award, be accepted as a part thereof.

Pending the report of the Commission upon the question or questions so referred and without awaiting such report, the Tribunal may make a separate award upon all or any other questions before it, and such separate award, if made, shall become immediately effective, provided that the report aforesaid shall not be incorporated in the award until it has been considered by the Tribunal. The expenses of such Commission shall be borne in equal moieties by the Parties hereto.

ARTICLE IV.

The Tribunal shall recommend for the consideration of the High Contracting Parties rules and a method of procedure under which all questions which may arise in the future regarding the exercise of the liberties above referred to may be determined in accordance with the principles laid down in the award. If the High Contracting Parties shall not adopt the rules and method of procedure so recommended, or if they shall not, subsequently to the delivery of the award, agree upon such rules and methods, then any differences which may arise

9 in the future between the High Contracting Parties relating to the interpretation of the Treaty of 1818 or to the effect and application of the award of the Tribunal shall be referred informally to the Permanent Court at The Hague for decision by the summary procedure provided in Chapter IV of The Hague Convention of the 18th October, 1907.

ARTICLE V.

The Tribunal of Arbitration provided for herein shall be chosen from the general list of members of the Permanent Court at The Hague, in accordance with the provisions of Article XLV of the Convention for the Settlement of International Disputes, concluded at the Second Peace Conference at The Hague on the 18th of October, 1907. The provisions of said Convention, so far as applicable and not inconsistent herewith, and excepting Articles LIII and LIV, shall govern the proceedings under the submission herein provided for.

The time allowed for the direct agreement of His Britannic Majesty and the President of the United States on the composition of such Tribunal shall be three months.

ARTICLE VI.

The pleadings shall be communicated in the order and within the time following:—

As soon as may be and within a period not exceeding seven months from the date of the exchange of notes making this agreement binding the printed case of each of the Parties hereto, accompanied by printed copies of the documents, the official correspondence, and all other evidence on which each Party relies, shall be delivered in duplicate (with such additional copies as may be agreed upon) to the agent of the other Party. It shall be sufficient for this purpose if such case is delivered at the British Embassy at Washington or at the American Embassy at London, as the case may be, for transmission to the agent for its Government.

Within fifteen days thereafter such printed case and accompanying evidence of each of the Parties shall be delivered in duplicate to each member of the Tribunal, and such delivery may be made by depositing within the stated period the necessary number of copies with the International Bureau at The Hague for transmission to the Arbitrators.

After the delivery on both sides of such printed case, either Party may, in like manner, and within four months after the expiration of

the period above fixed for the delivery to the agents of the case,
deliver to the agent of the other Party (with such additional
10   copies as may be agreed upon), a printed counter-case accompanied by printed copies of additional documents, correspondence, and other evidence in reply to the case, documents, correspondence, and other evidence so presented by the other Party, and within fifteen days thereafter such Party shall, in like manner as above provided, deliver in duplicate such counter-case and accompanying evidence to each of the Arbitrators.

The foregoing provisions shall not prevent the Tribunal from permitting either Party to rely at the hearing upon documentary or other evidence which is shown to have become open to its investigation or examination or available for use too late to be submitted within the period hereinabove fixed for the delivery of copies of evidence, but in case any such evidence is to be presented, printed copies of it, as soon as possible after it is secured, must be delivered, in like manner as provided for the delivery of copies of other evidence, to each of the Arbitrators and to the agent of the other Party. The admission of any such additional evidence, however, shall be subject to such conditions as the Tribunal may impose, and the other Party shall have a reasonable opportunity to offer additional evidence in rebuttal.

The Tribunal shall take into consideration all evidence which is offered by either Party.

ARTICLE VII.

If in the case or counter-case (exclusive of the accompanying evidence) either Party shall have specified or referred to any documents, correspondence, or other evidence in its own exclusive possession without annexing a copy, such Party shall be bound, if the other Party shall demand it within thirty days after the delivery of the case or counter-case respectively, to furnish to the Party applying for it a copy thereof; and either Party may, within the like time, demand that the other shall furnish certified copies or produce for inspection the originals of any documentary evidence adduced by the Party upon whom the demand is made. It shall be the duty of the Party upon whom any such demand is made to comply with it as soon as may be, and within a period not exceeding fifteen days after the demand has been received. The production for inspection or the furnishing to the other Party of official governmental publications, publishing, as authentic, copies of the documentary evidence referred to, shall be a sufficient compliance with such demand, if such governmental publications shall have been published prior to the 1st day of January, 1908. If the demand is not complied with, the reasons for the failure to comply must be stated to the Tribunal.

11

ARTICLE VIII.

The Tribunal shall meet within six months after the expiration of the period above fixed for the delivery to the agents of the case, and upon the assembling of the Tribunal at its first session each Party, through its agent or counsel, shall deliver in duplicate to each of the Arbitrators and to the agent and counsel of the other Party (with such additional copies as may be agreed upon) a printed argument showing the points and referring to the evidence upon which it relies.

The time fixed by this Agreement for the delivery of the case, counter-case, or argument, and for the meeting of the Tribunal, may be extended by mutual consent of the Parties.

ARTICLE IX.

The decision of the Tribunal shall, if possible, be made within two months from the close of the arguments on both sides, unless on the request of the Tribunal the Parties shall agree to extend the period.

It shall be made in writing, and dated and signed by each member of the Tribunal, and shall be accompanied by a statement of reasons.

A member who may dissent from the decision may record his dissent when signing.

The language to be used throughout the proceedings shall be English.

ARTICLE X.

Each Party reserves to itself the right to demand a revision of the award. Such demand shall contain a statement of the grounds on which it is made and shall be made within five days of the promulgation of the award, and shall be heard by the Tribunal within ten days thereafter. The Party making the demand shall serve a copy of the same on the opposite Party, and both Parties shall be heard in argument by the Tribunal on said demand. The demand can only be made on the discovery of some new fact or circumstance calculated to exercise a decisive influence upon the award and which was unknown to the Tribunal and to the Party demanding the revision at the time the discussion was closed, or upon the ground that the said award does not fully and sufficiently, within the meaning of this Agreement, determine any question or questions submitted. If the Tribunal shall allow the demand for a revision, it shall afford such opportunity for further hearings and arguments as it shall deem necessary.

12

ARTICLE XI.

The present Agreement shall be deemed to be binding only when confirmed by the two Governments by an exchange of notes.

In witness whereof this Agreement has been signed and sealed by His Britannic Majesty's Ambassador at Washington, the Right Honourable JAMES BRYCE, O.M., on behalf of Great Britain, and by the Secretary of State of the United States, ELIHU ROOT, on behalf of the United States.

Done at Washington on the 27th day of January, one thousand nine hundred and nine.

JAMES BRYCE. [SEAL.]
ELIHU ROOT. [SEAL.]

---

13   *Mr. Bacon to Mr. Bryce.*

N°. 541.]   DEPARTMENT OF STATE,
                                        February 21, 1909.

EXCELLENCY: I have the honor to inform you that the Senate, by its resolution of the 18th instant, gave its advice and consent to the ratification of the Special Agreement between the United States and Great Britain, signed on January 27, 1909, for the submission to the Permanent Court of Arbitration at The Hague of questions relating to fisheries on the North Atlantic Coast.

In giving this advice and consent to the ratification of the Special Agreement, and as a part of the act of ratification, the Senate states in the resolution its understanding:

That it is agreed by the United States and Great Britain that question 5 of the series submitted, namely, " from where must be measured the three marine miles of any of the coasts, bays, creeks or harbors referred to in said article," does not include any question as to the Bay of Fundy, considered as a whole apart from its bays or creeks, or as to innocent passage through the Gut of Canso, and that the respective views or contentions of the United States and Great Britain on either subject shall be in no wise prejudiced by anything in the present arbitration, and that this agreement on the part of the United States will be mentioned in the ratification of the special agreement and will, in effect, form part of this special agreement.

In thus formally confirming what I stated to you orally, I have the honor to express the hope that you will in like manner formally confirm the assent of His Majesty's Government to this understanding which you heretofore stated to me orally, and that you will be prepared at an early day to exchange the notes confirming the Special Agreement as provided for therein and in the general arbitration convention of June 5, 1908.

I have the honor to be, with the highest consideration,
        Your Excellency's most obedient servant,

ROBERT BACON.

His Excellency The Right Honorable JAMES BRYCE,
                                Etc., Etc., Etc.

Mr. Bryce to Mr. Bacon.

N°. 55.]   BRITISH EMBASSY,
                                                        Washington, March 4, 1909.

SIR: I have the honour to acknowledge the receipt of your note
informing me that the Senate of the United States has ap-
14   proved the Special Agreement for the reference to arbitration
of the questions relating to the fisheries on the North Atlantic
Coast and of the terms of the Resolution in which that approval is
given.

It is now my duty to inform you that the Government of His
Britannic Majesty confirms the Special Agreement aforesaid and in
so doing confirms also the understanding arrived at by us that Question V of the series of Questions submitted for arbitration, namely
from where must be measured the " three marine miles of any of the
coasts, bays, creeks, or harbours " referred to in the said article, is
submitted in its present form with the agreed understanding that no
question as to the Bay of Fundy considered as a whole apart from
its bays or creeks, or as to innocent passage through the Gut of Canso,
is included in this question as one to be raised in the present arbitration, it being the intention of the Parties that their respective views
or contentions on either subject shall be in no wise prejudiced by anything in the present arbitration.

This understanding is that which was embodied in notes exchanged
between your predecessor and myself on January 27th, and is that
expressed in the above-mentioned Resolution of the Senate of the
United States.

I have the honour to be, with the highest respect, Sir,
        Your most obedient, humble Servant,

                                                          JAMES BRYCE.

The Honourable, ROBERT BACON,
            Etc., Etc., Etc.

PROTOCOL I.

Meeting of Wednesday June 1st, 1910.

The Tribunal assembled at 4 p. m. at the Hague at the Permanent Court of Arbitration.

There were present the five Members of the Tribunal of Arbitration:

Mr. H. Lammasch, Doctor of Law, Professor of the University of Vienna, Aulic Councillor, Member of the Upper House of the Austrian Parliament;

His Excellency Jonkheer A. F. de Savornin Lohman, Doctor of Law, Minister of State, former Minister of the Interior, Member of the Second Chamber of the Netherlands;

The Honourable George Gray, Doctor of Law, formerly United States Senator, Judge of the United States Circuit Court of Appeals;

The Right Honourable Sir Charles Fitzpatrick, Doctor of Law, Chief Justice of Canada;

The Honourable Luis Maria Drago, Doctor of Law, former Minister of Foreign Affairs of the Argentine Republic, Member of the Law Academy of the University of Buenos Aires.

The Honourable Chandler P. Anderson and the Honourable Allen B. Aylesworth, Minister of Justice of Canada, King's Counsel, were present at the meeting as Agents for the Governments of the United States and Great Britain.

Mr. Lammasch took the chair as President and delivered the following address:

Your Excellencies, Gentlemen:

Ten years have elapsed since the Permanent Court of International Arbitration has been established by the first Conference of the Peace which has met under the reign of a glorious and all beloved Queen in this charming town.

16   In those few years already this novel institution has done a great deal of good all over the world. It has shown that, instead of appealing to brute force with all its casualties, cruelties, and injustices, differences, important differences between mighty States may be adjusted according to the laws of equity, justice, and humanity.

Tribunals instituted in virtue of the Convention of 1899 and 1907 have decided disputes touching all four continents, divided in various realms; differences which have arisen in the north of Europe, in Northern and in Southern America, in Japan, in Arabia, and in Morocco.

The greatest Powers of the world have submitted by their free will to this court and nations of minor forces have found their protection before it.

Governments which once had appealed to this high court have intrusted it a second and a third time with the decision of their conflicts; arbitrators who had been chosen in one case, have been nominated to decide other affairs, certainly the most convincing evidence, I think, that nations have been contented with the work that has been done here.

Matters of great importance have been adjusted in these modest, provisional rooms, some of them involving the most delicate questions of sovereignty and national pride, all implicating intricate problems of international law.

But perhaps never till now has there been intrusted to an arbitral tribunal a question of such gravity and of so complex a nature as in the present case of almost secular standing. Many of the documents in this case are prior to the independence of the United States of America, some of them go as far back as the seventeenth century. Upwards from 1818, during more than 90 years, the questions implicated in the present arbitration have been the subject of almost uninterrupted diplomatic correspondence and transaction, and more than once they have brought the two great seafaring nations of Europe and America to the verge of the extremities of war.

And now these two nations, to which the world is indebted for so much of its progress in every sphere of human thought and action, have agreed to submit their long-standing conflict to the arbitration of this Tribunal.

In doing so, they have expressed their full confidence in this peaceful mode of resolving international differences, which the first Conference of 1899 has recognized as the most efficacious and at the same time the most equitable method of deciding controversies which have not been settled by diplomatic means.

17   In doing so, these Governments have set an example for the whole community of nations and have acquired a new merit in the sublime cause of international justice and peace, to the progress of which they have contributed perhaps more than any other nation, especially under the peaceful reign of a great King, whose premature and sudden loss his vast Empire lamented in the last weeks, and under the presidency of that illustrious statesman who has the historical merit of having initiated the first meeting of this court in the " Pious Fund " case.

Having been appointed by agreement of the parties to be the umpire in this arbitration and being therefore called to the high honor of presiding at these debates, it is my first duty to thank their excellencies the President and the members of the Administrative Council of the Permanent Court for honoring the opening of these proceedings by their presence.

Then I may be permitted to offer a most hearty welcome to my eminent colleagues and to the honorable and distinguished agents and counsel of the two litigant parties.

Only consciousness of being at your side, my dear and most honored colleagues, and of being assisted by your experience, your tact, and your knowledge has inspired me with the courage to accept the functions so noble, but also so responsible and so difficult, incumbent on me in this arbitration.

Let me express to you once more in public, what I have said already to you in private, that I consider it the greatest distinction in my life to sit in your company in this historic proceeding.

My illustrious colleagues and myself have studied in these last months with all care and assiduity the voluminous and highly interesting documents which have been presented to us by the parties; but we have deliberately forborne to form a definite opinion on the arduous questions involved in the case, before having had the most valuable—I may say the indispensable—assistance from the speeches of those eminent lawyers and statesmen who have accepted the functions of counsel in this case.

Be assured, gentlemen representing the litigant parties, that all we arbitrators are imbued with the sense of our responsibility not only to the Governments which honored us with their confidence and to the two great nations they represent, but also to the noble idea of international arbitration, so dear to all of us.

We are fully aware that with the end of promoting this peaceful mode of settling international differences the award we have to pronounce must by the force of its motives meet with the ap-
18   proval of all who by their unbiased knowledge of international law are entitled to criticize us.

Every sentence rendered by this Court ought to be by virtue of its impartiality and equity a new marble pillar to sustain the ideal palace of Justice and Peace, the symbol of which is to be that noble edifice which has been dedicated to this town by the munificence of a man whose name is dear to both litigant nations.

Being conscious of our responsibilities, we shall do our best to render justice to those " captains courageous " and hardy fishermen of both nations, who in the uproar of the sea and at the risk of their lives pile the treasures of the Ocean for the benefit of men. In doing our duty in that way, we hope to settle peacefully and definitely a difference which for so long a time has agitated the two branches of the Anglo-Saxon race.

May we with the help of Him who bade His peace to all who are of good will succeed in promoting the progress of mankind through Justice to Peace, *per justitiam ad pacem.*

And now I beg the Secretary general of this Court, Baron Michiels van Verduynen, and the first Secretary of the International Bureau of this Court, Jonkheer Röell, to assist us with their rich experience in this arbitration as they have done to so great an advantage in former cases as Secretary general and Secretary of the Tribunal; and nominate as Secretaries of the Tribunal Mr. Charles D. White, Secretary of the Legation of the United States of America at Havana, and Mr. George Young, Secretary to His Majesty's Embassy at Washington.

At the request of the President, the Secretary general then read the list of the Agents, Counsel, and Secretaries of the interested Powers, viz:

For the *United States of America:*

The Honourable Chandler P. Anderson, *Agent;*

The Honourable Elihu Root, a Senator of the United States from the State of New York, formerly Secretary of War and Secretary of State of the United States, *Counsel;*

The Honourable George Turner, formerly a Senator of the United States from the State of Washington, *Counsel;*

The Honourable Samuel J. Elder, *Counsel;*

The Honourable Charles B. Warren, *Counsel;*

The Honourable James Brown Scott, Solicitor for the Department of State of the United States, *Counsel;*

19   The Honourable Robert Lansing, *Counsel;*

Mr. Otis Thomas Cartwright, *Secretary of the Agency.*

For *Great Britain:*

The Honourable Allen B. Aylesworth, King's Counsel, Minister of Justice of Canada, *Agent;*

The Right Honourable Sir William Snowdon Robson, Member of the Privy Council, King's Counsel, Member of Parliament, His Majesty's Attorney General, *Counsel;*

The Right Honourable Sir Robert Bannatyne Finlay, Member of the Privy Council, King's Counsel, Member of Parliament, *Counsel;*

The Honourable Sir Edward P. Morris, Doctor of Law, King's Counsel, Prime Minister of Newfoundland;

The Honourable Donald Morison, King's Counsel, Minister of Justice of Newfoundland;

Sir James S. Winter, King's Counsel, *Counsel;*

Mr. John S. Ewart, King's Counsel, *Counsel;*

Mr. George F. Shepley, King's Counsel, *Counsel;*

Sir H. Erle Richards, King's Counsel, *Counsel;*

Mr. A. F. Peterson, King's Counsel, *Counsel;*
Mr. W. N. Tilley, *Counsel;*
Mr. Raymond Asquith, *Counsel;*
Mr. Geoffrey Lawrence, *Counsel;*
Mr. Hamar Greenwood, *Counsel;*
Messrs. Blake and Redden, *Solicitors.*
Mr..H. E. Dale, of the British Colonial Office.
Mr. John D. Clarke, *Secretary of the Agency.*
By agreement of the Parties the meetings will be open to the public.
The meeting closed at 4.30 p. m.
The Tribunal of Arbitration adjourned till Monday 6th of June at 10 a. m.
Done at *The Hague*, the 1st of June 1910.
The President:

LAMMASCH.

The Secretary general:

MICHIELS VAN VERDUYNEN.

The Secretaries:

RÖELL.
CHARLES D. WHITE.
GEORGE YOUNG.

21   PROTOCOL II.

Meeting of Monday, June 6th, 1910.

The Tribunal assembled at The Hague at 10 a. m. in the Hall of the Knights.
There were present the Members of the Tribunal of Arbitration:
Mr. H. Lammasch, Doctor of Law, Professor of the University of Vienna, Aulic Councillor, Member of the Upper House of the Austrian Parliament;
His Excellency Jonkheer A. F. de Savornin Lohman, Doctor of Law, Minister of State, former Minister of the Interior, Member of the Second Chamber of the Netherlands;
The Honourable George Gray, Doctor of Law, formerly United States Senator, Judge of the United States Circuit Court of Appeals;
The Right Honourable Sir Charles Fitzpatrick, Doctor of Law, Chief Justice of Canada;
The Honourable Luis Maria Drago, Doctor of Law, former Minister of Foreign Affairs of the Argentine Republic, Member of the Law Academy of the University of Buenos Aires.
The President spoke as follows:
On holding our first meeting in this historical building of the Netherlands, where three years ago the important Sessions of the

Second Peace Conference were held, I have to thank, above all, His Excellency the Minister of Waterstaat, for having placed these comfortable rooms at our disposal; and I have to thank also the Secretary General and the First Secretary of this Court for having completed, in so short a time, the preparations necessary for our accommodation.

I will now beg the Secretary General to read the telegram which the Court at its first meeting, sent to Her Majesty, the Queen of the Netherlands, and the message by which Her Majesty deigned to answer.

22   The Secretary general then read, in both French and English, the following telegram:

A Sa Majesté la REINE DES PAYS-BAS,
Palais, Amsterdam.

Le Président et les Membres du Tribunal pour juger le différend entre les Etats-Unis d'Amérique et la Grande Bretagne au sujet des pêcheries atlantiques déposent aux pieds de Votre Majesté leurs hommages bien respectueux, ainsi que les vœux les plus sincères qu'ils forment pour Son bonheur et Son Auguste Famille.

(signé) Président:

H. LAMMASCH.

-Membres du Tribunal:

DE SAVORNIN LOHMAN.
G. GRAY.
Sir CH. FITZPATRICK.
L. M. DRAGO.

[Translation.]

To Her Majesty the QUEEN OF THE NETHERLANDS.
Palace, Amsterdam.

The President and the Members of the Tribunal for deciding the question pending between the United States of America and Great Britain in the matter of the Atlantic Coast Fisheries lay at Your Majesty's feet their respectful homage and the sincerest good wishes which they formulate for the happiness of Your Majesty and Your August Family.

(signed) President:

H. LAMMASCH.

Members of the Tribunal:

DE SAVORNIN LOHMAN.
G. GRAY.
Sir CH. FITZPATRICK.
L. M. DRAGO.

23   In reply the Tribunal of Arbitration has been honoured by the following telegram:

Au Tribunal arbitral réuni à La Haye. Het Loo.

Très sensible aux vœux que le Président et les Membres du Tribunal arbitral forment pour Moi et Ma Maison, Je leur donne l'assurance de Mon intérêt et de Ma vive sympathie pour leur tâche.

(signé)   WILHELMINA.

[Translation.]

To the Arbitral Tribunal assembled at The Hague. *Het Loo.*

Very grateful for the good wishes that the President and the Members of the Arbitral Tribunal offer to Myself and My House, I send them the assurance of My interest in and great sympathy with their task.

(signed) WILHELMINA.

The Right Honourable Sir Robert Finlay then opened his Argument at 10.10.

At 11.35 the Tribunal took a recess.

The Tribunal reassembled at 2 p. m., when the Right Honourable Sir Robert Finlay continued his Argument.

At 4 p. m. the Tribunal adjourned until Tuesday, June 7th, at 10 a. m.

Done at *The Hague*, the 6th of June, 1910.

The President:

LAMMASCH.

The Secretary general:

MICHIELS VAN VERDUYNEN.

The Secretaries:

RÖELL.
CHARLES D. WHITE.
GEORGE YOUNG.

25

PROTOCOL III.

Meeting of Tuesday, June 7th, 1910.

The Tribunal assembled at 10 a. m.

The Right Honourable Sir Robert Finlay resumed his Argument of the previous day.

At 12.03 the Tribunal took a recess.

The Tribunal reassembled at 2 p. m., when the Right Honourable Sir Robert Finlay continued his Argument.

At 4.02 p. m. the Tribunal adjourned until Thursday, June 9th, at 10 a. m.

Done at *The Hague*, June 7th, 1910.

The President:

LAMMASCH.

The Secretary general:

MICHIELS VAN VERDUYNEN.

The Secretaries:

RÖELL.
CHARLES D. WHITE.
GEORGE YOUNG.

27   PROTOCOL IV.

Meeting of Thursday, June 9th, 1910.

The Tribunal assembled at 10 a. m.

The Right Honourable Sir Robert Finlay resumed his Argument of the previous day.

At 12 the Tribunal took a recess.

The Tribunal reassembled at 2 p. m., when the Right Honourable Sir Robert Finlay continued his Argument.

At 4.05 p. m. the Tribunal adjourned until Friday, June 10th, at 10 a. m.

Done at *The Hague*, June 9th, 1910.

The President:

                                    LAMMASCH.

The Secretary general:

                                MICHIELS VAN VERDUYNEN.

The Secretaries:

                                RÖELL.
                                CHARLES D. WHITE.
                                GEORGE YOUNG.

29   PROTOCOL V.

Meeting of Friday, June 10th, 1910.

The Tribunal assembled at 10 a. m.

The Right Honourable Sir Robert Finlay resumed his Argument of the previous day.

The President, referring to a few questions which had been made by Members of the Tribunal, announced that, if in the course of the Arguments the Arbitrators were led to make observations or to address questions to the Agents and Counsel of the Parties, these observations or questions—in conformity with Article 72 of the Convention for the Pacific Settlement of International Disputes—can not be regarded as an expression of opinion by the Tribunal in general or by its Members in particular. They are simply, so far as the Tribunal is concerned, the means of obtaining from the Representatives of the Parties explanations on doubtful points.

At 12.02 the Tribunal took a recess.

The Tribunal reassembled at 2 p. m., when the Right Honourable Sir Robert Finlay continued his Argument.

At 4 p. m. the Tribunal adjourned until Monday, June 13th, at 10 a. m.

Done at *The Hague*, June 10th, 1910.

The President:

LAMMASCH.

The Secretary general:

MICHIELS VAN VERDUYNEN.

The Secretaries:

RÖELL.
CHARLES D. WHITE.
GEORGE YOUNG.

31 PROTOCOL VI.

Meeting of Monday, June 13th, 1910.

The Tribunal assembled at 10 a. m.

The Right Honourable Sir Robert Finlay resumed his Argument.

At 12.07 the Tribunal took a recess.

The Tribunal reassembled at 2 p. m., when the Right Honourable Sir Robert Finlay continued his Argument.

At 4.03 p. m. the Tribunal adjourned until Tuesday, June 14th, at 10 a. m.

Done at *The Hague*, June 13th, 1910.

The President:

LAMMASCH.

The Secretary general:

MICHIELS VAN VERDUYNEN.

The Secretaries:

RÖELL.
CHARLES D. WHITE.
GEORGE YOUNG.

33 PROTOCOL VII.

Meeting of Tuesday, June 14th, 1910.

The Tribunal assembled at 10 a. m.

The Right Honourable Sir Robert Finlay resumed his Argument of the previous day.

At 12.03 the Tribunal took a recess.

The Tribunal reassembled at 2 p. m., when the Right Honourable Sir Robert Finlay continued his Argument.

At 4.02 p. m. the Tribunal adjourned until Thursday, June 16th, at 10 a. m.

Done at *The Hague*, June 14th, 1910.

The President:

LAMMASCH.

The Secretary general:

MICHIELS VAN VERDUYNEN.

The Secretaries:

RÖELL.
CHARLES D. WHITE.
GEORGE YOUNG.

35   PROTOCOL VIII.

Meeting of Thursday, June 16th, 1910.

The Tribunal assembled at 10 a. m.

The Right Honourable Sir Robert Finlay resumed his Argument of the previous day.

At 12.05 the Tribunal took a recess.

The Tribunal reassembled at 2 p. m., when the Right Honourable Sir Robert Finlay continued his Argument.

At 4.07 p. m. the Tribunal adjourned until Friday, June 17th, at 10 a. m.

Done at *The Hague*, June 16th, 1910.

The President:

LAMMASCH.

The Secretary general:

MICHIELS VAN VERDUYNEN.

The Secretaries:

RÖELL.
CHARLES D. WHITE.
GEORGE YOUNG.

37   PROTOCOL IX.

Meeting of Friday, June 17th, 1910.

The Tribunal assembled at 10 a. m.

The Right Honourable Sir Robert Finlay resumed his Argument of the previous day.

At 12.10 the Tribunal took a recess.

The Tribunal reassembled at 2 p. m.

At the request of the President, the Secretary General announced that, on account of the festival at the University of Leiden, the

Tribunal will assemble on Wednesday, June 22nd, instead of Tuesday, June 21st.

The Right Honourable Sir Robert Finlay continued and concluded his Argument.

At 4.40 p. m. the Tribunal adjourned until Monday, June 20th, at 10 a. m.

Done at *The Hague*, June 17th, 1910.

The President:

LAMMASCH.

The Secretary general:

MICHIELS VAN VERDUYNEN.

The Secretaries:

RÖELL.
CHARLES D. WHITE.
GEORGE YOUNG.

39 PROTOCOL X.

Meeting of Monday, June 20th, 1910.

The Tribunal assembled at 10 a. m.

The Honourable George Turner began his Argument on behalf of the United States.

At 12.03 the Tribunal took a recess.

The Tribunal reassembled at 2 p. m., when the Honourable George Turner continued his Argument.

At 4.05 p. m. the Tribunal adjourned until Wednesday, June 22nd, at 10 a. m.

Done at *The Hague*, June 20th, 1910.

The President:

LAMMASCH.

The Secretary general:

MICHIELS VAN VERDUYNEN.

The Secretaries:

RÖELL.
CHARLES D. WHITE.
GEORGE YOUNG.

41 PROTOCOL XI.

Meeting of Wednesday, June 22nd, 1910.

The Tribunal assembled at 10 a.m.

The Honourable George Turner resumed his Argument.

At 12.03 the Tribunal took a recess.

The Tribunal reassembled at 2 p.m., when the Honourable George Turner continued his Argument.

At 4.07 p.m. the Tribunal adjourned until Thursday, June 23rd, at 10 a.m.

Done at *The Hague*, June 22nd, 1910.

The President:

LAMMASCH.

The Secretary general:

MICHIELS VAN VERDUYNEN.

The Secretaries:

RÖELL.
CHARLES D. WHITE.
GEORGE YOUNG.

43   PROTOCOL XII.

Meeting of Thursday, June 23rd, 1910.

The Tribunal assembled at 10 a.m.

The Honourable George Turner resumed his Argument.

At 12.03 the Tribunal took a recess.

The Tribunal reassembled at 2 p.m., when the Honourable George Turner continued his Argument.

At 3.52 p.m. the Tribunal adjourned until Friday, June 24th, at 10 a.m.

Done at *The Hague*, June 23rd, 1910.

The President:

LAMMASCH.

The Secretary general:

MICHIELS VAN VERDUYNEN.

The Secretaries:

RÖELL.
CHARLES D. WHITE.
GEORGE YOUNG.

45   PROTOCOL XIII.

Meeting of Friday, June 24th, 1910.

The Tribunal assembled at 10 a. m.

The Honourable George Turner resumed his Argument.

At 12.03 the Tribunal took a recess.

The Tribunal reassembled at 2 p. m., when the Honourable George Turner continued his Argument.

At 4.18 p. m. the Tribunal adjourned until Monday, June 27th, at 10 a. m.

Done at *The Hague*, June 24th, 1910.

The President:

LAMMASCH.

The Secretary general:

MICHIELS VAN VERDUYNEN.

The Secretaries:

RÖELL.
CHARLES D. WHITE.
GEORGE YOUNG.

47   PROTOCOL XIV.

Meeting of Monday, June 27th, 1910.

The Tribunal assembled at 10.10 a. m.

The Honourable George Turner resumed his Argument.

At 12.12 the Tribunal took a recess.

The Tribunal reassembled at 2 p. m., when the Honourable George Turner continued his Argument.

At 4.10 p. m. the Tribunal adjourned until Tuesday, June 28th, at 10 a. m.

Done at *The Hague*, June 27th, 1910.

The President:

LAMMASCH.

The Secretary general:

MICHIELS VAN VERDUYNEN.

The Secretaries:

RÖELL.
CHARLES D. WHITE.
GEORGE YOUNG.

49   PROTOCOL XV.

Meeting of Tuesday, June 28th, 1910.

The Tribunal assembled at 10.10 a. m.

The Honourable George Turner resumed his Argument.

At 12—the Tribunal took a recess.

The Tribunal reassembled at 2 p. m., when the Honourable George Turner continued his Argument.

At 4.15 p. m. the Tribunal adjourned until Thursday, June 30th, at 10 a. m.

Done at *The Hague*, June 28th, 1910.

The President:

LAMMASCH.

The Secretary general:

MICHIELS VAN VERDUYNEN.

The Secretaries:

RÖELL.

CHARLES D. WHITE.

GEORGE YOUNG.

51   PROTOCOL XVI.

Meeting of Thursday, June 30th, 1910.

The Tribunal assembled at 10 a. m.

The Honourable George Turner resumed his Argument.

At 12.15 the Tribunal took a recess.

The Tribunal reassembled at 2 p. m., when the Honourable George Turner continued his Argument.

At 4.40 p. m. the Tribunal adjourned until Friday, July 1st, at 10 a. m.

Done at *The Hague*, June 30th, 1910.

The President:

LAMMASCH.

The Secretary general:

MICHIELS VAN VERDUYNEN.

The Secretaries:

RÖELL.

CHARLES D. WHITE.

GEORGE YOUNG.

53   PROTOCOL XVII.

Meeting of Friday, July 1st, 1910.

The Tribunal assembled at 10 a. m.

The Honourable George Turner resumed his Argument.

At 12 the Tribunal took a recess.

The Tribunal reassembled at 2 p. m. when the Honourable George Turner continued and concluded his Argument.

At 3.35 p. m. the Tribunal adjourned until Monday, July 4th, at 10 a. m.

Done at *The Hague*, July 1st, 1910.

The President:

LAMMASCH.

The Secretary general:

MICHIELS VAN VERDUYNEN.

The Secretaries:

RÖELL.
CHARLES D. WHITE.
GEORGE YOUNG.

55   PROTOCOL XVIII.

Meeting of Monday, July 4th, 1910.

The Tribunal assembled at 10 a. m.

Sir James S. Winter began his Argument on behalf of Great Britain.

At the request of the President the Secretary General read the following:

The two Counsel who have opened the case for both Parties having discussed all the questions and some of them in all their details, the Court expresses the opinion that the four Counsel who are next to follow might content themselves with the discussion of those topics which have not so far been treated *ex professo* and might succeed in doing so by taking together not more than two weeks, that is to say, four days for each Party.

For the purpose of enlarging the time at the disposal of these Counsel the Court is willing, if wanted, to sit in the next two weeks in the afternoon till five o'clock.

Of course it is expected that the Counsel who close for the respective Parties will cover all the questions at issue without any limitation as to time.

At 12.10 the Tribunal took a recess.

The Tribunal reassembled at 2 p. m., when Sir James S. Winter continued his Argument.

At 4.10 p. m. the Tribunal adjourned until Tuesday, July 5th at 10 a. m.

Done at *The Hague*, July 4th, 1910.

The President:

LAMMASCH.

The Secretary general:

MICHIELS VAN VERDUYNEN.

The Secretaries:

RÖELL.
CHARLES D. WHITE.
GEORGE YOUNG.

57 ### PROTOCOL XIX.

Meeting of Tuesday, July 5th, 1910.

The Tribunal assembled at 10 a. m.

Sir James S. Winter resumed and concluded his Argument.

At 11.55 the Tribunal took a recess.

The Tribunal reassembled at 2 p. m., when the Honourable Charles B. Warren began his Argument on behalf of the United States.

At 4.05 p. m. the Tribunal adjourned until Thursday, July 7th, at 10 a. m.

Done at *The Hague*, July 5th, 1910.

The President:

LAMMASCH.

The Secretary general:

MICHIELS VAN VERDUYNEN.

The Secretaries:

RÖELL.
CHARLES D. WHITE.
GEORGE YOUNG.

59 ### PROTOCOL XX.

Meeting of Thursday, July 7th, 1910.

The Tribunal assembled at 10 a. m.

The Honourable Charles B. Warren resumed his Argument.

At 12 the Tribunal took a recess.

The Tribunal reassembled at 2 p. m., when the Honourable Charles B. Warren continued his Argument.

At the close of the meeting the President, on behalf of the Court, asked Counsel on both sides to state whether they understand the position of Great Britain to be that under the renunciation clause of the Treaty of 1818 the United States have renounced for their inhabitants the right to enter bays that are non-territorial as well as those that are territorial, that is to say bays in the geographical sense of the word without referring to their territoriality.

At 4.30 p. m. the Tribunal adjourned until Friday, July 8th at 10 a. m.

Done at *The Hague*, July 7th, 1910.

The President:

LAMMASCH.

The Secretary general:

MICHIELS VAN VERDUYNEN.

The Secretaries:

RÖELL.
CHARLES D. WHITE.
GEORGE YOUNG.

PROTOCOL XXI.

Meeting of Friday, July 8th, 1910.

The Tribunal assembled at 10 a. m.

The Honourable Elihu Root, Counsel for the United States, replying to the question put by the President at the end of the preceding sitting, read the following statement:

The Counsel of the United States have the honor to answer the question asked by the President, in behalf of the Tribunal, on the 7th of July, as follows:—

They understand the position of Great Britain to be that under the renunciation clause of the Treaty of 1818 the United States has renounced the right to have its inhabitants take fish in bays in the geographical sense of the word, without referring to their territoriality, as stated:

1. In the British Case, page 83:

His Majesty's Government contend that the negotiators of the treaty meant by "bays," all those waters which, at the time, everyone knew as bays.

2. In the British Case, page 103:

His Majesty's Government contends that the term "bays," as used in the renunciation clause of article one, includes all tracts of water on the non-treaty coasts which were known under the name of "bays" in 1818, and that the 3 marine miles must be measured from a line drawn between the headlands of those waters.

3. In the British Case, page 104:

The negotiators of the convention were dealing, therefore, with tracts of water on the shores of His Majesty's dominions which were known to everyone under the name of "bays"—tracts of varying size and of varying conformation, some with greater and some with less width between their headlands, ranging from inclosures of considerable extent to inlets of small size. They used the term 62 "bays" without any qualification whatever, and the inference is irresistible, as His Majesty's Government submits, that the term was intended to apply to all the waters on those shores which were known to the negotiators and to the public, and were marked on the maps at the time, as "bays." If it had been intended that the term should apply only to a limited class of the waters which were then called "bays," an express limitation would have been inserted to give effect to that intention.

4. In the British Counter Case, page 43:

There is no qualification of any kind in regard to bays, and the necessary conclusion is that the treaty meant what it said and applied to all those tracts of water on the British American coasts which were known as bays at the date of the treaty.

5. In the British Argument, page 92:

It has been suggested that the natural meaning of the term "bays" may be limited by the words which follow, namely, "of His Britannic Majesty's dominions in America." Great Britain contends that these words are merely descriptive of the locality of the bays, and that they have no other significance. In the Counter-Case of the United States the attitude of Great Britain on this point has been misunderstood. It is there stated that "the British Case is based on the assumption that the words, 'bays, creeks or harbours of His Britannic Majesty's Dominions in America,' as used in the renunciatory clause of the treaty, were intended to be descriptive of territorial waters of Great Britain," and an argument is thereupon formulated on that issue. This is a misapprehension. The contention of His Majesty's Government is stated quite clearly in the British Case, and has been stated in the same way on many occasions during the last seventy years. It is that the treaty relates to all bays on the British coasts. In that view no question can arise as to territorial jurisdiction: the words of the article are read in their natural sense as referring to all the tracts of water known as bays on the coasts of the British dominions in North America.

The Right Honourable Sir William Snowdon Robson, Counsel for Great Britain, spoke as follows:

63   I will just add to the extract that my learned friend, Mr. Root, has read the last sentence of that passage on page 92 of the British Argument. It follows on:

It is abundantly clear that all the bays on these coasts were within British jurisdiction, but, in the view that His Majesty's Government presents, the question is not material.

I think I may add to that passage the answer to the question that the learned President put in very simple and concise terms. It is that Great Britain, while contending that the bays in question (referred to by the President) are in fact territorial, says also that the United States by the terms of the treaty have renounced for their fishermen the right to enter these bays, except for the purposes mentioned in the treaty itself—whether apart from the treaty these bays be territorial or be not territorial. We say they are territorial, but we say that in view of the terms of the Treaty of 1818, which contain an express renunciation, their territoriality is immaterial, so far as this Tribunal is concerned.

The Honourable Charles B. Warren then resumed his Argument.

At 12 the Tribunal took a recess.

The Tribunal reassembled at 2 p. m., when the Honourable Charles B. Warren continued his Argument.

At 4.06 p. m. the Tribunal adjourned until Monday, July 11th, at 10 a. m.

Done at *The Hague*, July 8th, 1910.

The President:

LAMMASCH.

The Secretary general:

MICHIELS VAN VERDUYNEN.

The Secretaries:

RÖELL.
CHARLES D. WHITE.
GEORGE YOUNG.

65   PROTOCOL XXII.
Meeting of Monday, July 11th, 1910.

The Tribunal assembled at 10 a. m.
The Honourable Charles B. Warren resumed his Argument.
At 12 the Tribunal took a recess.
The Tribunal reassembled at 2 p. m., when the Honourable Charles
B. Warren continued and concluded his Argument.
At 5.45 p. m. the Tribunal adjourned until Tuesday, July 12th, at
10 a. m.
Done at *The Hague*, July 11th, 1910.
The President:

LAMMASCH.

The Secretary general:

MICHIELS VAN VERDUYNEN.

The Secretaries:

RÖELL.
CHARLES D. WHITE.
GEORGE YOUNG.

67   PROTOCOL XXIII.
Meeting of Tuesday, July 12th, 1910.

The Tribunal assembled at 10 a. m.
Mr. John S. Ewart began his Argument on behalf of Great
Britain.
At 12 the Tribunal took a recess.
The Tribunal reassembled. at 2 p. m., when Mr. John S. Ewart
continued his Argument.
At 4 p. m. the Tribunal adjourned until Thursday, July 14th, at
10 a. m.
Done at *The Hague*, July 12th, 1910.
The President:

LAMMASCH.

The Secretary general:

MICHIELS VAN VERDUYNEN.

The Secretaries:

RÖELL.
CHARLES D. WHITE.
GEORGE YOUNG.

69   PROTOCOL XXIV.

Meeting of Thursday, July 14th, 1910.

The Tribunal assembled at 10 a. m.
Mr. John S. Ewart resumed his Argument.
At 12 the Tribunal took a recess.
The Tribunal reassembled at 2 p. m., when Mr. John S. Ewart
continued his Argument.
At 4 p. m. the Tribunal adjourned until Monday, July 18th, at
10 a. m.
Done at *The Hague*, July 14th, 1910.
The President:

LAMMASCH.

The Secretary general:

MICHIELS VAN VERDUYNEN.

The Secretaries:

RÖELL.
CHARLES D. WHITE.
GEORGE YOUNG.

71   PROTOCOL XXV.

Meeting of Monday, July 18th, 1910.

The Tribunal assembled at 10 a. m.
Mr. John S. Ewart resumed his Argument.
At 12 the Tribunal took a recess.
The Tribunal reassembled at 2 p. m., when Mr. John S. Ewart
continued his Argument.
At 4.37 p. m. the Tribunal adjourned until Tuesday, July 19th, at
10 a. m.
Done at *The Hague*, July 18th, 1910.
The President:

LAMMASCH.

The Secretary general:

MICHIELS VAN VERDUYNEN.

The Secretaries:

RÖELL.
CHARLES D. WHITE.
GEORGE YOUNG.

73   PROTOCOL XXVI.

Meeting of Tuesday, July 19th, 1910.

The Tribunal assembled at 10 a. m.
Mr. John S. Ewart resumed and concluded his Argument.
At 12.20 the Tribunal took a recess.

The Tribunal reassembled at 2.15 p. m.

At the request of the President the Secretary general read the following:

In pursuance of the provisions of Article II of the Special Agreement of the 27th of January 1909 both parties have called the attention of the Tribunal to different legislative and executive acts of the other party for the purpose of asking the Tribunal to point out in what respects, if any, they are inconsistent with the true interpretation of the Treaty. Without in any way expressing an opinion on any of the questions submitted to the Tribunal, it believes that it would facilitate its work and expedite the final disposition of this case if the Parties supplied the Tribunal with a detailed statement of the particular provisions of the statutes and regulations to which they object, accompanied by an exposition of the grounds of such objection. The objection of each Party to be communicated to the other. The objections should be made known to the Tribunal and the adverse Party within one week from this day and the answer of the adverse Party within one week thereafter, so that the Tribunal before taking the question submitted under advisement may have the benefit of a complete statement of the objections from each Party with such answer as the other Party may desire to make. In addition to the written objections the Tribunal would be pleased to receive such further oral statement as either Party may choose to make.

74   If the Counsel of the respective Parties desire to submit to the Tribunal, either orally or in writing, any view or suggestions in regard to the subject matter of article 4 of the special agreement, they will be heard or received at the convenience of counsel.

The Honourable Samuel J. Elder began his Argument on behalf of the United States.

At 4.25 p. m. the Tribunal adjourned until Thursday, July 21st, at 10 a. m.

Done at *The Hague*, July 19th, 1910.

The President:

LAMMASCH.

The Secretary general:

MICHIELS VAN VERDUYNEN.

The Secretaries:

RÖELL.
CHARLES D. WHITE.
GEORGE YOUNG.

75   PROTOCOL XXVII.

Meeting of Thursday, July 21st, 1910.

The Tribunal assembled at 10 a. m.
The Honourable Samuel J. Elder resumed his Argument.
At 12 the Tribunal took a recess.

The Tribunal reassembled at 2 p. m., when the Honourable Samuel J. Elder continued his Argument.

At 4.02 p. m. the tribunal adjourned until Friday, July 22nd, at 10 a. m.

Done at *The Hague*, July 21st, 1910.

The President:

LAMMASCH.

The Secretary general:

MICHIELS VAN VERDUYNEN.

The Secretaries:

RÖELL.
CHARLES D. WHITE.
GEORGE YOUNG.

77   PROTOCOL XXVIII.

Meeting of Friday, July 22nd, 1910.

The Tribunal assembled at 10 a. m.

The Honourable Samuel J. Elder resumed his Argument.

At 12.10 the Tribunal took a recess.

The Tribunal reassembled at 2 p. m., when the Honourable Samuel J. Elder continued and concluded his Argument.

At 4.45 p. m. the Tribunal adjourned until Monday, July 25th, at 10 a. m.

Done at *The Hague*, July 22nd, 1910.

The President:

LAMMASCH.

The Secretary general:

MICHIELS VAN VERDUYNEN.

The Secretaries:

RÖELL.
CHARLES D. WHITE.
GEORGE YOUNG.

79   PROTOCOL XXIX.

Meeting of Monday, July 25th, 1910.

The Tribunal assembled at 10 a. m.

The Right Honourable Sir William Snowdon Robson began his Argument on behalf of Great Britain.

At 12 the Tribunal took a recess.

The Tribunal reassembled at 2 p. m., when the Right Honourable Sir William Snowdon Robson continued his Argument.

At 3.55 p. m. the Tribunal adjourned until Tuesday, July 26th, at 10 a. m.

Done at *The Hague*, July 25th, 1910.

The President:

LAMMASCH.

The Secretary general:

MICHIELS VAN VERDUYNEN.

The Secretaries:

RÖELL.
CHARLES D. WHITE.
GEORGE YOUNG.

81 PROTOCOL XXX.

Meeting of Tuesday, July 26th, 1910.

The Tribunal assembled at 10 a. m.

The Right Honourable Sir William Snowdon Robson continued his Argument on behalf of Great Britain.

At 12.05 the Tribunal took a recess.

The Tribunal reassembled at 2 p. m., when, pursuant to the request on the part of the Tribunal which is incorporated in the Protocol of July 19th, the Right Honourable Sir William Snowdon Robson said, with regard to the particulars of objection which had been delivered by Great Britain complaining of the executive act of the United States Government in sending warships to the territorial waters in question, that it would be unnecessary to trouble the Tribunal for any judgment upon that particular executive act in view of the recognized motives of the United States in taking this action and of the relations maintained by their representatives with the local authorities.

The Honourable Elihu Root presented to the Members of the Tribunal printed copies of a Statement of specific provisions of certain legislative and executive acts of Newfoundland and Canada called to the attention of the Tribunal by the United States for action pursuant to Articles II and III of the Special Agreement of January 27th, 1909, copies of which Statement were also put at the disposal of the other Party.

He further said in reply to the last clause of the aforesaid request of the Tribunal, which is in these words: " If the counsel of the respective Parties desire to submit to the Tribunal, either orally or in writing, any view or suggestions in regard to the subject matter of Article IV of the Special Agreement, they will be heard or received at the convenience of counsel," that the United States have under consideration the question, whether it would be practicable to
82 make any suggestion of any value upon that subject in advance of the Award. Any rules which may be formulated by the

Tribunal under Article IV would necessarily depend so largely upon the Award, that Counsel for the United States have not yet seen how they could make any useful suggestions. They have it under consideration, however, and will be at any time ready to conform to any further expression on the part of the Tribunal.

The Right Honourable Sir William Snowdon Robson then said, with regard to the particulars of objection put forward by the United States, that he had not had an opportunity yet of considering them and asked that consideration of them might be delayed.

The President stated that the Tribunal had no objection to offer to that course.

The Right Honourable Sir William Snowdon Robson then continued his Argument.

At 4 p. m. the Tribunal adjourned until Thursday, July 28th, at 10 a. m.

Done at *The Hague*, July 26th, 1910.

The President:

> LAMMASCH.

The Secretary general:

> MICHIELS VAN VERDUYNEN.

The Secretaries:

> RÖELL.
> CHARLES D. WHITE.
> GEORGE YOUNG.

83   PROTOCOL XXXI.

Meeting of Thursday, July 28th, 1910.

The Tribunal assembled at 10 a. m.

The Right Honourable Sir William Snowdon Robson resumed his Argument.

At 12.02 the Tribunal took a recess.

The Tribunal reassembled at 2 p. m., when the Right Honourable Sir William Snowdon Robson continued his Argument.

At 4 p. m. the Tribunal adjourned until Friday, July 29th, at 10 a. m.

Done at *The Hague*, July 28th, 1910.

The President:

> LAMMASCH.

The Secretary general:

> MICHIELS VAN VERDUYNEN.

The Secretaries:

> RÖELL.
> CHARLES D. WHITE.
> GEORGE YOUNG.

85
PROTOCOL XXXII.

Meeting of Friday, July 29th, 1910.

The Tribunal assembled at 10 a. m.

The Right Honourable Sir William Snowdon Robson resumed his Argument.

At 12 the Tribunal took a recess.

The Tribunal reassembled at 2 p. m., when the Right Honourable Sir William Snowdon Robson continued his Argument.

At 4.10 p. m. the Tribunal adjourned until Monday, August 1st, at 10 a. m.

Done at *The Hague*, July 29th, 1910.

The President:

LAMMASCH.

The Secretary general:

MICHIELS VAN VERDUYNEN.

The Secretaries:

RÖELL.
CHARLES D. WHITE.
GEORGE YOUNG.

87
PROTOCOL XXXIII.

Meeting of Monday, August 1st, 1910.

The Tribunal assembled at 10 a. m.

The Right Honourable Sir William Snowdon Robson resumed his Argument.

At 12 the Tribunal took a recess.

The Tribunal reassembled at 2 p. m., when the Right Honourable Sir William Snowdon Robson continued his Argument.

At 4 p. m. the Tribunal adjourned until Tuesday, August 2nd, at 10 a. m.

Done at *The Hague*, August 1st, 1910.

The President:

LAMMASCH.

The Secretary general:

MICHIELS VAN VERDUYNEN.

The Secretaries:

RÖELL.
CHARLES D. WHITE.
GEORGE YOUNG.

89

PROTOCOL XXXIV.

Meeting of Tuesday, August 2nd, 1910.

The Tribunal assembled at 10 a. m.

The Right Honourable Sir William Snowdon Robson resumed his Argument.

At 12.15 the Tribunal took a recess.

The Tribunal reassembled at 2.15 p. m., when the Right Honourable Sir William Snowdon Robson continued his Argument, concluding the same at 2.35, and laid before the Tribunal the Answer of Great Britain to the Statement of the United States as to the Statutes and Regulations to which objection is taken.

After a recess of five minutes the Honourable Elihu Root began his Argument on behalf of the United States.

At 4.30 p. m. the Tribunal adjourned until Thursday, August 4th, at 10 a. m.

Done at *The Hague*, August 2nd, 1910.

The President:

LAMMASCH.

The Secretary general:

MICHIELS VAN VERDUYNEN.

The Secretaries:

RöELL.
CHARLES D. WHITE.
GEORGE YOUNG.

91

PROTOCOL XXXV.

Meeting of Thursday, August 4th, 1910.

The Tribunal assembled at 10 a. m.

The Honourable Elihu Root resumed his Argument.

At 12.15 the Tribunal took a recess.

The Tribunal reassembled at 2.15 p. m., when the Honourable Elihu Root continued his Argument.

At 4.15 p. m. the Tribunal adjourned until Friday, August 5th, at 10 a. m.

Done at *The Hague*, August 4th, 1910.

The President:

LAMMASCH.

The Secretary general:

MICHIELS VAN VERDUYNEN.

The Secretaries:

RöELL.
CHARLES D. WHITE.
GEORGE YOUNG.

93
PROTOCOL XXXVI.

Meeting of Friday, August 5th, 1910.

The Tribunal assembled at 10 a. m.
The Honourable Elihu Root resumed his Argument.
At 12.15 the Tribunal took a recess.
The Tribunal reassembled at 2.15 p. m., when the Honourable Elihu Root continued his Argument.

Mr. Root announced, in response to the request of the Tribunal made June 20th to the Agent and Counsel of the respective Parties, that Mr. Hugh M. Smith, Deputy Commissioner of Fisheries of the United States was designated by the United States to act as member of the Commission provided for by Article III of the Special Agreement of January 27th, 1909.

At 4.15 p. m. the Tribunal adjourned until Monday, August 8th, at 10 a. m.

Done at *The Hague*, August 5th, 1910.
The President:

LAMMASCH.

The Secretary general:

MICHIELS VAN VERDUYNEN.

The Secretaries:

RÖELL.
CHARLES D. WHITE.
GEORGE YOUNG.

95
PROTOCOL XXXVII.

Meeting of Monday, August 8th, 1910.

The Tribunal assembled at 10 a. m.
The Honourable Elihu Root resumed his Argument.
At 12.15 the Tribunal took a recess.
The Tribunal reassembled at 2.15 p. m., when the Honourable Elihu Root continued his Argument.

At 4.15 p. m. the Tribunal adjourned until Tuesday, August 9th, at 10 a. m.

Done at *The Hague*, August 8th, 1910.
The President:

LAMMASCH.

The Secretary general:

MICHIELS VAN VERDUYNEN.

The Secretaries:

RÖELL.
CHARLES D. WHITE.
GEORGE YOUNG.

97   PROTOCOL XXXVIII.

Meeting of Tuesday, August 9th, 1910.

The Tribunal assembled at 10 a. m.

The Honourable Elihu Root resumed his Argument.

At 12.05 the Tribunal took a recess.

The Tribunal reassembled at 2 p. m., when the Honourable Elihu
Root continued his Argument.

At 3.50 p. m. the Tribunal adjourned until Thursday, August 11th,
at 10 a. m.

Done at *The Hague*, August 9th, 1910.

The President:

                                  LAMMASCH.

The Secretary general:

                                  MICHIELS VAN VERDUYNEN.

The Secretaries:

                                  RÖELL.
                                  CHARLES D. WHITE.
                                  GEORGE YOUNG.

99   PROTOCOL XXXIX.

Meeting of Thursday, August 11th, 1910.

The Tribunal assembled at 10 a. m.

The Honourable Elihu Root resumed his Argument.

At 12.15 the Tribunal took a recess.

The Tribunal reassembled at 2.15 p. m., when the Honourable
Elihu Root continued his Argument.

At 4.35 p. m. the Tribunal adjourned until Friday, August 12th,
at 10 a. m.

Done at *The Hague*, August 11th, 1910.

The President:

                                  LAMMASCH.

The Secretary general:

                                  MICHIELS VAN VERDUYNEN.

The Secretaries:

                                  RÖELL.
                                  CHARLES D. WHITE.
                                  GEORGE YOUNG.

101   PROTOCOL XL.

Meeting of Friday, August 12th, 1910.

The Tribunal assembled at 10 a. m.

The Honorable Elihu Root resumed his Argument.

At 12 the Tribunal took a recess.

The Tribunal reassembled at 2 p. m., when the Honourable Elihu
Root continued his Argument, concluding the same at 3.15.

The Right Honourable William Snowdon Robson thereupon made some further observations in regard to new evidence introduced by the Honourable Elihu Root.

The President then spoke as follows:

GENTLEMEN: There is a noble custom prevailing among the Members of the bar in Anglo-Saxon countries to address one another as friends, even if they represent the adverse parties of a litigation. So Counsel on one side and on the other have done in this international proceeding.

So much the more it may be my privilege, in the name of the Tribunal, to address Counsel on both sides as our friends and to thank you for all the friendly assistance you have lent us during these weeks and months. You have led us through the maze of a hundred years of diplomatic correspondence, through the jungle of entangled statutes, through the dark forest of almost metaphysical problems, in which it was sometimes difficult to see our path, up to the summit of the mountain, where we hope we may see the problem we have to deal with in the light of truth and of justice.

I thank you all for the most valuable assistance we have had from your speeches, for the courtesy you have shown us and especially for the courtesy you have shown to one another. I am sure that the chivalrous spirit in which you have treated the grave controversies existing between your countries will facilitate us to come to a just and happy solution of them.

102   It is with regret that we take leave of you, who have been our friends and our guides in this long and sometimes laborious journey.

I beg the Agents of both Parties as well as the Secretary General and his Colleagues to accept the preliminary expression of our thanks, preliminary, as we shall apply to their assistance still for some time in our future work.

I also consider it my duty, before leaving, to thank the gentlemen who have their places immediately before me—and I desire to have their names on the record: Mr. Nelson R. Butcher, Mr. F. R. Hanna, Mr. Geo. Simpson, Mr. G. van Casteel and Mr. John W. Hulse—and their assistants for the accuracy, intelligence and punctuality with which they have reported the case.

The day of the next meeting for publication of the Award will be communicated to the Agents and Counsel of the Parties at least 4 days in advance.

I declare the discussion closed; the Tribunal adjourns *sine die*.

Done at *The Hague*, August 12th, 1910.

The President:

LAMMASCH.

The Secretary general:

MICHIELS VAN VERDUYNEN.

The Secretaries:

RÖELL.
CHARLES D. WHITE.
GEORGE YOUNG.

AWARD OF THE TRIBUNAL.
PROTOCOL XLI.

FORTY-FIRST DAY: WEDNESDAY, SEPTEMBER 7, 1910.

The Tribunal met at 10 a. m., at the Permanent Court of Arbitration, with closed doors, all the Arbitrators being present.

The five Arbitrators signed the Final Award of the Tribunal in triplicate original, one for each of the Parties, and the third to be preserved in the archives of the International Bureau of the Permanent Court of Arbitration.

The meeting, with closed doors, was followed at 2.30 p. m. by a public meeting.

There were present the five members of the Tribunal of Arbitration.

There were also present at the meeting:—

For the United States of America:

The Honourable CHANDLER P. ANDERSON, Agent;

The Honourable GEORGE TURNER, formerly a Senator of the United States from the State of Washington, Counsel;

The Honourable SAMUEL J. ELDER, Counsel;

The Honourable CHARLES B. WARREN, Counsel;

The Honourable JAMES BROWN SCOTT, Solicitor for the Department of State of the United States, Counsel;

The Honourable ROBERT LANSING, Counsel;

MR. OTIS THOMAS CARTWRIGHT, Secretary of the Agency.

For Great Britain:

The Honourable ALLEN B. AYLESWORTH, King's Counsel, Minister of Justice of Canada, Agent;

The Right Honourable SIR WILLIAM SNOWDON ROBSON, Member of the Privy Council, King's Counsel, Member of Parliament, His Majesty's Attorney-General, Counsel;

The Honourable DONALD MORISON, King's Counsel, Minister of Justice of Newfoundland;

MR. GEORGE F. SHEPLEY, King's Counsel, Counsel;

MR. A. F. PETERSON, King's Counsel, Counsel;

MR. W. N. TILLEY, Counsel;

MR. F. A. C. REDDEN, Solicitor.

104   The President called on the Secretary-General of the Tribunal to read the Award of the Tribunal, which is as follows:—

THE NORTH ATLANTIC COAST FISHERIES.

Preamble.

Whereas a special agreement between the United States of America
and Great Britain, signed at Washington the 27th January, 1909,
and confirmed by interchange of notes dated the 4th March, 1909,
was concluded in conformity with the provisions of the General
Arbitration Treaty between the United States of America and Great
Britain, signed the 4th April, 1908, and ratified the 4th June, 1908;

And whereas the said special agreement for the submission of
questions relating to fisheries on the North Atlantic coast under the
General Treaty of Arbitration concluded between the United States
and Great Britain on the 4th day of April, 1908, is as follows:—

ARTICLE I.

Whereas by Article I of the convention, signed at London on the
20th day of October, 1818, between Great Britain and the United
States, it was agreed as follows:—

" Whereas differences have arisen respecting the liberty claimed
by the United States for the inhabitants thereof, to take, dry, and
cure fish on certain coasts, bays, harbours, and creeks of His Britannic Majesty's dominions in America, it is agreed between the High
Contracting Parties that the inhabitants of the said United States
shall have forever, in common with the subjects of His Britannic
Majesty, the liberty to take fish of every kind on that part of the
southern coast of Newfoundland which extends from Cape Ray to
the Rameau Islands, on the western and northern coast of Newfoundland, from the said Cape Ray to the Quirpon Islands, on the
shores of the Magdalen Islands. and also on the coasts, bays, harbours, and creeks from Mount Joly on the southern coast of Labrador, to and through the Straits of Belleisle, and thence northwardly
indefinitely along the coast, without prejudice, however, to any of
the exclusive rights of the Hudson Bay Company; and that the
American fishermen shall also have liberty forever, to dry and cure
fish in any of the unsettled bays, harbours, and creeks of the southern
part of the coast of Newfoundland hereabove described, and of the
coast of Labrador; but so soon as the same, or any portion thereof,
shall be settled, it shall not be lawful for the said fishermen to dry
or cure fish at such portion so settled, without previous agreement
for such purpose with the inhabitants. proprietors, or possessors of
the ground.—And the United States hereby renounce forever, any
liberty heretofore enjoyed or claimed by the inhabitants thereof, to
take, dry, or cure fish on, or within three marine miles of any of the
coasts, bays, creeks, or harbours of His Britannic Majesty's dominions in America not included within the above-mentioned limits;

provided, however, that the American fishermen shall be admitted to enter such bays or harbours for the purpose of shelter and of repairing damages therein, of purchasing wood, and of obtaining water, and for no other purpose whatever. But they shall be under such restrictions as may be necessary to prevent their taking, drying or curing fish therein, or in any other manner whatever abusing the privileges hereby reserved to them."

And, whereas, differences have arisen as to the scope and meaning of the said article, and of the liberties therein referred to, and otherwise in respect of the rights and liberties which the inhabitants of the United States have or claim to have in the waters or on the shores therein referred to:

It is agreed that the following questions shall be submitted for decision to a Tribunal of Arbitration constituted as hereinafter provided :—

Question 1.—To what extent are the following contentions or either of them justified?

It is contended on the part of Great Britain that the exercise of the liberty to take fish referred to in the said article, which the inhabitants of the United States have forever in common with the subjects of His Britannic Majesty, is subject, without the consent of the United States, to reasonable regulation by Great Britain, Canada, or Newfoundland in the form of municipal laws, ordinances, or rules, as, for example, to regulations in respect of (1) the hours, days, or seasons when fish may be taken on the treaty coasts; (2) the method, means, and implements to be used in the taking of fish or in the carrying on of fishing operations on such coasts; (3) any other matters of a similar character relating to fishing; such regulations being reasonable, as being, for instance—

(*a*.) Appropriate or necessary for the protection and preservation of such fisheries and the exercise of the rights of British subjects therein and of the liberty which by the said Article I the inhabitants of the United States have therein in common with British subjects;

(*b*.) Desirable on grounds of public order and morals;

(*c*.) Equitable and fair as between local fishermen and the inhabitants of the United States exercising the said treaty liberty, and not so framed as to give unfairly an advantage to the former over the latter class.

It is contended on the part of the United States that the exercise of such liberty is not subject to limitations or restraints by Great Britain, Canada, or Newfoundland in the form of municipal laws, ordinances, or regulations in respect of (1) the hours, days, or seasons when the inhabitants of the United States may take fish on the treaty coasts, or (2) the method, means, and implements used by them in taking fish or in carrying on fishing operations on such coasts, or (3) any other limitations or restraints of similar character—

(*a.*) Unless they are appropriate and necessary for the protection and preservation of the common rights in such fisheries and the exercise thereof; and

(*b.*) Unless they are reasonable in themselves and fair as between local fishermen and fishermen coming from the United States, and not so framed as to give an advantage to the former over the latter class; and

(*c.*) Unless their appropriateness, necessity, reasonableness, and fairness be determined by the United States and Great Britain by common accord and the United States concurs in their enforcement.

Question 2.—Have the inhabitants of the United States, while exercising the liberties referred to in said article, a right to employ as members of the fishing crews of their vessels persons not inhabitants of the United States?

Question 3.—Can the exercise by the inhabitants of the United States of the liberties referred to in the said article be subjected, without the consent of the United States, to the requirements of entry or report at custom-houses or the payment of light or harbour or other dues, or to any other similar requirement or condition or exaction?

Question 4.—Under the provision of the said article that the American fishermen shall be admitted to enter certain bays or harbours for shelter, repairs, wood, or water, and for no other purpose whatever, but that they shall be under such restrictions as may be necessary to prevent their taking, drying, or curing fish therein or in any other manner whatever abusing the privileges thereby reserved to them, is it permissible to impose restrictions making the exercise of such privileges conditional upon the payment of light or harbour or other dues, or entering or reporting at custom-houses or any similar conditions?

Question 5.—From where must be measured the "three marine miles of any of the coasts, bays, creeks, or harbours" referred to in the said article?

Question 6.—Have the inhabitants of the United States the liberty under the said article or otherwise to take fish in the bays, harbours, and creeks on that part of the southern coast of Newfoundland which extends from Cape Ray to Rameau Islands, or on the western and northern coasts of Newfoundland from Cape Ray to Quirpon Islands, or on the Magdalen Islands?

Question 7.—Are the inhabitants of the United States whose vessels resort to the Treaty Coasts for the purpose of exercising the liberties referred to in Article I of the treaty of 1818 entitled to have for those vessels, when duly authorized by the United States in that behalf, the commercial privileges on the Treaty Coasts accorded by agreement or otherwise to United States trading-vessels generally?

Article II.

Either Party may call the attention of the Tribunal to any legislative or executive act of the other Party, specified within three months of the exchange of notes enforcing this agreement, and 106   which is claimed to be inconsistent with the true interpretation of the treaty of 1818; and may call upon the Tribunal to express in its Award its opinion upon such acts, and to point out in what respects, if any, they are inconsistent with the principles laid down in the Award in reply to the preceding questions; and each Party agrees to conform to such opinion.

Article III.

If any question arises in the arbitration regarding the reasonableness of any regulation or otherwise which requires an examination of the practical effect of any provisions in relation to the conditions surrounding the exercise of the liberty of fishery enjoyed by the inhabitants of the United States, or which requires expert information about the fisheries themselves, the Tribunal may, in that case, refer such question to a Commission of three expert specialists in such matters; one to be designated by each of the Parties hereto, and the third, who shall not be a national of either Party, to be designated by the Tribunal. This Commission shall examine into and report their conclusions on any question or questions so referred to it by the Tribunal, and such report shall be considered by the Tribunal, and shall, if incorporated by them in the Award, be accepted as a part thereof.

Pending the report of the Commission upon the question or questions so referred, and without awaiting such report, the Tribunal may make a separate Award upon all or any other questions before it; and such separate Award, if made, shall become immediately effective, provided that the report aforesaid shall not be incorporated in the Award until it has been considered by the Tribunal. The expenses of such Commission shall be borne in equal moieties by the Parties hereto.

Article IV.

The Tribunal shall recommend for the consideration of the High Contracting Parties rules and a method of procedure under which all questions which may arise in the future regarding the exercise of the liberties above referred to may be determined in accordance with the principles laid down in the Award. If the High Contracting Parties shall not adopt the rules and method of procedure so recommended, or if they shall not, subsequently to the delivery of the Award, agree upon such rules and methods, then any differences which may arise in the future between the High Contracting Parties relating to the interpretation of the Treaty of 1818 or to the effect and application of the Award of the Tribunal shall be referred informally to the Permanent Court at The Hague for decision by the summary procedure provided in Chapter IV of The Hague Convention of the 18th October, 1907.

ARTICLE V.

The Tribunal of Arbitration provided for herein shall be chosen from the general list of members of the Permanent Court at The Hague, in accordance with the provisions of Article XLV of the Convention for the Settlement of International Disputes, concluded at the second Peace Conference at The Hague on the 18th October, 1907. The provisions of said convention, so far as applicable and not inconsistent herewith, and excepting Articles LIII and LIV, shall govern the proceedings under the submission herein provided for.

The time allowed for the direct agreement of His Britannic Majesty and the President of the United States on the composition of such Tribunal shall be three months.

ARTICLE VI.

The pleadings shall be communicated in the order and within the time following:—

As soon as may be and within a period not exceeding seven months from the date of the exchange of notes making this agreement binding the printed case of each of the Parties hereto, accompanied by printed copies of the documents, the official correspondence, and all other evidence on which each Party relies, shall be delivered in duplicate (with such additional copies as may be agreed upon) to the agent of the other Party. It shall be sufficient for this purpose if such case is delivered at the British Embassy at Washington or at the American Embassy at London, as the case may be, for transmission to the agent for its Government.

107 Within fifteen days thereafter such printed case and accompanying evidence of each of the Parties shall be delivered in duplicate to each member of the Tribunal, and such delivery may be made by depositing within the stated period the necessary number of copies with the International Bureau at The Hague for transmission to the Arbitrators.

After the delivery on both sides of such printed case, either Party may, in like manner, and within four months after the expiration of the period above fixed for the delivery to the agents of the case, deliver to the agent of the other Party (with such additional copies as may be agreed upon), a printed counter-case accompanied by printed copies of additional documents, correspondence, and other evidence in reply to the case, documents, correspondence, and other evidence so presented by the other Party, and within fifteen days thereafter such Party shall, in like manner as above provided, deliver in duplicate such counter-case and accompanying evidence to each of the Arbitrators.

The foregoing provisions shall not prevent the Tribunal from permitting either Party to rely at the hearing upon documentary or other evidence which is shown to have become open to its investigation or examination or available for use too late to be submitted within the period hereinabove fixed for the delivery of copies of evidence, but in case any such evidence is to be presented, printed copies of it, as soon as possible after it is secured, must be delivered, in like manner, as provided for the delivery of copies of other evidence, to each of the Arbitrators and to the agent of the other Party. The admission of any such additional evidence, however, shall be subject to such conditions as the Tribunal may impose, and the other Party shall have a reasonable opportunity to offer additional evidence in rebuttal.

The Tribunal shall take into consideration all evidence which is offered by either Party.

ARTICLE VII.

If in the case or counter-case (exclusive of the accompanying evidence) either Party shall have specified or referred to any documents, correspondence, or other evidence in its own exclusive possession without annexing a copy, such Party shall be bound, if the other Party shall demand it within thirty days after the delivery of the case or counter-case respectively, to furnish to the Party applying for it a copy thereof; and either Party may, within the like time, demand that the other shall furnish certified copies or produce for inspection the originals of any documentary evidence adduced by the Party upon whom the demand is made. It shall be the duty of the Party upon whom any such demand is made to comply with it as soon as may be, and within a period not exceeding fifteen days after the demand has been received. The production for inspection or the furnishing to the other Party of official governmental publications, publishing, as authentic, copies of the documentary evidence referred to, shall be a sufficient compliance with such demand, if such governmental publications shall have been published prior to the 1st day of January, 1908. If the demand is not complied with, the reasons for the failure to comply must be stated to the Tribunal.

ARTICLE VIII.

The Tribunal shall meet within six months after the expiration of the period above fixed for the delivery to the agents of the case, and upon the assembling of the Tribunal at its first session each Party, through its agent or counsel, shall deliver in duplicate to each of the Arbitrators and to the agent and counsel of the other Party (with such additional copies as may be agreed upon) a printed argument showing the points and referring to the evidence upon which it relies.

The time fixed by this Agreement for the delivery of the case, counter-case, or argument, and for the meeting of the Tribunal, may be extended by mutual consent of the Parties.

ARTICLE IX.

The decision of the Tribunal shall, if posible, be made within two months from the close of the arguments on both sides, unless on the request of the Tribunal the Parties shall agree to extend the period.

It shall be made in writing, and dated and signed by each member of the Tribunal, and shall be accompanied by a statement of reasons.

A member who may dissent from the decision may record his dissent when signing.

The language to be used throughout the proceedings shall be English.

108   ## ARTICLE X.

Each Party reserves to itself the right to demand a revision of the Award. Such demand shall contain a statement of the grounds on which it is made and shall be made within five days of the promulgation of the Award, and shall be heard by the Tribunal within ten days thereafter. The Party making the demand shall serve a copy of the same on the opposite Party, and both Parties shall be heard in argument by the Tribunal on said demand. The demand can only be made on the discovery of some new fact or circumstance calculated to exercise a decisive influence upon the Award and which was unknown to the Tribunal and to the Party demanding the revision at the time the discussion was closed, or upon the ground that the said Award does not fully and sufficiently, within the meaning of this Agreement, determine any question or questions submitted. If the Tribunal shall allow the demand for a revision, it shall afford such opportunity for further hearings and arguments as it shall deem necessary.

ARTICLE XI.

The present Agreement shall be deemed to be binding only when confirmed by the two Governments by an exchange of notes.

In witness whereof this Agreement has been signed and sealed by His Britannic Majesty's Ambassador at Washington, the Right Honourable James Bryce, O. M., on behalf of Great Britain, and by the Secretary of State of the United States, Elihu Root, on behalf of the United States.

Done at Washington, on the 27th day of January, 1909.

JAMES BRYCE.   [SEAL.]
ELIHU ROOT.   [SEAL.]

And whereas the parties to the said Agreement have by common accord, in accordance with Article V, constituted as a Tribunal of Arbitration the following members of the Permanent Court at The Hague: Mr. H. Lammasch, Doctor of Law, Professor of the University of Vienna, Aulic Councillor, Member of the Upper House of the Austrian Parliament; His Excellency Jonkheer A. F. De Savornin Lohman, Doctor of Law, Minister of State, former Minister of the Interior, Member of the Second Chamber of the Netherlands; the Honourable George Gray, Doctor of Laws, Judge of the United States Circuit Court of Appeals, former United States Senator; the Right Honourable Sir Charles Fitzpatrick, Member of the Privy Council, Doctor of Laws, Chief Justice of Canada; the Honourable Luis Maria Drago, Doctor of Law, former Minister of Foreign Affairs of the Argentine Republic, Member of the Law Academy of Buenos Ayres;

And whereas the agents of the Parties to the said Agreement have duly, and in accordance with the terms of the Agreement communicated to this Tribunal, their cases, counter-cases, printed arguments, and other documents;

And whereas counsel for the Parties have fully presented to this Tribunal their oral arguments in the sittings held between the first assembling of the Tribunal on the 1st June, 1910, to the close of the hearings on the 12th August, 1910;

Now, therefore, this Tribunal having carefully considered the said Agreement, cases, counter-cases, printed and oral arguments, and the documents presented by either side, after due deliberation makes the following decisions and awards:—

QUESTION I.

To what extent are the following contentions, or either of them, justified?

It is contended on the part of Great Britain that the exercise of the liberty to take fish referred to in the said article, which the inhabitants of the United States have for ever in common with the subjects of His Britannic Majesty, is subject, without the consent of the United States, to reasonable regulation by Great Britain, Canada, or Newfoundland in the form of municipal laws, ordinances, or rules, as, for example, to regulations in respect of (1) the hours, days, or seasons when fish may be taken on the treaty coasts; (2) the method, means, and implements to be used in the taking of fish or in the carrying on of fishing operations on such coasts; (3) any other matters of a similar character relating to fishing; such regulations being reasonable, as being, for instance—

109   (a.) Appropriate or necessary for the protection and preservation of such fisheries and the exercise of the rights of British subjects therein, and of the liberty which by the said Article I the inhabitants of the United States have therein in common with British subjects;

(b.) Desirable on grounds of public order and morals;

(c.) Equitable and fair as between local fishermen and the inhabitants of the United States exercising the said treaty liberty, and not so framed as to give unfairly an advantage to the former over the latter class.

It is contended on the part of the United States that the exercise of such liberty is not subject to limitations or restraints by Great Britain, Canada, or Newfoundland in the form of municipal laws, ordinances, or regulations in respect of (1) the hours, days, or seasons when the inhabitants of the United States may take fish on the treaty coasts, or (2) the method, means, and implements used by them in taking fish or in carrying on fishing operations on such coasts, or (3) any other limitations or restraints of similar character—

(a.) Unless they are appropriate and necessary for the protection and preservation of the common rights in such fisheries and the exercise thereof; and

(b.) Unless they are reasonable in themselves and fair as between local fishermen and fishermen coming from the United States, and not so framed as to give an advantage to the former over the latter class; and (*c.*) Unless their appropriateness, necessity, reasonableness, and fairness be determined by the United States and Great Britain by common accord and the United States concurs in their enforcement.

Question I, thus submitted to the Tribunal, resolves itself into two main contentions:

1st. Whether the right of regulating reasonably the liberties conferred by the treaty of 1818 resides in Great Britain;

2nd. And, if such right does so exist, whether such reasonable exercise of the right is permitted to Great Britain without the accord and concurrence of the United States.

The treaty of 1818 contains no explicit disposition in regard to the right of regulation, reasonable or otherwise; it neither reserves that right in express terms, nor refers to it in any way. It is therefore incumbent on this Tribunal to answer the two questions above indicated by interpreting the general terms of Article I of the treaty, and more especially the words "the inhabitants of the United States shall have, for ever, in common with the subjects of His Britannic Majesty, the liberty to take fish of every kind." This interpretation must be conformable to the general import of the instrument, the general intention of the parties to it, the subject matter of the contract, the expressions actually used and the evidence submitted.

Now in regard to the preliminary question as to whether the right of reasonable regulation resides in Great Britain:—

Considering that the right to regulate the liberties conferred by the treaty of 1818 is an attribute of sovereignty, and as such must be held to reside in the territorial sovereign, unless the contrary be provided; and considering that one of the essential elements of sovereignty is that it is to be exercised within territorial limits, and that, failing proof to the contrary, the territory is coterminous with the sovereignty, it follows that the burden of the assertion involved in the contention of the United States (viz., that the right to regulate does not reside independently in Great Britain, the territorial sovereign) must fall on the United States. And for the purpose of sustaining this burden, the United States have put forward the following series of propositions, each one of which must be singly considered.

It is contended by the United States:

(1.) That the French right of fishery under the treaty of 1713 designated also as a liberty, was never subjected to regulation by Great Britain, and therefore the inference is warranted that the American liberties of fishery are similarly exempted.

The Tribunal is unable to agree with this contention:

(*a.*) Because although the French right designated in 1713 merely "an allowance" (a term of even less force than that used in

110   regard to the American fishery) was nevertheless converted, in practice, into an exclusive right, this concession on the part of Great Britain was presumably made because France, before 1713, claimed to be the sovereign of Newfoundland, and, in ceding the island, had, as the American argument says, " reserved for the benefit of its subjects the right to fish and to use the strand;"

(*b.*) Because the distinction between the French and American right is indicated by the different wording of the statutes for the observance of treaty obligations towards France and the United States, and by the British Declaration of 1783;

(*c.*) And, also, because this distinction is maintained in the treaty with France of 1904, concluded at a date when the American claim was approaching its present stage, and by which certain common rights of regulation are recognised to France.

For the further purpose of such proof it is contended by the United States:

(2.) That the liberties of fishery, being accorded to the inhabitants of the United States " for ever," acquire, by being in perpetuity and unilateral, a character exempting them from local legislation.

The Tribunal is unable to agree with this contention:

(*a.*) Because there is no necessary connection between the duration of a grant and its essential status in its relation to local regulation; a right granted in perpetuity may yet be subject to regulation, or, granted temporarily, may yet be exempted therefrom; or being reciprocal may yet be unregulated, or being unilateral may yet be regulated: as is evidenced by the claim of the United States that the liberties of fishery accorded by the Reciprocity Treaty of 1854 and the treaty of 1871 were exempt from regulation, though they were neither permanent nor unilateral;

(*b*) Because no peculiar character need be claimed for these liberties in order to secure their enjoyment in perpetuity, as is evidenced by the American negotiators in 1818 asking for the insertion of the words " for ever." International law in its modern development recognises that a great number of treaty obligations are not annulled by war, but at most suspended by it;

(*c.*) Because the liberty to dry and cure is, pursuant to the terms of the treaty, provisional and not permanent, and is nevertheless, in respect of the liability to regulation, identical in its nature with, and never distinguished from, the liberty to fish.

For the further purpose of such proof, the United States allege:

(3.) That the liberties of fishery granted to the United States constitute an international servitude in their favour over the territory of Great Britain, thereby involving a derogation from the sovereignty of Great Britain, the servient State, and that therefore Great Britain is deprived, by reason of the grant, of its independent right to regulate the fishery.

The Tribunal is unable to agree with this contention:

(*a.*) Because there is no evidence that the doctrine of international servitudes was one with which either American or British statesmen were conversant in 1818, no English publicists employing the term before 1818, and the mention of it in Mr. Gallatin's report being insufficient;

(*b.*) Because a servitude in the French law, referred to by Mr. Gallatin, can, since the Code, be only real and cannot be personal (Code Civil, article 686);

(*c.*) Because a servitude in international law predicates an express grant of a sovereign right and involves an analogy to the relation of a *praedium dominans* and a *praedium serviens;* whereas by the treaty of 1818 one State grants a liberty to fish, which is not a sovereign right, but a purely economic right, to the inhabitants of another State;

(*d.*) Because the doctrine of international servitude in the sense which is now sought to be attributed to it originated in the peculiar and now obsolete conditions prevailing in the Holy Roman Empire of which the *domini terræ* were not fully sovereigns; they holding territory under the Roman Empire, subject at least theoretically, and in some respects also practically, to the courts of that Empire; their right being, moreover, rather of a civil than of a public nature, partaking more of the character of *dominium* than of *imperium*, and therefore certainly not a complete sovereignty. And because in contradistinction to this quasi-sovereignty with its incoherent attributes acquired at various times, by various means, and not impaired

111   in its character by being incomplete in any one respect or by being limited in favour of another territory and its possessor, the modern State, and particularly Great Britain, has never admitted partition of sovereignty, owing to the constitution of a modern State requiring essential sovereignty and independence;

(*e.*) Because this doctrine being but little suited to the principle of sovereignty which prevails in States under a system of constitutional government such as Great Britain and the United States, and to the present international relations of sovereign States, has found little, if any, support from modern publicists. It could therefore in the general interest of the community of nations, and of the Parties to this treaty, be affirmed by this Tribunal only on the express evidence of an international contract;

(*f.*) Because even if these liberties of fishery constituted an international servitude, the servitude would derogate from the sovereignty of the servient State only in so far as the exercise of the rights of sovereignty by the servient State would be contrary to the exercise of the servitude right by the dominant State. Whereas it is evident that, though every regulation of the fishery is to some extent a limitation, as it puts limits to the exercise of the fishery at will, yet such regulations as are reasonable and made for the purpose of securing and preserving the fishery and its exercise for the common benefit, are clearly to be distinguished from those restrictions and " molestations," the annulment of which was the purpose of the American demands formulated by Mr. Adams in 1782, and such regulations consequently cannot be held to be inconsistent with a servitude;

(g.) Because the fishery to which the inhabitants of the United States were admitted in 1783, and again in 1818, was a regulated fishery, as is evidenced by the following regulations:—

Act 15 Charles II, cap. 16, sec. 7 (1663), forbidding " to lay any seine or other net in or near any harbour in Newfoundland, whereby to take the spawn or young fry of the Poor-John, or for any other use or uses, except for the taking of bait only," which had not been superseded either by the Order-in-Council of March 10th, 1670, or by the statute 10 and 11 Wm. III, cap. 25, 1699. The Order-in-Council provides expressly for the obligation " to submit unto and to observe all rules and orders as are now, or hereafter shall be, established," an obligation which cannot be read as referring only to the rules established by this very Act, and having no reference to anteceding rules " as are now established." In a similar way the statute of 1699 preserves in force prior legislation, conferring the freedom of fishery only " as fully and freely as at any time heretofore." The Order-in-Council, 1670, provides that the admirals, who always were fishermen, arriving from an English or Welsh port, " see that His Majesty's rules and orders concerning the regulation of the fisheries are duly put in execution " (sec. 13). Likewise the Act 10 and 11 Wm. III, cap. 25 (1699) provides that the admirals do settle differences between the fishermen arising in respect of the places to be assigned to the different vessels. As to Nova Scotia, the proclamation of 1665 ordains that no one shall fish without licence; that the licensed fishermen are obliged " to observe all laws and orders which now are made and published, or shall hereafter be made and published, in this jurisdiction," and that they shall not fish on the Lord's Day, and shall not take fish at the time they come to spawn. The judgment of the Chief Justice of Newfoundland, October 26th, 1820, is not held by the Tribunal sufficient to set aside the proclamations referred to. After 1783 the statute 26 Geo. III, cap. 26, 1786, forbids " the use, on the shores of Newfoundland, of seines or nets for catching cod by hauling on shore or taking into boat with meshes less than 4 inches"; a prohibition which cannot be considered as limited to the bank fishery. The Act for regulating the fisheries of New Brunswick, 1793, which forbids " the placing of nets or seines across any cove or creek in the province so as to obstruct the natural course of fish," and which makes specific provision for fishing in the harbour of St. John, as to the manner and time of fishing, cannot be read as being limited to fishing from the shore.   The Act for regulating the fishing on the coast of Northumberland (1799) contains very elaborate dispositions concerning the fisheries in the Bay of Miramichi, which were continued in 1823, 1829 and 1834.   The statutes of Lower Canada, 1788 and 1807, forbid the throwing overboard of offal.   The fact that these Acts extend the prohibition over a greater distance than the first marine league from the shore may make them non-operative against foreigners without the territorial limits of Great Britain, but is certainly no reason to deny their obligatory character for foreigners within these limits;

(h.) Because the fact that Great Britain rarely exercised the right of regulation in the period immediately succeeding 1818 is to be explained by various circumstances, and is not evidence of the non-existence of the right;

112   (i.) Because the words "in common with British subjects" tend to confirm the opinion that the inhabitants of the United States were admitted to a regulated fishery;

(j.) Because the statute of Great Britain, 1819, which gives legislative sanction to the treaty of 1818, provides for the making of "regulations with relation to the taking, drying and curing of fish by inhabitants of the United States ' in common.' "

For the purpose of such proof it is further contended by the United States, in this latter connection:

4. That the words "in common with British subjects" used in the treaty should not be held as importing a common subjection to regulation, but as intending to negative a possible pretension on the part of the inhabitants of the United States to liberties of fishery exclusive of the right of British subjects to fish.

The Tribunal is unable to agree with this contention:

(a.) Because such an interpretation is inconsistent with the historical basis of the American fishing liberty.   The ground on which Mr. Adams founded the American right in 1782 was that the people then constituting the United States had always, when still under British rule, a part in these fisheries and that they must continue to enjoy their past right in the future.   He proposed "that the subjects of His Britannic Majesty and the people of the United States shall continue to enjoy unmolested the right to take fish . . . . where the inhabitants of both countries used, at any time heretofore, to fish."   The theory of the partition of the fisheries which, by the American negotiators, had been advanced with so much force, negatives the assumption that the United States could ever pretend to an exclusive right to fish on the British shores; and to insert a special disposition to that end would have been wholly superfluous;

(*b.*) Because the words " in common " occur in the same connection in the treaty of 1818 as in the treaties of 1854 and 1871. It will certainly not be suggested that in these treaties of 1854 and 1871 the American negotiators meant by inserting the words " in common " to imply that without these words American citizens would be precluded from the right to fish on their own coasts and that, on American shores, British subjects should have an exclusive privilege. It would have been the very opposite of the concept of territorial waters to suppose that, without a special treaty provision, British subjects could be excluded from fishing in British waters. Therefore that cannot have been the scope and the sense of the words " in common ";

(*c.*) Because the words " in common " exclude the supposition that American inhabitants were at liberty to act at will for the purpose of taking fish, without any regard to the co-existing rights of other persons entitled to do the same thing; and because these words admit them only as members of a social community, subject to the ordinary duties binding upon the citizens of that community, as to the regulations made for the common benefit; thus avoiding the *bellum omnium contra omnes* which would otherwise arise in the exercise of this industry;

(*d.*) Because these words are such as would naturally suggest themselves to the negotiators of 1818 if their intention had been to express a common subjection to regulations as well as a common right.

In the course of the Argument it has also been alleged by the United States:

(5.) That the treaty of 1818 should be held to have entailed a transfer or partition of sovereignty, in that it must in respect to the liberties of fishery be interpreted in its relation to the treaty of 1783; and that this latter treaty was an act of partition of sovereignty and of separation, and as such was not annulled by the war of 1812.

Although the Tribunal is not called upon to decide the issue whether the treaty of 1783 was a treaty of partition or not, the questions involved therein having been set at rest by the subsequent treaty of 1818, nevertheless the Tribunal could not forbear to consider the contention on acount of the important bearing the controversy has upon the true interpretation of the treaty of 1818. In that respect the Tribunal is of opinion:

(*a.*) That the right to take fish was accorded as a condition of peace to a foreign people; wherefore the British negotiators
113   refused to place the right of British subjects on the same footing with those of American inhabitants; and further, refused to insert the words also proposed by Mr. Adams—" continue to enjoy "—in the second branch of Article III of the treaty of 1783;

(*b.*) That the treaty of 1818 was in different terms, and very different in extent, from that of 1783, and was made for different considerations. It was, in other words, a new grant.

For the purpose of such proof it is further contended by the United States:

(6.) That as contemporary commercial treaties contain express provisions for submitting foreigners to local legislation, and the treaty of 1818 contains no such provision, it should be held, *a contrario*, that inhabitants of the United States exercising these liberties are exempt from regulation.

The Tribunal is unable to agree with this contention:

(*a.*) Because the commercial treaties contemplated did not admit foreigners to all and equal rights, seeing that local legislation excluded them from many rights of importance, *e. g.*, that of holding land; and the purport of the provisions in question consequently was to preserve these discriminations. But no such discriminations existing in the common enjoyment of the fishery by American and British fishermen, no such provision was required;

(*b.*) Because no proof is furnished of similar exemptions of foreigners from local legislation in default of treaty stipulations subjecting them thereto;

(*c.*) Because no such express provision for subjection of the nationals of either Party to local law was made either in this treaty, in respect to their reciprocal admission to certain territories as agreed in Article III, or in Article III of the treaty of 1794; although such subjection was clearly contemplated by the Parties.

For the purpose of such proof it is further contended by the United States:

(7.) That, as the liberty to dry and cure on the treaty coasts and to enter bays and harbours on the non-treaty coasts are both subjected to conditions, and the latter to specific restrictions, it should therefore be held that the liberty to fish should be subjected to no restrictions, as none are provided for in the treaty.

The Tribunal is unable to apply the principle of " *expressio unius exclusio alterius* " to this case:—

(*a.*) Because the conditions and restrictions as to the liberty to dry and cure on the shore and to enter the harbours are limitations of the rights themselves, and not restrictions of their exercise. Thus the right to dry and cure is limited in duration, and the right to enter bays and harbours is limited to particular purposes;

(*b.*) Because these restrictions of the right to enter bays and harbours applying solely to American fishermen must have been expressed in the treaty, whereas regulations of the fishery, applying equally to American and British, are made by right of territorial sovereignty.

For the purpose of such proof it has been contended by the United States:

(8.) That Lord Bathurst in 1815 mentioned the American right under the treaty of 1783 as a right to be exercised " at the discretion of the United States;" and that this should be held as to be derogatory to the claim of exclusive regulation by Great Britain.

But the Tribunal is unable to agree with this contention:

(*a.*) Because these words implied only the necessity of an express stipulation for any liberty to use foreign territory at the pleasure of the grantee, without touching any question as to regulation;

(*b.*) Because in this same letter Lord Bathurst characterised this right as a policy " temporary and experimental, depending on the use that might be made of it, on the condition of the islands and places where it was to be exercised, and the more general conveniences or inconveniences from a military, naval and commercial point of view;" so that it cannot have been his intention to acknowledge the exclusion of British interference with this right;

(*c.*) Because Lord Bathurst, in his note to Governor Sir C. Hamilton in 1819, orders the Governor to take care that the American fishery on the coast of Labrador be carried on *in the same manner* as previous to the late war; showing that he did not interpret the treaty just signed as a grant conveying absolute immunity from interference with the American fishery right.

114

For the purpose of such proof it is further contended by the United States:

(9.) That on various other occasions following the conclusion of the treaty, as evidenced by official correspondence, Great Britain made use of expressions inconsistent with the claim to a right of regulation.

The Tribunal, unwilling to invest such expressions with an importance entitling them to affect the general question, considers that such conflicting or inconsistent expressions as have been exposed on either side are sufficiently explained by their relations to ephemeral phases of a controversy of almost secular duration, and should be held to be without direct effect on the principal and present issues.

Now, with regard to the second contention involved in Question I, as to whether the right of regulation can be reasonably exercised by Great Britain without the consent of the United States:—

Considering that the recognition of a concurrent right of consent in the United States would affect the independence of Great Britain, which would become dependent on the Government of the United States for the exercise of its sovereign right of regulation, and considering that such a co-dominium would be contrary to the constitution of both sovereign States; the burden of proof is imposed on the United States to show that the independence of Great Britain was thus impaired by international contract in 1818 and that a co-dominium was created.

For the purpose of such proof it is contended by the United States:

(10.) That a concurrent right to co-operate in the making and enforcement of regulations is the only possible and proper security to their inhabitants for the enjoyment of their liberties of fishery, and that such a right must be held to be implied in the grant of those liberties by the treaty under interpretation.

The Tribunal is unable to accede to this claim on the ground of a right so implied:

(a.) Because every State has to execute the obligations incurred by treaty *bonâ fide*, and is urged thereto by the ordinary sanctions of international law in regard to observance of treaty obligations. Such sanctions are, for instance, appeal to public opinion, publication of correspondence, censure by Parliamentary vote, demand for arbitration with the odium attendant on a refusal to arbitrate, rupture of relations, reprisal, &c. But no reason has been shown why this treaty, in this respect, should be considered as different from every other treaty under which the right of a State to regulate the action of foreigners admitted by it on its territory is recognised;

(b.) Because the exercise of such a right of consent by the United States would predicate an abandonment of its independence in this respect by Great Britain, and the recognition by the latter of a concurrent right of regulation in the United States. But the treaty conveys only a liberty to take fish in common, and neither directly nor indirectly conveys a joint right of regulation;

(c.) Because the treaty does not convey a common right of fishery, but a liberty to fish in common. This is evidenced by the attitude of the United States Government in 1823, with respect to the relations of Great Britain and France in regard to the fishery;

(d.) Because if the consent of the United States were requisite for the fishery a general veto would be accorded them, the full exercise of which would be socially subversive and would lead to the consequence of an unregulatable fishery;

(e.) Because the United States cannot by assent give legal force and validity to British legislation;

(f.) Because the liberties to take fish in British territorial waters and to dry and cure fish on land in British territory are in principle on the same footing; but in practice a right of co-operation in the elaboration and enforcement of regulations in regard to the latter liberty (drying and curing fish on land) is unrealisable.

115   In any event, Great Britain, as the local sovereign, has the duty of preserving and protecting the fisheries. In so far as it is necessary for that purpose, Great Britain is not only entitled, but obliged, to provide for the protection and preservation of the

fisheries; always remembering that the exercise of this right of legislation is limited by the obligation to execute the treaty in good faith. This has been admitted by counsel and recognised by Great Britain in limiting the right of regulation to that of reasonable regulation. The inherent defect of this limitation of reasonableness, without any sanction except in diplomatic remonstrance, has been supplied by the submission to arbitral Award as to existing regulations in accordance with Articles II and III of the special agreement, and as to further regulation by the obligation to submit their reasonableness to an arbitral test in accordance with Article IV of the agreement.

It is finally contended by the United States:

That the United States did not expressly agree that the liberty granted to them could be subjected to any restriction that the grantor might choose to impose on the ground that in her judgment such restriction was reasonable. And that while admitting that all laws of a general character, controlling the conduct of men within the territory of Great Britain, are effective, binding and beyond objection by the United States, and competent to be made upon the sole determination of Great Britain or her colony, without accountability to anyone whomsoever; yet there is somewhere a line, beyond which it is not competent for Great Britain to go, or beyond which she cannot rightfully go, because to go beyond it would be an invasion of the right granted to the United States in 1818. That the legal effect of the grant of 1818 was not to leave the determination as to where that line is to be drawn to the uncontrolled judgment of the grantor, either upon the grantor's consideration as to what would be a reasonable exercise of its sovereignty over the British Empire, or upon the grantor's consideration of what would be a reasonable exercise thereof towards the grantee.

But this contention is founded on assumptions which this Tribunal cannot accept for the following reasons in addition to those already set forth :—

(a.) Because the line by which the respective rights of both parties accruing out of the treaty are to be circumscribed, can refer only to the right granted by the treaty; that is to say, to the liberty of taking, drying and curing fish by American inhabitants in certain British waters in common with British subjects, and not to the exercise of rights of legislation by Great Britain not referred to in the treaty;

(b.) Because a line which would limit the exercise of sovereignty of a State within the limits of its own territory can be drawn only on the ground of express stipulation, and not by implication from stipulations concerning a different subject-matter;

(c.) Because the line in question is drawn according to the principle of international law that treaty obligations are to be executed in perfect good faith, therefore excluding the right to legislate at *will* concerning the subject-matter of the treaty, and limiting the exercise of sovereignty of the States bound by a treaty with respect to that subject-matter of such acts as are consistent with the treaty;

(*d.*) Because on a true construction of the treaty the question does not arise whether the United States agreed that Great Britain should retain the right to legislate with regard to the fisheries in her own territory; but whether the treaty contains an abdication by Great Britain of the right which Great Britain, as the sovereign Power, undoubtedly possessed when the treaty was made, to regulate those fisheries;

(*e.*) Because the right to make reasonable regulations, not inconsistent with the obligations of the treaty, which is all that is claimed by Great Britain, for a fishery which both Parties admit requires regulation for its preservation, is not a restriction of or an invasion of the liberty granted to the inhabitants of the United States. This grant does not contain words to justify the assumption that the sovereignty of Great Britain upon its own territory was in any way affected; nor can words be found in the treaty transferring any part of that sovereignty to the United States. Great Britain assumed only duties with regard to the exercise of its sovereignty. The sovereignty of Great Britain over the coastal waters and territory of Newfoundland remains after the treaty as unimpaired as it was before. But from the treaty results an obligatory relation whereby the right of Great Britain to exercise its right of sovereignty by making regulations is limited to such regulations as are made in good faith, and are not in violation of the treaty;

116   (*f.*) Finally, to hold that the United States, the grantee of the fishing right, has a voice in the preparation of fishery legislation involves the recognition of a right in that country to participate in the internal legislation of Great Britain and her colonies, and to that extent would reduce these countries to a state of dependence.

While therefore unable to concede the claim of the United States as based on the treaty, this Tribunal considers that such claim has been and is to some extent, conceded in the relations now existing between the two Parties. Whatever may have been the situation under the treaty of 1818 standing alone, the exercise of the right of regulation inherent in Great Britain has been, and is, limited by the repeated recognition of the obligations already referred to, by the limitations and liabilities accepted in the special agreement, by the unequivocal position assumed by Great Britain in the presentation of its case before this Tribunal, and by the consequent view of this Tribunal that it would be consistent with all the circumstances, as revealed by this record, as to the duty of Great Britain, that she should submit the reasonableness of any future regulation to such an impartial arbitral test, affording full opportunity therefor, as is hereafter recommended under the authority of Article IV of the special agreement, whenever the reasonableness of any regulation is objected to or challenged by the United States in the manner, and within the time hereinafter specified in the said recommendation.

Now therefore this Tribunal decides and awards as follows:

The right of Great Britain to make regulations without the consent of the United States, as to the exercise of the liberty to take fish referred to in Article I of the treaty of October 20th, 1818, in the form of municipal laws, ordinances or rules of Great Britain, Canada or Newfoundland is inherent to the sovereignty of Great Britain.

The exercise of that right by Great Britain is, however, limited by the said treaty in respect of the said liberties therein granted to the inhabitants of the United States in that such regulations must be made bona fide and must not be in violation of the said treaty.

Regulations which are (1) appropriate or necessary for the protection and preservation of such fisheries, or (2) desirable or necessary on grounds of public order and morals without unnecessarily interfering with the fishery itself, and in both cases equitable and fair as between local and American fishermen, and not so framed as to give unfairly an advantage to the former over the latter class, are not inconsistent with the obligation to execute the treaty in good faith, and are therefore reasonable and not in violation of the treaty.

For the decision of the question whether a regulation is or is not reasonable, as being or not in accordance with the dispositions of the treaty and not in violation thereof, the treaty of 1818 contains no special provision. The settlement of differences in this respect that might arise thereafter was left to the ordinary means of diplomatic intercourse. By reason, however, of the form in which Question I is put, and by further reason of the admission of Great Britain by her counsel before this Tribunal that it is not now for either of the Parties to the treaty to determine the reasonableness of any regulation made by Great Britain, Canada or Newfoundland, the reasonableness of any such regulation, if contested, must be decided not by either of the Parties, but by an impartial authority in accordance with the principles hereinabove laid down, and in the manner proposed in the recommendations made by the Tribunal in virtue of Article IV of the agreement.

The Tribunal further decides that Article IV of the agreement is, as stated by counsel of the respective Parties at the argument, permanent in its effect, and not terminable by the expiration of the General Arbitration Treaty of 1908 between Great Britain and the United States.

In execution, therefore, of the responsibilities imposed upon this Tribunal in regard to Articles II, III and IV of the special agreement, we hereby pronounce in their regard as follows:—

AS TO ARTICLE II.

Pursuant to the provisions of this article hereinbefore cited, either Party has called the attention of this Tribunal to acts of the other claimed to be inconsistent with the true interpretation of the treaty of 1818.

But in response to a request from the Tribunal, recorded in Protocol No. 26 of 19th July, for an exposition of the grounds of such objections, the Parties replied as reported in Protocol No. 30 of 28th July to the following effect:—

His Majesty's Government considered that it would be unnecessary to call upon the Tribunal for an opinion under the second clause of Article II, in regard to the executive act of the United States of America in 117   sending war ships to the territorial waters in question, in view of the recognised motives of the United States of America in taking this action, and of the relations maintained by their representatives with the local authorities.   And this being the sole act to which the attention of this Tribunal has been called by His Majesty's Government, no further action in their behalf is required from this Tribunal under Article II.

The United States of America presented a statement in which their claim that specific provisions of certain legislative and executive acts of the Governments of Canada and Newfoundland were inconsistent with the true interpretation of the treaty of 1818 was based on the contention that these provisions were not " reasonable " within the meaning of Question I.

After calling upon this Tribunal to express an opinion on these acts, pursuant to the second clause of Article II, the United States of America pointed out in that statement that under Article III any question regarding the reasonableness of any regulation might be referred by the Tribunal to a Commission of expert specialists, and expressed an intention of asking for such reference under certain circumstances.

The Tribunal having carefully considered the counter-statement presented on behalf of Great Britain at the session of August 2nd, is of opinion that the decision on the reasonableness of these regulations requires expert information about the fisheries themselves and an examination of the practical effect of a great number of these provisions in relation to the conditions surrounding the exercise of the liberty of fishery enjoyed by the inhabitants of the United States, as contemplated by Article III. No further action on behalf of the United States is therefore required from this Tribunal under Article II.

AS TO ARTICLE III.

As provided in Article III, hereinbefore cited and above referred to, " any question regarding the reasonableness of any regulation, or otherwise, which requires an examination of the practical effect of any provisions surrounding the exercise of the liberty of fishery enjoyed by the inhabitants of the United States, or which requires expert information about the fisheries themselves, may be referred by this Tribunal to a Commission of expert specialists: one to be designated by each of the Parties hereto, and the third, who shall not be a national of either Party, to be designated by the Tribunal."

The Tribunal now, therefore, calls upon the Parties to designate within one month their national Commissioners for the expert examination of the questions submitted.

As the third non-national Commissioner this Tribunal designates Dr. P. P. C. Hoek, scientific adviser for the fisheries of the Netherlands, and if any necessity arises therefor a substitute may be appointed by the President of this Tribunal.

After a reasonable time, to be agreed on by the Parties, for the expert Commission to arrive at a conclusion, by conference, or, if necessary, by local inspection, the Tribunal shall, if convoked by the President at the request of either Party, thereupon at the earliest convenient date, reconvene to consider the report of the Commission, and if it be on the whole unanimous shall incorporate it in the Award.   If not on the whole unanimous—i.e., on all points which, in the opinion of the Tribunal, are of essential importance—the Tribunal shall make its Award as to the regulations concerned after consideration of the conclusions of the expert Commissioners and after hearing argument by counsel.

But while recognising its responsibilities to meet the obligations imposed on it under Article III of the special agreement, the Tribunal hereby recommends as an alternative to having recourse to a reconvention of this Tribunal, that the Parties should accept the unanimous opinion of the Commission or the opinion of the non-national Commissioner on any points in dispute as an arbitral Award rendered under the provisions of chapter iv of The Hague Convention of 1907.

AS TO ARTICLE IV.

Pursuant to the provisions of this article hereinbefore cited, this Tribunal recommends for the consideration of the Parties the following rules and method of procedure under which all questions which may arise in the future regarding the exercise of the liberties above referred to may be determined in accordance with the principles laid down in this Award.

1. All future municipal laws, ordinances or rules for the regulation of the fishery by Great Britain in respect of (1) the hours, days or seasons when fish may be taken on the treaty coasts; (2) the method, means and implements used in the taking of fish or in carrying on fishing operations; (3) any other regulation of a similar character shall be published in the "London Gazette" two months before going into operation.

118 Similar regulations by Canada or Newfoundland shall be similarly published in the "Canada Gazette" and the "Newfoundland Gazette" respectively.

2. If the Government of the United States considers any such laws or regulations inconsistent with the treaty of 1818, it is entitled to so notify the Government of Great Britain within the two months referred to in Rule No. 1.

3. Any law or regulation so notified shall not come into effect with respect to inhabitants of the United States until the Permanent Mixed Fishery Commission has decided that the regulation is reasonable within the meaning of this Award.

4. Permanent Mixed Fishery Commissions for Canada and Newfoundland respectively shall be established for the decision of such questions as to the reasonableness of future regulations, as contemplated by Article IV of the special agreement; these commissions shall consist of an expert national appointed by either Party for five years. The third member shall not be a national of either Party; he shall be nominated for five years by agreement of the Parties, or failing such agreement within two months, he shall be nominated by Her Majesty the Queen of the Netherlands. The two national members shall be convoked by the Government of Great Britain within one month from the date of notification by the Government of the United States.

5. The two national members having failed to agree within one month, within another month the full Commisison, under the presidency of the Umpire, is to be convoked by Great Britain. It must deliver its decision, if the two Governments do not agree otherwise, at the latest in three months. The Umpire shall conduct the procedure in accordance with that provided in chapter iv of the Convention for the Pacific Settlement of International Disputes, except in so far as herein otherwise provided.

6. The form of convocation of the Commission including the terms of reference of the question at issue shall be as follows:—

" The provision hereinafter fully set forth of an Act dated   , published in the   , has been notified to the Government of Great Britain by the Government of the United States, under date of   , as provided by the Award of The Hague Tribunal of September 7th, 1910.

" Pursuant to the provisions of that Award the Government of Great Britain hereby convokes the Permanent Mixed Fishery Commission for $\frac{(Canada)}{(Newfoundland)}$. composed of   Commissioner for the United States of America, and of   Commissioner for $\frac{(Canada)}{(Newfoundland)}$, which shall meet at   , and render a decision within one month as to whether the provision so notified is reasonable and consistent with the treaty of 1818, as interpreted by the Award of The Hague Tribunal of September 7th, 1910, and if not, in what respect it is unreasonable and inconsistent therewith.

" Failing an agreement on this question within one month the Commission shall so notify the Government of Great Britain in order that the further action required by that Award may be taken for the decision of the above question.

" The provision is as follows:

7. The unanimous decision of the two national Commissioners, or the majority decision of the Umpire and one Commissioner, shall be final and binding.

QUESTION II.

Have the inhabitants of the United States, while exercising the liberties referred to in said article, a right to employ as members of the fishing crews of their vessels persons not inhabitants of the United States?

In regard to this question the United States claim in substance:

1. That the liberty assured to their inhabitants by the treaty plainly includes the right to use all the means customary or appropriate for fishing upon the sea, not only ships and nets and boats, but crews to handle the ships and the nets and the boats;

119   2. That no right to control or limit the means which these inhabitants shall use in fishing can be admitted unless it is provided in the terms of the treaty and no right to question the nationality or inhabitancy of the crews employed is contained in the terms of the treaty.

And Great Britain claims:

1. That the treaty confers the liberty to inhabitants of the United States exclusively;

2. That the Governments of Great Britain, Canada or Newfoundland may, without infraction of the treaty, prohibit persons from engaging as fishermen in American vessels.

Now considering (1) that the liberty to take fish is an economic right attributed by the treaty; (2) that it is attributed to inhabitants of the United States, without any mention of their nationality; (3) that the exercise of an economic right includes the right to employ servants; (4) that the right of employing servants has not been limited by the treaty to the employment of persons of a distinct nationality or inhabitancy; (5) that the liberty to take fish as an economic liberty refers not only to the individuals doing the manual act of fishing, but also to those for whose profit the fish are taken.

But considering that the treaty does not intend to grant to individual persons or to a class of persons the liberty to take fish in certain waters " in common," that is to say in company, with individual British subjects, in the sense that no law could forbid British subjects to take service on American fishing-ships; (2) that the treaty intends to secure to the United States a share of the fisheries designated therein, not only in the interest of a certain class of individuals, but also in the interest of both the United States and Great Britain, as appears from the evidence and notably from the correspondence between Mr. Adams and Lord Bathurst in 1815; (3) that the inhabitants of the United States do not derive the liberty to take fish directly from the treaty, but from the United States Government as party to the treaty with Great Britain and moreover exercising the right to regulate the conditions under which its inhabitants may enjoy the granted liberty; (4) that it is in the interest of the inhabitants of the United States that the fishing liberty granted to them be restricted to exercise by them and removed from the enjoyment of other aliens not entitled by this treaty to participate in the fisheries; (5) that such restrictions have been throughout enacted in the British Statute of June 15, 1819, and that of June 3, 1824, to this effect, that no alien or stranger whatsoever shall fish in the waters designated therein, except in so far as by treaty thereto entitled, and that this exception will, in virtue of the treaty of 1818, as hereinabove interpreted by this Award, exempt from these statutes American fishermen fishing by the agency of non-inhabitant aliens employed in their service; (6) that the treaty does not affect the sovereign right of Great Britain as to aliens, non-inhabitants of the United States, nor the right of Great Britain to regulate the engagement of British subjects, while these aliens or British subjects are on British territory.

Now, therefore, in view of the preceding considerations this Tribunal is of opinion that the inhabitants of the United States while exercising the liberties referred to in the said article have a right to employ, as members of the fishing crews of their vessels, persons not inhabitants of the United States.

But in view of the preceding considerations the Tribunal, to prevent any misunderstanding as to the effect of its Award, expresses the opinion that non-inhabitants employed as members of the fishing crews of United States vessels derive no benefit or immunity from the treaty and it is so decided and awarded.

QUESTION III.

Can the exercise by the inhabitants of the United States of the liberties referred to in the said article be subjected, without the consent of the United States, to the requirements of entry or report at customhouses or the payment of light or harbour or other dues, or to any other similar requirement or condition or exaction?

The Tribunal is of opinion as follows:

It is obvious that the liberties referred to in this question are those that relate to taking fish and to drying and curing fish on certain coasts as prescribed in the treaty of October 20, 1818.

120

The exercise of these liberties by the inhabitants of the United States in the prescribed waters to which they relate, has no reference to any commercial privileges which may or may not attach to such vessels by reason of any supposed authority outside the treaty, which itself confers no commercial privileges whatever upon the inhabitants of the United States or the vessels in which they may exercise the fishing liberty. It follows, therefore, that when the inhabitants of the United States are not seeking to exercise the commercial privileges accorded to trading-vessels for the vessels in which they are exercising the granted liberty of fishing, they ought not to be subjected to requirements as to report and entry at custom-houses that are only appropriate to the exercise of commercial privileges. The exercise of the fishing liberty is distinct from the exercise of commercial or trading privileges and it is not competent for Great Britain or her colonies to impose upon the former exactions only appropriate to the latter. The reasons for the requirements enumerated in the case of commercial vessels, have no relation to the case of fishing-vessels.

We think, however, that the requirement that American fishing-vessels should report, if proper conveniences and an opportunity for doing so are provided, is not unreasonable or inappropriate. Such a report, while serving the purpose of a notification of the presence of a fishing-vessel in the treaty waters for the purpose of exercising the treaty liberty, while it gives an opportunity for a proper surveillance of such vessel by revenue officers, may also serve to afford to such fishing-vessel protection from interference in the exercise of the fishing liberty. There should be no such requirement, however, unless reasonably convenient opportunity therefor be afforded in person or by telegraph, at a custom-house or to a customs official.

The Tribunal is also of opinion that light and harbour dues, if not imposed on Newfoundland fishermen, should not be imposed on American fishermen while exercising the liberty granted by the treaty. To impose such dues on American fishermen only would constitute an unfair discrimination between them and Newfoundland fishermen and one inconsistent with the liberty granted to American fishermen to take fish, etc., " in common with the subjects of His Britannic Majesty."

Further, the Tribunal considers that the fulfilment of the requirement as to report by fishing-vessels on arrival at the fishery would be greatly facilitated in the interests of both parties by the adoption of a system of registration, and distinctive marking of the fishing-boats of both Parties, analogous to that established by Articles V to XIII, inclusive, of the International Convention signed at The Hague, 8th May, 1882, for the regulation of the North Sea Fisheries.

The Tribunal therefore decides and awards as follows:

The requirement that an American fishing vessel should report, if proper conveniences for doing so are at hand, is not unreasonable, for the reasons stated in the foregoing opinion. There should be no such requirement, however, unless there be reasonably convenient opportunity afforded to report in person or by telegraph, either at a custom-house or to a customs official.

But the exercise of the fishing liberty by the inhabitants of the United States should not be subjected to the purely commercial formalities of report, entry and clearance at a custom-house, nor to light, harbour or other dues not imposed upon Newfoundland fishermen.

QUESTION IV.

Under the provision of the said article that the American fishermen shall be admitted to enter certain bays or harbours for shelter, repairs, wood, or water, and for no other purpose whatever, but that they shall be under such restrictions as may be necessary to prevent their taking, drying, or curing fish therein or in any other manner whatever abusing the privileges thereby reserved to them, is it permissible to impose restrictions making the exercise of such privileges conditional upon the payment of light or harbour or other dues, or entering or reporting at custom-houses or any similar conditions?

The Tribunal is of opinion that the provision in the first article of the treaty of October 20, 1818, admitting American fishermen to enter certain bays or harbours for shelter, repairs, wood and water, and for no other purpose whatever, is an exercise in large measure of those duties of hospitality and humanity which all civilised nations impose upon themselves and expect the performance of from others. The enumerated purposes for which entry is permitted all relate to the exigencies in which those who pursue their perilous calling on the sea may be involved. The proviso which appears 121 in the first article of the said treaty immediately after the so-called renunciation clause, was doubtless due to a recognition by Great Britain of what was expected from the humanity and civilisation of the then leading commercial nation of the world. To impose restrictions making the exercise of such privileges conditional upon the payment of light, harbour or other dues, or entering and reporting at custom-houses, or any similar conditions would be inconsistent with the grounds upon which such privileges rest and therefore is not permissible.

And it is decided and awarded that such restrictions are not permissible.

It seems reasonable, however, in order that these privileges accorded by Great Britain on these grounds of hospitality and humanity should not be abused, that the American fishermen entering such bays for any of the four purposes aforesaid and remaining more than forty-eight hours therein, should be required, if thought necessary by Great Britain or the Colonial Government, to report, either in person or by telegraph, at a custom-house or to a customs official, if reasonably convenient opportunity therefor is afforded.

And it is so decided and awarded.

QUESTION V.

From where must be measured the " three marine miles of any of the coasts, bays, creeks, or harbours " referred to in the said article?

In regard to this question, Great Britain claims that the renunciation applies to all bays generally and

The United States contend that it applies to bays of a certain class or condition.

Now, considering that the treaty used the general term " bays " without qualification, the Tribunal is of opinion that these words of the treaty must be interpreted in a general sense as applying to every bay on the coast in question that might be reasonably supposed to have been considered as a bay by the negotiators of the treaty under the general conditions then prevailing, unless the United States can adduce satisfactory proof that any restrictions or qualifications of the general use of the term were or should have been present to their minds.

And for the purpose of such proof the United States contend:

(1) That while a State may renounce the treaty right to fish in foreign territorial waters, it cannot renounce the natural right to fish on the high seas.

But the Tribunal is unable to agree with this contention. Because though a State cannot grant rights on the high seas it certainly can abandon the exercise of its right to fish on the high seas within certain definite limits. Such an abandonment was made with respect to their fishing rights in the waters in question by France and Spain in 1763. By a convention between the United Kingdom and the United States in 1846, the two countries assumed ownership over waters in Fuca Straits at distances from the shore as great as 17 miles.

The United States contend, moreover:

2. That by the use of the term " liberty to fish," the United States manifested the intention to renounce the liberty in the waters referred to only in so far as that liberty was dependent upon or derived from a concession on the part of Great Britain, and not to renounce the right to fish in those waters where it was enjoyed by virtue of their natural right as an independent State.

But the Tribunal is unable to agree with this contention:

(a.) Because the term " liberty to fish " was used in the renunciatory clause of the treaty of 1818 because the same term had been previously used in the treaty of 1783 which gave the liberty; and it was proper to use in the renunciation clause the same term that was used in the grant with respect to the object of the grant; and, in view of the terms of the grant, it would have been improper to use the term " right " in the renunciation. Therefore the conclusion drawn from the use of the term " liberty " instead of the term " right " is not justified;

122 (b.) Because the term " liberty " was a term properly applicable to the renunciation which referred not only to fishing in the territorial waters, but also to drying and curing on the shore. This latter right was undoubtedly held under the provisions of the treaty and was not a right accruing to the United States by virtue of any principle of international law.

3. The United States also contend that the term " bays of His Britannic Majesty's Dominions " in the renunciatory clause must be read as including only those bays which were under the territorial sovereignty of Great Britain.

But the Tribunal is unable to accept this contention:

(a.) Because the description of the coast on which the fishery is to be exercised by the inhabitants of the United States is expressed throughout the treaty of 1818 in geographical terms and not by reference to political control; the treaty describes the coast as contained between capes.

(b.) Because to express the political concept of dominion as equivalent to sovereignty, the word " dominion " in the singular would have been an adequate term and not " dominions " in the plural; this latter term having a recognised and well settled meaning as descriptive of those portions of the earth which owe political allegiance to His Majesty, e. g., " His Britannic Majesty's Dominions beyond the Seas."

4. It has been further contended by the United States that the renunciation applies only to bays six miles or less in width " inter fauces terræ," those bays only being territorial bays because the three

mile rule is, as shown by this treaty, a principle of international law applicable to coasts and should be strictly and systematically applied to bays.

But the Tribunal is unable to agree with this contention:

(a) Because admittedly the geographical character of a bay contains conditions which concern the interests of the territorial sovereign to a more intimate and important extent than do those connected with the open coast. Thus conditions of national and territorial integrity, of defence, of commerce and of industry are all vitally concerned with the control of the bays penetrating the national coast line. This interest varies, speaking generally, in proportion to the penetration inland of the bay; but as no principle of international law recognises any specified relation between the concavity of the bay and the requirements for control by the territorial sovereignty, this Tribunal is unable to qualify by the application of any new principle its interpretation of the treaty of 1818 as excluding bays in general from the strict and systematic application of the three mile rule; nor can this Tribunal take cognisance in this connection of other principles concerning the territorial sovereignty over bays, such as ten mile or twelve mile limits of exclusion based on international acts subsequent to the treaty of 1818 and relating to coasts of a different configuration and conditions of a different character;

(b) Because the opinion of jurists and publicists quoted in the proceedings conduce to the opinion that, speaking generally, the three mile rule should not be strictly and systematically applied to bays;

(c) Because the treaties referring to these coasts, antedating the treaty of 1818, made special provisions as to bays, such as the treaties of 1686 and 1713 between Great Britain and France, and especially the treaty of 1778 between the United States and France. Likewise Jay's Treaty of 1794, article 25, distinguished bays from the space " within cannon-shot of the coast " in regard to the right of seizure in times of war. If the proposed treaty of 1806 and the treaty of 1818 contained no disposition to that effect, the explanation may be found in the fact that the first extended the marginal belt to five miles, and also in the circumstance that the American proposition of 1818 in that respect was not limited to " bays," but extended to " chambers formed by headlands " and to " five marine miles from a right line from one headland to another," a proposition which in the times of the Napoleonic wars would have affected to a very large extent the operations of the British navy;

(d.) Because it has not been shown by the documents and correspondence in evidence here that the application of the three mile rule to bays was present to the minds of the negotiators in 1818, and they could not reasonably have been expected either to presume it or to provide against its presumption;

      (e.) Because it is difficult to explain the words in Article III
123   of the treaty under interpretation "country . . . . together with its bays, harbours and creeks" otherwise than that all bays without distinction as to their width were, in the opinion of the negotiators, part of the territory;

(f.) Because from the information before this Tribunal it is evident that the three mile rule is not applied to bays strictly or systematically either by the United States or by any other Power;

(g.) It has been recognised by the United States that bays stand apart, and that in respect of them territorial jurisdiction may be exercised farther than the marginal belt in the case of Delaware Bay by the report of the United States Attorney-General of May 19th, 1793; and the letter of Mr. Jefferson to Mr. Genet of November 8th, 1793, declares the bays of the United States generally to be " as being landlocked, within the body of the United States."

5. In this latter regard it is further contended by the United States that such exceptions only should be made from the application of the three mile rule to bays as are sanctioned by conventions and established usage; that all exceptions for which the United States of America were responsible are so sanctioned; and that His Majesty's Government are unable to provide evidence to show that the bays concerned by the treaty of 1818 could be claimed as exceptions on these grounds either generally, or, except possibly in one or two cases, specifically.

But the Tribunal, while recognising that conventions and established usage might be considered as the basis for claiming as territorial those bays which on this ground might be called historic bays, and that such claim should be held valid in the absence of any principle of international law on the subject, nevertheless is unable to apply this, *a contrario*, so as to subject the bays in question to the three mile rule as desired by the United States:—

(a.) Because Great Britain has during this controversy asserted a claim to these bays generally, and has enforced such claim specifically in statutes or otherwise, in regard to the more important bays, such as Chaleurs, Conception and Miramichi;

(b.) Because neither should such relaxations of this claim, as are in evidence, be construed as renunciations of it; nor should omissions to enforce the claim in regard to bays as to which no controversy arose be so construed. Such a construction by this Tribunal would not only be intrinsically inequitable, but internationally injurious, in that it would discourage conciliatory diplomatic transactions and encourage the assertion of extreme claims in their fullest extent;

(c.) Because any such relaxations in the extreme claim of Great Britain in its international relations are compensated by recognitions of it in the same sphere by the United States; notably in relations with France, for instance in 1823 when they applied to Great Britain for the protection of their fishery in the bays on the western coast of Newfoundland, whence they had been driven by French war-vessels on the ground of the pretended exclusive right of the French. Though they never asserted that their fishermen had been disturbed within the three mile zone, only alleging that the disturbance had taken place in the bays, they claimed to be protected by Great Britain for having been molested in waters which were, as Mr. Rush stated, " clearly within the jurisdiction and sovereignty of Great Britain."

6. It has been contended by the United States that the words " coasts, bays, creeks or harbours " are here used only to express different parts of the coast, and are intended to express and be equivalent to the word " coast," whereby the three marine miles would be measured from the sinuosities of the coast and the renunciation would apply only to the waters of bays within three miles.

But the Tribunal is unable to agree with this contention:

(a.) Because it is a principle of interpretation that words in a document ought not to be considered as being without any meaning if there is not specific evidence to that purpose and the interpretation referred to would lead to the consequence, practically, of reading the words " bays, creeks and harbours " out of the treaty; so that it would read " within three miles of any. of the coasts " including therein the coasts of the bays and harbours;

(b.) Because the word " therein " in the proviso—" restrictions necessary to prevent their taking, drying or curing fish therein "— can refer only to " bays," and not to the belt of three miles along the coast; and can be explained only on the supposition that 124   the words " bays, creeks and harbours " are to be understood in their usual ordinary sense and not in an artificially restricted sense of bays within the three mile belt;

(c.) Because the practical distinction for the purpose of this fishery between coasts and bays and the exceptional conditions pertaining to the latter has been shown from the correspondence and the documents in evidence, especially the treaty of 1783, to have been in all probability present to the minds of the negotiators of the treaty of 1818;

(d.) Because the existence of this distinction is confirmed in the same article of the treaty by the proviso permitting the United States fishermen to enter bays for certain purposes;

(e.) Because the word " coasts " is used in the plural form, whereas the contention would require its use in the singular;

(f.) Because the Tribunal is unable to understand the term " bays " in the renunciatory clause in other than its geographical sense, by which a bay is to be considered as an indentation of the coast, bearing a configuration of a particular character, easy to determine specifically, but difficult to describe generally.

The negotiators of the treaty of 1818 did probably not trouble themselves with subtle theories concerning the notion of " bays "; they most probably thought that everybody would know what was a bay. In this popular sense the term must be interpreted in the treaty. The interpretation must take into account all the individual circumstances which, for any one of the different bays, are to be appreciated; the relation of its width to the length of penetration inland; the possibility and the necessity of its being defended by the State in whose territory it is indented; the special value which it has for the industry of the inhabitants of its shores; the distance which it is secluded from the highways of nations on the open sea and other circumstances not possible to enumerate in general.

For these reasons the Tribunal decides and awards:

In case of bays, the three marine miles are to be measured from a straight line drawn across the body of water at the place where it ceases to have the configuration and characteristics of a bay. At all other places the three marine miles are to be measured following the sinuosities of the coast.

But considering the Tribunal cannot overlook that this answer to Question V, although correct in principle, and the only one possible in view of the want of a sufficient basis for a more concrete answer, is not entirely satisfactory as to its practical applicability, and that it leaves room for doubts and differences in practice: Therefore the Tribunal considers it its duty to render the decision more practicable, and to remove the danger of future differences by adjoining to it a recommendation in virtue of the responsibilities imposed by Article IV of the special agreement.

Considering, moreover, that in treaties with France, with the North German Confederation and the German Empire, and likewise in the North Sea Convention, Great Britain has adopted for similar cases the rule that only bays of ten miles width should be considered as those wherein the fishing is reserved to nationals: And that in the course of the negotiations between Great Britain and the United States a similar rule has been on various occasions proposed and adopted by Great Britain in instructions to the naval officers stationed on these coasts: And that though these circumstances are not sufficient to constitute this a principle of international law, it seems reasonable to propose this rule with certain exceptions, all the more that this rule, with such exceptions, has already formed the basis of an agreement between the two Powers.

Now, therefore, this Tribunal, in pursuance of the provisions of Article IV, hereby recommends for the consideration and acceptance of the High

Contracting Parties the following rules and method of procedure for determining the limits of the bays hereinbefore enumerated:

1. In every bay not hereinafter specifically provided for the limits of exclusion shall be drawn three miles seaward from a straight line across the bay in the part nearest the entrance at the first point where the width does not exceed ten miles.

2. In the following bays, where the configuration of the coast and the local climatic conditions are such that foreign fishermen, when within the geographic headlands, might reasonably and bonâ fide believe themselves on the high seas, the limits of exclusion shall be drawn in each case between the headlands hereinafter specified as being those at and within which such fishermen might be reasonably expected to recognise the bay under average conditions.

125

For the Baie des Chaleurs the line from the light at Birch Point on Miscou Island to Macquereau Point Light; for the Bay of Miramichi, the line from the light at Point Escuminac to the light on the eastern point of Tabisintac Gully; for Egmont Bay, in Prince Edward Island, the line from the light at Cape Egmont to the light at West Point; and off St. Ann's Bay, in the province of Nova Scotia, the line from the light at Point Anconi to the nearest point on the opposite shore of the mainland.

For Fortune Bay, in Newfoundland, the line from Connaigre Head to the light on the southeasterly end of Brunet Island, thence to Fortune Head.

For or near the following bays the limits of exclusion shall be three marine miles seawards from the following lines, namely:

For or near Barrington Bay, in Nova Scotia, the line from the light on Stoddart Island to the light on the south point of Cape Sable, thence to the light at Baccaro Point; at Chedabucto and St. Peter's Bays, the line from Cranberry Island light to Green Island light, thence to Point Rouge; for Mira Bay, the line from the light on the east point of Scatari Island to the northeasterly point of Cape Morien; and at Placentia Bay, in Newfoundland, the line from Latine Point, on the eastern mainland shore, to the most southerly point of Red Island, thence by the most southerly point of Merasheen Island to the mainland.

Long Island and Bryer Island on St. Mary's Bay, in Nova Scotia, shall, for the purpose of delimitation, be taken as the coasts of such bays.

It is understood that nothing in these rules refers either to the Bay of Fundy considered as a whole apart from its bays and creeks or as to the innocent passage through the Gut of Canso, which were excluded by the agreement made by exchange of notes between Mr. Bacon and Mr. Bryce, dated February 21st, 1909, and March 4th, 1909; or to Conception Bay, which was provided for by the decision of the Privy Council in the case of the Direct United States Cable Company v. the Anglo-American Telegraph Company, in which decision the United States have acquiesced.

QUESTION VI.

Have the inhabitants of the United States the liberty under the said article or otherwise, to take fish in the bays, harbours, and creeks on that part of the southern coast of Newfoundland which extends from Cape Ray to Rameau Islands, or on the western and northern coasts of Newfoundland from Cape Ray to Quirpon Islands, or on the Magdalen Islands?

In regard to this question, it is contended by the United States that the inhabitants of the United States have the liberty under Article I of the treaty of taking fish in the bays, harbours, and creeks on that part of the southern coast of Newfoundland which extends from Cape Ray to Rameau Islands, or on the western and northern coasts of Newfoundland from Cape Ray to Quirpon Islands and on the Magdalen Islands. It is contended by Great Britain that they have no such liberty.

Now considering that the evidence seems to show that the intention of the parties to the treaty of 1818, as indicated by the records of the negotiations and by the subsequent attitude of the Governments was to admit the United States to such fishery, this Tribunal is of opinion that it is incumbent on Great Britain to produce satisfactory proof that the United States are not so entitled under the treaty.

For this purpose Great Britain points to the fact that whereas the treaty grants to American fishermen liberty to take fish " on the coasts, bays, harbours, and creeks from Mount Joly on the southern coast of Labrador " the liberty is granted to the " coast " only of Newfoundland and to the " shore " only of the Magdalen Islands; and argues that evidence can be found in the correspondence submitted indicating an intention to exclude Americans from Newfoundland bays on the treaty coast, and that no value would have been attached at that time by the United States Government to the liberty of fishing in such bays because there was no cod fishery there as there was in the bays of Labrador.

126   But the Tribunal is unable to agree with this contention:

(*a.*) Because the words " part of the southern coast . . . from . . . to " and the words " western and northern coast . . . from . . . to," clearly indicate one uninterrupted coast-line; and there is no reason to read into the words " coasts " a contradistinction to bays, in order to exclude bays. On the contrary, as already held in the answer to Question V, the words " liberty, forever, to dry and cure fish in any of the unsettled bays, harbours and creeks of the southern part of the coast of Newfoundland hereabove described," indicate that in the meaning of the treaty, as in all the preceding treaties relating to the same territories, the words coast, coasts, harbours, bays, &c., are used, without attaching to the word " coast " the specific meaning of excluding bays. Thus in the provision of the treaty of 1783 giving liberty " to take fish on such part of the coast of Newfoundland as British fishermen shall use," the word " coast " necessarily includes bays, because if the intention had been to prohibit the entering of the bays for fishing the following words " but not to dry or cure the same on that island," would have no meaning. The contention that in the treaty of 1783 the word " bays " is in-

serted lest otherwise Great Britain would have had the right to
exclude the Americans to the three mile line, is inadmissible, because in that treaty that line is not mentioned;

(b.) Because the correspondence between Mr. Adams and Lord
Bathurst also shows that during the negotiations for the treaty the
United States demanded the former rights enjoyed under the treaty
of 1783, and that Lord Bathurst in the letter of 30th October, 1815
made no objection to granting those " former rights " " placed under
some modifications," which latter did not relate to the right of fishing
in bays, but only to the " preoccupation of British harbours and
creeks by the fishing vessels of the United States and the forcible
exclusion of British subjects where the fishery might be most advantageously conducted," and " to the clandestine introduction of
prohibited goods into the British colonies." It may be therefore
assumed that the word " coast " is used in both treaties in the same
sense, including bays;

(c.) Because the treaty expressly allows the liberty to dry and
cure in the unsettled bays, &c., of the southern part of the coast of
Newfoundland, and this shows that, à fortiori, the taking of fish
in those bays is also allowed; because the fishing liberty was a lesser
burden than the grant to cure and dry, and the restrictive clauses
never refer to fishing in contradistinction to drying, but always to
drying in contradistinction to fishing. Fishing is granted without
drying, never drying without fishing;

(d.) Because there is not sufficient evidence to show that the
enumeration of the component parts of the coast of Labrador was
made in order to discriminate between the coast of Labrador and the
coast of Newfoundland;

(e.) Because the statement that there is no cod-fish in the bays of
Newfoundland and that the Americans only took interest in the cod-
fishery is not proved; and evidence to the contrary is to be found
in Mr. John Adams' Journal of Peace Negotiations of November 25,
1782;

(f.) Because the treaty grants the right to take fish of every kind,
and not only cod-fish;

(g.) Because the evidence shows that, in 1823, the Americans were
fishing in Newfoundland bays and that Great Britain when summoned to protect them against expulsion therefrom by the French
did not deny their right to enter such bays.

Therefore this Tribunal is of opinion that American inhabitants are entitled to fish in the bays, creeks and harbours of the treaty coasts of Newfoundland and the Magdalen Islands and it is so decided and awarded.

QUESTION VII.

Are the inhabitants of the United States whose vessels resort to the treaty coasts for the purpose of exercising the liberties referred to in Article I of the treaty of 1818, entitled to have for those vessels, when duly authorised by the United States in that behalf, the commercial privileges on the treaty coasts accorded by agreement or otherwise to United States trading vessels generally?

Now assuming that commercial privileges on the treaty coasts are accorded by agreement or otherwise to United States trading vessels generally, without any exception, the inhabitants of the United States, whose vessels resort to the same coasts for the purpose of exercising the liberties referred to in Article I of the treaty of 127 1818, are entitled to have for those vessels when duly authorised by the United States in that behalf, the above-mentioned commercial privileges, the treaty containing nothing to the contrary. But they cannot at the same time and during the same voyage exercise their treaty rights and enjoy their commercial privileges, because treaty rights and commercial privileges are submitted to different rules, regulations and restraints.

For these reasons this Tribunal is of opinion that the inhabitants of the United States are so entitled in so far as concerns this treaty, there being nothing in its provisions to disentitle them, provided the treaty liberty of fishing and the commercial privileges are not exercised concurrently, and it is so decided and awarded.

Done at The Hague, in the Permanent Court of Arbitration, in triplicate original, September 7th, 1910.

H. LAMMASCH.
A. F. DE SAVORNIN LOHMAN.
GEORGE GRAY.
C. FITZPATRICK.
LUIS M. DRAGO.

Signing the Award, I state pursuant to Article IX, clause 2, of the special agreement, my dissent from the majority of the Tribunal in respect to the considerations and enacting part of the Award as to Question V.

Grounds for this dissent have been filed at the International Bureau of the Permanent Court of Arbitration.

LUIS M. DRAGO.

GROUNDS FOR THE DISSENT TO THE AWARD ON QUESTION 5 BY DR. LUIS M. DRAGO.

Counsel for Great Britain have very clearly stated that, according to their contention, the territoriality of the bays referred to in the treaty of 1818 is immaterial, because, whether they are or are not territorial, the United States should be excluded from fishing in them by the terms of the renunciatory clause, which simply refers to " bays, creeks or harbours of His Britannic Majesty's dominions," without any other qualification or description. If that were so, the necessity might arise of discussing whether or not a nation has the right to exclude another by contract or otherwise from any portion or portions of the high seas. But in my opinion the Tribunal need not concern itself with such general question, the wording of the treaty being clear enough to decide the point at issue.

Article 1 begins with the statement that differences have arisen respecting the liberty claimed by the United States for the inhabitants thereof to take, dry and cure fish on " certain coasts, bays, harbours and creeks of His Britannic Majesty's dominions in America," and then proceeds to locate the specific portions of the coast with its corresponding indentations, in which the liberty of taking, drying and curing fish should be exercised. The renunciatory clause, which the Tribunal is called upon to construe, runs thus: "And the United States hereby renounce, forever, any liberty heretofore enjoyed or claimed by the inhabitants thereof, to take, dry or cure fish on, or within three marine miles of any of the coasts, bays, creeks or harbours of His Britannic Majesty's dominions in America not included within the above-mentioned limits." This language does not lend itself to different constructions. If the bays in which the liberty has been renounced are those " of His Britannic Majesty's dominions in America," they must necessarily be territorial bays, because, in so far as they are not so considered, they should belong to the high seas, and consequently form no part of His Britannic Majesty's dominions, which, by definition, do not extend to the high seas. It cannot be said, as has been suggested, that the use of the word " dominions," in the plural, implies a different meaning than would be conveyed by the same term as used in the singular, so that, in the present case, " the British dominions in America " ought to be considered as a mere geographical expression, without reference to any right of sovereignty or " *dominion*." It seems to

me, on the contrary, that " dominions," or " possessions," or " estates,"
or such other equivalent terms, simply designate the places over
which the " dominion " or property rights are exercised.   Where
there is no possibility of appropriation or dominion, as on the
128   the high seas, we cannot speak of dominions.   The " dominions " extend exactly to the point which the " dominion "
reaches; they are simply the actual or physical thing over which
the abstract power or authority, the *right*, as given to the proprietor
or the ruler, applies.   The interpretation as to the territoriality of
the bays as mentioned in the renunciatory clause of the treaty appears stronger when considering that the United States specifically
renounced the " liberty," not the " right," to fish or to cure and dry
fish.   " The United States renounce, forever, any *liberty* heretofore
enjoyed or claimed, to take, cure or dry fish on, or within three
marine miles of any of the coasts, bays, creeks or harbours of His
Britannic Majesty's dominions in America."   It is well known that
the negotiators of the treaty of 1783 gave a very different meaning
to the terms *liberty* and *right*, as distinguished from each other.
In this connection, Mr. Adams' journal may be recited.   To this
journal the British Counter-Case refers in the following terms:
" From an entry in Mr. Adams' journal it appears that he drafted
an article by which he distinguished the *right* to take fish (both on
the high seas and on the shores) and the *liberty* to take and cure
fish on the land.   But on the following day he presented to the
British negotiators a draft in which he distinguishes between the
' *right* ' to take fish on the high seas, and the ' *liberty* ' to take fish on
the ' *coasts*,' and to dry and cure fish on the land. . . . .   The British
Commissioner called attention to the distinction thus suggested by
Mr. Adams, and proposed that the word *liberty* should be applied
to the privileges both on the water and on the land.   Mr. Adams
thereupon rose up and made a vehement protest, as is recorded in
his diary, against the suggestion that the United States enjoyed the
fishing on the banks of Newfoundland by any other title than that
of *right*. . . . .   The application of the word *liberty* to the coast
fishery was left as Mr. Adams proposed."   " The incident," proceeds the British Case, " is of importance, since it shows that the
difference between the two phrases was intentional " (British
Counter-Case, p. 17).   And the British Argument emphasises again
the difference.   " More cogent still is the distinction between the
words *right* and *liberty*.   The word *right* is applied to the sea fisheries, and the word *liberty* to the shore fisheries.   The history of
the negotiations shows that this distinction was advisedly adopted."
If, then, a *liberty* is a grant and not the recognition of a *right*, if, as
the British Case, Counter-Case, and Argument recognise, the United
States had the right to fish in the open sea in contradistinction with

the *liberty* to fish near the shores or portions of the shores, and if what has been renounced in the words of the treaty is the *liberty* to fish on or within three miles of the bays, creeks and harbours of His Britannic Majesty's dominions, it clearly follows that such *liberty* and the corresponding renunciation refers only to such portions of the bays which were under the sovereignty of Great Britain and not to such other portions, if any, as form part of the high seas.

And thus it appears that, far from being immaterial, the territoriality of bays is of the utmost importance. The treaty not containing any rule or indication upon the subject, the Tribunal cannot help a decision as to this point, which involves the second branch of the British contention that all so-called bays are not only geographical, but wholly territorial as well, and subject to the jurisdiction of Great Britain. The situation was very accurately described on almost the same lines as above stated by the British memorandum sent in 1870 by the Earl of Kimberley to Governor Sir John Young: " The right of Great Britain to exclude American fishermen from waters within three miles of the coasts is unambiguous and, it is believed, uncontested. But there appears to be some doubt what are the waters described as within three miles of bays, creeks or harbours. When a bay is less than six miles broad its waters are within the three-mile limit, and therefore clearly within the meaning of the treaty; *but when it is more than that breadth, the question arises whether it is a bay of Her Britannic Majesty's dominions.* This is a question which has to be considered in each particular case with regard to international law and usage. When such a bay is not a bay of Her Majesty's dominions, the American fishermen shall be entitled to fish in it, except within three marine miles of the ' coast ' ; when it is a bay of Her Majesty's dominions, they will not be entitled to fish within three miles of it, that is to say (it is presumed), within three miles of a line drawn from headland to headland." (United States Case Appendix, p. 629.)

Now, it must be stated in the first place that there does not seem to exist any general rule of international law which may be considered final, even in what refers to the marginal belt of territorial waters. The old rule of the cannon-shot, crystallised into the present three marine miles measured from low water mark, may be modified at a later period, inasmuch as certain nations claim a wider jurisdiction, and an extension has already been recommended by the Institute of International Law. There is an obvious reason for that. The marginal strip of territorial waters, based originally on the cannon-shot, was founded on the necessity of the riparian State to protect itself from outward attack, by providing something in the nature of an insulating zone, which very reasonably should be ex-

tended with the accrued possibility of offence due to the wider range
of modern ordnance.   In what refers to bays it has been proposed as a
general rule (subject to certain important exceptions) that the marginal belt of territorial waters should follow the sinuosities of the
coast more or less in the manner held by the United States in the
present contention, so that the marginal belt being of three miles,
as in the treaty under consideration, only such bays should be held
as territorial as have an entrance not wider than six miles.   (See Sir
Thomas Barclay's report to Institute of International Law, 1894, p.
129, in which he also strongly recommends these limits.)   This is the
doctrine which Westlake, the eminent English writer on international
law, has summed up in very few words: "As to bays," he says,
" if the entrance to one of them is not more than twice the width of
the littoral sea enjoyed by the country in question—that is, not more
than six sea miles in the ordinary case, eight in that of Norway, and
so forth—there is no access from the open sea to the bay except
through the territorial water of that country, and the inner part of
the bay will belong to that country, no matter how widely it may
expand.   The line drawn from shore to shore at the part where, in
approaching from the open sea, the width first contracts to that
mentioned, will take the place of the line of low water, and the littoral sea belonging to the State will be measured outwards from that
line to the distance of three miles or more proper to the State; "
(Westlake, vol. i, p. 187).   But the learned author takes care to add:
" But although this is the general rule, it often meets with an exception in the case of bays which penetrate deep into the land and are
called gulfs.   Many of these are recognized by immemorial usage as
territorial sea of the States into which they penetrate, notwithstanding that their entrance is wider than the general rule for bays would
give as a limit for such appropriation."   And he proceeds to quote as
examples of this kind the Bay of Conception in Newfoundland, which
he considers as wholly British, Chesapeake and Delaware Bays,
which belong to the United States, and others.   (*Ibid.*, p. 188.)   The
Institute of International Law, in its annual meeting of 1894, recommended a marginal belt of six miles for the general line of the coast,
and as a consequence established that for bays the line should be
drawn up across at the nearest portion of the entrance toward the sea
where the distance between the two sides do not exceed twelve miles.
But the learned association very wisely added a proviso to the effect
" that bays should be so considered and measured *unless a continuous
and established usage* has sanctioned a greater breadth."   Many great
authorities are agreed as to that.   Counsel for the United States
proclaimed the right to the exclusive jurisdiction of certain bays, no
matter what the width of their entrance should be, when the littoral
nation has asserted its right to take it into their jurisdiction upon

reasons which go always back to the doctrine of protection. Lord Blackburn, one of the most eminent of English judges, in delivering the opinion of the Privy Council about Conception Bay, in Newfoundland, adhered to the same doctrine when he asserted the territoriality of that branch of the sea, giving as a reason for such finding " that the British Government for a long period had exercised dominion over this bay, and its claim had been acquiesced in by other nations, so as to show that the bay had been for a long time occupied exclusively by Great Britain, a circumstance which, in the tribunals of any country, would be very important." "And moreover," he added, " the British Legislature has, by Acts of Parliament, declared it to be part of the British territory and part of the country made subject to the legislation of Newfoundland." (*Direct United States Cable Company* v. *the Anglo-American Telegraph Company*, Law Reports, 2 Appeal Cases, 374.)

So it may safely be asserted that a certain class of bays, which might be properly called the historical bays, such as Chesapeake Bay and Delaware Bay, in North America, and the great estuary of the River Plate, in South America, form a class distinct and apart, and undoubtedly belong to the littoral country, whatever be their depth of penetration and the width of their mouths, when such country has asserted its sovereignty over them, and particular circumstances, such as geographical configuration, immemorial usage, and, above all, the requirements of self-defence, justify such a pretension. The right of Great Britain over the bays of Conception, Chaleur, and Miramichi are of this description. In what refers to the other bays, as might be termed the common, ordinary bays, indenting the coasts, over which no special claim or assertion of sovereignty has been made, there does not seem to be any other general principle to be applied than the one resulting from the custom and usage of each individual nation, as shown by their treaties and their general and time honoured practice.

130   The well-known words of Bynkershoek might be very appropriately recalled in this connection when so many and divergent opinions and authorities have been recited: " The common law of nations," he says, " can only be learnt from reason and custom. I do not deny that authority may add weight to reason, but I prefer to seek it in a constant custom of concluding treaties in one sense or another, and in examples that have occurred in one country or another." (*Quæstiones Juris Publici*, vol. i, cap. 3.)

It is to be borne in mind in this respect that the Tribunal has been called upon to decide, as the subject matter of this controversy, the construction to be given to the fishery treaty of 1818 between Great Britain and the United States. And so it is that from the usage and the practice of Great Britain in this and other like fisheries, and from treaties entered into by them with other nations as to fisheries, may be evolved the right interpretation to be given to the particular convention which has been submitted. In this connection the following treaties may be recited:—

Treaty between Great Britain and France, 2nd August, 1839. It reads as follows:—

"Article 9. The subjects of Her Britannic Majesty shall enjoy the exclusive right of fishery within the distance of three miles from low water mark along the whole extent of the coasts of the British Islands.

" It is agreed that the distance of three miles fixed as the general limit for the exclusive right of fishery upon the coasts of the two countries shall, with respect to bays, the mouths of which do not exceed ten miles in width, be measured from a straight line drawn from headland to headland.

"Article 10. It is agreed and understood that the miles mentioned in the present convention are geographical miles, whereof 60 make a degree of latitude." (Hertslet's Treaties and Conventions, vol. v, p. 89.)

Regulations between Great Britain and France, 24th May, 1843 :—

"Art. 2. The limits within which the general right of fishery is exclusively reserved to the subjects of the two kingdoms respectively are fixed (with the exception of those in Granville Bay) at 3 miles distance from low water mark.

" With respect to bays, the mouths of which do not exceed ten miles in width, the 3 mile distance is measured from a straight line drawn from headland to headland.

"Art. 3. The miles mentioned in the present regulations are geographical miles, of which 60 make a degree of latitude." (Hertslet, vol. vi, p. 416.)

Treaty between Great Britain and France, November 11, 1867 :—

"Art. 1. British fishermen shall enjoy the exclusive rights of fishery within the distance of 3 miles from low-water mark, along the whole extent of the coasts of the British islands.

" The distance of 3 miles fixed as the general limit for the exclusive right of fishery upon the coasts of the two countries shall, with respect to bays, the mouths of which do not exceed ten miles in width be measured from a straight line drawn from headland to headland.

" The miles mentioned in the present convention are geographical miles, whereof 60 make a degree of latitude." (Hertslet's Treaties, vol. xii, p. 1126, British Case Appendix, p. 38.)

Great Britain and North German Confederation. British notice to fishermen by the Board of Trade. Board of Trade, November 1868 :—

" Her Majesty's Government and the North German Confederation having come to an agreement respecting the regulations to be observed by British fishermen fishing off the coasts of the North German Confederation, the following notice is issued for the guidance and warning of British fishermen:—

" 1. The exclusive fishery limits of the German Empire are designated by the Imperial Government as follows: That tract of the sea which extends to a distance of 3 sea miles from the extremest limits which the ebb leaves dry of the German North Sea Coast of the German islands or flats lying before it, as well as those bays and incurvations of the coast which are ten sea miles or less in breadth reckoned from the extremest points of the land and the flats, must be considered as under the territorial sovereignty of North Germany."
    (Hertslet's Treaties, vol. xiv, p. 1055.)

131   Great Britain and German Empire. British Board of Trade, December 1874.

(Same recital referring to an arrangement entered into between Her Britannic Majesty and the German Government.)

Then the same articles follow with the alteration of the words " German Empire " for " North Germany." (Hertslet, vol. xiv, p. 1058.)

Treaty between Great Britain, Belgium, Denmark, France, Germany and the Netherlands for regulating the police of the North Sea Fisheries, May 6, 1882:—

" 2. Les pêcheurs nationaux jouiront du droit exclusif de pêche dans le rayon de 3 milles, à partir de la laisse de basse mer, le long de toute l'étendue des côtes de leurs pays respectifs, ainsi que des îles et des bancs qui en dépendent.

" Pour les baies le rayon de 3 milles sera mesuré à partir d'une ligne droite, tirée, en travers de la baie, dans la partie la plus rapprochée de l'entrée, au premier point où l'ouverture n'excédera pas 10 milles." (Hertslet, vol. xv, p. 794.)

British Order-in-Council, October 23, 1877:—

Prescribes the obligation of not concealing or effacing numbers or marks on boats, employed in fishing or dredging for purposes of sale on the coasts of England, Wales, Scotland and the Islands of Guernsey, Jersey, Alderney, Sark and Man, and not going outside—

"(a.) The distance of 3 miles from low-water mark along the whole extent of the said coasts;
"(b.) In cases of bays less than 10 miles wide the line joining the headlands of said bays." (Hertslet, vol. xiv, p. 1032.)

To this list may be added the unratified treaty of 1888 between Great Britain and the United States, which is so familiar to the Tribunal. Such unratified treaty contains an authoritative interpretation of the convention of October 20th, 1818, *sub judice:* " The 3 marine miles mentioned in article 1 of the convention of October 20th, 1818, shall be measured seaward from low-water mark; but at every bay, creek or harbour, not otherwise specifically provided for in this treaty, such three marine miles shall be measured seaward from a straight line drawn across the bay, creek or harbour, in the part nearest the entrance at the first point where the width does not exceed ten marine miles," which is recognising the exceptional bays as aforesaid and laying the rule for the general and common bays.

It has been suggested that the treaty of 1818 ought not to be studied as hereabove in the light of any treaties of a later date, but rather be referred to such British international conventions as preceded it and clearly illustrate, according to this view, what were, at the time, the principles maintained by Great Britain as to their sovereignty over the sea and over the coast and the adjacent territorial waters. In this connection the treaties of 1686 and 1713 with France and of 1763 with France and Spain have been recited and offered as examples also of exclusion of nations by agreement from fishery rights on the high seas. I cannot partake of such a view. The treaties of 1686, 1713, and 1763 can hardly be understood with respect to this, otherwise than as examples of the wild, obsolete claims over the common ocean which all nations have of old abandoned with the progress of an enlightened civilisation. And if certain nations accepted long ago to be excluded by convention from fishing on what is to-day considered a common sea, it is precisely because it was then understood that such tracts of water, now free and open to all, were the exclusive property of a particular Power, who, being the owners, admitted or excluded others from their use. The treaty of 1818 is in the meantime one of the few which mark an era in the diplomacy of the world. As a matter of fact it is the very first which commuted the rule of the cannon-shot into the three marine miles of coastal jurisdiction. And it really would appear unjustified to explain such an historic document by referring it to international agreements of a hundred and two hundred years before when the doctrine of Selden's *Mare Clausum* was at its height, and when the coastal waters were fixed at such distances as sixty miles, or a hundred miles, or two days' journey from the shore and the like. It seems very appropriate, on the contrary, to explain the meaning of the treaty of 1818 by comparing it with those which immediately followed and established the same limit of coastal jurisdiction. As a general rule a treaty of a former date may be very safely construed by referring it to the provisions of like treaties made by the same nation on the same matter at a later time. Much more so when, as occurs in the present case, the later conventions, with no exception, starting from the same premise of the three miles coastal jurisdiction arrive always to an uniform policy and line of action in what refers to bays. As a matter of fact, all authorities approach and connect the modern fishery treaties of Great Britain, and refer them to the treaty of 1818. The second edition of Klüber, for instance, quotes in the same sentence the treaties of October 20th,

1818, and August 2nd, 1839, as fixing a distance of three miles from low water mark for coastal jurisdiction. And Fiori, the well-known Italian jurist, referring to the same marine miles of coastal jurisdiction, says: "This rule recognized as early as the treaty of 1818 between the United States and Great Britain, and that between Great Britain and France in 1839, has again been admitted in the treaty of 1867." ("Nouveau Droit international public," Paris, 1885, section 803.)

This is only a recognition of the permanency and the continuity of States. The treaty of 1818 is not a separate fact unconnected with the later policy of Great Britain. Its negotiators were not parties to such international convention, and their powers disappeared as soon as they signed the document on behalf of their countries. The Parties to the treaty of 1818 were the United States and Great Britain, and what Great Britain meant in 1818 about bays and fisheries, when they, for the first time, fixed a marginal jurisdiction of three miles, can be very well explained by what Great Britain, the same permanent political entity, understood in 1839, 1843, 1867, 1874, 1878 and 1882, when fixing the very same zone of territorial waters. That a bay in Europe should be considered as different from a bay in America, and subject to other principles of international law, cannot be admitted in the face of it. What the practice of Great Britain has been outside the treaties is very well known to the Tribunal, and the examples might be multiplied of the cases in which that nation has ordered its subordinates to apply to the bays on these fisheries the ten mile entrance rule or the six miles according to the occasion. It has been repeatedly said that such have been only relaxations of the strict right, assented to by Great Britain in order to avoid friction on certain special occasions. That may be. But it may also be asserted that such relaxations have been very many, and that the constant, uniform, never contradicted, practice of concluding fishery treaties from 1839 down to the present day, in all of which the ten miles entrance bays are recognised, is the clear sign of a policy. This policy has but very lately found a most public, solemn, and unequivocal expression. "On a question asked in Parliament on the 21st February, 1907," says Pitt Cobbett, a distinguished English writer, with respect to the Moray Firth Case, "it was stated that, according to the view of the Foreign Office, the Admiralty, the Colonial Office, the Board of Trade and the Board of Agriculture and Fisheries, the term 'territorial waters' was deemed to include waters extending from the coast line of any part of the territory of a State to three miles from the low-water mark of such coast line, and the waters of all bays, the entrance to which is not more than *six miles*, and of which the entire land boundary forms part of the territory of the same State." (Pitt Cobbett, "Cases and Opinions on International Law," vol. i, p. 143.)

Is there a contradiction between these six miles and the ten miles of the treaties just referred to? Not at all. The six miles are the consequence of the three miles marginal belt of territorial waters in their coincidence from both sides at the inlets of the coast and the ten miles far from being an arbitrary measure are simply an extension, a margin given for convenience to the strict six miles with fishery purposes. Where the miles represent sixty to a degree in latitude the ten miles are besides the sixth part of the same degree. The American Government, in reply to the observations made to Secretary Bayard's memorandum of 1888, said very precisely: "The width of ten miles was proposed not only because it had been followed in conventions between many other Powers, but also because it was deemed reasonable and just in the present case; this Government, recognising the fact that while it might have claimed a width of six miles as a basis of settlement, fishing within bays and harbours only slightly wider would be confined to areas so narrow as to render it practically valueless and almost necessarily expose the fishermen to constant danger of carrying their operations into forbidden waters." (British Case Appendix, p. 416.) And Professor John Basset Moore, a recognised authority on international law, in a communication addressed to the Institute of International Law, said very forcibly: "Since you observe that there does not appear to be any convincing reason to prefer the ten mile line in such a case to that of double three miles, I may say that there have been supposed to exist reasons both of convenience and of safety. The ten mile line has been adopted in the cases referred to as a practical rule. The transgression of an encroachment upon territorial waters by fishing vessels is generally a grave offence, involving in many instances the forfeiture of the offending vessel, and it is obvious that the narrower the space in which it is permissible to fish, the more likely the offence is to be committed. In order, therefore, that fishing may be practicable and safe, and not constantly attended with the risk of violating territorial waters, it has been thought to be expedient not to allow it where the extent of free waters between the three miles drawn on each side of the bay is less than four miles. This is the reason of the ten mile line. Its intention is not to hamper or restrict the right to fish, but to render its exercise practicable and safe. When fishermen fall in with a shoal of fish the impulse to follow it is so strong as to make the possibilities of transgression very serious within narrow limits of free waters. Hence it has been deemed wiser to exclude them from space less than four miles each way from the forbidden lines. In spaces less than this operations are not only hazardous, but so circumscribed as to render them of little practical value." ("Annuaire de l'Institut de Droit international," 1894, p. 146.)

So the use of the ten mile bays so constantly put into practice by Great Britain in its fishery treaties has its root and connection with the marginal belt of three miles for the territorial waters. So much so that the Tribunal having decided not to adjudicate in this case the ten miles entrance to the bays of the treaty of 1818, this will be the only one exception in which the ten miles of the bays do not follow as a consequence the strip of three miles of territorial waters, the historical bays and estuaries always excepted.

And it is for that reason that an usage so firmly and for so long a time established ought, in my opinion, be applied to the construction of the treaty under consideration, much more so, when custom, one of the recognised sources of law, international as well as municipal, is supported in this case by reason and by the acquiescence and the practice of many nations.

The Tribunal has decided that: " In case of bays the three miles " (of the treaty) " are to be measured from a straight line drawn across the body of water at the place where it ceases to have the configuration characteristic of a bay. At all other places the three miles are to be measured following the sinuosities of the coast." But no rule is laid out or general principle evolved for the parties to know what the nature of such configuration is or by what methods the points should be ascertained from which the bay should lose the characteristics of such. There lies the whole contention and the whole difficulty, not satisfactorily solved, to my mind, by simply recommending, without the scope of the Award and as a system of procedure for resolving future contestations under article 4 of the Treaty of Arbitration, a series of lines, which practical as they may be supposed to be, cannot be adopted by the Parties without concluding a new treaty.

These are the reasons for my dissent, which I much regret, on Question Five.

Done at The Hague, September 7th, 1910.

LUIS M. DRAGO.

THE PRESIDENT then asked the agents of both Parties whether they wished to make any declaration or communication to the Tribunal.

The Honorable CHANDLER P. ANDERSON, agent for the United States, said that in case he should desire to present any communication to the Tribunal, on behalf of his Government, in regard to the Award or any part of it, he would do so within the period fixed by article 10 of the special agreement, reserving any rights which his Government might have in the premises.

The Right Honourable SIR WILLIAM SNOWDON ROBSON, Counsel for Great Britain, said that he had nothing to add.

THE PRESIDENT then spoke as follows:

After more than three months of uninterrupted work a sentence has been pronounced which is destined to put an end to controversies of almost secular standing, involving not only great economic, but still more important political questions and interests.

134 During three months the temple of international arbitration has been open and in three weeks it will be opened again; while two new arbitrations are already in preparation.

So that it seems that one of the features of a really Permanent Court of Arbitration is already established, as such a Court was proposed at the Second Peace Conference in 1907 by the two Powers which are the Parties in the present litigation, that is, the feature of continuity in the work, though the personnel of the Court may change.

It is not to be expected that at first sight the Award which has just been read will entirely satisfy either of the Parties, especially if it is considered not as a whole, but in its different parts.

In questions so complicated and involving interests so conflicting and important it is not likely that the right should be all on one side. The Tribunal has endeavoured to find out where the right is in every special point according to the conviction at which it arrived on the basis of a most careful and conscientious examination of the whole matter. We hope and are of the conviction that, if not at the first moment, yet certainly after a reasonable time, both Parties will agree that the solution is fair, just and equitable to both of them.

Before concluding, I consider it my duty to renew the expression of our thanks to the Secretary-General, Baron Michiels van Verduynen, and the First Secretary of the Court, Jonkheer Röell, for all the pains they have taken and the assistance they have afforded us, and also to Messrs. Charles D. White and George Young, Secretaries of the Tribunal.

I avail myself of this opportunity to thank Messrs. van Langenhuysen Brothers, printers at The Hague, for the expeditious and precise manner in which they have executed the difficult printing in a language foreign to their employees.

And now I beg the Secretary-General to deliver the originals of the Award, signed by the Arbitrators, to the Agents of the Parties.

THE SECRETARY-GENERAL then handed to the Honourable Chandler P. Anderson, Agent of the United States, and to the Honourable Allen B. Aylesworth, Agent of Great Britain, the Award of the Tribunal destined for their respective Governments.

The Court adjourned *sine die.*

NORTH ATLANTIC COAST FISHERIES

THE

CASE OF THE UNITED STATES

BEFORE

THE PERMANENT COURT OF ARBITRATION
AT THE HAGUE

UNDER THE

PROVISIONS OF THE SPECIAL AGREEMENT BETWEEN
THE UNITED STATES OF AMERICA AND GREAT BRITAIN
CONCLUDED JANUARY 27, 1909

CONTENTS OF THE CASE.

THE CASE OF THE UNITED STATES.

INTRODUCTORY STATEMENT.

In the general arbitration treaty entered into by the United States and Great Britain on April 4, 1908, it was agreed:

ARTICLE I.

Differences which may arise of a legal nature or relating to the interpretation of treaties existing between the two Contracting Parties and which it may not have been possible to settle by diplomacy, shall be referred to the Permanent Court of Arbitration established at The Hague by the Convention of the 29th of July, 1899, provided nevertheless, that they do not affect the vital interests, the independence, or the honor of the two Contracting States, and do not concern the interests of third Parties.

ARTICLE II.

In each individual case the High Contracting Parties, before appealing to the Permanent Court of Arbitration, shall conclude a special Agreement defining clearly the matter in dispute, the scope of the powers of the Arbitrators, and the periods to be fixed for the formation of the Arbitral Tribunal and the several stages of the procedure. It is understood that such special agreements on the part of the United States will be made by the President of the United States, by and with the advice and consent of the Senate thereof; His Majesty's Government reserving the right before concluding a special agreement in any matter affecting the interests of a self-governing Dominion of the British Empire to obtain the concurrence therein of the Government of that Dominion.

Such Agreements shall be binding only when confirmed by the two Governments by an Exchange of Notes.

Subsequently, the United States and Great Britain as signatory parties to the Convention for the pacific settlement of international disputes entered into on the 18th day of October, 1907, agreed, by Article 91 thereof, that such Convention duly ratified "shall replace as between the Contracting Powers the Convention for the pacific settlement of international disputes of July 29, 1899," and such Convention has since been duly ratified by the United States and Great Britain.

1

Thereafter, on the 29th day of January, 1909, the United States and Great Britain entered into a Special Agreement for the submission of questions relating to the fisheries on the North Atlantic coast under the general treaty of arbitration above referred to, concluded between the United States and Great Britain on the 4th day of April, 1908, which Special Agreement, pursuant to the requirement of Article II of the aforesaid general arbitration treaty defines "the matter in dispute, the scope of the powers of the arbitrators, and the periods to be fixed for the formation of the arbitral tribunal and the several stages of the procedure," and notes confirming it were exchanged by the two Governments on March 4, 1909.

The provisions of this Special Agreement, so far as they relate to the matter in dispute and the scope of the powers of the arbitrators, are as follows:

ARTICLE I.

Whereas, by Article I of the Convention signed at London on the 20th day of October, 1818, between Great Britain and the United States, it was agreed as follows:

Whereas differences have arisen respecting the Liberty claimed by the United States for the Inhabitants thereof, to take, dry and cure Fish on Certain Coasts, Bays, Harbours and Creeks of His Britannic Majesty's Dominions in America, it is agreed between the High Contracting Parties, that the Inhabitants of the said United States shall have forever, in common with the Subjects of His Britannic Majesty, the Liberty to take Fish of every kind on that part of the Southern Coast of Newfoundland which extends from Cape Ray to the Rameau Islands, on the Western and Northern Coast of Newfoundland, from the said Cape Ray to the Quirpon Islands, on the shores of the Magdalen Islands, and also on the Coasts, Bays, Harbours, and Creeks from Mount Joly on the Southern Coast of Labrador, to and through the Straits of Belleisle and thence Northwardly indefinitely along the Coast, without prejudice however, to any of the exclusive Rights of the Hudson Bay Company; and that the American Fishermen shall also have liberty forever, to dry and cure Fish in any of the unsettled Bays, Harbours, and Creeks of the Southern part of the Coast of Newfoundland hereabove described, and of the Coast of Labrador; but so soon as the same, or any Portion thereof, shall be settled, it shall not be lawful for the said Fishermen to dry or cure Fish at such Portion so settled, without previous agreement for such purpose with the Inhabitants, Proprietors, or Possessors of the ground.—And the United States hereby renounce forever, any Liberty heretofore enjoyed or claimed by the Inhabitants thereof, to take, dry, or cure Fish on, or within three marine Miles of any of the Coasts, Bays, Creeks, or Harbours of His Britannic Majesty's Dominions in America not included within the above mentioned limits; provided, however, that the American Fishermen shall be admitted to enter such Bays or Harbours for the purpose of Shelter and of repairing Damages therein, of purchasing Wood, and of obtaining Water, and for no other purpose whatever. But they shall be under such Restrictions as may be necessary to prevent their taking, drying or curing Fish therein, or in any other manner whatever abusing the Privileges hereby reserved to them.

And, whereas, differences have arisen as to the scope and meaning of the said Article, and of the liberties therein referred to, and otherwise in respect of the rights and liberties which the inhabitants of the United States have or claim to have in the waters or on the shores therein referred to:

It is agreed that the following questions shall be submitted for decision to a tribunal of arbitration constituted as hereinafter provided:

Question 1. To what extent are the following contentions or either of them justified?

It is contended on the part of Great Britain that the exercise of the liberty to take fish referred to in the said Article, which the inhabitants of the United States have forever in common with the subjects of His Britannic Majesty, is subject, without the consent of the United States, to reasonable regulation by Great Britain, Canada, or Newfoundland in the form of municipal laws, ordinances, or rules, as, for example, to regulations in respect of (1) the hours, days, or seasons when fish may be taken on the treaty coasts; (2) the method, means, and implements to be used in the taking of fish or in the carrying on of fishing operations on such coasts; (3) any other matters of a similar character relating to fishing; such regulations being reasonable, as being, for instance—

(*a*) Appropriate or necessary for the protection and preservation of such fisheries and the exercise of the rights of British subjects therein and of the liberty which by the said Article I the inhabitants of the United States have therein in common with British subjects;

(*b*) Desirable on grounds of public order and morals;

(*c*) Equitable and fair as between local fishermen and the inhabitants of the United States exercising the said treaty liberty and not so framed as to give unfairly an advantage to the former over the latter class.

It is contended on the part of the United States that the exercise of such liberty is not subject to limitations or restraints by Great Britain, Canada, or Newfoundland in the form of municipal laws, ordinances, or regulations in respect of (1) the hours, days, or seasons when the inhabitants of the United States may take fish on the treaty coasts, or (2) the method, means, and implements used by them in taking fish or in carrying on fishing operations on such coasts, or (3) any other limitations or restraints of similar character—

(*a*) Unless they are appropriate and necessary for the protection and preservation of the common rights in such fisheries and the exercise thereof; and

(*b*) Unless they are reasonable in themselves and fair as between local fishermen and fishermen coming from the United States, and not so framed as to give an advantage to the former over the latter class; and

(*c*) Unless their appropriateness, necessity, reasonableness, and fairness be determined by the United States and Great Britain by common accord and the United States concurs in their enforcement.

Question 2. Have the inhabitants of the United States, while exercising the liberties referred to in said Article, a right to employ as members of the fishing crews of their vessels persons not inhabitants of the United States?

Question 3. Can the exercise by the inhabitants of the United States of the liberties referred to in the said Article be subjected, without the consent of the United States, to the requirements of entry or report at custom-houses or the payment of light or harbor or other dues, or to any other similar requirement or condition or exaction?

Question 4. Under the provision of the said Article that the American fishermen shall be admitted to enter certain bays or harbors for shelter, repairs, wood, or water, and for no other purpose whatever, but that they shall be under such restrictions as may be necessary to prevent their taking, drying, or curing fish therein or in any other manner whatever abusing the privileges thereby reserved to them, is it permissible to impose restrictions making the exercise of such privileges conditional upon the payment of light or harbor or other dues, or entering or reporting at custom-houses or any similar conditions?

Question 5. From where must be measured the " three marine miles of any of the coasts, bays, creeks, or harbors " referred to in the said Article?

Question 6. Have the inhabitants of the United States the liberty under the said Article or otherwise, to take fish in the bays, harbors, and creeks on that part of the southern coast of Newfoundland which extends from Cape Ray to Rameau Islands, or on the western and northern coasts of Newfoundland from Cape Ray to Quirpon Islands, or on the Magdalen Islands?

Question 7. Are the inhabitants of the United States whose vessels resort to the treaty coasts for the purpose of exercising the liberties referred to in Article I of the treaty of 1818 entitled to have for those vessels, when duly authorized by the United States in that behalf, the commercial privileges on the treaty coasts accorded by agreement or otherwise to United States trading vessels generally?

ARTICLE II.

Either Party may call the attention of the Tribunal to any legislative or executive act of the other Party, specified within three months of the exchange of notes enforcing this agreement, and which is claimed to be inconsistent with the true interpretation of the treaty of 1818; and may call upon the Tribunal to express in its award its opinion upon such acts, and to point out in what respects, if any, they are inconsistent with the principles laid down in the award in reply to the preceding questions; and each Party agrees to conform to such opinion.

ARTICLE III.

If any question arises in the arbitration regarding the reasonableness of any regulation or otherwise which requires an examination of the practical effect of any provisions in relation to the conditions surrounding the exercise of the liberty of fishery enjoyed by the inhabitants of the United States, or which requires expert information about the fisheries themselves, the Tribunal may, in that case, refer such question to a commission of three expert specialists in such matters; one to be designated by each of the Parties hereto, and the third, who shall not be a national of either Party, to be designated by the Tribunal. This Commission shall examine into and report their conclusions on any question or questions so referred to it by the Tribunal and such report shall be considered by the Tribunal and shall, if incorporated by them in the award, be accepted as a part thereof.

Pending the report of the Commission upon the question or questions so referred and without awaiting such report, the Tribunal may make a separate award upon all or any other questions before it, and such separate award, if made, shall become immediately effective, provided that the report aforesaid shall not be incorporated in the award until it has been considered by the Tribunal. The expenses of such Commission shall be borne in equal moieties by the Parties hereto.

ARTICLE IV.

The Tribunal shall recommend for the consideration of the High Contracting Parties rules and a method of procedure under which all questions which may arise in the future regarding the exercise of the liberties above referred to may be determined in accordance with the principles laid down in the award. If the High Contracting Parties shall not adopt the rules and method of procedure so recommended, or if they shall not, subsequently to the delivery of the award, agree upon such rules and methods, then any differences which may arise in the future between the High Contracting Parties relating to the interpretation of the treaty of 1818 or to the effect and application the award of the Tribunal shall be referred informally to the Permanent Court at The Hague for decision by the summary procedure provided in Chapter IV of The Hague Convention of the 18th of October, 1907.

ARTICLE V.

The Tribunal of Arbitration provided for herein shall be chosen from the general list of members of the Permanent Court at The Hague, in accordance with the provisions of Article XLV of the Convention for the Settlement of International Disputes, concluded at the Second Peace Conference at The Hague on the 18th of October, 1907. The provisions of said Convention, so far as applicable and not inconsistent herewith, and excepting Articles LIII and LIV, shall govern the proceedings under the submission herein provided for.

The time allowed for the direct agreement of His Britannic Majesty and the President of the United States on the composition of such Tribunal shall be three months.

The Special Agreement of January 27, 1909, was entered into upon the express stipulation and understanding on both sides—

That it is agreed by the United States and Great Britain that question 5 of the series submitted, namely, "from where must be measured the three marine miles of any of the coasts, bays, creeks or harbors referred to in said article," does not include any question as to the Bay of Fundy, considered as a whole apart from its bays or creeks, or as to innocent passage through the Gut of Canso, and that the respective views or contentions of the United States and Great Britain on either subject shall be in no wise prejudiced by anything in the present arbitration.[a]

The printed Case on the part of the United States, accompanied by printed copies of the documents, the official correspondence and other evidence on which it relies, is delivered pursuant to Article

---

[a] Appendix, p. 9.

VI of the Special Agreement, the accompanying documents, correspondence and evidence being contained in an Appendix to the Case together with a set of two maps.

A list of charts published at the British Admiralty appears in the Appendix at page 1308, copies of which will be furnished to the Tribunal upon the oral argument, if required for geographical information of a character more detailed than can be obtained from the maps above referred to.

The text of the Special Agreement and of so much of the Convention for the pacific settlement of international disputes of October 18, 1907, as is adopted thereby, are printed in full in the Appendix to this Case.[a]

The subject of this controversy, as presented in the printed Case, is divided into Part I. covering the status prior to the treaty of 1818, including the negotiations resulting in that treaty, and an examination of the provisions of Article I. thereof; and Part II. covering the subsequent actions of the United States and Great Britain having a bearing upon the interpretation of its provisions in accordance with their true intent and meaning. Each of these parts is subdivided under sub-headings, for convenience of reference, which are set forth in the table of contents and do not require repetition here.

The position of the United States on each of the seven questions submitted for decision is stated at the end of the Case under the heading Statement in Conclusion, and it will remain for the printed and oral arguments on the part of the United States to marshal and present, in response to each of these questions, the reasons and grounds of law and fact on which the position of the United States with respect thereto should be sustained.

---

[a] Appendix, p. 3.

PART I.

STATUS PRIOR TO THE TREATY OF 1818.

The Special Agreement of January 27, 1909, between the United States and Great Britain, under which this case is presented, requires the Tribunal of Arbitration thereby constituted to answer a series of questions submitted for its decision growing out of differences which have arisen between the United States and Great Britain as to the scope and meaning of Article I of their treaty of October 20, 1818 " and of the liberties therein referred to and otherwise in respect of the rights and liberties which the inhabitants of the United States have or claim to have in the waters or on the shores therein referred to."

It will be observed that the differences under consideration include not only those which have arisen as to the scope and meaning of the said Article and of the liberties therein referred to, but also those which have arisen otherwise in respect of the rights and liberties which the inhabitants of the United States have or claim to have in the waters or on the shores mentioned in that Article. It will also be observed upon an examination of Article I of the treaty of 1818 that its provisions which are now the occasion of differences were themselves the outcome of differences existing with respect to these fisheries when that treaty was made, the introductory recital of Article I of that treaty being as follows:

Whereas differences have arisen respecting the liberty claimed by the United States for the inhabitants thereof to take, dry and cure fish on certain coasts, bays, harbors and creeks of His Britannic Majesty's Dominions in America, its is agreed, etc.

Therefore, before discussing the provisions of Article I of the treaty of 1818 and in order that the various differences above referred to and their relation to that Article may be clearly understood, it will be convenient to examine into the antecedent conditions and course of events leading up to the treaty of 1818 with a view to showing the respective positions of the two Governments at that time so far as they relate to the questions now in controversy.

THE TREATY OF SEPTEMBER 3, 1783.

The first discussion with Great Britain of the interests of the United States in these fisheries will be found in the negotiations for the treaty of peace at the close of the Revolution in 1782.

The Commissioners who took part in these negotiations were John Adams, Benjamin Franklin, John Jay and Henry Laurens on the part of the United States, and Richard Oswald on the part of Great Britain assisted by Mr. Strachey and Mr. Fitzherbert who were present and took part in the discussions during the closing conferences.

In entering upon these negotiations the United States stipulated as an indispensible condition that at the outset Great Britain should acknowledge their independence and should treat with them as an independent nation.[a] In Franklin's report of these negotiations, made immediately after the treaty was signed, he says that the use of any expressions in the powers given by Great Britain to its commissioners which might imply an acknowledgment of American independence seemed at first to be industriously avoided, and much of the summer was taken up in removing these objections, but that the refusal otherwise to treat finally induced Great Britain to overcome that difficulty and the negotiations were then entered upon.[b] Great Britain having finally acquiesced in this demand, such acknowledgment of independence was incorporated in the original draft of the proposed treaty and was carried without change through the negotiations and into the treaty as finally agreed upon, where it appears as Article I in the following form:

His Britannic Majesty acknowledges the s[d] United States, viz. New Hampshire, Massachusetts Bay, Rhode-Island & Providence Plantations, Connecticut, New York, New Jersey, Pennsylvania, Delaware, Maryland, Virginia, North Carolina, South Carolina, & Georgia, to be free sovereign & Independent States; that he treats with them as such, and for himself his Heirs and Successors, relinquishes all claim to the Government Propriety & Territorial Rights of the same & every Part thereof.[c]

The United States and Great Britain thus met as independent nations negotiating for the purpose of concluding a treaty of peace

---

[a] Appendix, pp. 227–235.   [b] Appendix, p. 226.   [c] Appendix, p. 24.

dividing between them the British Empire in North America; and standing on this basis the Commissioners on the part of the United States asserted and insisted throughout the negotiations that the British interests in the North Atlantic Coast fisheries were subject to such division and that the pre-existing rights of the Colonies therein must be recognized and continued by the treaty.

The people of the Massachusetts Bay Colony and of the other Colonies had continuously and freely resorted to these fisheries and exercised unrestricted fishing rights and liberties there until the time of the Revolution, and had borne almost unaided the burden of maintaining and defending their own and British interests in these fisheries against the aggressions of the French during the wars between Great Britain and France. In view of such continuous usage and enjoyment and by virtue of the services rendered by them in defence of these fisheries, the American Colonies asserted and insisted that they had in them at least the equal rights of joint owners with Great Britain and the other British Colonies. John Adams, one of the American Commissioners in the peace negotiations, bears witness, in a statement written by him in 1822 in review of these negotiations, that the grounds and principles on which the fisheries article of the treaty of 1783 was contended for on their part and finally yielded on the part of Great Britain were among others the following:

That New England, and especially Massachusetts, had done more in defence of them than all the rest of the British empire. That the various projected expeditions to Canada, in which they were defeated by British negligence, the conquest of Louisburg, in 1745, and the subsequent conquest of Nova Scotia, in which New England had expended more blood and treasure than all the rest of the British empire, were principally effected with a special view to the security and protection of the fisheries.

That the inhabitants of the United States had as clear a right to every branch of those fisheries, and to cure fish on land, as the inhabitants of Canada or Nova Scotia; that the citizens of Boston, New York, or Philadelphia, had as clear a right to those fisheries, as the citizens of London, Liverpool, Bristol, Glasgow, or Dublin.

And further:

We considered that treaty as a division of the empire. Our independence, our rights to territory and to the fisheries, as practised before the Revolution were no more a grant from Britain to us than the treaty was a grant from us of Canada, Nova Scotia, England,

Scotland, and Ireland to the Britons.   The treaty was nothing more than mutual acknowledgment of antecedent rights.[a]

The course of the negotiations was briefly as follows:

Before the arrival of the other American Commissioners, Messrs. Franklin and Jay proposed a series of articles which, under date of October 8, 1782, were agreed upon *ad referendum* by the British Commissioner and sent to England by him for the King's consideration, in which articles it was provided—

3rd. That the subjects of his Britannic Majesty and people of the said United States, shall continue to enjoy unmolested, the rights to take fish of every kind on the banks of Newfoundland, and other places where the inhabitants of both countries used formerly, to wit, before the last war between France and Britain, to fish and also to dry and cure the same at the accustomed places, whether belonging to his said Majesty or to the United States; and his Britannic Majesty and the said United States will extend equal privileges and hospitality to each other's fishermen as to their own.[b]

The articles thus proposed were not approved by the British Government and a new series of articles, under date of November 5, 1782, was agreed upon and signed by the British and American Commissioners, in which series the fisheries article appeared in the following form:

That the subjects of his Britannic Majesty and the people of the said United States shall continue to enjoy unmolested the right to take fish of every kind on all the banks of Newfoundland, also in the Gulf of St. Lawrence, and all other places where the inhabitants of both countries used at any time heretofore to fish; and also to dry and cure their fish on the shores of the Isle of Sables; Cape Sables, and the shores of any of the unsettled bays, harbors, or creeks of Nova Scotia, and of the Magdalen Islands.   And his Britannic Majesty and the said United States will extend equal privileges and hospitality to each other's fishermen as to their own.[c]

It will be noted that the chief difference between these articles is that the Gulf of St. Lawrence is specifically mentioned as among the places where the inhabitants of both countries used formerly to fish and where, under the provisions of both articles, they are to continue to enjoy unmolested such right; and that the places to be used for drying and curing fish, which in the first proposal were described as the "accustomed places," whether belonging to his Majesty or to the United States, in the second proposal are specifically named, and that all of the places thus named are on the

---

[a] Appendix, p. 318.   [b] Appendix, p. 217.   [c] Appendix, p. 218.

coasts which fell to Great Britain in the division of territory. So that, although still reciprocal in form as in the original proposal, the article was no longer reciprocal in effect with respect to the drying and curing of fish.

The articles thus agreed upon were again sent to England for the King's consideration and having proved unacceptable there fresh proposals from the British Ministry were delivered by Mr. Oswald to the American Commissioners on November 25, 1782, containing the following fisheries article:

Article III. The citizens of the said United States shall have the liberty of taking fish of every kind on all the banks of Newfoundland, and also in the Gulf of St. Lawrence; and also to dry and cure their fish on the shores of the Isle of Sables and on the shores of any of the unsettled bays, harbors, and creeks of the Magdalen Islands, in the Gulf of St. Lawrence, so long as such bays, harbors, and creeks shall continue and remain unsettled; on condition that the citizens of the said United States do not exercise the fishery, but at the distance of three leagues from all the coast belonging to Great Britain, as well those of the continent as those of the islands situated in the Gulf of St. Lawrence. And as to what relates to the fishery on the coast of the Island of Cape Breton out of the said gulf, the citizens of the said United States shall not be permitted to exercise the said fishery, but at the distance of fifteen leagues from the coasts of the Island of Cape Breton.[a]

It is evident from this proposal that Great Britain acquiesced in the elimination under the previous proposal of any reciprocal right of using the coasts of the United States for drying and curing fish, for no attempt is made to renew such provision, and even the provision for the extension of equal privileges and hospitality to each other's fishermen, which is found at the end of the previous proposals, is omitted here. In all other respects, however, this proposal shows a marked departure by Great Britain from the proposals previously agreed upon by the British Commissioner. Not only does it fail to reserve to the inhabitants of the United States any of the inshore or coast fisheries which were provided for in the earlier proposals, but it greatly reduces the shore space open to the Americans for drying and curing fish and it fails to recognize the American rights in the off-shore fisheries as a continuation of pre-existing rights in such fisheries, and further it proposes that American fishermen should not be permitted to enjoy such off-shore fisheries " but at the distance of three leagues from all the coast belonging to Great Britain as well

---

[a] Appendix, p. 219.

those of the continent as those of the islands situated in the Gulf of St. Lawrence " and outside of said Gulf " but at the distance of fifteen leagues from the coasts of the Island of Cape Breton." By reference to Article V of the Treaty of Paris (1763) between Great Britain and France,[a] it will be seen that this suggestion with respect to the three leagues and fifteen leagues limit of exclusion was based upon a similar limitation established by that treaty upon the French fishing rights.

The American Commissioners refused to consider any such limitations and the suggestion was abandoned by Great Britain for the reason, as stated by Mr. Richard Oswald, commissioner on the part of Great Britain in his letter of November 30, 1782, reporting the conclusion of the negotiations to his Government, that—

If we had not given way in the article of the fishery, we should have had no treaty at all, Mr. Adams having declared that he would never put his hand to any treaty, if the restraints regarding the three leagues and fifteen leagues were not dispensed with, as well as denying his countrymen the privilege of drying fish on the unsettled parts of Nova Scotia.[b]

The agreement finally arrived at appears in the treaty as Article III and is as follows:

It is agreed that the people of the United States shall continue to enjoy unmolested the right to take fish of every kind on the Grand Bank, and on all the other banks of Newfoundland; also in the Gulph of Saint Lawrence, and at all other places in the sea where the inhabitants of both countries used at any time heretofore to fish. And also that the inhabitants of the United States shall have liberty to take fish of every kind on such part of the coast of Newfoundland as British fishermen shall use (but not to dry or cure the same on that island) and also on the coasts, bays and creeks of all other of His Britannic Majesty's dominions in America; and that the American fishermen shall have liberty to dry and cure fish in any of the unsettled bays, harbours and creeks of Nova Scotia, Magdalen Islands, and Labrador, so long as the same shall remain unsettled; but so soon as the same or either of them shall be settled, it shall not be lawful for the said fishermen to dry or cure fish at such settlements, without a previous agreement for that purpose with the inhabitants, proprietors or possessors of the ground.[c]

The first clause of this article relating to the off-shore fisheries is in almost the identical language of the two proposals originally agreed upon by the British Commissioner, except that here all reference to the British rights in these fisheries is omitted. The American rights

---

[a] Appendix, p. 52.   [b] Appendix, p. 234.   [c] Appendix, p. 24.

are recognized, however, as the continuation of pre-existing rights—
" shall continue to enjoy unmolested " can have no different meaning—and instead of the limitation of three leagues or fifteen leagues
from the coast proposed by Great Britain there is no limit of
exclusion whatsoever.

This clause of the article is of particular importance inasmuch
as Great Britain has never asserted that the right of the United
States therein referred to was not of a permanent character, and has
never denied that these provisions are still in force; on the contrary
it will appear later that Great Britain has admitted that when this
treaty was made she had no exclusive jurisdiction or right in such
fisheries and that the United States as an independent nation would
have been equally entitled to their use and enjoyment independently
of any treaty provisions.[a]

The remaining portion or second clause of this article applies only
to the inshore or coast fisheries and does not require particular attention at this time because it was superseded by the provisions of the
treaty of 1818 and its relation to that treaty is considered later. For
the present it is sufficient to note with respect to this second clause of
the article that after the War of 1812 Great Britain asserted and the
United States denied that these provisions were abrogated by that
war. This question and its bearing on the present case may more
conveniently be considered in connection with the negotiations for
the treaty of peace at the close of that war and the discussions leading up to the treaty of 1818, which are hereinafter reviewed. It
will there appear that this question was not settled by the treaty
of peace of 1814 and was still unsettled when the treaty of 1818 was
entered into, and that it furnished the grounds for the differences
which are referred to in the opening clause of Article 1 of that
treaty, and in consequence of which that Article was negotiated.

---

[a] Appendix, p. 276.

THE CONTROVERSY AS TO THE EFFECT OF THE WAR OF 1812 UPON THE FISHERIES ARTICLE OF THE TREATY OF 1783.

Negotiations for the Treaty of Ghent.

No question with respect to the fisheries article of the treaty of 1783 between the United States and Great Britain or the use of these fisheries under it arose until the close of the War of 1812 when Great Britain took the position in the negotiations leading up to the treaty of peace signed at Ghent on December 24, 1814, that the provisions of the second clause of that article, relating to the inshore or coast fisheries, were abrogated by that war and that the future use of such fisheries by the United States would depend upon new treaty stipulations. The United States refused to assent to this proposition and contended that there was no justification for discriminating against- this particular portion of the treaty; and that, like any other provision of the treaty which was intended to secure to the United States the continued enjoyment of pre-existing rights upon the partition of the British North American Empire at the close of the Revolution, this particular provision survived the War of 1812, and consequently that no declaration or provision in the new treaty was required to continue it in force.

At the opening conference in these negotiations on August 8, 1814, the British Plenipotentiaries who were Lord Gambier, Henry Goulburn and William Adams, after enumerating the subjects proposed by them for discussion and after asking whether the American Plenipotentiaries were instructed to enter into negotiations on these subjects, stated that—

before they desired any answer they felt it right to communicate the intentions of their Government as to the North American Fisheries, viz: that the British Government did not intend to grant to the United States gratuitously the privileges formerly granted by treaty to them of fishing within the limits of the British Sovereignty and of using the shores of the British territories for purposes connected with the fisheries.[a]

In response to this inquiry, the United States Plenipotentiaries who were John Quincy Adams, James A. Bayard, Henry Clay, Jonathan Russell and Albert Gallatin, informed the British Plenipo-

---

[a] Appendix, p. 242.

tentiaries, at a conference held on August 9th, that the point raised by them with respect to the fisheries was not provided for in their instructions.[a] The American Plenipotentiaries were forbidden by their instructions to permit the right of the United States to the enjoyment of the fisheries under the treaty of 1783 to be brought into question,[b] and in consequence of these instructions they declined to entertain any suggestion that a new basis for the enjoyment of these fisheries be adopted or that their rights under the former treaty be continued conditionally or in exchange for some equivalent, and they explicitly declined to enter into any stipulation which could be construed as a renunciation either directly or indirectly of their rights under that treaty. The negotiations on their part were conducted throughout on the basis that the fisheries provisions under consideration had not been abrogated by the War of 1812. Notice of the position of each Government on this subject seems to have been given to the other at the second conference, held on August 9, 1814. No official record of the discussion on the subject at that conference is found further than appears from two brief references to it in the notes subsequently exchanged between the Plenipotentiaries. In their note of October 21, 1814, to the American Plenipotentiaries the British Plenipotentiaries said:

On the subject of the fisheries the undersigned expressed, with so much frankness, at the conference already referred to the views of their Government, that they consider any further observation on that topic as unnecessary at the present time.[c]

The American Plenipotentiaries in their note of November 10th, wrote in response:

In answer to the declaration made by the British Plenipotentiaries respecting the fisheries, the undersigned, referring to what passed in the conference of the 9th August, can only say that they are not authorized to bring into discussion any of the rights or liberties which the United States have heretofore enjoyed in relation thereto. From their nature, and from the peculiar character of the treaty of 1783, by which they were recognized, no further stipulation has been deemed necessary by the Government of the United States to entitle them to the full enjoyment of all of them.[d]

The position of the United States as presented at this conference and as adhered to throughout the negotiations is stated in the report

---

[a] Appendix, p. 243.   [c] Appendix, p. 247.
[b] Appendix, p. 242.   [d] Appendix, p. 250.

made by the American Plenipotentiaries to their Government after the close of the negotiations as follows:

Our instructions had forbidden us to suffer our right to the fisheries to be brought into discussion, and had not authorized us to make any distinction in the several provisions of the third article of the treaty of 1783, or between that article and any other of the same treaty. We had no equivalent to offer for a new recognition of our right to any part of the fisheries, and we had no power to grant any equivalent which might be asked for it by the British Government. We contended that the whole treaty of 1783 must be considered as one entire and permanent compact, not liable, like ordinary treaties, to be abrogated by a subsequent war between the parties to it; as an instrument recognising the rights and liberties enjoyed by the people of the United States as an independent nation, and containing the terms and conditions on which the two parts of one empire had mutually agreed, thenceforth, to constitute two distinct and separate nations. In consenting by that treaty, that a part of the North American continent should remain subject to the British jurisdiction, the people of the United States had reserved to themselves the liberty, which they had ever before enjoyed, of fishing upon that part of its coasts, and of drying and curing fish upon the shores, and this reservation had been agreed to by the other contracting party. We saw not why this liberty, then no new grant, but the mere recognition of a prior right always enjoyed, should be forfeited by war, any more than any other of the rights of our national independence; or why we should need a new stipulation for its enjoyment more than we needed a new article to declare that the King of Great Britain treated with us as free, sovereign, and independent States. We stated this principle in general terms to the British plenipotentiaries, in the note, which we sent to them with our *projet* of the treaty, and we alleged it as the ground upon which no new stipulation was deemed by our Government necessary to secure to the people of the United States all the rights and liberties stipulated in their favor by the treaty of 1783.[a]

No other reference to the fisheries is found in the protocols of the conferences or in the correspondence between the British and American Plenipotentiaries until the closing days of the negotiations. Meanwhile, however, Great Britain had brought into the negotiations a proposal for renewing and enlarging the privileges which British subjects had enjoyed in the navigation of the Mississippi River under Article VIII of the treaty of 1783, which Article was as follows:

The navigation of the Mississippi River, from its source to the ocean, shall forever remain free and open to the subjects of Great Britain and the citizens of the United States.

---

[a] Appendix, p. 258.

It will be remembered that under that treaty the western boundary of the United States was a line drawn along the middle of the Mississippi River and that the mouth of the Mississippi was then in the possession of Spain, and that its source was at that time erroneously supposed to be far enough north to carry it into British territory. Under that treaty it was further provided that the northern boundary of the United States should extend due west from the northwesternmost point of the Lake of the Woods to the Mississippi River. It having subsequently been ascertained that a line so drawn would run north of the source of the Mississippi River, it became necessary to make a change in the treaty provisions in respect to that portion of the boundary; and the United States having extended its borders west of the Mississippi by the purchase of the Louisiana Territory in 1803 and no treaty agreement having been made fixing the northern boundary of the possessions of the United States to the west of the Mississippi River, that portion of the line also required treaty definition. An attempt had been made in connection with the treaty negotiated in 1806, but left unratified by the United States, to agree upon the description of this section of the boundary extending from the Lake of the Woods to the Rocky Mountains; [a] and the location of such boundary line being one of the subjects which had been proposed for settlement in the negotiations now under consideration, an article in respect thereto was included by the American Plenipotentiaries in a *projet* of the treaty submitted by them to the British Plenipotentiaries with their letter above referred to of November 10th. [b] This boundary proposal constituted Article VIII of the *projet* and was almost identical with the article proposed by the American Commissioners for the unratified treaty of 1806, [c] and in it no mention was made of the Mississippi River. On November 26th, the British Plenipotentiaries returned this *projet* with their proposed alterations and additions noted in the margin, [b] and with respect to this article they inserted, as a substitute for the form proposed by the United States, the identical form, with some minor changes, previously proposed by the British Commissioners in the negotiations for the unratified treaty of 1806, [c] with the addition, however, of this provision:

And it is further agreed the subjects of His Britannic Majesty shall at all times have access from His Britannic Majesty's territories by

---

[a] Appendix, p. 236.   [b] Appendix, p. 251.   [c] Appendix, p. 238.

land or inland navigation, into the aforesaid territories of the United States to the River Mississippi with their goods, effects and merchandise, and that His Britannic Majesty's subjects shall have and enjoy the free navigation of the said river.[a]

So far as it concerns the location of the boundary the form of the article is of no particular importance in the present connection, but it will be observed that as a condition for agreeing upon it even in the form which had been acceptable to them in 1807, Great Britain insisted upon coupling with it a clause providing, among other things, for continuing the British right to navigate the Mississippi River, although it was then known that this river did not extend into British territory. The American Plenipotentiaries were unwilling to recognize the necessity, which this would have implied, of renewing by special provision in this treaty a right established by the treaty of 1783, unless at the same time the continuation of the American fishing rights under that treaty was also provided for, and in response to the suggestion of the British Plenipotentiaries, they proposed as an amendment, at the conference of December 1, 1814, the following:

The inhabitants of the United States shall continue to enjoy the liberty to take, dry, and cure fish in places within the exclusive jurisdiction of Great Britain, as secured by the former treaty of peace; and the navigation of the river Mississippi within the exclusive jurisdiction of the United States shall remain free and open to the subjects of Great Britain, in the manner secured by the said treaty; and it is further agreed, that the subjects of His Britannic Majesty shall, at all times, have access from such place as may be selected for that purpose in His Britannic Majesty's aforesaid territories, west, and within three hundred miles of the Lake of the Woods, in the aforesaid territories of the United States, to the river Mississippi, in order to enjoy the benefit of the navigation of that river with their goods, effects and merchandise, whose importations into the said States shall not be entirely prohibited, on the payment of the same duties as would be payable on the importation of the same into the Atlantic ports of the said States, and on conforming with the usual custom-house regulations.[b]

In proposing this amendment the American Plenipotentiaries, as stated in the protocol of this conference, also intimated their willingness to omit Article VIII altogether if that course should appear more advisable to the British Plenipotentiaries.[c]

The next step in the negotiations is reported in the protocol of the conference which was held on December 10th, as follows:

---

[a]Appendix, p. 251.   [b]Appendix, p. 253.   [c]Appendix, p. 254.

The British plenipotentiaries then stated that with respect to the 8th Article, their Government offered in lieu of the American proposals to retain the amended article as far as the words "Stony mountains," and insert the following stipulation:

"His Britannic Majesty, agrees to enter into negotiation with the United States of American, respecting the terms, conditions, and regulations under which the inhabitants of the said United States shall have the liberty of taking fish on certain parts of the coast of Newfoundland, and other of His Britannic Majesty's dominions in North America, and of drying and curing fish, in the unsettled bays, harbors and creeks of Nova Scotia, Magdalen islands, and Labrador; as stipulated in the latter part of the third article of the treaty of 1783, in consideration of a fair equivalent to be agreed upon between His Majesty and the said United States, and granted by the said United States, for such liberty as aforesaid."

"The United States of America agree to enter into negotiation with His Britannic Majesty respecting the terms, conditions, and regulations under which the navigation of the river Mississippi from its source to the ocean, as stipulated in the eighth article of the treaty of 1783, shall remain free and open to the subjects of Great Britain, in consideration of a fair equivalent, to be agreed upon between His Majesty and the United States, and granted by His Majesty."[a]

The protocol of the conference of December 12th reports that after much discussion relative to this article and others, the American Plenipotentiaries undertook to return an answer in writing to the propositions brought forward by the British Plenipotentiaries,[b] and this they did in their note of December 14, to the British Plenipotentiaries as follows:

To the stipulation now proposed by the British plenipotentiaries as a substitute for the last paragraph of the eighth article, the undersigned cannot accede.

The proposition made respecting the navigation of the Mississippi, in the alteration first proposed by the British plenipotentiaries to that article, was unexpected. In their note of the 31st of October they had stated that they had brought forward, in their note of the 21st of the same month, all the propositions which they had to offer; and that subject was not mentioned either in this last mentioned note, or in the first conference to which it referred. In order to obviate any difficulty arising from a presumed connexion between that subject and that of the boundary proposed by the eighth article, the undersigned expressed their willingness to omit the article altogether. For the purpose of meeting what they believed to be the wishes of the British Government, they proposed the insertion of an article which should recognize the right of Great Britain to the navigation of that river, and that of the United States to a liberty in certain fisheries, which the British Government considered as abrogated by the war. To such an article, which they viewed as merely declaratory, the undersigned had no objection, and have offered to accede. They do not, however, want any new article on either of those subjects; they have

---

offered to be silent with regard to both. To the stipulation now proposed, or to any other, abandoning, or implying the abandonment of any right in the fisheries claimed by the United States, they can not subscribe. As a stipulation merely that the parties will hereafter negotiate concerning the subjects in question, it appears also unnecessary. Yet to an engagement, couched in general terms, so as to embrace all the subjects of difference not yet adjusted, or so expressed as to imply in no manner whatever an abandonment of any right claimed by the United States, the undersigned are ready to agree.[a]

In answer to this note from the American Plenipotentiaries the British Plenipotentiaries withdrew their proposals relative to the fisheries and offered to omit the boundary article altogether, reverting to their position announced at the outset of the negotiations, as appears from the following extract from their note of December 22nd:

So far as regards the substitution proposed by the undersigned for the last clause of the 8th article, as it was offered solely with the hope of attaining the object of the amendment tendered by the American plenipotentiaries at the conference of the 1st instant, no difficulty will be made in withdrawing it.

The undersigned, returning to the declaration made by them at the conference of the 8th of August, that the privileges of fishing within the limits of the British sovereignty, and of using the British territories for purposes connected with the fisheries, were what Great Britain did not intend to grant without equivalent, are not desirous of introducing any article upon the subject.

With a view of removing what they consider as the only objection to the immediate conclusion of the treaty, the undersigned agree to adopt the proposal made by the American plenipotentiaries at the conference of the 1st instant, and repeated in their last note, of omitting the 8th article altogether.[b]

At the final conference held December 23rd the American Plenipotentiaries intimated their readiness to accede to the propositions contained in the note of the British Plenipotentiaries of the 22nd instant, namely, that no mention be made in the treaty of either the fisheries or the Mississippi.[b]

This completed the negotiations, and the treaty which was signed on the following day contains no reference either to the use of the inshore fisheries by the United States, or to the navigation of the Mississippi by British subjects.

The position maintained by the American Plenipotentiaries on this feature of the negotiations is set forth in their official report of the negotiations to their Government, dated December 25, 1814, as follows:

---

[a] Appendix, p. 255.   [b] Appendix, p. 256.

Without adverting to the ground of prior and immemorial usage, if the principle were just that the treaty of 1783, from its peculiar character, remained in force in all its parts, notwithstanding the war, no new stipulation was necessary to secure to the subjects of Great Britain the right of navigating the Mississippi, so far as that right was secured by the treaty of 1783, as, on the other hand, no stipulation was necessary to secure to the people of the United States the liberty to fish, and to dry and cure fish, within the exclusive jurisdiction of Great Britain. If they asked the navigation of the Mississippi as a new claim, they could not expect we should grant it without an equivalent; if they asked it because it had been granted in 1783, they must recognize the claim of the people of the United States to the liberty to fish and to dry and cure fish, in question. To place both points beyond all future controversy, a majority of us determined to offer to admit an article confirming both the rights, or we offered at the same time to be silent in the treaty upon both, and to leave out altogether the article defining the boundary from the Lake of the Woods westward. They finally agreed to this last proposal, but not until they had proposed an article stipulating for a future negotiation for an equivalent to be given by Great Britain for the navigation of the Mississippi, and by the United States for the liberty as to the fisheries within British jurisdiction. This article was unnecessary with regard to its professed object, since both Governments had it in their power, without it, to negotiate upon these subjects if they pleased. We rejected it, although its adoption would have secured the boundary of the forty-ninth degree of latitude west of the Lake of the Woods, because it would have been a formal abandonment, on our part, of our claim to the liberty as to the fisheries, recognised by the treaty of 1783.[a]

Although no reference is made in this treaty to the fisheries, it is evident from the foregoing examination of the negotiations that nothing was settled by it with respect to the effect of the War of 1812 upon the inshore fisheries provisions of the treaty of 1783. The United States had explicitly refused to renounce them or to bring them into question by discussing any change in them, and in signing the treaty without any provision referring to them maintained that they had survived the War of 1812 and were still in force and required no declaration or provision in the treaty for their continuance.

Great Britain, on the other hand, had expressly refused in the negotiations to agree to any stipulation renewing the inshore fisheries provisions under the former treaty without some equivalent, and in omitting any reference thereto in the treaty maintained that such provisions had been abrogated by the War of 1812, and that, in the absence of an express provision renewing or continuing them, they must be regarded as no longer in force.

---

[a]Appendix, p. 258.

The question, therefore, of the effect of the War of 1812 upon the continued enjoyment of the rights of the United States in these inshore fisheries under the second clause of Article III of the treaty of 1783 was left open by the treaty of 1814 as an unsettled subject of difference between the two Governments.

The Jaseur Incident.

Within six months after the signing of the Treaty of Ghent, occasion arose for the renewal of the controversy as to whether or not the inshore fisheries clause of the treaty of 1783 had survived the War of 1812. The question was ably and fully presented in the diplomatic correspondence exchanged, and as a result of the discussion Great Britain made overtures to the United States for a new treaty arrangement on the subject, which led to a series of negotiations, the final outcome of which was the fisheries article of the treaty of October 20, 1818.

The occasion for the renewal of the controversy was the action of Captain Lock of H. M. S. *Jaseur* in warning on June 19, 1815 an American vessel, engaged in cod-fishing about forty-five miles distant from Cape Sable, not to come within sixty miles of the coast. The captain of the fishing vessel promptly reported the incident to his Government with the further information that all the other American fishing vessels in sight at that time were warned off by the *Jaseur* in the same manner.[a]

Mr. Monroe, then Secretary of State, immediately called the incident to the attention of the British Chargé d'Affaires at Washington,[a] and at the same time, by note of July 21, 1815, informed Mr. John Quincy Adams, the American Minister at London, of the action of the *Jaseur* which, he says, " it is presumed, has been done under a construction of the late treaty of peace," and he adds that—

The measure thus promptly taken by the British Government without any communication with this Government, notwithstanding the declaration of our ministers at Ghent that our right would not be affected by the silence of the treaty, indicates a spirit which excites equal surprise and regret.[b]

That the position taken on the subject by the American Plenipotentiaries at Ghent was still maintained and insisted upon by the United States Government as indisputably right is clearly shown

---

[a] Appendix, p. 262.   [b] Appendix, p. 263.

in the following extract from Mr. Monroe's instructions of July 21, 1815, to Mr. Adams:

As you are well acquainted with the solidity of our right to the fisheries in question, as well as to those on the Grand Bank, and elsewhere on the main ocean, to the limit of a marine league only from the coast, (for the pretension to remove us twenty leagues is too absurd to be discussed,) I shall not dilate on it, especially at this time. It is sufficient to observe here, that the right of the United States to take fish on the coast of Newfoundland, and on the coasts, bays, and creeks of all other of His Britannic Majesty's dominions in America, and to dry and cure fish in any of the unsettled bays, harbors and creeks of Nova Scotia, Magdalen islands, and Labrador— in short, that every right appertaining to the fisheries, which was secured by the treaty of 1783, stands now as unshaken and perfect as it then did, constituting a vital part of our political existence, and resting on the same solid foundation as our independence itself. In the act of dismemberment and partition, the rights of each party were distinctly defined. So much of territory and incidental rights were allotted to one, so much to the other; and as well might it be said, because our boundary had not been retraced in the late treaty, in every part, that certain portions of our territory had reverted to England, as that our right to fish, by whatever name secured, had experienced that fate. A liberty of unlimited duration, thus secured, is as much a right as if it had been stipulated by any other term. Being to be enjoyed by one, adjoining the territory allotted by the partition to the other party, it seemed to be the appropriate term. I have made these remarks to show the solid ground on which this right is deemed to rest by this Government, relying on your thorough knowledge of the subject to illustrate and support it in the most suitable manner.[a]

The importance which the American Government attached to this assertion of the right to the continued enjoyment of the inshore fisheries under the treaty of 1783 is disclosed by the view expressed by Mr. Monroe in this instruction that this incident may eventuate in a breach of friendly relations and a renewal of hostilities.

The British Chargé replied on August 31, 1815, to Mr. Monroe's note on the subject of the interference by the *Jaseur* with American fishing vessels, stating that—

This measure was, as you have justly presumed in your note, totally unauthorized by His Majesty's Government; and I have the satisfaction to acquaint you that orders have been given by the naval commanders-in-chief on the Halifax and Newfoundland stations, which will effectually prevent the recurrence of any similar interruption to the vessels belonging to the United States engaged in fishing on the high seas.[b]

---

[a] Appendix, p. 263. [b] Appendix, p. 264.

Meanwhile, however, Mr. Adams, the American Minister at London, had taken up the question with the British Foreign Office, and in his letter of September 19, 1815, to Mr. Monroe he reports an interview with Lord Bathurst, then Under Secretary of State for Colonial and War Departments, in which Lord Bathurst stated, as the substance of an answer already sent to the British Chargé at Washington, that—

it had been that as, on the one hand, Great Britain could not permit the vessels of the United States to fish within the creeks and close upon the shores of the British territories, so, on the other hand, it was by no means her intention to interrupt them in fishing anywhere in the open sea, or without the territorial jurisdiction, a marine league from the shore; and, therefore, that the warning given at the place stated, in the case referred to, was altogether unauthorized.[a]

The question of where the line of demarcation should be drawn between the inshore and the off-shore fisheries had not as yet been raised in the discussion, the American contention for the right to use all the fisheries making it unnecessary, but as this demarcation later became a question of importance in the interpretation of the true meaning of the word "bays" as used in the treaty of 1818, it is desirable, in anticipation of that question, that attention be directed, in reviewing this controversy, to several significant indications of the views on that subject which were held at this time by the two Governments. It should be noted, therefore, that in the extract above quoted from the report by Mr. Adams of his interview with Lord Bathurst, the inshore fisheries are referred to as " close upon the shores of the British territories," and the off-shore fisheries are referred to as " without the territorial jurisdiction, a marine league from the shore." It should also be noted that later in the same despatch Mr. Adams reiterates and emphasizes Lord Bathurst's statement of the British position as follows:

The answer which was so promptly sent to the complaint relative to the warning of the fishing vessels by the captain of the *Jaseur*, will probably be communicated to you before you will receive this letter. You will see whether it is so precise, as to the limits within which they are determined to adhere to the exclusion of our fishing vessels, as Lord Bathurst's verbal statement of it to me, namely, to the extent of one marine league from their shores. Indeed, it is to the curing and drying upon the shore that they appear to have the strongest objection.[b]

---

[a] Appendix, p. 265.   [b] Appendix, p. 268.

The evidence of Mr. Adams on this point is of special value in that his despatch was an official communication to the Secretary of State, and this particular question referred to was not a matter of controversy when the letter was written. It will be further noted in confirmation of Mr. Adams' report of Lord Bathurst's statement on this subject, that in Mr. Adams' note of September 25th to Lord Bathurst, referring to this interview, Mr. Adams quotes him on this point as follows:

Your lordship did also express it as the intention of the British Government to exclude the fishing vessels of the United States, hereafter, from the liberty of fishing within one marine league of the shores of all the British territories in North America.[a]

This statement of Lord Bathurst's position is accepted by Lord Bathurst, in his note in reply, without question.

The Adams-Bathurst Correspondence.

Although it was evident from the attitude of Great Britain on the *Jaseur* incident that it did not involve any question of dispute with respect to American rights either in the inshore or off-shore fisheries, yet Mr. Monroe's instructions to Mr. Adams on the subject and Great Britain's announced intention of excluding American fishermen from the inshore fisheries made it incumbent on Mr. Adams to take up with the British Government the question of the continued enjoyment by the United States of the liberties in those inshore fisheries reserved in the second clause of Article III of the treaty of 1783. Therefore, Mr. Adams, at his conference with Lord Bathurst on September 14, and in his note to him of September 25, undertook—

to present to the consideration of His Majesty's Government the grounds upon which the United States conceive those liberties to stand, and upon which they deem that such exclusion cannot be effected without an infraction of the rights of the American people.[a]

In this correspondence Mr. Adams restated the position taken by the American Plenipotentiaries at Ghent, which has already been made clear in the foregoing review of those negotiations, and after showing that, although notice of the position of the United States had been explicitly given at that time, the question of the rightfulness of that position had not as yet been discussed between the two Governments, he proceeded to enter upon such discussion.

---

[a] Appendix, p. 269.

The issue presented was whether or not the provisions of the second clause of Article III of the treaty of 1783, reserving to the United States certain fishing liberties on and within three marine miles of land on the British coasts, survived the War of 1812. As will appear from the correspondence by which this discussion was carried on, Mr. Adams contended throughout the discussion that such provisions had survived owing to the character of the treaty, and the language used, and the nature of the liberties, and the relation of the American Colonies to them before the Revolution, and that as these liberties had never been renounced by the United States, either in the treaty of Ghent or otherwise, they were still in force. As will appear from Lord Bathurst's reply, he seems to have rested the British contention almost wholly on the ground that no treaties survive subsequent war between the parties; and, although he admits that treaties may contain obligations of an irrevocable nature and does not claim that any of the provisions of this treaty, except the one under consideration, could be revoked without the consent of the United States, he maintains that owing to the language used in respect to the inshore fisheries, the enjoyment of them was intended to be temporary and experimental, and being dependent upon the treaty provisions, terminated with the termination of the treaty. A considerable portion of his argument is devoted to showing that the right of the United States to exercise these liberties was dependent upon the treaty, and that, therefore, they would not survive the treaty, all of which might well be admitted without affecting the question at issue, which was, not whether such rights would continue independently of the treaty, but whether or not the treaty obligations were revocable without the consent of the United States.

Lord Bathurst seems to have failed to recognize the distinction between the extent of the American interest in these inshore fisheries and the title under which such interest was held. The interest reserved therein by the United States was the right to the enjoyment of certain liberties which were clearly defined, and the title of the United States to such interest was complete and absolute upon the signing of the treaty of 1783, and such title could not be destroyed without the consent of the United States.

The Tribunal is not called upon to decide the issue presented in that controversy or to pass upon the merits of the arguments, the questions involved having been laid at rest by the subsequent treaty of 1818; nevertheless the respective positions of the two Governments in the controversy have an important bearing upon the true interpretation of the treaty of 1818. Out of that controversy grew the negotiations which finally resulted in the treaty of 1818, and the question as to whether or not the fisheries provisions under consideration were terminated by the War of 1812, constituted the " differences " which are referred to in the first clause of the fisheries article of that treaty and in consequence of which that article was negotiated. The attention of the Tribunal is therefore directed to Mr. Adams' notes of September 19, and 25, and to Lord Bathurst's answer of October 30, 1815, and to Mr. Adams' reply of January 22, 1816, which are too voluminous to quote here at length, but are printed in full at pages 264 to 287 of the Appendix.

Before passing from the subject, however, special reference must be made to Lord Bathurst's statement in regard to the inshore fisheries provisions of the treaty that—

The grant of this liberty has all the aspect of a policy temporary and experimental, depending on the use that might be made of it, on the condition of the islands and places where it was to be exercised, and the more general conveniences or inconveniences, in a military, naval, or commercial point of view, resulting from the access of an independent nation to such islands and places.[a]

As pointed out by Mr. Adams in his reply, this statement is wholly erroneous and unsupported by the terms of the treaty, and it would require no further attention were it not that Lord Bathurst makes this erroneous assumption as to the terms of the treaty the basis for the following argument:

When, therefore, Great Britain, admitting the independence of the United States, denies their right to the liberties for which they now contend, it is not that she selects from the treaty, articles, or parts of articles, and says, at her own will, this stipulation is liable to forfeiture by war, and that is irrevocable; but the principle of her reasoning is, that such distinctions arise out of the provisions themselves, and are founded on the very nature of the grants. But the rights acknowledged by the treaty of 1783 are not only distinguishable from the liberties conceded by the same treaty, in the foundation upon which they stand, but they are carefully distinguished in the treaty of 1783 itself. The undersigned begs to call the attention of the American minister to the wording of the first and third articles, to which he has often referred, for the foundation of his arguments. In the first article, Great Britain acknowledges an independence already expressly recognised by the Powers of Europe, and by herself, in her consent to enter into provisional articles, of November, 1782.

---

[a]Appendix, p. 276.

In the third article, Great Britain acknowledged the *right* of the United States to take fish on the Banks of Newfoundland and other places, from which Great Britain has no right to exclude an independent nation. But they are to have the *liberty* to cure and dry them in certain unsettled places within His Majesty's territory. If these liberties, thus granted, were to be as perpetual and indefeasible as the rights previously recognised, it is difficult to conceive that the plenipotentiaries of the United States would have admitted a variation of language so adapted to produce a different impression; and, above all, that they should have admitted so strange a restriction of a perpetual and indefeasible right as that with which the article concludes, which leaves a right so practical and so beneficial as this is admitted to be, dependent on the will of British subjects in their character of inhabitants, proprietors or possessors of the soil, to prohibit its exercise altogether.

It is surely obvious that the word right is, throughout the treaty, used as applicable to what the United States were to enjoy, in virtue of a recognised independence; and the word liberty to what they were to enjoy, as concessions strictly dependent on the treaty itself.[a]

Mr. Adams' reply to Lord Bathurst's argument on this point is as follows:

The answer of Lord Bathurst denies that Great Britain has made such a selection, and affirms that the whole treaty of 1783 was annulled by the late war. It admits, however, that the recognition of independence and the boundaries was in the nature of a perpetual obligation; and that, with the single exception of the liberties in and connected with the fisheries within British jurisdiction on the coasts of North America, the United States are entitled to all the benefits of all the stipulations in their favor contained in the treaty of 1783, although the stipulations themselves are supposed to be annulled. The fishing liberties within British jurisdiction alone are considered as a temporary grant, liable not only to abrogation by war, but, as it would seem from the tenor of the argument, revocable at the pleasure of Great Britain, whenever she might consider the revocation suitable to her interest. The note affirms that "the liberty to fish within British limits, or to use British territory, is essentially different from the right to independence in all that can reasonably be supposed to regard its intended duration; that the grant of this liberty has all the aspect of a policy, *temporary and experimental*, depending on the use that might be made of it, on the condition of the islands and places where it was to be exercised, and the more general conveniences or inconveniences, in a military, naval, or commercial point of view, resulting from the access of an independent nation to such islands and places."

The undersigned is induced, on this occasion, to repeat his lordship's own words, because, on a careful and deliberate review of the article in question, he is unable to discover in it a single expression indicating, even in the most distant manner, a policy, temporary or experimental, or having the remotest connexion with military, naval or commercial conveniences or inconveniences to Great Britain. He has not been inattentive to the variation in the terms, by which

---

[a] Appendix, p. 276.

the enjoyment of the fisheries on the main ocean, the common possession of both nations, and the same enjoyment within a small portion of the special jurisdiction of Great Britain, are stipulated in the article, and recognized as belonging to the people of the United States. He considers the term *right* as importing an advantage to be enjoyed in a place of common jurisdiction, and the term *liberty* as referring to the same advantage, incidentally leading to the borders of a special jurisdiction. But, evidently, neither of them imports any limitation of time. Both were expressions no less familiar to the understandings than dear to the hearts of both the nations parties to the treaty. The undersigned is persuaded it will be readily admitted that, wherever the English language is the mother tongue, the term *liberty*, far from including in itself either limitation of time or precariousness of tenure, is essentially as permanent as that of *right*, and can, with justice, be understood only as a modification of the same thing; and as no limitation of time is implied in the term itself, so there is none expressed in any part of the article to which it belongs. The restriction at the close of the article is itself a confirmation of the permanency which the undersigned contends belongs to every part of the article. The intention was, that the people of the United States should continue to enjoy all the benefits of the fisheries which they had enjoyed theretofore, and, with the exception of drying and curing fish on the island of Newfoundland, all that *British* subjects should enjoy thereafter. Among them, was the liberty of drying and curing fish on the shores, then uninhabited, adjoining certain bays, harbors, and creeks. But, when those shores should become settled, and thereby become private and individual property, it was obvious that the liberty of drying and curing fish upon them must be conciliated with the proprietary rights of the owners of the soil. The same restriction would apply to British fishermen; and it was precisely because no grant of a new right was intended, but merely the continuance of what had been previously enjoyed, that the restriction must have been assented to on the part of the United States. But, upon the common and equitable rule of construction for treaties, the expression of one restriction implies the exclusion of all others not expressed; and thus the very limitation which looks forward to the time when the unsettled deserts should become inhabited, to modify the enjoyment of the same liberty conformably to the change of circumstances, corroborates the conclusion that the whole purport of the compact was permanent and not temporary—not experimental, but definitive.

That the term *right* was used as applicable to what the United States were to enjoy in virtue of a recognised independence, and the word *liberty* to what they were to enjoy as *concessions* strictly dependant on the treaty itself, the undersigned not only cannot admit, but considers as a construction altogether unfounded. If the United States would have been entitled, *in virtue of a recognised independence*, to enjoy the fisheries to which the word *rights* is applied, no article upon the subject would have been required in the treaty. Whatever their right might have been, Great Britain would not have felt herself bound, without a specific article to that effect, to acknowledge it as included among the appendages to their independence. Had she not acknowledged it, the United States must have been reduced to the alternative of resigning it, or of maintaining it by

force; the result of which must have been *war*—the very state from
which the treaty was to redeem the parties. That Great Britain
would not have acknowledged these rights as belonging to the United
States in virtue of their independence, is evident; for, in the cession
of Nova Scotia by France to Great Britain, in the twelfth article
of the treaty of Utrecht, it was expressly stipulated that, as a consequence of that cession, French subjects should be thenceforth
" excluded from all kind of fishing in the said seas, bays, and other
places on the coasts of Nova Scotia; that is to say, on those which
lie towards the east, within thirty leagues, beginning from the island
commonly called Sable, inclusively, and thence stretching along
towards the southwest." The same exclusion was repeated, with
some slight variation, in the treaty of peace of 1763; and, in the
eighteenth article of the same treaty, Spain explicitly renounced all
pretensions to the right of fishing " in the neighborhood of the island
of Newfoundland." It was not, therefore, as a necessary result of
their independence that Great Britain recognised the *right* of the
people of the United States to fish on the Banks of Newfoundland,
in the " Gulf of St. Lawrence " and at all other places in the sea
where " the inhabitants of both countries used, at any time theretofore, to fish." She recognised it, by a special stipulation, as a right
which they had theretofore enjoyed as a part of the British nation,
and which, as an independent nation, they were to continue to enjoy
unmolested; and it is well known that, so far from considering it
as recognised by virtue of her acknowledgment of independence, her
objections to admitting it at all formed one of the most prominent
difficulties in the negotiation of the peace of 1783. It was not asserted by the undersigned, as Lord Bathurst's note appears to suppose, that either the right or the liberty of the people of the United
States in these fisheries was *indefeasible*. It was maintained that,
after the recognition of them by Great Britain, in the treaty of 1783,
neither the right nor the liberty could be forfeited by the United
States, but by their own consent; that no act or declaration of Great
Britain alone could divest the United States of them; and that no
exclusion of them from the enjoyment of either could be valid, unless
expressly stipulated by themselves, as was done by France in the
treaty of Utrecht, and by France and Spain in the peace of 1763.[a]

      *   *   *   *   *   *   *

It was precisely because they might have lost their portion of this
joint national property, to the acquisition of which they had contributed more than their share, unless a formal article of the treaty should
secure it to them, that the article was introduced. By the British
municipal laws, which were the laws of both nations, the property of
a fishery is not necessarily in the proprietor of the soil where it is
situated. The soil may belong to one individual, and the fishery to
another. The right to the soil may be exclusive, while the fishery
may be free or held in common. And thus, while in the partition of
the national possessions in North America, stipulated by the treaty
of 1783, the jurisdiction over the shores washed by the waters where
this fishery was placed was reserved to Great Britain, the fisheries
themselves, and the accommodations essential to their prosecution,
were, by mutual compact, agreed to be continued in common.[b]

---

[a] Appendix, p. 282.   [b] Appendix, p. 286.

Supplementing Mr. Adams' reply to the portion of Lord Bathurst's argument, in which the use of the word "liberty" instead of the word "right" with respect to these fisheries is claimed to have a special significance, attention is called to the letter written in 1822 by John Adams, in which, speaking for himself and the other commissioners who negotiated the treaty of 1783, he says with reference to the use of the words "right" and "liberty:"

We demanded it [this article of the treaty] as a right and we demanded an explicit acknowledgment of that as an indispensable condition of peace; and the word *right* was in the article as agreed to by the British Ministers, but they afterwards requested that the word *liberty* might be substituted instead of *right*. They said it amounted to the same thing, for liberty was right and privilege was right; but the word *right* might be more unpleasing to the people of England than *liberty*, and we did not think it necessary to contend for a word.[a]

NEGOTIATIONS FOR A NEW TREATY.

In the controversy above reviewed Mr. Adams not only argued that the United States was entitled as a matter of right to the continued enjoyment of the inshore fisheries reserved to the United States under the treaty of 1783, but he also urged considerations of policy and expediency as an inducement for Great Britain to recognize such right. In his despatch of September 19, 1815, to the Secretary of State reporting his interview of September 14, 1815, with Lord Bathurst he says:

There were, also, considerations of policy and expediency, to which I hoped they would give suitable attention, before they should come to a final decision upon this point. * * * These fisheries afforded the means of subsistence to multitudes of people who were destitute of any other; they also afforded the means of remittance to Great Britain in payment for articles of her manufactures exported to America. It was well understood to be the policy of Great Britain that no unnecessary stimulus should be given to the manufactures in the United States, which would diminish the importation of those from Great Britain. But, by depriving the fishermen of the United States of this source of subsistence, the result must be to throw them back upon the country, and drive them to the resort of manufacturing for themselves; while, on the other hand, it would cut off the means of making remittances in payment for the manufactures of Great Britain.[b]

These considerations were further urged by Mr. Adams in his despatch of September 25, 1815, to Lord Bathurst, as follows:

In the interview with which your lordship recently favored me, I suggested several other considerations, with the hope of con-

---

[a] Appendix, p. 318.   [b] Appendix, p. 267.

vincing your lordship that, independent of the question of rigorous right, it would conduce to the substantial interests of Great Britain herself, as well as to the observance of those principles of benevolence and humanity which it is the highest glory of a great and powerful nation to respect, to leave to the American fishermen the participation of those benefits which the bounty of nature has thus spread before them; which are so necessary to their comfort and subsistence; which they have constantly enjoyed hitherto; and which, far from operating as an injury to Great Britain, had the ultimate result of pouring into her lap a great portion of the profits of their hardy and laborious industry; that these fisheries afforded the means of subsistence to a numerous class of people in the United States whose habit of life had been fashioned to no other occupation, and whose fortunes had allotted them no other possession; that to another, and, perhaps, equally numerous class of our citizens, they afforded the means of remittance and payment for the productions of British industry and ingenuity, imported from the manufactures of this united kingdom; that, by the common and received usages among civilized nations, fishermen were among those classes of human society whose occupations, contributing to the general benefit and welfare of the species, were entitled to a more than ordinary share of protection; that it was usual to spare and exempt them even from the most exasperated conflicts of national hostility; that this nation had, for ages, permitted the fishermen of another country to frequent and fish upon the coasts of this island, without interrupting them, even in times of ordinary war; that the resort of American fishermen to the barren, uninhabited, and, for the great part, uninhabitable rocks on the coasts of Nova Scotia, the Gulf of St. Lawrence, and Labrador, to use them occasionally for the only purposes of utility of which they are susceptible, if it must, in its nature, subject British fishermen on the same coasts to the partial inconvenience of a fair competition, yet produces, in its results, advantages to other British interests equally entitled to the regard and fostering care of their sovereign. By attributing to motives derived from such sources as these the recognition of these liberties by His Majesty's Government in the treaty of 1783, it would be traced to an origin certainly more conformable to the fact, and surely more honorable to Great Britain, than by ascribing it to the improvident grant of an unrequited privilege, or to a concession extorted from the humiliating compliance of necessity.[a]

In response to these suggestions, Lord Bathurst says, in his note of October 30, 1815, to Mr. Adams:

But, though Great Britain can never admit the claim of the United States to enjoy those liberties with respect to the fisheries, as matter of right, she is by no means insensible to some of those considerations with which the letter of the American minister concludes.

Although His Majesty's Government cannot admit that the claim of the American fishermen to fish within British jurisdiction, *and* to use the British territory for purposes connected with their fishery, is analogous to the indulgence which has been granted to enemy's

---

[a] Appendix, p. 272.

subjects engaged in fishing on the high seas, for the purpose of conveying fresh fish to market, yet they do feel that the enjoyment of the liberties, formerly used by the inhabitants of the United States, may be very conducive to their national and individual prosperity, though they should be placed under some modifications; and this feeling operates most forcibly in favor of concession. But Great Britain can only offer the concession in a way which shall effectually protect her own subjects from such obstructions to their lawful enterprises as they too frequently experienced immediately previous to the late war, and which are, from their very nature, calculated to produce collision and disunion between the two states.

It was not of fair competition that His Majesty's Government had reason to complain, but of the preoccupation of British harbors and creeks, in North America, by the fishing vessels of the United States, and the forcible exclusion of British vessels from places where the fishery might be most advantageously conducted. They had, likewise, reason to complain of the clandestine introduction of prohibited goods into the British colonies by American vessels ostensibly engaged in the fishing trade, to the great injury of the British revenue.

The undersigned has felt it incumbent on him thus generally to notice these obstructions, in the hope that the attention of the Government of the United States will be directed to the subject; and that they may be induced, amicably and cordially, to co-operate with His Majesty's Government in devising such regulations as shall prevent the recurrence of similar inconveniences.

His Majesty's Government are willing to enter into negotiations with the Government of the United States for the modified renewal of the liberties in question; and they doubt not that an arrangement may be made satisfactory to both countries, and tending to confirm the amity now so happily subsisting between them.[a]

It appears, therefore, that although Great Britain was unwilling to admit " the claim of the United States to enjoy those liberties with respect to the fisheries, as matter of right," yet that Government was willing as a matter of policy to enter into a new arrangement for a " modified renewal of the liberties in question." It further appears that the modification required did not relate to " fair competition " by American fishermen, but to their " preoccupation of British harbors and creeks " and to " the forcible exclusion of British vessels from places where the fishery might be most advantageously conducted " and likewise to " the clandestine introduction of prohibited goods into the British colonies by American vessels ostensibly engaged in the fishing trade," which were assigned as the grounds of objection to the methods of the American fishermen.

Further light is thrown on the British views on this subject by Mr. Adams in his despatch of September 19, 1815, to the Secretary of

---

[a] Appendix, p. 277.

State, reporting that Lord Bathurst in their conference of September 14th, said:

It was not so much the fishing, as the drying and curing on the shores, that had been followed by bad consequences. It happened that our fishermen, by their proximity, could get to the fishing stations sooner in the season than the British, who were obliged to go from Europe, and who, upon arriving there, found all the best fishing places and drying and curing places pre-occupied. This had often given rise to disputes and quarrels between them, which in some instances had proceeded even to blows. It had disturbed the peace among the inhabitants on the shores; and, for several years before the war, the complaints to this Government had been so great and so frequent, that it had been impossible not to pay regard to them.[a]

It will be further noted that, in proposing to Mr. Adams that negotiations be entered upon for a new arrangement, Lord Bathurst called attention to the above objections to the arrangement under the treaty of 1783 in the hope that the United States might be induced " amicably and cordially, to co-operate with His Majesty's Government in devising such regulations as shall prevent the recurrence of similar inconveniences." [b]

To Lord Bathurst's proposal that negotiations for a new arrangement be undertaken, Mr. Adams, in his note of January 22, 1816, replied:

It is for the Government of the United States alone to decide upon the proposal of a negotiation upon the subject. That they will at all times be ready to agree upon arrangements which may obviate and prevent the recurrence of those inconveniences stated to have resulted from the exercise by the people of the United States of these rights and liberties, is not to be doubted.[c]

He added at the close of the same note, after further urging the recognition of the right claimed by the United States to the enjoyment of the liberties secured under the treaty of 1783:

In submitting these reflections to the consideration of His Majesty's Government, the undersigned is duly sensible to the amicable and conciliatory sentiments and dispositions towards the United States manifested at the conclusion of Lord Bathurst's note, which will be met by reciprocal and corresponding sentiments and dispositions on the part of the American Government. It will be highly satisfactory to them to be assured that the conduciveness of the object to the national and individual prosperity of the inhabitants of the United States operates with His Majesty's Government as a forcible motive to concession. Undoubtedly, the participation in the liberties of which their right is now maintained is far more important to the

---

[a] Appendix, p. 268.   [b] Supra, p. 33.   [c] Appendix, p. 279.

interests of the people of the United States than the exclusive enjoyment of them can be to the interests of Great Britain. The real, general, and ultimate interests of both the nations on this object, he is fully convinced, are the same. The collision of particular interests which heretofore may have produced altercations between the fishermen of the two nations, and the clandestine introduction of prohibited goods by means of American fishing vessels, may be obviated by arrangements duly concerted between the two Governments. That of the United States, he is persuaded, will readily cooperate in any measure to secure those ends compatible with the enjoyment by the people of the United States of the liberties to which they consider their title as unimpaired, inasmuch as it has never been renounced by themselves.[a]

Meanwhile Mr. Adams had reported to the Secretary of State the position taken by Lord Bathurst and Lord Bathurst's proposal that negotiations for a new arrangement be undertaken, and on February 27, 1816, the Secretary of State wrote to Mr. Adams in reply as follows:

It appears by these communications that, although the British Government denies our right of taking, curing and drying fish within their jurisdiction, and on the coast of the British provinces in North America, it is willing to secure to our citizens the liberty stipulated by the treaty of 1783, under such regulations as will secure the benefit to both parties, and will likewise prevent the smuggling of goods into the British provinces by our vessels engaged in the fisheries.

It is hoped that the reply which you intimate you intended giving to Lord Bathurst's note may have produced some change in the sentiments of the British Government on this interesting subject; it is nevertheless, thought proper to enclose you an instruction, to be shown to the British Government, authorizing you to negotiate a convention providing for the objects contemplated.

It is very important that this trust should be executed in a manner not to weaken our right, which, it is presumed, may be done with the concurrence of the British Government, either by the reservation of mutual rights, or making the instrument a remedy for abuses.[b]

The instructions enclosed are as follows:

DEPARTMENT OF STATE, *February 27, 1816.*

SIR: It being represented, by your letter of the 8th of November, that the British Government was disposed to regulate, in concert with the United States, the taking of fish on the coasts, bays and creeks of all His Britannic Majesty's dominions in America, and the curing and drying of fish by their citizens on the unsettled bays, harbors, and creeks of Nova Scotia, Magdalen islands, and Labrador, in such manner as to promote the interest of both nations, you will consider

---

[a] Appendix, p. 286.   [b] Appendix, p. 287.

this letter an authority and instruction to negotiate a convention for these purposes.

I have the honor to be &c　　　　　JAMES MONROE.[a]

Negotiations at Washington in 1816–1817.

Meanwhile, without waiting for Mr. Adams to receive the necessary authority from his Government to undertake the negotiations proposed by Great Britain, it appears that instructions had been sent by Great Britain to the British Minister at Washington to open direct negotiations there upon the subject with the Secretary of State. Pursuant to these instructions Mr. Bagot, the British Minister, early in July, 1816, submitted a proposal on the subject to Mr. Monroe, the Secretary of State, who thereupon wrote to Mr. Adams on July 8, 1816, informing him of this circumstance and, in consequence of the transfer of the negotiations to Washington, revoking the authority given him to carry on such negotiations at London under the instructions of February 27th above quoted.[a]

The motives and desires which induced Great Britain to undertake this negotiation were stated by Mr. Bagot in his note of November 27, 1816, to Mr. Monroe as follows:

It will be in your recollection that, early in the month of July last, I had the honor to acquaint you that I had received instructions from my Government to assure you that, although it had been felt necessary to resist the claim which had been advanced by Mr. Adams, the determination had not been taken in any unfriendly feeling towards America, or with any illiberal wish to deprive her subjects of adequate means of engaging in the fisheries; but that, on the contrary, many of the considerations which had been urged by Mr. Adams, on behalf of the American citizens formerly engaged in this occupation, had operated so forcibly in favor of granting to them such a concession as might be consistent with the just rights and interests of Great Britain, that I had been furnished with full powers from His Royal Highness the Prince Regent to conclude an arrangement upon the subject, which it was hoped might at once offer to the United States a pledge of His Royal Highness's goodwill, and afford to them a reasonable participation in those benefits of which they had formerly the enjoyment.[b]

The arrangements which were proposed by Mr. Bagot, however, in order to afford to the American fishermen " a reasonable participation in those benefits of which they had formerly the enjoyment " fell far short of meeting the requirements of the United States. An

---

[a] Appendix, p. 288.　　　　　[b] Appendix, p. 290.

examination of the correspondence exchanged at that time will show that three proposals in all were made during this negotiation, and that they all came from the British Minister and were all promptly declined by the United States.

Mr. Bagot in his note of November 27, 1816, to the Secretary of State, reviews the course of the negotiations up to that time, and with respect to his first proposal he says:

It being the object of the American Government, that, in addition to the right of fishery, as declared by the first branch of the fourth article [a] of the treaty of 1783 permanently to belong to the citizens of the United States, they should also enjoy the privilege of having an adequate accommodation, both in point of harbors and drying grounds, on the unsettled coasts within the British sovereignty, I had the honor to propose to you that that part of the southern coast of Labrador which extends from Mount Joli, opposite the eastern end of the island of Anticosti, in the Gulf of St. Lawrence, to the bay and isles of Esquimaux, near the western entrance of the straits of Belleisle, should be allotted for this purpose, it being distinctly agreed that the fishermen should confine themselves to the unsettled parts of the coast, and that all pretensions to fish or dry within the maritime limits, or on any other of the coasts of British North America, should be abandoned.[b]

Mr. Bagot then goes on to say in the same note that this proposal was declined by the United States and he sets forth his second proposal as follows:

Upon learning from you, some weeks afterwards, that, from the information which you had received upon the subject of this coast, you were apprehensive that it would not afford, in a sufficient degree, the advantages required, I did not delay to acquaint you that I was authorized to offer another portion of coast, which it was certainly not so convenient to the British Government to assign, but which they would nevertheless be willing to assign, and which, from its natural and local advantages, could not fail to afford every accommodation of which the American Fishermen could stand in need. I had then the honor to propose to you as an alternative that, under similar conditions, they should be admitted to that portion of the southern coast of Newfoundland which extends from Cape Ray eastward to the Ramea islands, or to about the longitude of 57° west of Greenwich.

The advantages of this portion of coast are accurately known to the British Government; and, in consenting to assign it to the uses of the American fishermen, it was certainly conceived that an accommodation was afforded as ample as it was possible to concede, without abandoning that control within the entire of His Majesty's own harbors and coasts which the essential interests of His Majesty's dominions required. That it should entirely satisfy the wishes of

---

[a] This should be the third article, which is the fisheries article.
[b] Appendix, p. 290.

those who have for many years enjoyed, without restraint, the privilege of using for similar purposes all the unsettled coasts of Nova Scotia and Labrador, is not to be expected; but in estimating the value of the proposal, the American Government will not fail to recollect that it is offered without any equivalent, and notwithstanding the footing upon which the navigation of the Mississippi has been left by the treaty of Ghent, and the recent regulations by which the subjects of His Majesty have been deprived of the privileges which they so long enjoyed, of trading with the Indian nations within the territory of the United States.[a]

Replying to Mr. Bagot's note of November 27, 1816, from which the above extract is taken, Mr. Monroe wrote to him on December 30, 1816, pointing out that the purpose of the negotiations was to reach a mutually advantageous basis of settlement rather than to renew the previous discussion of the respective rights of the two countries in the inshore fisheries, and stating that the United States entered into the negotiations neither claiming nor making any concession in respect of its rights in the premises. The following extract from his note indicates the position of the United States on this point:

In providing for the accommodation of the citizens of the United States engaged in the fisheries on the coast of His Britannic Majesty's colonies, on conditions advantageous to both parties, I concur in the sentiment that it is desirable to avoid a discussion of their respective rights, and to proceed, in a spirit of conciliation, to examine what arrangement will be adequate to the object. The discussion which has already taken place between our Governments has, it is presumed, placed the claim of each party in a just light. I shall, therefore, make no remark on that part of your note which relates to the right of the parties, other than by stating that this Government entered into this negotiation on the equal ground of neither claiming nor making any concessions in that respect.[a]

In the same note Mr. Monroe rejected the proposals made by Mr. Bagot as a basis of settlement. He wrote:

You have made two propositions, the acceptance of either of which must be attended with the relinquishment of all other claims on the part of the United States, founded on the first branch of the fourth article [c] of the treaty of 1783. In the first you offer the use of the territory on the Labrador coast, lying between Mount Joli and the bay of Esquimaux, near the entrance of the strait of Belleisle; and, in the second, of such part of the southern coast of the island of Newfoundland as lies between Cape Ray and the Ramea islands.

I have made every inquiry that circumstances have permitted respecting both these coasts, and find that neither would afford to the

---

[a] Appendix, p. 291.

[b] See note of November 27, 1816, from Bagot to Monroe, to which this is an answer, *supra*, p. 37.

citizens of the United States, the essential accommodation which is desired; neither having been much frequented by them heretofore, nor likely to be in the future. I am compelled, therefore, to decline both propositions.[a]

On the following day Mr. Bagot replied by note under date of December 31, 1816, suggesting as his third proposal—

that if, upon examination of the local circumstances of the coasts, which I have had the honor to propose, the American Government should be of opinion that neither of them, taken separately, would afford, in a satisfactory degree, the conveniences which are deemed requisite, His Royal Highness will be willing that the citizens of the United States should have the full benefit of both of them, and that, under the conditions already stated, they should be admitted to each of the shores which I have had the honor to point out.[b]

This proposal was likewise declined by Mr. Monroe, who stated with respect to it in his note to Mr. Bagot of January 7, 1817:

Having stated, in my letter, of the 30th of December, that, according to the best information which I had been able to obtain, neither of those coasts had been much frequented by our fishermen, or was likely to be so in future, I am led to believe that they would not, when taken conjointly, as proposed in your last letter, afford the accommodation which is so important to them, and which it is very satisfactory to find it is the desire of your Government that they should possess. From the disposition manifested by your Government, which corresponds with that of the United States, a strong hope is entertained that further inquiry into the subject will enable His Royal Highness the Prince Regent to ascertain that an arrangement, on a scale more accommodating to the expectation of the United States will not be inconsistent with the interest of Great Britain.

In the mean time, this Government will persevere in its measures for obtaining such further information as will enable it to meet yours in the conciliatory views which are cherished on both sides[b]—

That Mr. Bagot's authority under his instructions was not sufficiently extensive to enable him to negotiate on a basis satisfactory to the United States, is evident from the statement made by Lord Castlereagh in his note of May 7, 1817, to Mr. Adams, after the close of this negotiation, that—

it appears that the American Secretary, in February last, had it in contemplation to offer, for the consideration of the British Government, some specific proposition on the subject, which Mr. Bagot did not then feel himself authorized to take, *ad referendum* but which he has since been instructed to receive, and transmit for the information of his court.[c]

What the proposition here referred to was, does not appear and it is of interest to note as a significant feature of this negotiation that no-

---

[a] Appendix, p. 292.   [b] Appendix, p. 293.   [c] Appendix, p. 295.

where in the course of the negotiation was any statement made on the part of the United States of the terms or conditions which were regarded by that Government as essential to meet the requirements of the American fishermen, and that none of the proposals made on the part of Great Britain elicited a counter-proposal on the part of the United States.

The purpose of the negotiation having been, as stated by Mr. Monroe in the extract from his note to Mr. Bagot of December 30, 1816, above quoted, to arrange for " the accommodation of the citizens of the United States engaged in the fisheries on the coast of His Britannic Majesty's Colonies, on conditions advantageous to both parties," and the accommodations proposed by Mr. Bagot having been inadequate so far as the United States was concerned, Mr. Monroe, recognizing the necessity for a further examination of the subject on both sides, expressed the hope in his note of January 7, 1817, to Mr. Bagot that—

further inquiry into the subject will enable His Royal Highness the Prince Regent to ascertain that an arrangement, on a scale more accommodating to the expectation of the United States, will not be inconsistent with the interest of Great Britain.[a]

And he added in closing this note—

In the meantime, this Government will persevere in its measures for obtaining such further information as will enable it to meet yours in the conciliatory views which are cherished on both sides.[a]

Again in his instruction of February 5, 1817, to Mr. Adams, advising him that the negotiation on the fisheries " has not had the desired result," which instruction was written by Mr. Monroe within a month after he had declined Mr. Bagot's third proposal, Mr. Monroe says:

Mr. Bagot professes on the part of his Government the most conciliatory disposition in regard to this affair, and it is yet to be hoped that it may be satisfactorily settled. With this view, the President intends to renew the negotiation as soon as he can obtain the information necessary to enable him to decide what arrangement would be best calculated to reconcile the interests of both parties, which he hopes to do in the course of a few months.[b]

An attempt was made by Great Britain, in the month of May following, to ascertain the terms which would be satisfactory to the United States as a basis of settlement. Mr. Bagot was instructed, as stated by Lord Castlereagh in the extract hereinabove quoted from his

---

[a] Supra, p. 39. [b] Appendix, p. 294.

note of May 7, 1817, to Mr. Adams, to receive and transmit, for the information of his court, a specific proposition which he understood Mr. Monroe had in mind to offer in February preceding, but which Mr. Bagot did not then feel himself authorized to take *ad referendum.* Pursuant to these instructions Mr. Bagot wrote to Mr. Monroe on May 27, 1817, as follows:

In laying before my Government the correspondence which passed last year between the Secretary of the Department of State and myself, upon the subject of the accommodation which His Royal Highness the Prince Regent was willing to afford to the Citizens of the United States for the purpose of their Fishery, I did not fail to represent, that, in the conversations which had taken place upon the propositions which I had been authorized to make, and which were finally declined, the Secretary of the Department of State had intimated a wish to communicate to me some particular arrangement which would be satisfactory upon the subject to the American Government.[a]

In the same note, after alluding to the regret of His Royal Highness that the accommodation which had been offered should not have been regarded as affording the advantages which the American Government desired, and also to the continued disposition cherished by His Royal Highness to admit the citizens of the United States to such participation of the conveniences afforded to their fishery by the neighboring coasts of His Majesty's dominions as may justly consist with His Majesty's rights and the interests of his own subjects, he says:

His Royal Highness is willing to receive in a sincere spirit of friendly accommodation whatever suggestion the American Government may have to offer which they may conceive to be reconcilable with these primary considerations—His Royal Highness feels assured, that the Government of the United States must know so well the nature and value of those interests of His Majesty's subjects which it is the first object of His Royal Highness to protect and preserve, that they will not fail to frame any proposition which they may be desirous of making in such a spirit of moderation as will not impose upon His Royal Highness the necessity of declining to entertain it. His Royal Highness has therefore commanded me to ascertain from the American Government the extent of the accommodation which they seek to obtain, and at the same time to give the assurance of his Royal Highness that it will be considered with the sincere and earnest hope that it may not be found irreconcilable with those important objects to which I have adverted.

I shall be happy to receive the proposition which the President may wish to make whenever you will do me the honor to communicate it.[a]

---

[a] Appendix, p. 296.

In answer to this note Mr. Rush, the Acting Secretary of State, wrote to Mr. Bagot on May 30, 1817:

I had the honor to receive, and have laid before the President, your note of the 27th of this month. In answer to it, I have the honor to state that this Government is not yet prepared to make known, in any definite and final shape, the nature and extent of the accommodation desired by its citizens engaged in the fisheries along the coast of His Britannic Majesty's dominions, according to the invitation held out, by order of the Prince Regent, in your note. At the same time, I am directed by the President to inform you that he recognizes, in the terms of this invitation, not less than in the general scope of your note, a spirit of friendly accommodation, which this Government, not foregoing rights which it feels itself bound to look to, will nevertheless be desirous, in the fullest extent, to reciprocate.

On the return of the President from a tour through part of the United States, which he is now upon the eve of commencing, it is expected that this Department will be enabled to offer such propositions as taking for their basis the principles stated in your note, it is confidently hoped may end in an adjustment of this important interest, upon terms reconcilable with the views of both nations, and serve to strengthen the harmony and good understanding which it is so desirable to cultivate and preserve between them.[a]

SEIZURES IN 1817.

Within two months after the date of Mr. Rush's note, above quoted, and before he had been able to submit to Mr. Bagot the proposition for the adjustment of the question under consideration upon terms reconcilable with the views of both nations, as proposed in his note, these negotiations were interrupted by a discussion between the two Governments concerning the seizure of a number of American fishing vessels by the British sloop-of-war *Dee* in the month of June preceding, and the negotiations thus interrupted were not resumed again at Washington.

An examination of the correspondence and proceedings had with reference to these seizures will show that they were all made within less than three marine miles from the shore, and that the offense charged was resorting to such inshore waters for the purpose of fishing or of procuring bait there. It appears from the official

----
[a] Appendix, p. 297.

records that nine of these vessels were seized while at anchor in Ragged Island harbor and one vessel at the entrance of that harbor; seven vessels were seized either in Cape Negro harbor or while entering or leaving that harbor; one vessel in the basin of Annapolis and one vessel in the Gut of Annapolis, within half a mile of land, and one vessel in the Bay of Fundy, one mile distant from Trout Cove.[a] By reference to the map [b] showing these localities it will be found that not only the places of seizure but also the places where the offenses were alleged to have occurred were in every instance within three marine miles of the shore.

Here again, therefore, was presented the question which had been in controversy since the close of the War of 1812, though temporarily held in abeyance while the negotiation for a new treaty was in progress, namely, whether or not the pre-existing right of the American fishermen to resort to the waters within three marine miles of the shores of the British provinces for fishing purposes had survived the War of 1812. The decision rendered in the judicial proceedings which were instituted in the courts of Nova Scotia for the condemnation and forfeiture of these vessels did not turn on this question. Nevertheless, these proceedings served to disclose the interesting situation that the contentions of the British Ministry on this question had not been authorized or supported by the British Parliament, it being found that no legislation had been adopted by Parliament excluding American fishermen from these waters; and the condemnation proceedings resulted in a judicial decree directing the restitution of these vessels to their owners on the ground that the seizures had been illegally made.[c]

It appears that at the commencement of the conferences between Mr. Bagot and Mr. Monroe, Mr. Bagot, in the expectation that their discussions would lead to a satisfactory issue, had secured the revocation of an order issued by the British admiral to the British cruisers in regard to the treatment of American fishing vessels on the coasts of the British Provinces.[d]

It does not appear that a copy of this order was shown to Mr. Monroe or delivered to the United States Government. Mr. Monroe says

[a] Appendix, pp. 300, 1076–1077.
[b] See U. S. Case Map No. 1.
[c] *Infra*, p. 47.
[d] Appendix, pp. 289, 294, 295.

with regard to it in his instruction of August 13, 1816, to Mr. Adams merely that—

At the commencement of our conferences Mr. Bagot informed me of an order which had been issued by Admiral Griffith to the British cruisers to remove our fishing vessels from the coasts of those provinces which he would endeavor to have revoked pending the negotiation. His attempt succeeded. I shall endeavor to have this revocation extended so as to afford the accommodation desired until the negotiation is concluded. All the information which has been or may be obtained on this subject shall be transmitted to you.[a]

Subsequently, upon the temporary suspension of the negotiations after Mr. Monroe's rejection, in January, 1817, of Mr. Bagot's third proposal and in anticipation of the renewal of such negotiations as soon as the President "could obtain the information necessary to ascertain what arrangement would be best calculated to reconcile the interests of both parties, which he hoped to do in the course of a few months," Mr. Adams, pursuant to instructions from Mr. Monroe, wrote to Lord Castlereagh on April 21, 1817, using the language above quoted in regard to the intention of the President to renew the negotiations in the course of a few months and stating:

In the meantime he relied that no measures would be taken by his Majesty's Government to alter the existing state of things; and particularly, that the order to the naval officer commanding on that station, not to interrupt or disturb the American fishermen during the approaching season, would be renewed.[b]

In reply Lord Castlereagh wrote to Mr. Adams on May 7, 1817:

The undersigned, His Majesty's principal Secretary of State for Foreign Affairs, in reply to Mr. Adams's note of the 21st ultimo, has the honor to acquaint him that, as soon as the proposition which Mr. Bagot was authorized in July last, to make to the Government of the United States, for arranging the manner in which American citizens might be permitted to carry on the fisheries within the British limits, had been by them declined, viz: in the month of February, the same was immediately notified by His Majesty's minister in America to the British admiral commanding at Halifax; the effect of which notification was to revive the orders which Mr. Bagot had taken upon himself to suspend, in the expectation that the discussions in which he was then employed with the American Government would have led to a satisfactory issue.

These discussions having failed of success, and the orders above alluded to being consequently now in full force, the British Government cannot but feel some reluctance again to suspend them, without being in possession of more precise grounds for expecting an adjustment. Persuaded, however, from the official communication received from Mr. Adams, that it is not only the sincere desire of the President of the United States to come to an amicable arrangement, but also

---

[a] Appendix, p. 289.   [b] Appendix, p. 295.

that he, being already in possession of the views of Great Britain, is now lead to entertain a strong expectation that a settlement which shall reconcile the interests of both parties may, without any material delay, be effectuated, the Prince Regent, under these impressions, is willing to give to the American Government this additional proof of his earnest wish that the negotiation should proceed, under circumstances the most favorable to a speedy and amicable conclusion, by acceding to the application of the Government of the United States, as brought forward by Mr. Adams. Instructions will, accordingly, be expedited to the naval commanders on the American station to suspend the execution of the said orders during the approaching season.[a]

Meanwhile, however, and before the revocation of the order to the naval officers on the American station could be communicated to them, as promised by Lord Castlereagh, the British sloop-of-war *Dee* had made the seizures of the American vessels above referred to. The order under which the captain of the *Dee* acted in making these seizures was communicated by Mr. Bagot to Mr. Rush, Acting Secretary of State, in his note of August 8, 1817, and was in the following form:

By Sir David Milne, K. C. B. and K. W. N., Rear Admiral of the Blue, and commander-in-chief of His Majesty's ships and vessels employed, and to be employed, in North America, and on the lakes of Canada, &c. &c.

You are hereby required and directed to proceed, in His Majesty's ship under your command, to Halifax; and having received on board a pilot at that port, you will repair and cruise between Sambro lighthouse and Cape Sable, using every means in your power for the protection of the revenue, as also the fisheries on the coast, against the encroachment of foreigners.

On your meeting with any foreign vessel fishing or at anchor in any of the harbors or creeks in His Majesty's North American provinces or within our maritime jurisdiction, you will seize and send such vessel so trespassing to Halifax for adjudication, unless it should clearly appear that they have been obliged to put in there in consequence of distress; acquainting me with the cause of such seizure, and every other particular, to enable me to give all information to the lords commissioners of the admiralty.

You are to come within sight of signals from Sambro light-house every fourteen days, if the wind and weather will permit, and wait eight hours at that distance. You will continue on this service for six weeks from your sailing from Halifax, at the expiration of which time you will return to that port for further orders.

Given on board His Majesty's ship *Leander*, Bermuda, the 12th day of May, 1817.

DAVID MILNE, *Rear Admiral.*

To Captain SAMUEL CHAMBERS, of His Majesty's ship *Dee.*

By command of the Rear Admiral:

J. P. LAMEY.[b]

---

[a] Appendix, p. 295.   [b] Appendix, p. 299.

In the same note in which the order above quoted was enclosed, Mr. Bagot also inclosed a copy of the report from the captain of the *Dee* to his admiral, dated June 8, 1817, stating his reasons for making the seizures, which report is in full as follows:

In compliance with your order of the 12th ultimo, I sailed from Halifax on the 30th ultimo, but did not meet or receive any intelligence of foreign fishing vessels being within our jurisdiction until the 3d instant; when, being off the Isle Maten, I was informed that the whole of the banks to the westward (off Cape Sable and Shelburne) were fished by American schooners; and that they continually resorted to the creeks on this coast in order to catch their bait, clean their fish, wood, water, &c.; this, of course, is highly detrimental to the interest of the industrious fishermen on this coast. I was also informed that the intricate harbors of Cape Negro and Ragged island were their resort most evenings, several going in; but more particularly on Saturdays, when they remain till Monday, to procure bait for the ensuing week. At the former place they had not been well received; at the latter, I suspect, much encouragement had been given them by an individual. I intended having our boats into Ragged island harbor before daylight on the 4th, but light winds prevented our getting that length. I, therefore, in the course of the day, put into Shelburne; and, in the evening, despatched the boats, under the charge of Lieutenant Hooper, into Ragged island, with the order I enclose; the weather preventing any boats returning until the 7th, when I received information that nine American vessels had been found at Ragged island harbor, lying with their nets set. Lieutenant Hooper remained at this place, and despatched Lieutenant Lechenere, with a gig and cutter, to Cape Negro, with the enclosed order. He found two American fishing vessels in the harbor, and seven others came in in the course of Saturday. The whole joined me this day with two others that came into Ragged island. I have, therefore, in obedience to your directions, sent them into Halifax for adjudication; as any distress they may plead might, with more ease, be relieved at the regular harbor of Shelburne, which has been avoided for two intricate harbors in its immediate neighborhood.

I beg further to state, that, without the use of our harbors, it appears impossible for any foreigners to carry on successful fishing on this coast, which fishing has much injured our fishermen; and I have every reason to believe that considerable smuggling of tobacco, shoes, &c. is carried on by their boats. I beg leave to enclose a list of the detained vessels, and also to inform you that, from some of the Americans attempting to tamper with some of our boats' crews, and the riotous conduct of others, I have been obliged to take precautionary measures to prevent any of the vessels being run away with.[a]

The reports received by the United States Government in regard to these seizures differ materially from Captain Chambers' report, as

---

[a] Appendix, p. 300.

will appear from Mr. Rush's note of August 4, 1817, to Mr. Bagot.[a]
It is evident, however, that no question of fishing outside of the limit
of three marine miles from the shore was involved in those seizures.
Mr. Bagot in his answer of August 8, 1817, to Mr. Rush, after referring to Captain Chambers' instructions and report, copies of which
he encloses, says:

By these papers you will perceive that the vessels in question were
in the habit of occupying, and were, at the time of their seizure
actually occupying, for the purposes of their fishery, the settled
harbors of His Majesty's dominions, in violation of the orders at all
times enforced against all foreign vessels detected in making similar
encroachments, and of which it is not to be supposed that the masters
of these vessels could have been ignorant.[b]

Notwithstanding Lord Castlereagh's promise to revoke the orders
under which these fishing vessels were seized, every effort was made
to secure their condemnation and forfeiture, and proceedings for
that purpose were instituted in the courts of Nova Scotia.[b]

All of these seizures were ultimately held by the courts to have
been illegal and the vessels were restored to their owners.[c] The
results of these proceedings and the position taken by the United
States on the questions presented were subsequently stated by John
Quincy Adams, after he became Secretary of State, in his instructions of July 28, 1818, to Messrs. Gallatin and Rush, the Plenipotentiaries on the part of the United States in the negotiation of the
treaty of 1818, as follows:

By the decree of the judge of the vice-admiralty court at Halifax, on the 29th of August last, in the case of several American
fishing vessels which had been captured and sent into that port, a
copy of which is also now transmitted to you, it appears that all
those captures have been *illegal*. An appeal from this decree was
entered by the captors to the appellate court in England, and the
owners of the captured vessels were obliged to give bonds to stand
the issue of the appeal. Mr. Rush was instructed to employ suitable counsel for these cases if the appeals should be entered, and, as
we have been informed by him, has accordingly done so. If you do
not succeed in agreeing upon an article on this subject, it will be
desirable that the question *upon the right* should be solemnly argued
before the lords of appeals, and that counsel of the first eminence
should be employed in it. Judge Wallace agreed with the advocate
general that the late war completely dissolved every right of the
people of the United States acquired by the treaty of 1783. But it
does not appear that this question had been argued before him, and
the contrary opinion is not to be surrendered on the part of the

---

United States upon the *dictum* of a vice-admiralty court. Besides this, we claim the rights in question not *as acquired* by the treaty of 1783; but as having always before enjoyed them, and as only recognised as belonging to us by that treaty, and therefore never to be divested from us but by our own consent. Judge Wallace, however, explicitly says that he does not see how he can condemn these vessels without *an act of Parliament;* and whoever knows any thing of the English constitution must see that on this point he is unquestionably right. He says, indeed, something about an order in council, but it is very clear that would not answer. It is a question of forfeiture for a violated *territorial* jurisdiction; which forfeiture can be incurred not by the law of nations, but only by the *law of the land.* There is obviously no such law.

The argument which has been so long and so ably maintained by Mr. Reeves, that the rights of antenati Americans, as British subjects, even within the Kingdom of Great Britain, have never been divested from them, because there has been no act of Parliament to declare it, applies in its fullest force to this case; and, connected with the article in the treaty of 1783, by which this particular right was recognised, confirmed and placed out of the reach of an act of Parliament, corroborates the argument in our favor. How far it may be proper and advisable to use these suggestions in your negotiation, must be left to your sound discretion; but they are thrown out with the hope that you will pursue the investigation of the important question of British law involved in this interest, and that every possible advantage may be taken of them, preparatory for the trial before the lords of appeals, if the case should ultimately come to their decision. The British Government may be well assured that not a particle of these rights will be finally yielded by the United States without a struggle, which will cost Great Britain more than the worth of the prize.[a]

It was subsequently found to be unnecessary that the question presented by these seizures, with respect to the effect of the War of 1812 upon the fisheries article of the treaty of 1783, " should be solemnly argued before the Lords of Appeals ", for, as stated by Mr. Rush in his despatch of October 27, 1818, to Mr. Adams after the conclusion of the negotiations for the treaty of 1818, Mr. Slade, the proctor employed to represent the interests of the American fishermen, reported that " no appeal has been entered by the captors from the sentences of restitution; and that the time having now gone by allowed by the practice of the admiralty for entering appeals, none can be entered." [b]

---

[a] Appendix, p. 305.   [b] Appendix, p. 308.

SEIZURES IN 1818.

Notwithstanding the decision of the Vice Admirality Court of Halifax, rendered in August, 1817, holding that the seizures above referred to were illegal, and notwithstanding the assurance given by Lord Castlereagh to Mr. Adams in his note of May 7, 1817, hereinabove quoted, that pending the negotiations for a new treaty instructions would be issued to the naval commanders on the American station suspending the execution of the orders under which the aforesaid seizures had been made, four additional seizures of American fishing vessels were made by British warships in the months of July and August, 1818, and here again in every instance the vessels were seized within three marine miles from the shore and the offences charged were alleged to have occurred within that limit.[a] As appear from the official records of these seizures, one of the vessels was seized while lying at anchor in Mackerel Cove, Beaver Island; one off Pope's Harbor, and two in Lipscomb harbor, one of which was released after the following notice had been endorsed upon its license:

It is hereby notified, that it is the earnest desire of rear admiral Sir David Milne, commander in chief of his Majesty's ships and vessels in North America, and in the lakes of Canada, in endeavouring to preserve the maritime rights of his majesty from infringement, to avoid, as much as possible, subjecting the vessels and people of the United States of America engaged in the fisheries to any loss or interruption which they have made themselves liable as to the just rights which belong to the maritime dominions of his majesty in North America. You are therefore allowed to pursue your voyage without further detention, taking notice, however, that if you are again found trespassing on his majesty's rights you cannot expect to receive further indulgences: and you are requested to notify to the vessels of your nation, as far as in your power, to avoid interferring with these fisheries which exclusively appertain to his majesty's subjects, as they will be hereafter proceeded against as the law directs. Given under my hand at Halifax, 58 year of H. M. reign, 1818.

(Signed) DAVID MILNE, *Commander in Chief.*[a]

---

[a] Appendix, p. 1076.

The renewal of the orders under which these vessels were seized does not appear to have been made the subject of official correspondence between the two Governments, but it is reported by Mr. Bagot in his despatch of April 7, 1818, to Lord Castlereagh that prior to the renewal of such orders he communicated to Mr. Adams, then Secretary of State, "the orders which Sir David Milne proposed to give to the ships under his command, in regard to the American vessels found fishing upon our coast during the present season," and he then proceeds to state " some part of the conversation which then passed " between him and Mr. Adams, which, he adds, " was not a little remarkable." This conversation as reported by Mr. Bagot with his comments thereon is as follows:

I met Mr. Adams accidentally on the street, and when I told him of the letter which I had received from Sir David Milne, he showed some surprise, but certainly no irritation. In the course, however, of our conversation, which lasted about ten minutes, he said, not with a tone of anger, but with the ordinary tone of earnestness with which he usually speaks upon business, that, after all, " he believed that they should have to fight about it, and that his opinion was, that they ought to do so."

I deprecated in some common-place phrase a resort to such an extremity, when he proceeded to say that, " holding as he did the right of participation in the United States to be unequivocal, undeniable, and absolute, it was a matter only to be settled by agreement or by force; and, all arrangement by assignment of coast being out of the question, he did not see distinctly what proposition of arrangement could be made, which would promise a satisfactory result."

He then said that " we could have no right to seize their ships; that all the lawyers in England with whom he had spoken on the subject were of that opinion; that our own judge had last year released the vessels which had been captured by the *Dee*, and that, without an Act of Parliament for the purpose, they could not be taken; or, if they were taken, the American Government would have a claim upon Great Britain for full indemnity for them."

The more I have reflected upon this conversation, the more extraordinary I have thought it. Mr. Adams is, I presume, much too cautious a man to have suffered himself, in his official situation, to be betrayed by mere temper into the use of such expressions to me. On the other hand, I equally presume that he cannot seriously believe that the point itself is a ground of war for this country; or, even if it were, that this country could now be excited to a war with Great Britain upon a point in which two States at the utmost have any immediate interest whatever. The only explanation which I can conceive of his conversation is either that, being himself of the State of Massachusetts, the only State which is deeply interested in the question, he is anxious to hold a very high tone upon the subject; or that it is the policy of the Government not to let the matter be brought to any arrangement but to reserve it as a grievance, to be used as it may hereafter be wanted.   Whatever may have been the motive which prompted Mr. Adams' expressions, they are, as coming from him, somewhat extraordinary, and it is certainly my duty to report them to your lordship.[a]

THE NEGOTIATIONS RESULTING IN THE TREATY OF 1818.

The Commercial Convention of July 3, 1815, between the United States and Great Britain was, by its terms, to remain in force for four years from that date, its period of duration thus extending to July 3, 1819.   In anticipation of the expiration of this treaty, instructions were issued as early as November, 1817, by Mr. Adams, then Secretary of State, to Mr. Rush, the American Minister at London, authorizing him to enter upon negotiations with the British Government for a new commercial treaty; and subsequently, in May, 1818, Mr. Rush was authorized to propose to Great Britain an immediate general negotiation for a commercial treaty covering the continuance of the treaty of 1815 for a further term of years, and also to embrace the following unsettled questions then in discussion between the two Governments: the impressment of seamen and the regulation of maritime neutrality; commercial intercourse between the United States and the British West Indies and North American Colonies; indemnity to the owners of the slaves carried away from the United States by British officers after the ratification of the treaty of peace of Ghent and contrary to the stipulation in the first article of that treaty; the location of the international boundary line from the northwest corner of the Lake of the Woods to the Rocky Mountains and beyond; the title to the American settlement at the mouth of the Columbian River; and the fisheries.[b]   At the same time the Secretary of State sent instructions to Mr. Gallatin, the American Minister to France, authorizing him to take part with Mr. Rush in these negotiations.   The reasons for entering upon the negotiations at that time are stated in the letter of instructions, dated May 22, 1818, from Mr. Adams to Mr. Gallatin as follows:

---

[a] Appendix, p. 301.   [b] Appendix, p. 302.

The present state of the relations between the United States and Great Britain has suggested to the President the expediency of proposing to the British Government the negotiation of a treaty of amity and commerce, to embrace the continuance for eight years longer of the commercial convention of July 3, 1815, and to attempt the adjustment of other objects interesting to the two countries, and upon which the Governments have not yet been able to come to an agreement. It is desirable that this negotiation should take place in the course of the ensuing summer, and that its result should be transmitted here for the commencement of the next session of Congress, fixed for the third Monday of November; for as the convention, unless continued, will expire in July, 1819, and as it is due to the interests of the merchants on both sides affected by it that early notice should be given whether its provisions are to be continued or to cease, it appears that no time is to be lost in bringing the question of its renewal or cessation to an immediate issue. As the motives for taking up the subject thus early are operative alike upon both parties, and as, in the event of the expiration of the convention of July, 1815, legislative measures preparatory to that contingency will doubtless be necessary as well in Parliament as in Congress, it is expected that this proposal will be acceded to by the British Government, and that plenipotentiaries on their part will be appointed to treat with you and Mr. Rush, to whom jointly the President proposes to commit the trust of this negotiation.[a]

In the present examination of these negotiations it is unnecessary to refer to any of the subjects embraced in them other than the fisheries.

On the subject of the fisheries Mr. Adams says in his letter of instructions to Mr. Gallatin:

The correspondence between the two Governments on this subject leaves it still in the unsettled state in which it was left at the peace [of Ghent]. Two proposals have been made, on the part of the British Government, neither of which proving acceptable, a counterproposal from us has been promised, and will be contained in the further detailed instructions which will be prepared and forwarded to Mr. Rush, to assist you in the conduct of the negotiation.[b]

These instructions were supplemented by further instructions sent by Mr. Adams to Messrs. Gallatin and Rush on July 28, 1818, which, so far as they relate to the fisheries, were as follows:

In the expectation that the Government of Great Britain have accepted the proposal which Mr. Rush was instructed to make for negotiating a treaty of commerce, embracing the continuance of the convention of 3d July, 1815, for an additional term of years, and including other objects of interest to the two nations, I have now the honor of transmitting to you the President's instructions to you for the conduct of the negotiation.

* * * * * * *

---

[a] Appendix, p. 302.   [b] Appendix, p. 303.

5. Fisheries.

The proceedings, deliberations, and communications upon this subject, which took place at the negotiation of Ghent, will be fresh in the remembrance of Mr. Gallatin. Mr. Rush possesses copies of the correspondence with the British Government relating to it after the conclusion of the peace, and of that which has passed here between Mr. Bagot and this Government. Copies of several letters received by members of Congress during the late session, from the parts of the country most deeply interested in the fisheries, are now transmitted.[a]

The President authorizes you to agree to an article whereby the United States will desist from the liberty of fishing and curing and drying fish, within the British jurisdiction *generally*, upon condition that it shall be secured as a permanent right, not liable to be impaired by any future war, from Cape Ray to the Ramea islands, and from Mount Joli, on the Labrador coast, through the strait of Belle-isle, indefinitely north, along the coast; the right to extend as well to curing and drying the fish as to fishing.[b]

Negotiations were accordingly entered upon, and Messrs. Frederick John Robinson and Henry Goulburn, who had meanwhile been appointed plenipotentiaries on the part of Great Britain, met Messrs. Albert Gallatin and Richard Rush, plenipotentiaries on the part of the United States, for their first formal conference on August 27, 1818.[c] As a result of the negotiations so undertaken the treaty of October 20, 1818, was concluded, and the agreement arrived at upon the fisheries question will be found in Article I of that treaty, which is as follows:

Whereas differences have arisen respecting the Liberty claimed by the United States for the Inhabitants thereof, to take, dry and cure Fish on Certain Coasts, Bays, Harbours and Creeks of His Britannic Majesty's Dominions in America, it is agreed between the High Contracting Parties, that the Inhabitants of the said United States shall have forever, in common with the Subjects of His Britannic Majesty, the Liberty to take Fish of every kind on that part of the Southern Coast of Newfoundland which extends from Cape Ray to the Rameau Islands, on the Western and Northern Coast of Newfoundland, from the said Cape Ray to the Quirpon Islands, on the shores of the Magdalen Islands, and also on the Coasts, Bays, Harbours, and Creeks from Mount Joly on the Southern Coast of Labrador, to and through the Straits of Belleisle and thence Northwardly indefinitely along the Coast, without prejudice however, to any of the exclusive Rights of the Hudson Bay Company; and that the American Fishermen shall also have liberty forever, to dry and cure Fish in any of the unsettled Bays, Harbours, and Creeks of the Southern

---

[a] A thorough search for the inclosures referred to has been made in the records and files of the United States Government and elsewhere but no trace of them has been found.

[b] Appendix, p. 304. [c] Appendix, p. 308.

part of the Coast of Newfoundland hereabove described, and of the Coast of Labrador; but so soon as the same, or any Portion thereof, shall be settled, it shall not be lawful for the said Fishermen to dry or cure Fish at such Portion so settled, without previous agreement for such purpose with the Inhabitants, Proprietors, or Possessors of the ground.—And the United States hereby renounce forever, any Liberty heretofore enjoyed or claimed by the Inhabitants thereof, to take, dry, or cure Fish on, or within three marine Miles of any of the Coasts, Bays, Creeks, or Harbours of His Britannic Majesty's Dominions in America not included within the above mentioned limits; provided, however, that the American Fishermen shall be admitted to enter such Bays or Harbours for the purpose of Shelter and of repairing Damages therein, of purchasing Wood, and of obtaining Water, and for no other purpose whatever. But they shall be under such Restrictions as may be necessary to prevent their taking, drying or curing Fish therein, or in any other manner whatever abusing the Privileges hereby reserved to them.[a]

Before reviewing the course of these negotiations, and in order that they may be clearly understood, attention is called at this point to the report made by Messrs. Gallatin and Rush to Mr. Adams on the same day that the treaty was signed, which states the position taken by them with respect to the various proposals exchanged with regard to the fisheries, and shows clearly the purpose and meaning of the fishery article as finally agreed upon in the treaty. This report is as follows, so far as it relates to the subject of the fisheries:

We have the honor to transmit a convention which we concluded this day with the British plenipotentiaries.

Lord Castlereagh having expressed a wish that the negotiations might be opened before his departure for Aix-la-Chapelle, Mr. Gallatin left Paris as soon as he had received our full powers, and arrived here on the 16th of August. Our joint instructions contained in your despatch of the 28th of July did not, however, reach us till the 3d of September. We had long conversations with Lord Castlereagh at his country seat, on the 22d and 23d of August, but could not, owing to our instructions not having arrived, discuss with him the question of the fisheries and of the West India intercourse. He left London on the 1st of September. The official conferences had begun on the 27th of August, and, for the progress of the negotiation, we beg leave to refer to the enclosed copies of the protocol, and documents annexed to it, and of two unofficial notes sent by us to the British plenipotentiaries. We will add some observations on the several objects embraced by the convention.

1. FISHERIES.

We succeeded in securing, besides the rights of taking and curing fish within the limits designated by our instructions, as a *sine qua non*, the liberty of fishing on the coasts of the Magdalen islands, and

---

[a] Appendix, p. 25.

of the western coast of Newfoundland, and the privilege of entering for shelter, wood, and water, in all the British harbors of North America. Both were suggested as important to our fishermen, in the communications on that subject which were transmitted to us with our instructions.[a] To the exception of the exclusive rights of the Hudson's Bay Company we did not object, as it was virtually implied in the treaty of 1783, and we had never, any more than the British subjects, enjoyed any right there; the charter of that company having been granted in the year 1670. The exception applies only to the coasts and their harbors, and does not affect the right of fishing in Hudson's Bay beyond three miles from the shores, a right which could not exclusively belong to, or be granted by, any nation.

The most difficult part of the negotiation related to the permanence of the right. To obtain the insertion in the body of the convention of a provision declaring expressly that that right should not be abrogated by war, was impracticable. All that could be done was to express the article in such manner as would not render the right liable to be thus abrogated. The words "for ever" were inserted for that purpose, and we also made the declaration annexed to the protocol of the third conference, the principal object of which was to provide in any event for the revival of all our prior rights. The insertion of the words "for ever" was strenuously resisted. The British plenipotentiaries urged that, in case of war, the only effect of those words being omitted, or of the article being considered as abrogated would be the necessity of inserting in the treaty of peace a new article renewing the present one; and that, after all that had passed, it would certainly be deemed expedient to do it, in whatever manner the condition was now expressed. We declared that we would not agree to any article on the subject, unless the words were preserved, or in case they should enter on the protocol a declaration impairing their effect.

It will also be perceived that we insisted on the clause by which the United States renounce their right to the fisheries relinquished by the convention, that clause having been omitted in the first British counter-project. We insisted on it with the view—1st. Of preventing any implication that the fisheries secured to us were a new grant, and of placing the permanence of the rights secured and of those renounced precisely on the same footing. 2d. Of its being expressly stated that our renunciation extended only to the distance of three miles from the coasts. This last point was the more important, as, with the exception of the fishery in open boats within certain harbors, it appeared, from the communications above mentioned, that the fishing ground, on the whole coast of Nova Scotia, is more than three miles from the shores; whilst, on the contrary, it is almost universally close to the shore on the coasts of Labrador. It is in that point of view that the privilege of entering the ports for shelter is useful, and it is hoped that, with that provision, a considerable portion of the actual fisheries on that coast (of Nova Scotia) will, notwithstanding the renunciation, be preserved.[b]

---

[a] See note on page 53 *supra* with reference to these communications.
[b] Appendix, p. 306.

The protocols of the conferences [a] show that three drafts in all of the fisheries article were proposed during these negotiations. The first was proposed by the American Plenipotentiaries at the third conference, which was held on September 17, 1818, and was accompanied by an explanatory memorandum. A counter proposal was made by the British Plenipotentiaries at the fifth conference, which was held on October 6, 1818. To this counter proposal the American Plenipotentiaries raised objections which were set forth in a memorandum submitted by them to the British Plenipotentiaries on the following day, and at the sixth conference, which was held on the 9th of October, 1818, the American Plenipotentiaries declared " that they could not agree to the article upon the fisheries brought forward by the British Plenipotentiaries at the preceding conference." The third proposal, which proved to be the final one, was made by the British Plenipotentiaries at the next following conference which was held on the 13th of October, 1818. The fisheries articles thus proposed was agreed to practically without change at the next conference, held on the 19th of October, 1818, and became Article I of the treaty which was signed on the following day.

The first draft of the article as proposed by the American Plenipotentiaries was in the following form:

ARTICLE A.

Whereas differences have arisen respecting the liberty claimed by the United States for the inhabitants thereof to take, dry and cure fish on certain coasts, bays, harbors, and creeks of His Britannic Majesty's dominions in America: It is agreed between the high contracting parties that the inhabitants of the said United States shall continue to enjoy unmolested, for ever, the liberty to take fish, of every kind, on that part of the southern coast of Newfoundland which extends from Cape Ray to the Ramea islands, and the western and northern coast of Newfoundland, from the said Cape Ray to the Quirpon island, on the Magdalen islands; and also on the coasts, bays, harbors, and creeks from Mount Joli, on the southern coast of Labrador, to and through the straits of Belleisle, and thence, northwardly, indefinitely, along the coast; and that the American fishermen shall also have liberty for ever to dry and cure fish in any of the unsettled bays, harbors, and creeks of the southern part of the coast of Newfoundland here above described, of the Magdalen islands, and of Labrador, as here above described; but so soon as the same, or either of them, shall be settled, it shall not be lawful for the said fishermen to dry or cure fish at such settlement, without previous

---

[a] Appendix, p. 308-317.

agreement for that purpose with the inhabitants, proprietors, or possessors of the ground; and the United States hereby renounce any liberty heretofore enjoyed or claimed by the inhabitants thereof to take, dry, or cure fish on or within three marine miles of any of the coasts, bays, creeks, and harbors of His Britannic Majesty's dominions in America not included within the above-mentioned limits: *Provided, however,* That the American fishermen shall be admitted to enter such bays and harbors for the purpose only of obtaining shelter, wood, water, and bait, but under such restrictions as may be necessary to prevent their drying or curing fish therein, or in any other manner abusing the privilege hereby reserved to them.[a]

The explanatory memorandum which accompanied this draft was as follows:

EXPLANATORY MEMORANDUM.

The American plenipotentiaries presented for consideration an article on the subject of certain fisheries. They stated, at the same time, that as the United States considered the liberty of taking, drying, and curing fish, secured to them by the treaty of peace of 1783, as being unimpaired, and still in full force for the whole extent of the fisheries in question, whilst Great Britain considered that liberty as having been abrogated by war; and as, by the article now proposed, the United States offered to desist from their claim to a certain portion of the said fisheries, that offer was made with the understanding that the article now proposed, or any other on the same subject which might be agreed on, should be considered as permanent, and, like one for fixing boundaries between the territories of the two parties, not to be abrogated by the mere fact of a war between them; or that, if vacated by any event whatever, the rights of both parties should revive and be in full force, as if such an article had not been agreed to.[b]

The counter proposal made by the British Plenipotentiaries was in the following form:

ARTICLE A.

It is agreed that the inhabitants of the United States shall have liberty to take fish, of every kind, on that part of the western coast of Newfoundland which extends from Cape Ray to the Quirpon islands, and on that part of the southern and eastern coasts of Labrador which extends from Mount Joli to Huntingdon island; and it is further agreed that the fishermen of the United States shall have liberty to dry and cure fish in any of the unsettled bays, harbors and creeks of the said south and east coasts of Labrador, so long as the same shall remain unsettled; but as soon as the same, or any part of them, shall be settled, it shall not be lawful for the said fishermen to dry or cure fish without a previous agreement for that purpose with the inhabitants, proprietors, or possessors of the ground.

And it is further agreed that nothing contained in this article shall be construed to give to the inhabitants of the United States any liberty to take fish within the rivers of His Britannic Majesty's

---

[a]Appendix, p. 310.   [b]Appendix, p. 311.

territories, as above described; and it is agreed, on the part of the United States, that the fishermen of the United States resorting to the mouths of such rivers shall not obstruct the navigation thereof, nor wilfully injure nor destroy the fish within the same, either by setting nets across the mouths of such rivers, or by any other means whatever.

His Britannic Majesty further agrees that the vessels of the United States, *bona fide* engaged in such fishery, shall have liberty to enter the bays, and harbors of any of His Britannic Majesty's dominions in North America, for the purpose of shelter, or of repairing damages therein, and of purchasing wood and obtaining water, and for no other purpose; and all vessels so resorting to the said bays, and harbors shall be under such restrictions as may be necessary to prevent their taking, drying, or curing fish therein.

It is further well understood that the liberty of taking, drying, and curing fish, granted in the preceding part of this article, shall not be construed to extend to any privilege of carrying on trade with any of His Britannic Majesty's subjects residing within the limits hereinbefore assigned for the use of the fishermen of the United States, for any of the purposes aforesaid.

And in order the more effectually to guard against smuggling, it shall not be lawful for the vessels of the United States, engaged in the said fishery, to have on board any goods, wares, or merchandise whatever, except such as may be necessary for the prosecution of the fishery, or the support of the fishermen whilst engaged therein or in the prosecution of their voyages to and from the said fishing grounds. And any vessel of the United States which shall contravene this regulation may be seized, condemned, and confiscated, together with her cargo.[a]

The objections raised by the American Plenipotentiaries to the British counter proposal were as follows:

Mr. Gallatin and Mr. Rush present their compliments to Mr. Robinson and Mr. Goulburn, and beg leave to send them the enclosed paper containing some remarks on the articles handed to them at the conference yesterday. They are to be considered as unofficial, according to the intimation given yesterday, when they were promised, and have been drawn up merely under the hope that, by possessing the British plenipotentiaries of some of the views of the American plenipotentiaries before the next meeting on the 9th, the progress of the negotiation may be accelerated.

FISHERIES.

The American plenipotentiaries are not authorized by their instructions to assent to any article on that subject which shall not secure to the inhabitants of the United States the liberty of taking fish of every kind on the southern coast of Newfoundland, from Cape Ray to the Ramea islands, and on the coasts, bays, harbors, and creeks from Mount Joli, on the southern coast of Labrador, to and through the straits of Belleisle, and thence northwardly, indefinitely, along the coast; and, also, the liberty of drying and curing fish in any of

---

[a] Appendix, p. 312.

the unsettled bays, harbors, and creeks of Labrador and of the southern coast of Newfoundland, as above described; with the proviso respecting such of the said bays, harbors, and creeks as may be settled.

The liberty of taking fish within rivers is not asked. A positive clause to except them is unnecessary, unless it be intended to comprehend under that name waters which might otherwise be considered as bays or creeks. Whatever extent of fishing-ground may be secured to American fishermen, the American plenipotentiaries are not prepared to accept it on a tenure or on conditions différent from those on which the whole has heretofore been held. Their instructions did not anticipate that any new terms or restrictions would be annexed, as none were suggested in the proposals made by Mr. Bagot to the American Government. The clauses forbidding the spreading of nets, and making vessels liable to confiscation in case any articles not wanted for carrying on the fishery should be found on board, are of that description, and would expose the fishermen to endless vexations.[a]

The revised draft brought forward by the British Plenipotentiaries after the article as previously proposed by them had been rejected by the American Plenipotentiaries was in the form finally agreed upon with some slight typographical changes, and became Article I of the treaty.

ARTICLE I OF THE TREATY OF 1818.

It will be observed that the general scope and purpose of Article I of this treaty is indicated by the introductory clause, which is in the exact form proposed by the American Plenipotentiaries in their first draft and recites:

Whereas differences have arisen respecting the liberty claimed by the United States for the inhabitants thereof, to take, dry and cure fish on certain coasts, bays, harbors and creeks of His Britannic Majesty's dominions in America, it is agreed, etc.[b]

The recitals of this clause appropriately set forth, by way of explanation of what follows, the situation out of which the article grew and upon which it was predicated.

As has already been shown in the review of the course of events and negotiations leading up to this treaty, the only fishing liberties claimed by the United States which were disputed by Great Britain, and, therefore, the only ones with respect to which differences had

---

[a] Appendix, p. 313.   [b] Appendix, p. 25.

arisen, were the liberties under the second clause of Article III of the treaty of 1783, relating to the inshore or coast fisheries, which clause, it will be remembered, Great Britain asserted, and the United States denied, had been terminated by the War of 1812. It is evident, therefore, that the liberties referred to in the introductory clause of the new article were the liberties claimed by the United States under the second clause of Article III of the treaty of 1783, and it will further appear from an examination of the negotiations and of the stipulations of the new article that, so far as it reserves liberties in these fisheries to the inhabitants of the United States, the liberties so reserved were intended to be the identical liberties to which the American fishermen were previously entitled under the second clause of Article III of the treaty of 1783, and that, so far as liberties are relinquished or renounced by it, such relinquishment or renunciation applies only to liberties which were covered by the clause referred to of the treaty of 1783, which Great Britain contended had been terminated by the War of 1812. In this connection attention is called to the explanatory memorandum which accompanied the first draft of the article as proposed by the American Plenipotentiaries in which it is clearly set forth that the United States considered the liberty of taking, drying, and curing fish, secured to them by the treaty of peace of 1783, as being unimpaired and still in full force for the whole extent of the fisheries in question, while Great Britain considered that liberty as having been abrogated by war; and that, by the article proposed, the United States offered to desist from their claim to a certain portion of the said fisheries.

Attention is further called to the note already quoted, which was sent by the American Plenipotentiaries to the British Plenipotentiaries, and in which their reason for rejecting the British counterproposal containing some conditions upon the enjoyment of the liberties to be reserved to the American fishermen is stated to be:

Whatever extent of fishing ground may be secured to American fishermen, the American plenipotentiaries are not prepared to accept it on a tenure or on conditions different from those on which the whole has heretofore been held. Their instructions did not anticipate that any new terms or restrictions would be annexed, as none was suggested in the proposals made by Mr. Bagot to the American Government.[a]

---

a *Supra*, p. 59.

The question of the extent of the coasts on which such liberties were to be reserved was the subject of discussion in the negotiations, but it was settled beyond the possibility of question that the fishing rights to be exercised on such coasts were to be the same as those exercised on the same coasts under the provisions of the treaty of 1783.

The intimate relationship between the provisions of the new fisheries article and the provisions of the second clause of Article III of the treaty of 1783 will become evident from a comparison of the corresponding provisions of the two treaties.

The second clause of Article III of the treaty of 1783 provides:

And also [it is agreed] that the inhabitants of the United States shall have liberty to take fish of every kind on such part of the coast of Newfoundland as British fishermen shall use (but not to dry or cure the same on that island) and also on the coasts, bays and creeks of all other of His Britannic Majesty's dominions in America; and that the American fishermen shall have liberty to dry and cure fish in any of the unsettled bays, harbours and creeks of Nova Scotia, Magdalen Islands, and Labrador, so long as the same shall remain unsettled; but so soon as the same or either of them shall be settled, it shall not be lawful for the said fishermen to dry or cure fish at such settlements, without a previous agreement for that purpose with the inhabitants, proprietors or possessors of the ground.[a]

The corresponding provisions of the new article are as follows:

It is agreed between the High Contracting Parties, that the Inhabitants of the said United States shall have forever, in common with the Subjects of His Britannic Majesty, the Liberty to take Fish of every kind on that part of the Southern Coast of Newfoundland which extends from Cape Ray to the Rameau Islands, on the Western and Northern Coast of Newfoundland, from the said Cape Ray to the Quirpon Islands, on the shores of the Magdalen Islands, and also on the Coasts, Bays, Harbours, and Creeks from Mount Joly on the Southern Coast of Labrador, to and through the Straits of Belleisle and thence Northwardly indefinitely along the Coast, without prejudice however, to any of the exclusive Rights of the Hudson Bay Company; and that the American Fishermen shall also have liberty forever, to dry and cure Fish in any of the unsettled Bays, Harbours and Creeks of the Southern part of the Coast of Newfoundland hereabove described, and of the Coast of Labrador; but so soon as the same or any Portion thereof, shall be settled, it shall not be lawful for the said Fishermen to dry or cure Fish at such Portion so settled, without previous agreement for such purpose with the Inhabitants, Proprietors, or Possessors of the ground.[b]

By a comparison of the provisions above quoted from these two articles, it will be seen that, in effect, there are only three points of difference between them.

---

[a] Appendix, p. 24.　　　　　[b] Appendix, p. 25.

One of these differences is that the coasts on which the liberty of fishing is reserved to American fishermen are described in the earlier treaty as "such part of the coast of Newfoundland as British fishermen shall use" and also "the coasts, bays, and creeks of all other of his Britannic Majesty's dominions in America" and in the later treaty, such coasts are described as "that part of the southern coast of Newfoundland which extends from Cape Ray to the Rameau Islands, on the western and northern coast of Newfoundland, from the said Cape Ray to the Quirpon Islands, on the shores of the Magdalen Islands, and also on the coasts, bays, harbors, and creeks from Mount Joly on the southern coast of Labrador, to and through the straits of Belleisle, and thence northwardly indefinitely along the coast." It is apparent that the only effect of this difference is to substitute the particular coasts mentioned in the later treaty in place of all the coasts mentioned in the earlier treaty, wherever the liberty of taking fish was to be exercised by the inhabitants of the United States.

The clause in the new article providing that the liberties of the American fishermen shall be without prejudice to any of the exclusive rights of the Hudson Bay Company was not regarded by the American Plenipotentiaries as imposing any additional restriction upon the rights previously enjoyed under the earlier treaty. It will be remembered that in their report of the negotiations sent to Mr. Adams on the day the treaty was signed, they made the following statement with respect to this clause:

To the exception of the exclusive rights of the Hudson's Bay Company we did not object, as it was virtually implied in the treaty of 1783, and we had never, any more than the British subjects, enjoyed any right there; the charter of that Company having been granted in the year 1670. The exception applies only to the coasts and their harbors and does not affect the right of fishing in Hudson's Bay beyond three miles from the shores, a right which could not exclusively belong to, or be granted by, any nation.[a]

It is true that in the draft of the new article as first proposed by the American Plenipotentiaries, the provision now under consideration contained the expression: "the inhabitants of the United States shall continue to enjoy unmolested for ever", etc., which expression was changed in the article as finally agreed upon to "the inhabitants of the said United States shall have for ever." It will be remembered

_____

[a] *Supra,* p. 55.

that this expression "shall continue to enjoy unmolested" was used in the earlier treaty with respect to the right to the enjoyment of the off-shore fisheries in distinction from the inshore or coast fisheries, and that with respect to the latter, the same expression was used which, as above pointed out, was finally adopted in the new treaty. This change was proposed by the British Plenipotentiaries in their final draft, and as it was in effect merely the adoption of the identical phrase used in the earlier treaty with respect to these same liberties, it could not well be refused by the American Plenipotentiaries, any objection which they might otherwise have had being obviated by the use in connection with it of the word "forever" which was added to the phrase in the new treaty. As stated by the American Plenipotentiaries in their report hereinabove quoted "the most difficult part of the negotiation related to the permanence of the right" and "the insertion of the words 'for ever' was strenuously resisted," but "we declared that we would not agree to any article on the subject unless the words were preserved."

The second point of difference between the above quoted provisions of the treaty of 1783 and the new treaty is found in the use in the new treaty of the expression "in common with the subjects of His Britannic Majesty," which does not appear in the earlier treaty.

It will be noted that the words "in common" are used for the first time in the second draft prepared by the British plenipotentiaries, and that in proposing this draft no suggestion was made that these words were not to have the usual and well-known meaning which attached to them as used in legal phraseology, to which Mr. Adams refers in his note of January 22, 1816, to Lord Bathurst as follows:

By the British municipal laws, which were the laws of both nations, the property of a fishery is not necessarily in the proprietor of the soil where it is situated. The soil may belong to one individual, and the fishery to another. The right to the soil may be exclusive, while the fishery may be free or held in common. And thus, while in the partition of the national possessions in North America, stipulated by the treaty of 1783, the jurisdiction over the shores washed by the waters where this fishery was placed was reserved to Great Britain, the fisheries themselves, and the accommodations essential to their prosecution, were, by mutual compact, agreed to be continued in common.[a]

---

[a] *Supra*, p. 30.

It is not to be supposed that the British Plenipotentiaries inserted the words " in common " in this article for any purpose other than to negative the presumption, which otherwise might have arisen, that the American fishermen in the exercise of the fishing liberties reserved to them by the treaty were at liberty to take precedence over the British fishermen in those waters or crowd out the British fishermen from the fishing grounds, the possibility of which, it will be remembered, Lord Bathurst informed Mr. Adams was the chief reason for objecting to the admission of American fishermen to those waters.[a] In any event, however, it is not permissible to attribute to these words inserted by the British Plenipotentiaries any unusual meaning which was not disclosed to the American Plenipotentiaries at the time of the negotiations.

The third point of difference between the provisions above quoted of the treaty of 1783 and the new treaty is found in the specification of the bays, harbors, and creeks wherein the liberty of drying and curing fish may be exercised by the American fishermen, " the unsettled bays, harbors and creeks of Nova Scotia, Magdalen Islands and Labrador " being specified in the earlier treaty, and " the unsettled bays, harbors and creeks of the southern part of the coast of Newfoundland here above described and of the coast of Labrador " being specified in the new treaty. In both treaties alike it is provided that so soon as the same or any portion thereof (in the earlier treaty " or either of them ") shall be settled, it shall not be lawful for the said fishermen to dry or cure fish at such portion so settled (in the earlier treaty " at such settlements ") without previous agreement for that purpose with the inhabitants, proprietors or possessors of the ground. Here again, as in the case of the differences first noted between the provisions of these two paragraphs, the only effect of the differences here noted is to change the locality wherein the liberty referred to is to be exercised by the American fishermen without changing the character or tenure of such liberty.

Passing now to the remaining provisions of the fisheries article of the new treaty, it will be found that there are no corresponding provisions in the fisheries article of the earlier treaty with which to compare them, the obvious reason being that the purpose of the new provisions was to renounce certain liberties theretofore enjoyed or claimed by the inhabitants of the United States under the provisions

---

[a] *Supra*, pp. 33, 34.

already examined of the second clause of Article III of the earlier treaty.   The new provisions referred to are as follows:

And the United States hereby renounce forever, any Liberty heretofore enjoyed or claimed by the Inhabitants thereof, to take, dry, or cure Fish on, or within three marine Miles of any of the Coasts, Bays, Creeks, or Harbours of His Britannic Majesty's Dominions in America not included within the above mentioned limits; provided, however, that the American Fishermen shall be admitted to enter such Bays or Harbours for the purpose of Shelter and of repairing Damages therein, of purchasing Wood, and of obtaining Water, and for no other purpose whatever.   But they shall be under such Restrictions as may be necessary to prevent their taking, drying or curing Fish therein, or in any other manner whatever abusing the Privileges hereby reserved to them.[a]

It will be remembered that no question had at any time been raised throughout the entire history of this controversy as to the fisheries covered by the first clause of the fisheries article of the treaty of 1783, and in fact the word " right " and not the word " liberty," is used, with reference to those fisheries, so that the word " liberty " here used could not have been intended to refer to any other fisheries than those covered by the second clause.   In this connection attention is again called to the following statement made in the report of the American Plenipotentiaries with respect to the purpose and effect of the renunciation of the liberty referred to:

It will also be perceived that we insisted on the clause by which the United States renounce their right to the fisheries relinquished by the convention, that clause having been omitted in the first British counter-projet.   We insisted on it with the view—1st. Of preventing any implication that the fisheries secured to us were a new grant, and of placing the permanence of the rights secured and of those renounced precisely on the same footing.   2d. Of its being expressly stated that our renunciation extended only to the distance of three miles from the coasts.   This last point was the more important, as, with the exception of the fishery in open boats within certain harbors, it appeared, from the communications above mentioned, that the fishing-ground, on the whole coast of Nova Scotia, is more than three miles from the shores; whilst, on the contrary, it is almost universally close to the shore on the coasts of Labrador.   It is in that point of view that the privilege of entering the ports for shelter is useful, and it is hoped that, with that provision, a considerable portion of the actual fisheries on that coast (of Nova Scotia) will, notwithstanding the renunciation, be preserved.[b]

As has been shown in reviewing the course of events which led up to this treaty, Great Britain throughout the entire controversy

---

[a] Appendix, p. 25.   [b] *Supra*, p 55.

never claimed that any part of the fisheries article of the treaty of 1783 except the provisions of the second clause thereof was abrogated by the War of 1812 and never asserted that the alleged abrogation of that article affected American fishing liberties beyond the distance of three marine miles from the shore; and in confirmation of the view expressed by the American Plenipotentiaries, in the extract above quoted from their report of these negotiations, that the renunciation in the fisheries article of the new treaty did not extend beyond three miles from the shores, attention is called to the further statement in their report that the exception in the new treaty with respect to the exclusive rights of the Hudson Bay Company " applies only to the coasts and their harbors and does not affect the right of fishing in Hudson's Bay beyond three miles from the shores, a right which could not exclusively belong to, or be granted by, any nation." [a]

This renunciatory clause was drafted by the American Plenipotentiaries, omitted in the British counter projet, and finally insisted upon by the Plenipotentiaries of the United States, because " of its being expressly stated that our renunciation extended only to the distance of three miles from the coasts," with the explanation that the importance of this was that " the fishing ground, on the whole coast of Nova Scotia, is more than three miles from the shores," and that " it is hoped that, with that provision, a considerable portion of the actual fisheries on that coast (of Nova Scotia) will, notwithstanding the renunciation, be preserved." [a]

Great Britain had never in any of the negotiations claimed jurisdiction beyond a marine league from shore, and it is not conceivable that the American Plenipotentiaries should have drafted a clause which under its true interpretation would have surrendered historic rights continuously claimed and insisted upon by the United States, and the surrender of which was not demanded by Great Britain.

Before passing from the consideration of the provisions of the renunciatory clause of the new treaty, it must be noted that the provisions of this clause relate only to the enjoyment of the liberties and privileges referred to in it on the coasts other than those mentioned in the earlier provisions of the article. It is, therefore, unnecessary to examine here the effect of the provisions of this clause

---

[a] *Supra*, p. 55.

in relation to commercial privileges, inasmuch as the only question involving commercial privileges in this case concerns the enjoyment of such privileges on the coasts other than those mentioned in this clause.

With reference, however, to the enjoyment of commercial privileges by American fishermen on the coasts not covered by the renunciatory clause of the treaty, which is the subject of Question 7 submitted for decision in this Arbitration, it is important, while these negotiations are under consideration, that attention be directed to one feature of them in connection with this question.

It will be remembered that the British counter proposal, after describing the coasts on which the liberty of fishing was to be enjoyed by the American fishermen, contained the following provisions:

It is further well understood that the liberty of taking, drying, and curing fish, granted in the preceding part of this article, shall not be construed to extend to any privilege of carrying on trade with any of His Britannic Majesty's subjects residing within the limits hereinbefore assigned for the use of the fishermen of the United States, for any of the purposes aforesaid.

And in order the more effectually to guard against smuggling, it shall not be lawful for the vessels of the United States, engaged in the said fishery, to have on board any goods, wares, or merchandise whatever, except such as may be necessary for the prosecution of the fishery, or the support of the fishermen whilst engaged therein or in the prosecution of their voyages to and from the said fishing grounds. And any vessel of the United States which shall contravene this regulation may be seized, condemned, and confiscated, together with her cargo.[a]

To these provisions the American Plenipotentiaries objected, as has already been shown, stating that—

Whatever extent of fishing-ground may be secured to American fishermen, the American plenipotentiaries are not prepared to accept it on a tenure or on conditions different from those on which the whole has heretofore been held. Their instructions did not anticipate that any new terms or restrictions would be annexed, as none were suggested in the proposals made by Mr. Bagot to the American Government. The clauses forbidding the spreading of nets, and making vessels liable to confiscation in case any articles not wanted for carrying on the fishery should be found on board, are of that description, and would expose the fishermen to endless vexations.[b]

The draft, as finally accepted, was proposed by the British Plenipotentiaries after the receipt of these objections, and it will be observed that the objectionable provisions were omitted from it.

---

[a] *Supra*, p. 58.　　　　　[b] *Supra*, p. 59.

Inasmuch, therefore, as the coasts to which the objectionable provisions related in the first British proposal were, with some additions, the coasts designated in the final draft as those upon which the American fishermen should have liberty to take fish, it is evident that with respect to these coasts, at least, it cannot be claimed on the part of Great Britain that it was

understood that the liberty of taking, drying, and curing fish, granted in the preceding part of this article, shall not be construed to extend to any privilege of carrying on trade with any of His Britannic Majesty's subjects residing within the limits hereinbefore assigned for the use of the fishermen of the United States, for any of the purposes aforesaid.

MAPS.

The attention of the Tribunal is here directed to Maps No. I and No. II, which form part of this Case, and on which the coasts covered by the renunciatory clause of the treaty are colored light brown, and the coasts referred to as "treaty coasts" in the Special Agreement of January 27, 1909 are colored green and red; those colored green being the coasts on which the American fishermen have the liberty both of taking fish and of drying and curing them, and those colored red being the coasts on which they have the liberty of taking fish but not of drying or curing them.

PART II.

THE INTERPRETATION OF ARTICLE I OF THE TREATY OF 1818.

The terms of Article I of the treaty of October 20, 1818, having been examined in the light of the circumstances leading up to and surrounding the negotiation of that treaty, there still remains to be considered the subsequent actions of the two Governments having a bearing upon the interpretation of its provisions in accordance with their true intent and meaning.

BRITISH ACTS OF PARLIAMENT AND ORDERS IN COUNCIL.

Act of June 14, 1819.

On June 14, 1819, within five months after the exchange of ratifications of the treaty of 1818, an act of parliament was passed (59 Geo. III Cap. 38) entitled "An act to enable His Majesty to make regulations with respect to the taking and curing of fish on certain parts of the coasts of Newfoundland, Labrador and His Majesty's other possessions in North America, according to a convention made between His Majesty and the United States of America."[a] In this act, after the recital of so much of the fisheries article of the treaty of 1818 as relates to the taking and drying and curing of fish, followed by the further recital "And Whereas it is expedient that His Majesty should be enabled to carry into execution so much of the said convention as is above recited and to make regulations for that purpose," it is provided, in the first section of the act, that it shall be lawful for His Majesty by orders in council to be made from time to time for that purpose "to make such regu-

---

[a] Appendix, p. 112.

lations and to give such directions, orders and instructions to the Governor of Newfoundland, or to any officer or officers on that station, or to any other person or persons whomsoever, as shall or may be from time to time deemed proper and necessary for the carrying into effect *the purpose of the said convention, with relation to the taking, drying and curing of fish by the inhabitants of the United States of America, in common with British subjects,* within the limits set forth in the said article of the said convention and heretofore recited."

Section II of the act provides that

it shall not be lawful for any Person or Persons, not being a natural born Subject of His Majesty, in any Foreign Ship, Vessel or Boat, nor for any Person in any Ship, Vessel or Boat, other than such as shall be navigated according to the Laws of the United Kingdom of Great Britain and Ireland, to fish for, or to take, dry or cure any Fish of any Kind whatever within Three Marine Miles of any Coasts, Bays, Creeks or Harbours whatever, in any Part of His Majesty's Dominions in America, not included within the Limits specified and described in the first Article of the said Convention, and hereinbefore recited; and that if any such Foreign Ship, Vessel or Boat, or any Persons on board thereof, shall be found fishing or to have been fishing, or preparing to fish within such Distance of such Coasts, Bays, Creeks or Harbours, within such Parts of His Majesty's Dominions in America out of the said Limits as aforesaid, all such Ships, Vessels and Boats, together with their Cargoes, and all Guns, Ammunition, Tackle, Apparel, Furniture and Stores, shall be forfeited, and shall and may be seized, taken, sued for, prosecuted, recovered and condemned by such and the like Ways, Means and Methods, and in the same Courts, as Ships, Vessels or Boats may be forfeited, seized, prosecuted and condemned for any Offence against any Laws relating to the Revenue of Customs, or the Laws of Trade and Navigation, under any Act or Acts of the Parliament of Great Britain, or of the United Kingdom of Great Britain and Ireland; provided that nothing in this Act contained shall apply, or be construed to apply to the Ships or Subjects of any Prince, Power or State in Amity with His Majesty, who are entitled by Treaty with His Majesty to any Privilege of taking, drying or curing Fish on the Coasts, Bays, Creeks or Harbours, or within the Limits in this Act described.[a]

This section will be considered in connection with the seizures made under it which are elsewhere reviewed.

Section III of the act provides—

That it shall and may be lawful for any Fisherman of the said United States to enter into any such Bays or Harbours of His Britannic Majesty's Dominions in America as are last mentioned, for the purpose of Shelter and repairing Damages therein, and of purchasing Wood and of obtaining Water, and for no other purpose whatever;

---

[a]Appendix, p. 113.

subject nevertheless to such restrictions as may be necessary to prevent such Fishermen of the said United States from taking, drying or curing Fish in the said Bays or Harbours, or in any other manner whatever abusing the said Privileges by the said Treaty and this Act reserved to them, and as shall for that purpose be imposed by any Order or Orders to be from time to time made by His Majesty in Council under the Authority of this Act, and by any Regulations which shall be issued by the Governor or Person exercising the Office of Governor in any such Parts of His Majesty's Dominions in America, under or in pursuance of any such Order in Council as aforesaid.[a]

With respect to the regulations above referred to it should be noted in passing that, so far as the United States has been informed, no order in council was ever adopted under this section of the act and that no attempt was made to impose restrictions upon American fishermen resorting to the bays and harbors on the coasts where the liberty of fishing was renounced, for the four purposes mentioned in the treaty, until the year 1836, when the adoption of so-called regulations became the subject of provincial legislation, as is elsewhere shown in reviewing that branch of the question.

Regulations by Orders in Council.

It will be observed that the regulations which are to be imposed by orders in council under the authority of this act refer to two distinct branches of the treaty Article: those under the first section of the act, relating only to the coasts on which the liberty of fishing is secured to American fishermen by the treaty, and those under the third section of the act, relating only to the coasts on which the liberty of fishing is renounced by the United States.

In the latter case the regulations to be imposed were obviously intended to apply to American fishermen, for the treaty itself expressly provides for the imposition of restrictions upon them.

In the former case, however, no express authority is found in the treaty for imposing restrictions or regulations upon American fishermen. On the contrary, the express purpose of the portion of the treaty referred to in this section of the act was, not to regulate the American fishermen, but to admit them to the enjoyment of a fishing liberty in common with British subjects their right to which had been disputed by Great Britain since the War of 1812. The regulations which are authorized by the terms of the act are such only "as shall or may be from time to time deemed proper and necessary for

---

[a] Appendix, p. 113.

the carrying into effect the purposes of the said convention." It is evident, therefore, that this section of the act was intended to authorize the adoption of regulations for the purpose of preventing interference by British subjects with the fishing liberties which were secured to the American fishermen by the treaty and which had been denied them since the War of 1812.

This interpretation of the meaning of the act is confirmed by the action of the British Government in giving it practical application, and an examination of the regulations adopted by orders in council under this section of the act will show that in every instance such regulations have applied to British subjects and not to American fishermen and that this section of the act has never been interpreted in such orders as authorizing the imposition of regulations upon American fishermen.

It appears, therefore, both from the terms of the act and from the construction placed upon it by the orders in council adopted under it, that the purpose of the first section of the act was to insure the enjoyment by the inhabitants of the United States of the fishing liberties secured to them under the treaty, by imposing such regulations upon British subjects as were necessary to prevent them from interfering with such liberties.

Order in Council of June 19, 1819.

On June 19, 1819, five days after the date of the act above mentioned, an order in council was adopted which, so far as appears, is the only order in council adopted under the first section of the act for a period of nearly ninety years from the date of the treaty. This order, after reciting the authority of His Majesty, pursuant to the act, to make regulations for the purpose of carrying into execution the provisions of the treaty relating to the liberty in common which the inhabitants of the United States had with British subjects on the treaty coasts, provides as follows:

It is ordered by His Royal Highness the Prince Regent, in the name and on the behalf of His Majesty, and by and with the advice of His Majesty's Privy Council, in pursuance of the powers vested in His Majesty by the said Act, that the Governor of Newfoundland do *give notice to all His Majesty's subjects being in or resorting to the said ports that they are not to interrupt in any manner the aforesaid fishery so as aforesaid allowed to be carried on by the inhabitants of the said United States in common with His Majesty's subjects on the said coasts,* within the limits assigned to them by the said Treaty; and that the Governor of Newfoundland do conform himself to the said Treaty, and to such instructions as he shall from time to time receive thereon in conformity to the said Treaty, and to the above-recited Act, from one of His Majesty's Principal Secretaries of State, anything in His Majesty's Commission under the Great Seal, constituting him Governor and Commander-in-Chief in and over the said island of Newfoundland in America, and of the islands and territories thereunto belonging, or in His Majesty's general instructions to the said Governor, to the contrary notwithstanding; and His Royal Highness, in the name and on the behalf of His Majesty doth hereby annul and make void each and every of the said general instructions which are or shall be deemed contrary to the intent and meaning of the said Convention and of the said Act.   And the Right Honorable Earl Bathurst, one of His Majesty's Principal Secretaries of State, is to take the necessary measures therein accordingly.[a]

This action taken by the British Government within five months after the ratification of the treaty is of peculiar significance as showing that, in the opinion of those who were responsible for making the treaty and were thoroughly familiar with its purpose and meaning, the appropriate regulations to be adopted for giving effect to the fishing liberty which the American fishermen had in common with British subjects under the treaty, were regulations requiring British subjects "not to interrupt in any manner the aforesaid fishery so as aforesaid allowed to be carried on by the inhabitants of the said United States" and to require the Governor of Newfoundland to "conform himself to the said Treaty," anything in his commission or general instructions to the contrary notwithstanding, and in fact the order even went further than this and annulled and made void "each and every of the said general instructions which are or shall be deemed contrary to the intent and meaning of the said Convention and of the said Act."

The action taken at that time by the British Government is of particular importance in connection with the contention which many years later was brought forward by the Newfoundland Government that because the American fishing liberty on these coasts was a liberty held in common with British subjects, the Newfoundland Government was entitled to impose restrictions without the consent of the United States upon the exercise of such liberty upon the treaty coasts of Newfoundland, this contention being one of the questions in controversy in the present Case.

---

[a] Appendix, p. 115.

Order in Council of September 9, 1907.

By an order in council dated September 9, 1907 regulations were again adopted under the authority given by the first section of the Act of June 14, 1819 and, as will later appear, this order in council was adopted by Great Britain after Newfoundland had asserted the right to impose restrictions without the concurrence of the United States upon American fishermen in the exercise of the fishing liberties claimed by the United States on the Newfoundland coast under the treaty of 1818. It is, therefore, of interest in this connection to find that here again, as before, the regulations made by this order in council applied to British subjects and not to American fishermen and were designed to prevent British subjects from interfering with American fishermen and that the authority for adopting such regulations was stated by the terms of the order to be the Act of June 14, 1819, the purpose of which act was, as heretofore shown, to provide for the adoption of such regulations "as shall or may be from time to time deemed proper and necessary for the carrying into effect the purposes of the said convention with relation to the taking, drying and curing of fish by inhabitants of the United States of America in common with British subjects within the limits set forth in the said article of the said convention and hereinbefore recited."

The following recitals in the order referred to will show the character of the regulations adopted:

And whereas by an Order in Council made on the 19th June, 1819, in pursuance of the powers vested in His Majesty by the said Act, certain directions were given to the Governor of Newfoundland,

And whereas His Majesty by and with the advice of His Majesty's Privy Council deems it proper and necessary for the carrying into effect the purposes of the said Convention, to give further directions with relation to the taking, drying, and curing of fish by the inhabitants of the United States of America in common with British subjects on the coasts of Newfoundland:

Now therefore, His Majesty, in pursuance of the powers vested in His Majesty by Section I. of the Act 59 George III., cap. 38, by and with the advice of His Majesty's Privy Council is pleased to order and it is hereby ordered as follows:—

I. No provisions, rules, or enactments which may be in force with regard to the boarding and bringing into port of foreign fishing vessels found in the waters of Newfoundland shall, within the limits prescribed by the said Convention of 1818, apply to vessels in which inhabitants of the United States of America resort to the waters of Newfoundland for the purpose of exercising the liberty assured to them by Article I. of the said Convention.

II. If any question should arise before any Magistrate, Justice of the Peace, Judge or Court in Newfoundland, in relation to, concerning, or in anywise in respect of the presence on board any such vessel of any caplin, squid, or other bait fishes, or of ice, lines, seines, or other outfit or supplies for the fishery, the burden of proof that the said bait fishes and supplies and outfits have been purchased within the waters of Newfoundland shall rest upon the person or persons alleging the same.

III. It shall not be lawful for any person without the consent of His Majesty's Senior Naval Officer on the Newfoundland Station, in any proceedings against inhabitants of the United States exercising or claiming to exercise the liberty to take fish assured to them by the First Article of the Convention of 1818, or against any of their boats or vessels or against any persons engaged by them to form part of the crew of the vessels used or employed by such inhabitants in the exercise of such right.

A. To serve any process of law upon any boat or vessel so used or employed for any act or thing done in the exercise or alleged exercise of the said right, or which may, in the opinion of the said Naval Officer, give rise to any question or dispute in relation to the common fishery established or referred to in the said Convention, or to go on board any such vessel or boat for the purpose of serving such a process.

B. To arrest or seize any such vessel or boat or to seize, remove, or disturb any gear, nets, apparel, or other furniture or stores belonging to such vessel or boat.

IV. This Order shall commence and come into operation forthwith.

V. The Governor of Newfoundland, His Majesty's Senior Naval Officer on the Newfoundland Station, all Judges, Magistrates, Justices of the Peace, Constables, and all other persons whatsoever in Newfoundland shall take notice hereof and govern themselves accordingly.[a]

PERIOD FROM 1818 TO 1836.

During the eighteen years from 1818 to 1836 and in fact for several years thereafter no question arose between Great Britain and the United States under this treaty involving the interpretation of the meaning of its provisions. As has already been shown, the regulations established by the order in council of June 19, 1819, adopted under the first section of the act above referred to, had no application to American fishermen and, so far as the United States has been informed, no further order in council under that section of the act was adopted during this period, and no order in council

[a] Appendix, p. 117.

establishing regulations under the third section of the act was ever adopted, and no attempt was made prior to 1836 to establish by provincial legislation any regulations or restrictions upon American fishmen resorting for the four purposes mentioned in the treaty to the bays and harbors referred to in the last part of the fisheries article of the treaty.

It appears, therefore, that, except for the provisions of section II of the act referred to, there was no British or Colonial legislation in force during this period authorizing the seizure of American vessels for alleged violations of the treaty; and under the provisions of section II, which have been quoted, the only seizures authorized were of foreign fishing vessels found fishing or to have been fishing or preparing to fish within a distance of three marine miles from the coasts, bays, creeks and harbors where the liberty of fishing was renounced by the United States under the treaty.

The only seizures of American vessels during this period were made between the years 1821 and 1824 for alleged violations of the provisions of this section of the act. It will be found upon an examination of the circumstances surrounding these seizures that in every instance they were made under the direction of British naval officers on the charge of fishing within three miles of the shore in waters wherein the liberty of fishing had been renounced by the treaty, or of being within three miles of the shore in such waters for purposes other than the four purposes of shelter, repairs, wood and water provided for in the treaty. It will also be found that the objections raised to such seizures were in every instance that the vessel seized had not been fishing in such waters and that it had gone there for one or more of the four purposes for which it was entitled under the treaty to resort to such waters.

The only questions presented by these seizures, therefore, were disputed questions of fact as to the circumstances surrounding the seizures, and the only bearing which they have upon the interpretation of the treaty provisions will be found in the fact that the orders, under which they were made, show that Great Britain did not dispute the right, freely asserted and exercised at that time by the American fishermen, of fishing in any of the bays along the coast referred to provided that such fishing was not carried on within three marine miles of the shore.[a] It will be found that all of the

---

[a] Appendix, pp. 335, 338, 355, 375.

seizures in 1824, (and no subsequent seizures occurred during this period), were made under an order issued to the officers of the boats making the seizures "that any American vessels they may find *within three marine miles of the shore*, except in evident cases of distress or in want of wood or water, they are to detain and send or carry them to St. Andrews." [a]

It is evident, therefore, that none of the seizures made during this period had any bearing upon the question which afterwards arose as to whether or not, in renouncing the *liberty* of fishing in bays under the provisions of this treaty, the United States intended to renounce the *right* of fishing more than three miles from the shore in such bays, which right, as has already been shown, was secured to American fishermen under the first clause of Article III of the treaty of 1783 and had never been questioned by Great Britain.

Seizures in 1821–1824.

It is reported in an official return made in 1852 by the Registrar of the Vice Admiralty Court at Halifax, N. S., that in 1821 six American fishing vessels were seized at Gulliver's Hole, Bay of Fundy, three of which were condemned and three restored.[b] As will be found upon an examination of the map showing this locality, Gulliver's Hole is less than six miles in width throughout its entire extent.[c]

The attention of the United States Government does not appear to have been called to these seizures and they were not made the subject of diplomatic correspondence between the two governments.

The first seizure which was called to the attention of the Department of State for redress occurred on May 9, 1823, when the American fishing schooner *Charles* was seized in Shelburne Harbor by the British sloop *Argus;* and on the facts set forth in the protest filed with the Department of State at that time Mr. Adams, the Secretary of State, promptly wrote, on June 25, 1823, to the British Minister at Washington requesting restitution and indemnity.[d] The circumstances surrounding this seizure, as reported by the master and crew of the American vessel, differed in many respects from those reported by the British officer making the seizure, but they all agreed that the seizure was made for an offense alleged to have occurred within three miles from the shore; and the British report, which alone

---

[a] Appendix, pp. 375, 338, 357, 367, 377.
[b] Appendix, p. 1076, 1077.
[c] U. S. Case Map No. 1.
[d] Appendix, p. 325.

requires examination in the present connection as showing the British position at that time, sets forth the particulars of the seizure as follows:

The American fishing schooner *Charles*, William Stover, master, belonging to York, state of Maine, detained by the *Argus* at Shelburne on Friday, 9th of May, 1823, for a breach of the act of 59 Geo. III, chapter 38, for the protection of the British fisheries, and to enable his Majesty to make regulations respecting the same, according to a convention made between his Majesty and the United States, 20th October, 1818. The said schooner was found at anchor in Shelburne harbor, into which she had not been driven by stress of weather or any other fortuitous circumstance. Information had been received of this schooner having put into that same harbor on the Tuesday previous to the seizure, and anchored below Sandy Point, the weather being fine and moderate at that time, as well as on the day of seizure. She went out on Wednesday and returned again on Thursday, where she was found by the *Argus* on Friday; and having remained hovering upon the coast instead of proceeding on her fishing voyage, when there was no pretence whatever for her putting into port, she was detained.[a]

This report was made by the captain of the sloop *Argus*, which made the seizure, and was communicated to Mr. Adams by Mr. Addington, the British Chargé at Washington, in his note of October 12, 1823, with the following explanatory statement:

By the report of Captain Arabin it appears that the said schooner was found at anchor in Shelburne Harbor, into which she had not been driven by stress of weather. From that harbor she had already sailed once, after having previously anchored there, and had returned a second time, before she was captured by the *Argus*, the weather being fine and moderate the whole time.

It was disclosed in the reports of this case that while the schooner *Charles* was in possession of the British and before she had been condemned by judicial proceedings she was used for capturing an American vessel, the *Dolphin*. The particulars of this seizure are not reported, as the vessel was released on account of the illegality of the use of the *Charles* for that purpose.[b]

In June and July, 1824, seven American fishing vessels were seized under orders issued by the commander of the British war vessel *Dotterell*, charged with fishing or being at anchor without justification within three miles of the shores of the Island of Grand Menan. These seizures were promptly reported to the Department of State, and on September 8, 1824, Mr. Brent, the Assistant Secretary of State, wrote to Mr. Addington, calling them to his attention and

---

[a] Appendix, p. 333.　　　　[b] Appendix, p. 333, 349.

requesting indemnity and the prevention of similar interruptions in the future.[a] In the ensuing correspondence full statements, which had been procured on each side, showing the circumstances of the seizures, were exchanged. It will be found that here, as in the earlier cases, the British[b] and American[c] statements differed widely as to the justification for the seizures, but it is unnecessary to examine these differences. In the present connection the grounds assigned by Great Britain for such seizures are alone of importance as showing the acquiesence of Great Britain in the right claimed by American fishermen of fishing in the Bay of Fundy, beyond three miles from the shore. It will be remembered that the orders of the commander of the *Dotterell*, which have already been quoted and under which all these seizures were made, authorized seizures only within three miles of the shore, and it will be found that in each case Great Britain produced carefully prepared evidence to show that the alleged offenses for which the seizures were made occurred within three miles of the shore.[d]

The circumstances surrounding these seizures, as set forth in the evidence presented on the part of Great Britain, may be briefly summarized as follows:

The *Hero* and the *Pilgrim* were seized on June 16, 1824, within three miles of the shore, for fishing within one or two miles of the shore. On behalf of the vessels it was alleged that they were more than three miles from the shore, which was denied by the British officers making the seizures.[e]

The *Rebecca* was seized on July 6, 1824, in Gull Cove, Grand Menan, charged with being within three miles of the shore without justification. On behalf of the vessel it was alleged that she had gone in to procure wood of which she was in need, which was denied by the British officers making the seizure.[f]

The *William* and the *Galeon* were seized on July 15, 1824, the former at anchor in Gull Cove, Grand Menan, and the latter at anchor in Beale's Passage, Grand Menan, both charged with being within three miles of the shore without justification. On behalf of both vessels it was alleged that they had gone in for the purpose of procuring

---

[a] Appendix, p. 334.
[b] Appendix, pp. 348–353, 373–406.
[c] Appendix, pp. 334–348, 353–373.
[d] Appendix, pp. 380–406.
[e] Appendix, pp. 339, 341, 352, 362, 370, 379, 392–397.
[f] Appendix, pp. 339, 358, 372, 377, 380–385.

wood and water of which they were in need, but this was denied by the British officers making the seisure.[a]

The *Reindeer* and the *Ruby* were seized on July 6, 1824, at anchor in Two Island Harbor, Grand Menan, charged with being within three miles of the shore without justification. On behalf of these vessels it was alleged that they had gone in for the purpose of procuring wood and water of which they were in need, which was denied by the British officers making the seizures.[b]

While the *Reindeer* and the *Ruby* were on their way to St. Andrews N. S., in charge of a prize crew they were boarded and rescued by two American fishing vessels, the *Diligence* and the *Madison*, which had put out from Eastport, Maine, for that purpose. According to the British accounts of this incident, the rescuing party numbered about one hundred men with muskets and fixed bayonets, headed by Mr. Howard, a captain of the United States militia, and it was asserted that as the vessels approached shots were fired at the British crews in charge of the seized vessels.[c] According to the American account, on the other hand, the rescuing party numbered about twenty-five in all, twelve on board the *Diligence* and ten men and two or three boys on the *Madison*, and not a shot was fired until after the boats were retaken, when the American colors were hoisted and saluted by a discharge of muskets.[d] It appears that Mr. Howard, who is referred to as the leader in the British reports, was a boy of seventeen or eighteen who had never been a captain in the militia but had trained a company of boys at Eastport with wooden guns and swords. It is further stated in the American reports that the British officer in charge of the prize crew went on board the *Madison* after the rescue and drank the health of the rescuing party, saying that "we were good fellows for having retaken them; he took them according to his orders but without any provocation and was glad we had got them."[e]

The *Pilgrim*, which, as above noted, was seized on June 16th, escaped on the same day by sailing off with the prize crew, but was afterwards retaken by the *Dotterell* on August 29th, and on the same day the *Madison*, which had taken part in the rescue of the *Ruby* and the *Reindeer*, was seized by the *Dotterell* on that ground. Both of these seizures

---

[a] Appendix, pp. 339, 342–344, 348, 356–359, 377, 385–392.
[b] Appendix, pp. 336, 339, 350, 354, 366, 378, 397–406.
[c] Appendix, pp. 349, 350, 398, 401.
[d] Appendix, pp. 354, 355, 367–371.
[e] Appendix, pp. 369, 355.

occurred in the Bay of Fundy outside of the three miles limit from shore, but it is obvious that in the circumstances these seizures have no bearing upon the question of the rights of American fishermen to fish in the waters where the seizures were made.[a]

Three other seizures were made by the *Dotterell* during that season: The *Seaflower* was seized on September 29th at anchor in Kent's Island Harbor, Grand Menan, charged with being within three miles of the shore without justification. It was asserted on behalf of the vessel that she had gone in there for the purpose of shelter and repairs of which she was in need, but this was denied by the British officers making the seizure.[b]

The *Rover* and the *Escape* were seized in the latter part of October, charged with fishing within three miles of the shore of Grand Menan. The distance of these vessels from the shore at the time of the seizure seems to have been a matter of dispute, the Americans claiming that they were more than three miles from the shore, but in any event the seizures were made under the orders above referred to, which authorized seizures only within three miles from the shore.[c]

These later seizures were not made the subject of diplomatic correspondence, for meanwhile Mr. Addington had written to Mr. Adams, on October 5, 1824, demanding reparation "for the act of violence perpetrated on persons bearing His Majesty's commissions" during the rescue of the *Reindeer* and the *Ruby*. He wrote: "whether the vessels were legally detained or not, such an act of violence will bear no justification. If individuals are permitted to expound the stipulations and treaties for themselves, with arms in their hands, the preservation of harmony and good understanding between nations can no longer be hoped for."[d] No response was made to this note, and the correspondence on this subject was not carried further.

No further seizures appear to have been made until the year 1838, when different conditions prevailed which require separate consideration.

---

[a] Appendix, pp. 350, 351, 362, 369–371.
[b] Appendix, p. 360.

[c] Appendix, pp. 361, 377.
[d] Appendix, p. 349.

PERIOD FROM 1836 TO 1841.

Nova Scotia Hovering Act.

The Legislature of the Province of Nova Scotia adopted, early in the year 1836, a joint address to His Majesty King William IV, reciting:

That, by the Statute of the Imperial Parliament, passed in the 59th year of the Reign of our late Most Gracious Sovereign George the Third, power was given to His Majesty, by and with the advice of His Privy Council, by any order or orders in Council to be from time to time made for that purpose, to make such Regulations and give such Directions, as may be necessary to prevent Fishermen of the United States from taking, drying or curing Fish, in the Bays or Harbors of His Majesty's Dominions in America, or in any other manner whatever abusing the privileges by the Treaty and Act of the Imperial Parliament reserved to them.

That, as no such Order in Council has passed, it may be presumed that it may be extremely difficult for Your Majesty's Council to submit such Order for Your Majesty's consideration, as may be best adapted to meet the exigencies of the case in all Your Majesty's Dominions in America. That your Majesty's subjects in this Province have experienced great inconvenience and loss in this branch of Industry, by Foreign interference—and the Province is injuriously affected by the Illicit Trade carried on by Vessels ostensibly engaged in the Fisheries, who hover on the Coast, and, in many cases, combine Trade with the Fishery—a traffic, prejudicial alike to the Revenue— the importation of British Manufactures—the honest Trader, and the political and moral sentiments, habits and manners, of the people.

To prevent the continuance and extension of such evils, the Legislature of this Your Majesty's loyal Province of Nova-Scotia, have embodied in an Act such Regulations and Restrictions as they conceive will most effectually prevent such interference in the Fishery, and the Illicit Trade connected with it,—and, thereby secure the Rights and Privileges recognized by the Treaty, and intended to be guarded by the Statute.[a]

The act, to which reference is made in the above address, was passed by the Legislature of Nova Scotia on March 12, 1836 (6 Wm. IV. Chap. 8) and is entitled:

AN ACT Relating to the fisheries, and for the prevention of illicit trade in the province of Nova Scotia and the coasts and harbors thereof.[b]

This act provides in part as follows:

Whereas, by the convention made between his late Majesty, King George the Third, and the United States of America, signed at London on the twentieth day of October, in the year of our Lord one thousand eight hundred and eighteen, and the statute made and passed in the

---

[a]Appendix, pp. 1040–1041.   [b]Appendix, p. 119.

Parliament of Great Britain in the fifty-ninth year of the reign of his late Majesty, King George the Third, all foreign ships, vessels or boats, or any ships, vessel or boat, other than such as shall be navigated according to the laws of the United Kingdom of Great Britain and Ireland, found fishing, or to have been fishing, or preparing to fish within certain distances of any coasts, bays, creeks or harbors whatever, in any part of his Majesty's dominions in America, not included within the limits specified in the first article of the said convention, are liable to seizure:

Whereas the United States did, by the said Convention, renounce forever any liberty enjoyed or claimed by the inhabitants thereof to take, dry or cure fish on or within three marine miles of any of the coasts, bays, creeks or harbors of his Britannic Majesty's dominions in America not included within the above mentioned limits; Provided, however, that the American fishermen should be admitted to enter such bays or harbours for the purpose of shelter, and of repairing damages therein, of purchasing wood and of obtaining water, and for no other purpose whatever, but under such restrictions as might be necessary to prevent their taking, drying or curing fish therein, or in any other manner whatever abusing the privileges thereby reserved to them; and whereas no rules or regulations have been made for such purpose, and the interests of the inhabitants of this province are materially impaired; and whereas the said act does not designate the persons who are to make such seizure as aforesaid, and it frequently happens that persons found within the distance of the coasts aforesaid, infringing the articles of the convention aforesaid, and the enactments of the statute aforesaid, on being taken possession of, profess to have come within said limits for the purpose of shelter, and repairing damages therein, or to purchase wood and obtain water, by which the law is evaded, and the vessels and cargoes escape confiscation, although the cargoes may be evidently intended to be smuggled into this province, and the fishery carried on contrary to said convention and statute.

I. Be it therefore enacted by the Lieutenant Governor, Council and Assembly, That from and after the passage of this act, it shall be lawful for the officers of his Majesty's customs, the officers of impost and excise, the sheriffs and magistrates throughout the province, and any person holding a commission for that purpose from his excellency the Lieutenant Governor, for the time being, to go on board any ship, vessel or boat, within any port, bay, creek or harbor in this province; and also, to go on board of any ship, vessel or boat, hovering within three marine miles of any of the coasts, bays, creeks or harbors thereof, and in either case freely to stay on board such ship, vessel or boat, as long as she shall remain within such port or distance; and if any such ship, vessel or boat be bound elsewhere, and shall continue so hovering for the space of twenty-four hours after the master shall have been required to depart, it shall be lawful for any of the above enumerated officers or persons to bring such ship, vessel or boat into port, and to search and examine her cargo, and to examine the master on oath touching the cargo and voyage, and if there be any goods on board prohibited to be imported into the province, such ship, vessel or boat, and the cargo laden on board thereof, shall be forfeited; and if the said ship, vessel or boat shall be foreign, and not navigated according to the laws of Great Britain and Ireland, and shall have been found fishing or preparing to fish, or to have been fishing within such distance of such coasts, bays, creeks or harbors of this province, such ship, vessel or boat, and their respective cargoes, shall be forfeited; and if the master, or person in command thereof, shall not truly answer the questions which shall be demanded of him in such examination, he shall forfeit the sum of one hundred pounds.[a]

It will be observed that the preamble of the act recites as reasons for its adoption that no rules or regulations had been made under the third section of the British Act of June 14, 1819, heretofore quoted, and that "the said act does not designate the persons who are to make such seizure as aforesaid." In these two respects, the situation under the old act was changed by the new act so far as the coasts of Nova Scotia were concerned.

The first section of the act designates the persons authorized to carry out its provisions and relates to the treatment and seizure of foreign vessels in waters wherein the liberty of fishing was renounced by the United States under the treaty, and in the treatment of such vessels a notable distinction is drawn between vessels "within any port, bay, creek or harbor in this province" and vessels "hovering within three marine miles of any of the coasts, bays, creeks or harbors thereof." Although in either of these cases the persons designated to carry out the provisions of the act may board such vessel and freely stay on board "as long as she shall remain within such port or distance," it is provided in the case of the vessels found hovering that if they "be bound elsewhere, and shall continue so hovering for the space of twenty-four hours after the master shall have been required to depart, it shall be lawful for any of the above enumerated officers or persons to bring such ship, vessel or boat into port, and to search and examine her cargo, and to examine the master on oath touching the cargo and voyage, and if there be any goods on board prohibited to be imported into the province, such ship, vessel or boat, and the cargo laden on board thereof, shall be forfeited." In the case, however, of vessels found within a port, bay, creek or harbor, such provisions do not apply, and the seizure of such vessels was authorized only under the general provision authorizing the seizure of foreign vessels not navigated according to the laws of Great Britain and Ireland "found fishing or preparing to fish, or to have been fishing" within three marine miles of such coasts, bays, creeks or harbors.

---

[a] Appendix, pp. 119, 120.

The remaining sections of the act, from II to XVII inclusive, relate to judicial proceedings after seizure.

Sections II to VII direct the course to be taken in such proceedings by the courts and the government representatives and do not require special consideration here, further than to note the exceedingly significant provision in section IV giving the officer making the seizure half of the proceeds resulting from the condemnation and sale of the vessel seized.

Sections VIII to XVII relate to the rights of the claimants in such proceedings and impose upon them the most unusual and extraordinary disabilities.

Section VIII provides that in any dispute as to the legality of a seizure the burden of proof shall lie on the owner or claimant, so that the mere fact of seizure is made *prima facie* evidence that the vessel seized had committed an offense under the law.

Section X provides that no person may enter a claim for anything seized until he has given security in a penalty not exceeding sixty pounds for costs and in default of such security the vessel seized shall be adjudged forfeited and condemned.

Section XI provides, among other things, that no evidence can be produced by a claimant in a proceeding against the officer or person making the seizure unless notice of such evidence is given to such officer or person in writing thirty days before the writ, under which the proceedings are taken, is sued out against such officer or person, and, unless it is proved at the trial that the notice containing this and certain other information has been so served, judgment must be awarded against the claimant.

Section XII provides that every such action must be brought within three months after the cause thereof, and that if the claimant is nonsuited or judgment is awarded against him the defendant shall receive treble costs.

Section XIII provides that in any case where the judge or court grants a certificate of probable cause of seizure the claimant shall not be entitled to costs even if a verdict is found in his favor for the recovery of the vessel seized, nor shall the officer or person making the seizure be sued or prosecuted on account of such seizure; and in any case where a verdict is given against the defendant the claimant, in addition to recovering the thing seized, shall not be entitled to more than two pence damages, nor shall the defendant in any case be fined more than one shilling.

Section XIV provides that if the person making the seizure tenders amends to the claimant such tender may be pleaded in bar to any action; and if the jury finds the amends tendered sufficient, they shall give a verdict for the defendant and the defendant shall be entitled to costs.

Section XV provides that if the judge or court shall certify that the defendant acted upon probable cause the plaintiff shall not be entitled to more than two pence damages or to any costs.

Sections XVI and XVII fix the periods within which actions must be brought and appeals taken.

The purpose of these provisions of the act would seem to have been to deprive the owners of American vessels seized under it of the usual fair and impartial treatment, which is generally extended equally to all parties in courts of justice, and to discourage American fishermen from attempting to secure justice by judicial proceedings in that province. As these provisions of the act will speak for themselves they do not require further comment here. Attention is called, however, to the statements as to the effects of this act in a letter of June 15, 1839, from United States Consul Morrow to Lieutenant Governor Campbell[a] and in a letter of December 29, 1839, from Lieutenant Paine to Secretary of State Forsyth,[b] and it may be added that in almost every case of the condemnation of an American fishing vessel under this law such condemnation was obtained by default.

The final section of the act is as follows:

XVIII. And be it further enacted, That this act shall not go into force or be of any effect until His Majesty's assent shall be signified thereto, and an order made by his Majesty, in council that the clauses and provisions of this act shall be the rules, regulations and restrictions respecting the fisheries on the coasts, bays, creeks or harbors of the province of Nova Scotia.[c]

An order made by His Majesty in Council to the effect proposed in this section was adopted on July 6, 1836.[d] By such order in council, therefore, the provisions of the act were adopted as "the rules, regulations and restrictions respecting the fisheries on the coasts, bays, creeks or harbors of the province of Nova Scotia."

---

a Appendix, p. 416.   c Appendix, p. 123.
b Appendix, p. 451.   dAppendix, p. 116.

So far as these so-called rules, regulations, and restrictions are concerned, it will be remembered that the only authority found in the treaty for imposing any restrictions upon American fishermen is found in the last part of the renunciatory clause where provision is made for imposing in the waters wherein the liberty of fishing is renounced by the treaty "such restrictions as may be necessary to prevent them from taking, drying or curing fish therein, or in any other manner whatever abusing the privileges hereby reserved to them." It will also be remembered that under the treaty the American fishing vessels have the right of entering, for four specified purposes, the bays and harbors on the coasts where the right of fishing was renounced.

The act above referred to was in force until 1851, when it was substantially re-enacted by chapter 94 of the Nova Scotia Revised Statutes of that year.[a]

In the province of Prince Edward Island, an act was adopted on April 15, 1843, similar in all its essential features to the Nova Scotia act of 1836, but no attempt was ever made to enforce this act against American fishermen.[b]

In the province of New Brunswick, an act was adopted on May 3, 1853, which closely follows the provisions of the Nova Scotia act of 1836.[c]

These acts were all superseded by the act of the Dominion of Canada passed May 22, 1868, entitled "An act respecting fishing by foreign vessels."[d]

This entire series of acts grew out of the Nova Scotia act of 1836 on which they were modelled and, so far as they have any relation to the fisheries article of the treaty of 1818, it will be found that all the questions presented by them were discussed in the diplomatic correspondence between the United States and Great Britain following the objections raised in 1841 by the United States against the treatment to which American vessels were subjected by Nova Scotia under the provisions of the act of 1836, which correspondence is herein elsewhere reviewed.

It may be noted in passing, however, that section one of the act of the Dominion of Canada of May 22, 1868, authorized the Governor

---

[a] Appendix, p. 123.
[b] Appendix, p. 128.
[c] Appendix, p. 126.
[d] Appendix, p. 133.

General to grant to foreign vessels a license for a period not exceeding one year "to fish for or take, dry or cure any fish of any kind whatever, in British waters, within three marine miles of any of the coasts, bays, creeks or harbors whatever, of Canada, not included within the limits specified and described in the first article" of the treaty of 1818. This provision for licenses will be considered in reviewing the period following the date of this act.

The act was further amended by the acts of May 12 and April 14, 1870, but no material change was made in the original act so far as it relates to the questions presented in this Case until 1886 when an amendment was adopted on November 26th of that year authorizing, for the first time, the search and seizure of vessels "being within any harbor of Canada," in case such vessel "has entered such waters for any purpose not permitted by treaty or convention, or by any law of the United Kingdom or of Canada for the time being in force."

All the Newfoundland legislation with respect to the fisheries which was in force at this time or adopted later contained a proviso that nothing therein should affect the rights and privileges granted by tréaty, and so far as the rights of American fishermen under the treaty of 1818 are concerned no attempt was made to apply such legislation to them until a very recent period. Such legislation will be reviewed in its appropriate place.

United States Treasury Circular of January 21, 1836.

A note was written by the British Chargé at Washington to Mr. Forsyth, the Secretary of State, on January 6, 1836, calling his attention to complaints which had been preferred by the officers of customs at Quebec and Gaspé against fishermen of the United States "for encroaching on the limits of the British fisheries carried on in the river and gulf of St. Lawrence."[a] An examination of the complaints referred to, which were enclosed with this note, will show that the only actual encroachments specified in such complaints are those set forth as follows:

On a recent voyage in the custom-house boat, down the bay of Gaspé, I met three large schooners fishing for mackerel between the shores and the fishing barges, not two miles from land, and remonstrated with the master of one (the *Bethel*, of Provincetown.) They were all in the act of fishing, and although I advised the said

---

[a] Appendix, p. 407.

master to go off, he declined doing so, offering nothing in vindication but scurrilous contempt, and my means were inadequate to enforce any measures of redress.[a]

The Secretary of State replied to the British Chargé, on January 18, 1836, stating that although the case of the schooner *Bethel* was the only encroachment specifically mentioned—

the President, desirous of avoiding just ground of complaint on the part of the British government on this subject, and preventing the injury which might result to American fishermen from trespassing on the acknowledged British fishing grounds, has, without waiting for an examination of the general complaint, or into that respecting the *Bethel*, directed the Secretary of the Treasury to instruct the collectors to inform the masters, owners, and others engaged in the fisheries, that complaints have been made, and to enjoin upon those persons a strict observance of the limits assigned for taking, drying, and curing fish by the American fishermen, under the convention of 1818.[b]

Pursuant to the direction of the President as above stated, the Secretary of the Treasury issued, under date of January 21, 1836, the following circular letter of instructions:

Representations have been made to our government through the chargé d'affaires of his Britannic Majesty, of encroachments by the American fishermen upon the fishing-grounds secured exclusively to British fishermen by the convention between the United States and Great Britain, bearing date the 20th day of October, 1818.

The President, being desirous of avoiding any just cause of dissatisfaction on the part of the British government on this subject, and with a view of preventing the injury which might result to the American fishermen from trespassing upon the acknowledged British fishing-grounds, directs that you will inform the masters, owners, and others employed in the fisheries in your district, of the foregoing complaints; and that they be enjoined to observe strictly the limits assigned for taking, drying, and curing fish, by the fishermen of the United States, under the convention before stated.

In order that persons engaged in the fisheries may be furnished with the necessary information, the first article of the convention, containing the provision upon this subject, is annexed to this circular.[c]

Seizures in 1838–1840.

The only seizures of American fishing vessels which occurred during the period from 1836 to 1840 were made on the Nova Scotia coast in the years 1838, 1839, and 1840 under the Nova Scotia Act of 1836. It has already been shown that the only part of the treaty to which the provisions of this act related was the renunciatory clause, including the provision in respect of restrictions at the

---

[a] Appendix, p. 409. [b] Appendix, p. 410. [c] Appendix, p. 410.

end of that clause; and it will be found upon an examination of the circumstances surrounding these seizures that they were all made for offenses alleged to have occurred under this clause of the treaty and within three marine miles of the shore.

In 1838 two vessels are reported to have been seized: the *Hero* and the *Combine*. The former was seized in June of that year at Turney's Cove, Gut of Canso and the latter in November, about three quarters of a mile from the western shore of the Gut of Canso.[a]

In 1839 ten vessels were seized: the *Hart*, the *Magnolia* and the *Independence*, seized in May in Tusket Island Harbor; the *Java*, seized in June in Beaver Island Harbor; the *Eliza*, the *Battelle*, the *Hyder Ally* and the *Mayflower*, seized in June at Beaver Harbor; and the *Charles*, seized at Canso.[b]

As the result of an inquiry made on the part of the United States the Assistant Secretary of State, Mr. Vail, wrote to Mr. Fox, the British Chargé at Washington, on July 10, 1839, communicating to him information received by the Department showing that "some, at least, of those seizures were made for causes of a trivial character, and with a rigor not called for by circumstances," and he stated that his object in sending this communication was

to invoke your good offices in calling the attention of Her Majesty's provincial authorities to the ruinous consequences of those seizures to our fishermen, whatever may be the issue of the legal proceedings founded upon them, and to the consequent expediency of great caution and forbearance in future, in order that American citizens, not manifestly encroaching upon British rights, be not subjected to interruption in the lawful pursuit of their profession.[c]

On August 14th of the same year Mr. Vail made a report to the President, in obedience to his direction requiring him to report, among other things, the seizure of American fishing vessels on the coast of Nova Scotia and "the nature and circumstances of the cases which have been presented to this government by our citizens as infractions of right on the part of the British authorities." In this report, after referring to a statement made on June 18, 1839, by the United States Consular Agent at Yarmouth,[d] as containing the most detailed information in possession of the Department in relation to the "nature and circumstances of the cases," Mr. Vail says:

---

[a] Appendix, p. 412.
[b] Appendix, pp. 415, 419–423, 434, 1076, 1077.
[c] Appendix, p. 424.
[d] Appendix, pp. 430–434.

According to that statement, the *Independence* is alleged to have anchored in the Tusket islands, and, while there, hired her nets to an English fisherman, for the purpose of taking fish on shares. The crew state that they were forced to anchor there by stress of weather; and that their nets had been lent, and not hired, for which they had received a few herrings.

The *Magnolia* is charged with having been engaged in fishing while at anchor in the Tusket islands, and with the fact having been acknowledged by the crew. This is denied; and the reason alleged for anchoring within British grounds is, want of shelter, wood and water.

The charge against the *Java*, of having been engaged in taking fish in the Tusket islands, is admitted by the master.

Against the *Hart* is alleged that her crew were seen cleaning fish on board, while at anchor in the islands, and that her master had acknowledged that he had procured a quantity of herrings. The taking of fish is denied; and the fact of the crew having been seen cleaning fish is explained by stating that two barrels of herrings had been received from a British fisherman in recompense of services rendered.

On the 20th of July, a letter from the consul of the United States at Halifax, dated the 27th of June, was received at this department, informing it of the seizure of the four vessels above referred to, and of seven others, viz: the *"Shetland,"* seized at Whitehead, near Canso; the *"Charles,"* at Canso; the *"Mayflower,"* and a schooner, name unknown, at Guysborough; the *"Battelle,"* *"Hyder Ally,"* and *"Eliza,"* at Beaver harbor.

The *"Shetland"* was seized on the ground of the master having sold to a lad who came on board, while the vessel lay at anchor in the harbor of Whitehead, whither she had been forced by stormy weather, a pair of oil-cloth trousers, and small quantities of tea and tobacco. The master states that in doing so he yielded to the importunities of the lad, whom he believes to have been sent purposely to entrap him into an attempt at smuggling. He denies having caught fish within British limits.

With the exception of the *"Eliza,"* which was likewise compelled to make a harbor by bad weather, and the crew of which deny having taken fish within the British limits, or having sold or bartered any articles whatever, the particulars of the cases are not given; but in communications addressed by the consul to the Lieutenant Governor of Nova Scotia, asking his interference in behalf of the owners of the seized vessels, he urges the exercise of indulgence and mercy, on the ground that some of the sufferers had only erred in a slight degree either from ignorance or temptation, and without intention to violate regulations, of the existence of which they might, perhaps, never have heard.[a]

In closing his report on these seizures, Mr. Vail sums up the situation as follows:

From these statements it will appear that the only cases of seizure of which anything is known at the department, not being made on the coasts of Newfoundland or Labrador occurred at places in which,

a Appendix, p. 438.

under the convention of 1818, the United States had forever renounced the right of their vessels to take, dry and cure fish; retaining only the privilege of entering them for the purposes of shelter, repairs, purchasing wood and obtaining water, and no other.   In the absence of information of a character sufficiently precise to ascertain either, on the one side, the real motives which carried the American vessels into British harbors, or, on the other, the reasons which induced their seizure by British authorities, the department is unable to state whether, in the cases under consideration, there has been any flagrant infraction of the existing treaty stipulations.   The presumption is, that if, on the part of citizens of the United States, there has been a want of caution or care in the strict observance of those stipulations, there has been, on the other hand, an equal disregard of their spirit, and of the friendly relations which they were intended to promote and perpetuate, in the haste and indiscriminate rigor with which the British authorities have acted.[a]

The grounds assigned for the seizure of the *Mayflower*, *Battelle* and *Hyder Ally* are set forth in a report made by the Advocate General of Nova Scotia on June 20, 1839, as follows:

The three American schooners seized at Beaver harbor, by Mr. Darby, have been proceeded against by me as advocate general, and the examination duly taken; whereby it appears that the crews of two of them had actually fished with set nets in that harbor, and had taken fish on board therefrom on the night before the seizure; and this evidence is confirmed by the mate of one of those vessels, an American subject.   In the case of the third, which is one of those noticed by Mr. Morrow, the evidence at present is not so conclusive.[b]

In addition to the vessels mentioned in Mr. Vail's report several other American fishing vessels appear to have been subjected to interference and detention on the Nova Scotia coast during the year 1839; but as these were afterwards released, they do not require more than passing mention here, with two exceptions, the *Charles* and the *Amazon*. The *Charles* was seized in June, 1839, at Canso, although the alleged offense apparently occurred at the Magdalen Islands, which were outside of the jurisdiction of Nova Scotia.   It is reported in a letter to the Secretary of State from the United States Collector at Frenchman's Bay, dated July 15, 1839, that "the only pretense for this seizure was that the schooner was under cod-fishing license and had on board herrings".[c]   After being detained for about nineteen days she was discharged without any expenses under instructions for her release from the Attorney General of the province.[d]

---

a Appendix, p. 440.   c Appendix, pp. 417, 425.
b Appendix, p. 424.   d Appendix, pp. 423, 434.

The *Amazon* was seized in July, 1839, at the Gut of Canso, by the Collector of Light Dues. The facts surrounding the seizure as set forth in an affidavit sworn to by the master and crew of the vessel before the United States Consul at Pictou, Nova Scotia, were—

that the said vessel arrived at the Gut of Canso on the 4th day of July last, and came to anchor there at Steep Creek cove, for the purpose of procuring wood and water; that, on the next day, said appearers took on board said vessel two barrels of water, and two cords of wood; that, thereafter, said vessel remained at anchor there until the morning of Sunday, (the 7th,) on account of the weather being so very foggy that at no time during the said period could appearers discern objects at a distance of thirty or forty yards; that, on the morning of the said 7th, one Duncan McMillan came on board and seized the said vessel, and turned all the said appearers, except the master, on shore in a destitute condition; and the said appearers do severally most solemnly declare that there were no articles on board the said vessel when she left Gloucester aforesaid, but such as are usual and necessary for such voyages.[a]

After being detained about two weeks she was released under an order from the Attorney General of the province in which he states: "I cannot see any just ground for her longer detention".[b]

Several seizures of American vessels other than fishing vessels are reported to have been made on the Nova Scotia coast, which stand on a different footing from those above mentioned. The seizures referred to were apparently made for the purpose of enforcing the payment of light dues by American trading vessels passing through the Gut of Canso. Inasmuch as such seizures involve the question of the right of innocent passage through the Gut of Canso which, by express stipulation, is excluded from the questions submitted in this Case, it is unnecessary to review here the circumstances surrounding them. The only question presented for decision in this Case with respect to the imposition of light dues on this portion of the coast relates to the imposition of such dues on American fishing vessels exercising their treaty right of entering bays or harbors for shelter, repairs, wood or water, and it will be perceived that this question differs from that presented by the seizures above considered in that such vessels were not exercising a treaty right.

---

[a] Appendix, p. 445.   [b] Appendix, p. 446.

In the year 1840 a number of American vessels are reported to have been seized on the Nova Scotia coast, charged with offenses under the Act of 1836 alleged to have been committed within three miles of the shore, all of which vessels, however, appear to have been released, except two: the *Ocean* and the *Alms*. These two with one other, the *Pallas*, which was afterwards released, were the only cases reported to the Department of State at that time for diplomatic intervention.

According to the reports made by the United States Consul, the circumstances surrounding these three last mentioned seizures were briefly as follows:

The *Pallas* was seized on the 4th of August off the Highlands of Chetecam on the northwestern side of the Island of Cape Breton for fishing within three miles of the shore, it being assumed by the officer making the seizure that she was within that distance. The captain and crew, however, maintained that they were considerably more than a league from the shore, most of them estimating the distance to be four miles, and they denied that they had taken any fish within three miles of the shore.[a] The *Pallas* was released, but not until the captain had been subjected to heavy expenses.[b]

The *Ocean* was seized on August 31st while at anchor off Cheticamp Harbor, abreast of Friar Head, charged with fishing within two miles of the shore. Here again there was a dispute as to the distance of the vessel from shore, the master contending that she was six or seven miles distant therefrom and charging the officer who made the seizure with being drunk at the time and unable to judge the distance. Apparently the only fishing that had been done was by the cook who caught two mackerel and a cod-fish for the crew's breakfast.[c]

The *Alms* was seized on September 11th, while lying to, about two miles from land, where she had run in for shelter. She was charged with having been fishing there, although the captain maintained that no fish had been caught nearer the shore than seven miles.[d]

---

[a] Appendix, p. 455.　　　　　　　[c] Appendix, pp. 457, 1076, 1077.
[b] Appendix, p. 456.　　　　　　　[d] Appendix, pp. 457, 1076, 1078.

The situation in 1840.

It appears, therefore, from the foregoing review of the seizures made during this period that of the great number of American fishing vessels resorting annually to the Bay of Fundy and to other bays along the coast of Nova Scotia the only vessels seized for fishing in alleged violation of the treaty were those charged with fishing within three miles from the shore; and it will be perceived that in enforcing the Nova Scotia Act of 1836, as was the case under the British Act of 1819, the provisions relating to bays, as interpreted by the seizures made under them, were not regarded as authorizing seizures for fishing in bays except within three miles of the shore.

It must further be noted in this connection that all the seizures above reviewed were made under orders for the strict enforcement of the laws enacted for the purpose of protecting to the fullest extent the British fishing rights under the treaty of 1818 on the coasts where the United States had renounced the liberty of taking fish.

Such was the situation up to the end of the year 1839 when a hitherto unheard of interpretation of the treaty was proposed by Nova Scotia.

The desire of driving American fishermen away from their coasts altogether, and the opportunity of securing half the profits from seizures under the act of 1836 offered every inducement to the people of Nova Scotia for searching the treaty for some new meaning favorable to their purposes, and although it had never before been asserted, even as a possible interpretation of the renunciatory clause of the treaty, that American fishermen were not at liberty to fish in bays, as elsewhere on the coast, up to within three marine miles of the shore, such an interpretation was evolved and began to be advocated at this time. This new interpretation was not officially communicated to the United States by Great Britain until several years later, but rumors of its purpose and effect soon reached the United States, as will appear.

The situation at this time is presented with clearness and the developments to be expected in the near future are predicted with great foresight in a report made by Lieutenant Paine of the United States Navy under date of December 29, 1839, following an investigation made by him under the direction of the Secretary of State, from which report the following extract is taken:

I visited the seat of government of Nova Scotia, and that of Prince Edward's Island, and St. John's, the principal city of New Brunswick, where I communicated with the principal government officers, with our consuls, with Admiral Sir Thomas Harvey, and the commander of the British vessels of war with whom I met; as also with the collectors of Portland and Eastport, Maine, and such other persons as from their situations seemed qualified to impart information on the questions arising.

I had believed the vessels seized had been generally guilty of systematic violation of the revenue laws; but I was soon led to suspect that this was not the cause, so much as a pretence, for seizing.

A vessel once seized must be condemned, unless released as a favor; because the owners will not claim her under the present laws of Nova Scotia, where the only seizures have taken place.

The questions on which dispute may arise, are—

1st. The meaning of the word *bay*, in the convention of 1818, where the Americans relinquish the rights before claimed or exercised, of fishing in or upon any of the coasts, bays, &c., of her Britannic Majesty's provinces, not before described, nearer than three miles.

The authorities of Nova Scotia seem to claim a right to exclude Americans from all bays, including those large seas such as the Bay of Fundy and the Bay of Chaleurs; and also to draw a line from headland to headland; the Americans not to approach within three miles of this line.

The fishermen, on the contrary, believe they have a right to work anywhere, if not nearer than three miles to the land.

The orders of Admiral Sir Thomas Harvey, as he informed me, are only to prevent their fishing nearer than three miles.

According to this construction, Americans may fish in the Bay of Fundy, Bay of Chaleurs, and the Bay of Miramichi; while their right would be doubtful in Chedabucto Bay, and they would be prohibited in the other bays of Nova Scotia.

On that part of the coast of Newfoundland where the right of fishing is relinquished, there are several bays in which fisheries may be prosecuted at three or more miles from the land.

On that part of the coast of Newfoundland where the right of taking and curing fish is secured by the convention of 1818, it is to be feared that troubles may arise with the French, who assume an exclusive right, and who have gone so far as to drive off even English fishermen.

The right of fishing on the shores of the Magdalen islands, though sometimes questioned, seems so secured by the convention of 1818 that I think it unnecessary to lengthen this communication by further discussing it.

2d. The right of resorting to ports for shelter, and to procure wood and water. The provincial authorities claim a right to exclude vessels, unless in actual distress; and the subordinates, as well as the naval forces of her Majesty, warn, as they term it, vessels to depart, or order them to get under weigh and leave a harbor when they suppose a vessel has lain a reasonable time; but this is often done without examining or knowing much of the circumstances under which the vessel entered, or how long she has been in port.

The English men-of-war also endorse the papers of the fishermen as if they had violated the blockade, or committed some other illegal act.

The fishermen claim a right, under the convention, to resort to the ports for shelter whenever from rough weather, calms or fogs, they cannot prosecute, without risk or inconvenience, their labors at sea; and the navigation on some parts of the coast is, on account of the extraordinary tides, as perilous in calms and fogs as in rough weather.

The Nova Scotia courts would exact that American fishermen shall have been supplied, on leaving home, with wood and water for the cruise; but the Americans believe they can, by the terms of the convention, resort to the ports to procure wood and water at their convenience during the cruise; and they do not, on account of the inconvenience, as well as the high price, take on board either water-casks or wood for the whole cruise.

If the grounds assumed by the British provincial authorities be carried out, it will be in their power to drive the Americans from those parts of the coast where are some of the most valuable fisheries; whereas, if the ground maintained by the Americans be admitted, it will be difficult to prevent their procuring articles of convenience, and particularly bait; from which they are precluded by the convention, and which a party in the provinces seems resolved to prevent.

The questions will, I doubt not, ere long be brought to a crisis; and it seems probable that the vexatious course pursued towards the fishermen, with the object of fostering their own at the expense of our fisheries, and the care taken by the French to protect and encourage theirs, will tend to injure, perhaps destroy those of this country; a result to be deprecated in connexion with the navy, for there is no branch of commerce which supplies so large a portion of hardy and efficient seamen.

Although several of the vessels seized by authority of the province of Nova Scotia were afterwards released, the great expense incurred and the time they were detained made the injury to the owners nearly equal to a total loss.

The person who made the most of these seizures, (a Mr. Darby, who commands a chebacco boat, with ten or twelve men armed with muskets) is prompted, as well by his interest as by a certainty of impunity, to seize all he can find.

The law of this province, entitled William IV., chap. viii, 1836, which seems solely intended to persecute our fishermen, could only have been approved by orders in council through an oversight.

It is not possible that Great Britain intends, when the property of citizens of a nation in amity is seized on false pretences, or with no pretence, to force the lawful owner to give heavy bonds, liable to be forfeited, in addition to vessel and cargo, before he can claim his property.

To give a month's notice to the seizing officer; the notice to contain every thing intended to be proved against him, before a suit can be instituted; and, again, to prove that the notice has been given:

To force the owner to bring his action or claim within three
months—one of which is expended in thus giving notice, and the other
two may well expire, owing to the infrequency and uncertainty of
communications, before the distant owner can transfer funds and
give the requisite bonds to precede his suit, or lay claim to his illegally seized property, which property will thus be condemned by
default:

To force the owner, if he cannot prove the illegality of the seizure,
to pay treble costs:

To screen the officer seizing, by providing that, if the judge shall
say there was probable cause, he shall be liable to no prosecution;
the plaintiff only entitled to 2d. damages; the defendant only liable
to costs.

The whole of this act, and the proceedings on the subject, as
detailed in the journals of the assembly, display an unfriendly disposition towards Americans, or rather a determination to quarrel
or drive them from the exercise of rights secured by solemn treaty.

The injustice and annoyance suffered by the fishermen have so
irritated them, that there is ground to believe that violence will be
resorted to, unless some understanding be had before the next
season.[a]

PERIOD FROM 1841 TO 1854.

*Controversy arising from Nova Scotia's proposed interpretation of the
renunciatory clause of the treaty.*

As has been shown in reviewing the treatment of American fishermen by the Province of Nova Scotia up to this time, their treaty
right of entering the bays and harbors on the Nova Scotia coast for
shelter, repairs, wood, and water had been unwarrantably interfered
with, and in effect destroyed by the indiscriminate seizure of their
vessels by the provincial authorities for trivial offences alleged to
have been committed within three miles of the shore in violation of
the so-called "rules, regulations and restrictions respecting the
fisheries on the coasts, bays, creeks or harbors of the Province of
Nova Scotia" established under the Act of 1836.   Not content, however, with their efforts to prevent the American fishermen from exercising the treaty right referred to, the provincial authorities proceeded to devise a new and far reaching interpretation of the renunciatory clause of the treaty in order if possible to deprive the American

---

[a] Appendix, pp. 451–453.

fishermen of their right of fishing in the outer portions of the great bays or indentations of the Nova Scotia coast, in which the American fishermen had always claimed and exercised the right of fishing beyond the limit of three miles from the shore. The United States had never regarded the great bays or indentations on these coasts as "bays of His Britannic Majesty's Dominions" within the meaning of the treaty; and ever since the date of the treaty the American fishermen had freely and openly resorted to such bays for the purpose of fishing outside of the three mile limit from the shore. This practical interpretation of the effect of the treaty with respect to the great bays and indentations had always been acquiesced in by Great Britain, and no attempt had been made by the British Government to interpret the treaty otherwise, until the new interpretation about to be considered was brought forward, the first suggestion of which, it will be noted, originated not with the British Government but with the provincial authorities, who had taken no part in negotiating the treaty and were not even consulted about its provisions before it was entered into.

In further confirmation of Great Britain's assent to the practical effect of the treaty as understood by the United States at that time, attention is called to a statement made by Richard Rush, one of the American Plenipotentiaries who negotiated the treaty of 1818, in a letter written by him to the Secretary of State on July 18, 1853, in which, after mentioning the fact that he remained as American Minister at London for seven years after signing the treaty of 1818, he says:

Opportunities of complaint were therefore never wanting. If intimated to me, it would have been my duty to transmit at once every such communication to our government. Nor did I ever hear of complaint through the British Legation in Washington. It would have been natural to make objections when our misconstruction of the instrument was *fresh*, if we *did* misconstrue it. The occasion would have been especially opportune when I was subsequently engaged in extensive negotiations with England in 1823–4, which brought under consideration the whole relations, commercial and territorial, between the two countries including our entire intercourse by sea and land, with her North American colonies. Still, silence was never broken in the metropolitan atmosphere of London whilst I remained there. Your letter informs me that for more than twenty years after the convention, there was no serious attempt to exclude us from those large bays; and Mr. Everett, writing as Secretary of State, only on the 4th of December last to Mr. Ingersoll, minister in England, renders more definite the time you would indicate by saying, that, "it was just a *quarter of a century* after the date of the convention before the *first* American fisherman was captured for fishing at large in the Bay of Fundy!"   I find it difficult, under any lights at present before me, to explain the extraordinary circumstances which environ this international question, consistently with all that is due to the high party on the other side; feelings the most friendly being due to her from the magnitude of the interests bound up in the subsistence of relations the most harmonious at all points between the two countries, and which all ought to cherish and improve.

It is impossible for me to doubt that the convention as *we* now construe it, and have *always* construed it, was entirely acceptable to the British government *at the time of its adoption*.   But I remember also that other feelings were afloat at that epoch beyond the pale of the government in London.   The fishery article was sharply assailed out of doors.   Journals of prominence in the capital represented it as sacrificing high maritime interests of England, following up like sacrifices which they said had been made in the treaties of Vienna.   The Legislative Assembly and Council of Nova Scotia, sent forward murmurs deep and loud from that quarter. They alleged, that the prospects of British Colonial industry and advantage in North America were exposed to a shock in the competition which this fishery article opened up to the Americans.[a]

The novel interpretation, devised by Nova Scotia with respect to the meaning of the word "bays" was called to the attention of Mr. Forsyth, then Secretary of State, by the United States Consul at Pictou in his letter of November 25, 1840, in which he says, referring to certain documents enclosed, "these documents possess considerable interest but more particularly that part of the Assembly's interpretation of the Convention of 1818, by which it asserts that the prescribed distance of 'three marine miles' therein expressed, is to be measured from the *headlands* and not from the shores of the Provinces."   This seems to have been understood to mean that the "prescribed distance of three marine miles" should be measured from a line drawn between the headlands instead of following the indentations of the coast.

On the 20th of February following, the Secretary of State wrote to Mr. Stevenson, the American Minister in London, calling attention to this novel interpretation and to the proceedings of the authorities of Nova Scotia, which had taken place under the provincial Act of 1836, in relation to the seizures and interruptions of the American fishing vessels in the prosecution of the fisheries on the coasts of that Province, and instructed him to bring these matters to the notice of the British Government without

---

[a] Appendix, p. 555.

delay. Pursuant to these instructions, Mr. Stevenson wrote to Lord Palmerston on March 27, 1841, directing his attention to the proceedings of the provincial authorities, which he says "in the opinion of the American Government demand the prompt interposition of Her Majesty's Government." This note deals with the new interpretation proposed by Nova Scotia with respect to the meaning of the word "bays," and with the interference by the provincial authorities with American fishermen in the exercise of their right to enter the bays and harbors on that coast for the purpose of repairs, shelter, wood, and water, and with the attempt on the part of the provincial authorities to exclude American fishermen from innocent passage through the Gut of Canso. The provincial contention on this latter question having subsequently been abandoned and the question being, by express stipulation, excluded from the present Case, it is unnecessary to review it here, and all reference to it in the subsequent correspondence will be omitted. With respect to the other two questions above mentioned, Mr. Stevenson's note, after reciting the stipulations of Article I of the treaty of 1818, states the position of the United States as follows:

Such are the stipulations of the treaty, and they are believed to be too plain and explicit to leave room for doubt or misapprehension, or render the discussion of the respective rights of the two countries at this time necessary. Indeed it does not appear that any conflicting questions of right between them have as yet arisen out of differences of opinion regarding the true intent and meaning of the treaty. It appears, however, that in the actual application of the provisions of the convention, (committed on the part of Great Britain to the hands of subordinate agents, subject to and controlled by local legislation,) difficulties, growing out of individual acts, have unfortunately sprung up from time to time, among the most important of which have been recent seizures of American vessels for supposed violations of the treaty. These have been made, it is believed, under color of a provincial law of 6 William IV., chapter 8, 1836, passed doubtless with a view to restrict vigorously, if not intended to aim a fatal blow at the fisheries of the United States on the coasts of Newfoundland.

It also appears, from information recently received by the government of the United States, that the provincial authorities assume a right to exclude the vessels of the United States from all their bays, (even including those of Fundy and Chaleurs,) and likewise to prohibit their approach within three miles of a line drawn from headland to headland, instead of from the indents of the shores of the provinces. They also assert the right of excluding them from British ports, unless in actual distress; warning them to depart, or get under weigh and leave harbor, whenever the provincial custom-house or British naval officer shall suppose that they have remained a reasonable time; and this without a full examination of the circumstances under which they may have entered the port. Now, the fishermen of the United States believe (and it would seem that they are right in their opinion, if uniform practice is any evidence of correct construction,) that they can with propriety take fish any where on the coasts of the British provinces *if not nearer than three marine miles to land*, and have the right to resort to their ports for shelter, wood and water; nor has this claim, it is believed, ever been seriously disputed, based as it is on the plain and obvious terms of the convention. Indeed, the main object of the treaty was not only to secure to American fishermen, in the pursuit of their employment, the right of fishing, but likewise to insure to them as large a proportion of the conveniences afforded by the neighboring coasts of British settlements, as might be reconcilable with the just rights and interests of British settlements, and the due administration of her Majesty's dominions. The construction, therefore, which has been attempted to be put upon the stipulations of the treaty by the authorities of Nova Scotia, is directly in conflict with their object, and entirely subversive of the rights and interests of the citizens of the United States. It is one moreover, which would lead to the abandonment, to a great extent, of a highly important branch of American industry, which could not for a moment be admitted by the government of the United States. The undersigned has also been instructed to acquaint Lord Palmerston that the American government has received information that in the House of Assembly of Nova Scotia during the session of 1839–40, an address to her Majesty was voted, suggesting the extension to adjoining British colonies of rules and regulations relating to the fisheries, similar to those in actual operation in that province, and which have proved so onerous to the fishermen of the United States; and that efforts, it is understood, are still making to induce the other colonies to unite with Nova Scotia in this restrictive system. Some of the provisions of her code are of the most extraordinary character. Among these is one which declares that any foreign vessel *preparing* to fish within three miles of the coast of her Majesty's dominions in America shall, together with her cargo, be forfeited; that in all cases of seizure, the owner or claimant of the vessel, &c., shall be held to prove his innocence, or pay treble costs; that he shall be forced to try his action within three months, and give one month's notice at least to the seizing officer, containing everything intended to be proved against him, before any suit can be instituted; and also prove that the notice has been given. The seizing officer, moreover, is almost wholly irresponsible, inasmuch as he is liable to no prosecution if the judge certifies that there was probable cause; and the plaintiff, if successful in his suit, is only entitled to two pence damages without costs, and the defendant fined not more than one shilling. In short, some of these rules and regulations are violations of well established principles of the common law of England, and of the principles of the just laws of all civilized nations, and would seem to have been designed to enable her Majesty's authorities to seize and confiscate with impunity American vessels, and embezzle indiscriminately the property of American citizens employed in the fisheries on the coasts of the British provinces.[a]

---

[a] Appendix, pp. 463, 464.

Mr. Stevenson s note closes with the request—

that measures may be forthwith adopted by her Majesty's government to remedy the evils arising out of the misconstruction on the part of its provincial authorities of their conventional obligations, and prevent the possibility of the recurrence of similar acts.[a]

The course pursued by the British Government in dealing with the protest of the United States as expressed in Mr. Stevenson's note throws considerable light upon Great Britain's understanding of the true intent and meaning of the treaty provisions under which these questions arose. It will be found that instead of expressing any dissent or protest in answer to Mr. Stevenson's criticism of Nova Scotia's proposed interpretation of the treaty, Great Britain promptly referred his note to the Provincial Government with a request for a report on which to base its reply. This delay obviously would have been wholly unnecessary if the understanding of the British Government at that time as to the meaning of these treaty provisions had differed materially from that expressed by Mr. Stevenson. Moreover, as will appear in the later correspondence, after this report was received, the British Government still refrained from stating its position on the subject of Nova Scotia's novel interpretation of the meaning of the word "bays" in reply to Mr. Stevenson's inquiry until that question could be submitted to the Law Officers of the Crown for an opinion, and even after their opinion was rendered in support of the Nova Scotian construction, Great Britain showed a decided inclination to avoid the effect of such opinion by proposing a relaxation of the narrow construction recommended by it, and was only prevented from so doing by vigorous protests from Nova Scotia.[b] It will also appear from the subsequent correspondence that no answer whatever was made by Great Britain to the other question presented by Mr. Stevenson.

By note of April 2, 1841, Lord Palmerston acknowledged the receipt of Mr. Stevenson's note of March 27, 1841, and informed him that he had "lost no time in referring Mr. Stevenson's representation to the Secretary of State for the Colonial Department,"[a] and on the 28th of the same month he wrote again "to inform Mr. Stevenson that he has since received from the Colonial Department a letter informing him that copies of the papers received from Mr.

---

[a] Appendix, p. 465. [b] Infra, pp. 117, 118.

92909°—S. Doc. 870, 61–3, vol 1——15

Stevenson would be forwarded to Lord Falkland, with instructions to enquire into the allegations contained therein and to furnish a detailed report upon the subject."*   Lord Russell was at that time the Secretary of State for the Department referred to in Lord Palmerston's note, and on April 9, 1841, upon receipt of Mr. Stevenson's note, by reference from Lord Palmerston, he wrote to Lord Falkland, then Lieutenant Governor of Nova Scotia, transmitting a copy of Mr. Stevenson's note and requesting him to make immediate inquiry into the allegations contained therein, and to furnish "a detailed report on the subject, for the information of Her Majesty's Government."*

Nova Scotia's Case and the Opinion of the Crown Officers.

Meanwhile the House of Assembly of Nova Scotia had prepared "a case stated (raising the necessary questions as to the right of fishery which the people of these Colonies possess) for the purpose of being referred to the Crown Officers in England, in order that the existing treaties and the rights of these North American Provinces may be more strictly defined."*

This case was forwarded by Lord Falkland with his letter of April 28, 1841, to Lord Russell, in which letter he says—

I shall feel obliged by your Lordship's allowing the opinion of the Crown Officers to be taken on the said case, and I am authorized by the House of Assembly here to defray any expense that may be incurred in obtaining such opinion.*

This "case" after reciting the provisions of the fisheries articles of the treaties of 1783 and 1818, and making reference to the British Act of June 14, 1819 (59 Geo. III. Cap. 38), and the Nova Scotia Act of March 12, 1836 (6 William IV., Chap. 8), proceeds as follows:

Nova Scotia is indented with Bays, many of which reach from 60 to 100 miles into the interior, such as the Bay of Fundy, St. Mary's Bay, the Bras d'Or Lake, and Manchester Bay; the land on the shores is entirely British territory, and Nova Scotia proper is separated from the Island of Cape Breton by a narrow strait called the Gut of Canso, in some parts not wider than three quarters of a mile.   In the Bay of Fundy, St. Mary's Bay, and the Gut of Canso, Americans conduct the Fishery, and their Fishing vessels pass also through the latter, or anchor there, and not only fish, but by using bait, toll the mackerel into deep waters, thereby injuring the profitable Seine Fisheries of Fox Island and Crow Harbor, Arichat, St. Peter's Bay

---

a Appendix, p. 466.   *b* Appendix, p. 1043.   *c* Appendix, p. 1044.

and other stations in the neighborhood of Canso which formerly were the most productive Fisheries of Nova Scotia. They also land on the Magdalen Islands, set nets and sweep seines in the spring of the year, at a time when the Herrings resort to those waters to spawn, thereby destroying the spawn and young fish, and consequently ruining the Fishery.

The opinion of the Law Officers of the Crown in England is requested on the following points:

1st.—Whether the Treaty of 1783 was annulled by the War of 1812, and whether citizens of the United States possess any right of Fishery in the waters of the Lower Provinces other than ceded to them by the convention of 1818, and if so, what right. 2d.—Have American citizens the right under that Convention, to enter any of the Bays of this Province to take Fish; if after they have so entered they prosecute the Fishery more than three marine miles from the shores of such Bays; or should the prescribed distance of three marine miles be measured from the headlands, at the entrance of such Bays, so as to exclude them. 3d.—Is the distance of three marine miles to be computed from the indents of the coast of British America, or from the extreme headlands, and what is to be considered a headland. 4th.— Have American vessels, fitted out for a Fishery, a right to pass through the Gut of Canso, which they cannot do without coming within the prescribed limits, or to anchor there or to Fish there; and is casting bait to lure fish in the tract of the vessels fishing, within the meaning of the Convention. 5th.—Have American citizens a right to land on Magdalen Islands and conduct the Fishery from the shores thereof by using nets and seines; or what right of Fishery do they possess on the shores of those Islands and what is meant by the term shore. 6th.—Have American Fishermen the right to enter the Bays and Harbors of this Province for the purpose of purchasing wood or obtaining water, having provided neither of these articles at the commencement of their voyages, in their own countries; or have they the right of entering such Bays and Harbors in cases of distress, or to purchase wood and obtain water, after the usual stock of those articles for the voyage of such Fishing craft has been exhausted or destroyed. 7th.—Under existing Treaties, what rights of Fishery are ceded to the citizens of the United States of America, and what reserved for the exclusive enjoyment of British subjects.[a]

On August 30, 1841, the opinion of the Law Officers of the Crown was rendered, the text of which, omitting the introductory clauses, is as follows:

Query 1st.—In obedience to your Lordship's commands, we have taken these papers into consideration, and have the honor to report, that we are of opinion, that the Treaty of 1783 was annulled by the war of 1812; and we are also of opinion, that the rights of Fishery of the citizens of the United States must now be considered as defined and regulated by the Convention of 1818; and with respect to the general question "if so, what right", we can only refer to the terms of the convention, as explained and elucidated by the observations which will occur in answering the other specific queries.

---

[a] Appendix, p. 1045.

2d. **Except** within certain defined limits to which the query put to us does not apply, we are of opinion that by the terms of the Treaty, American citizens are excluded from the right of fishing within three miles of the Coast of British America, and that the prescribed distance of three miles is to be measured from the headlands or extreme points of land next the sea of the coast, or of the entrance of the Bays, and not from the interior of such Bays or Indents of the coast, and consequently that no right exists on the part of American citizens to enter the Bays of Nova Scotia there to take fish, although the fishing being within the Bay may be at a greater distance than three miles from the shore of the Bay, *as we are of opinion the term headland is used in the Treaty* to express the part of land we have before mentioned, excluding the interior of the Bays and the indents of the coast.

4th. By the treaty of 1818 it is agreed that American citizens should have the liberty of fishing in the Gulf of St. Lawrence, within certain defined limits, in common with British subjects; and such treaty does not contain any words negativing the right to navigate the passage or Gut of Canso, and therefore it may be conceded that such right of navigation is not taken away by that Convention; but we have now attentively considered the course of navigation to the Gulf, by Cape Breton, and likewise the capacity and situation of the passage of Canso, and of the British Dominions on either side, and we are of opinion that, independently of Treaty, no Foreign country has the right to use or navigate the passage of Canso; and attending to the terms of the convention relating to the liberty of Fishery to be enjoyed by the Americans, we are also of opinion that that convention did not either expressly or by implication, concede any such right of using or navigating the passage in question. We are also of opinion that casting bait to lure Fish in the track of any American vessels navigating the passage, would constitute a fishing within the negative terms of the convention.

5th. With reference to the claim of a right to land on the Magdalen Islands, and to fish from the shores thereof, it must be observed, that by the Treaty, the liberty of drying and curing Fish (purposes which could only be accomplished by landing) in any of the unsettled Bays, etc., of southern part of Newfoundland, and of the coast of Labrador is specifically provided for; but such liberty is distinctly negatived in any settled Bay, etc., and it must therefore be inferred, that if the liberty of landing on the shores of the Magdalen Islands had been intended to be conceded, such an important concession would have been the subject of express stipulation, and would necessarily have been accompanied with a description of the inland extent of the shore over which such liberty was to be exercised, and whether in settled or unsettled parts, but neither of these important particulars are provided for, even by implication, and that, among other considerations leads us to the conclusion that American citizens have no right to land or conduct the Fishery from the shores of the Magdalen Islands. The word "shore" does not appear to be used in the Convention in any other than the general or ordinary sense of the word, and must be construed with reference to the liberty to be exercised upon it, and would therefore comprise the land covered with water, as far as could be available for the due enjoyment of the liberty granted.

6th. By the Convention, the liberty of entering the Bays and Harbors of Nova Scotia for the purpose of purchasing wood and obtaining water, is conceded in general terms, unrestricted by any condition expressed or implied, limiting it to vessels duly provided at the commencement of the voyage; and we are of opinion that no such condition can be attached to the enjoyment of the liberty.

7th. The rights of Fishery ceded to the citizens of the United States and those reserved for the exclusive enjoyment of British subjects, depend altogether upon the Convention of 1818, the only existing Treaty on this subject between the two countries, and the material points arising thereon have been specifically answered in our replies to the preceding Queries.

We have, etc.,

(Signed)   J. DODSON,
THOS. WILDE.[a]

This opinion was never officially communicated to the United States Government, but some ten years later, having been published at Halifax, it came to the attention of Mr. Everett, then Secretary of State, who as American Minister at London during the controversy on the questions under consideration, having succeeded Mr. Stevenson in 1843, was entitled to speak with authority on the subject, and he then took occasion to comment on it as follows:

Now, neither the term "headland", nor anything equivalent or synonymous, occurs in the convention of 1818; and this legal authority, which, no doubt, was mainly instrumental in leading the home government to adopt the colonial construction of the treaty, rests in this respect, upon an imaginary basis. The law officers of the Crown appear to have mistaken a sentence in the ex parte case made up at Halifax, in which the word "headland" appears for a part of the treaty between the United States and Great Britain, which they were required to expound. The government of the United States cannot but regret that an official opinion which had the effect of reversing the construction of the convention on which Great Britain had acted from 1818 to 1842, which excluded our fishermen from some of the best fishing-ground, after the undisturbed enjoyment of a quarter of a century, and finally brought the countries to the verge of a deplorable collision, should have been given by the law officers of the Crown without a more careful perusal of the text of the treaty.[b]

In connection with the restrictions imposed by the province of Nova Scotia upon the treaty right of American fishermen to enter the bays and harbors of that coast for shelter, repairs, wood, and water, to which Mr. Stevenson particularly called Lord Palmerston's

---

[a] Appendix, p. 1047.

It will be noted that the paragraphs of the opinion are numbered to correspond with the numbers of the questions in the "case" to which they refer, and that the reprint of this opinion found in the Journal of the Legislative Assembly of Nova Scotia does not contain a 3d paragraph, but whether or not the opinion as originally rendered contained a 3d paragraph specifically answering the 3d question does not appear.

[b] Appendix, p. 540.

attention in his note of March 27, 1841, and upon which, as above stated, the British Government never expressed their views in reply to Mr. Stevenson's note, attention is particularly directed to the 6th paragraph of the opinion, which holds that under the treaty this right "is conceded in general terms, unrestricted by any condition expressed or implied, limiting it to vessels duly provided at the commencement of the voyage; and we are of opinion that no such condition can be attached to the enjoyment of the liberty."

The opinion of the Law Officers was withheld from the Colonial Government by the British Government until November 28, 1842, when Lord Stanley forwarded it to Lord Falkland at Halifax with a letter of that date in which he says—

I enclose for your information a copy of the Report, which on the 30th August was received from the Queen's Advocate and Her Majesty's Attorney General, on the case drawn up by Your Lordship; since that date the subject has frequently engaged the attention of myself and my colleagues, with the view of adopting further measures if necessary, for the protection of British interest in accordance with the law as laid down in the enclosed Report. We have, however, on full consideration come to the conclusion, as regards the Fisheries of Nova Scotia, that the precautions taken by the Provincial Legislature appear adequate to the purpose, and that being now practically acquiesced in by the Americans, no further measures are required.[a]

Inasmuch as Great Britain had not as yet replied to Mr. Stevenson's protest against the adoption of Nova Scotia's proposed "headland theory" and the United States had not been informed of the opinion on the subject rendered by the Law Officers of the Crown, Lord Stanley's statement that the precautions taken by the Provincial Government were "now practically acquiesced in by the Americans" was a wholly unwarranted assumption on his part, and neither then nor subsequently was it justified by the facts.

Seizure of the Washington and the Argus.

Upon the strength of the Crown Officers' opinion sustaining the "headland theory" interpretation and regardless of the unfinished state of the negotiations on the subject between Great Britain and the United States, the provincial authorities of Nova Scotia proceeded to put the new interpretation into practical operation, and on the 10th of May, 1843, an officer of the provincial customs service

---

[a] Appendix, p. 1046.

seized the American fishing schooner *Washington* while engaged in fishing in the Bay of Fundy at a place ten miles distant from the coast of Nova Scotia.[a]

Pursuant to instructions dated June 30, 1843, from Mr. Upshur, Secretary of State, to Mr. Everett, then American Minister at London, the seizure of the *Washington* and the failure of Great Britain to reply to Mr. Stevenson's note of March 27, 1841, were called to the attention of Lord Aberdeen, Secretary of State for Foreign Affairs, on August 10, 1843, by Mr. Everett in his note of that date, from which the following extract is taken:

From the construction attempted to be placed, on former occasions, upon the first article of the treaty of 1818, by the colonial authorities, the undersigned supposes that the "*Washington*" was seized because she was found fishing in the Bay of Fundy, and on the ground that the lines within which American vessels are forbidden to fish, are to run from headland to headland, and not to follow the shore. It is plain, however, that neither the words nor the spirit of the convention admits of any such construction; nor, it is believed, was it set up by the provincial authorities for several years after the negotiation of that instrument. A glance at the map will show Lord Aberdeen that there is, perhaps, no part of the great extent of the seacoasts of her Majesty's possessions in America, in which the right of an American vessel to fish can be subject to less doubt than that in which the "*Washington*" was seized.

For a full statement of the nature of the complaints which have, from time to time, been made by the government of the United States against the proceedings of the colonial authorities of Great Britain, the undersigned invites the attention of Lord Aberdeen to a note of Mr. Stevenson addressed to Lord Palmerston on the 27th March, 1841. The receipt of this note was acknowledged by Lord Palmerston on the 2d of April, and Mr. Stevenson was informed that the subject was referred by his lordship to the Secretary of State for the colonial department.

On the 28th of the same month Mr. Stevenson was further informed by Lord Palmerston, that he had received a letter from the colonial department, acquainting his lordship that Mr. Stevenson's communication would be forwarded to Lord Falkland with instructions to inquire into the allegations contained therein, and to furnish a detailed report upon the subject. The undersigned does not find on the files of this legation any further communication from Lord Palmerston in reply to Mr. Stevenson's letter of the 27th March, 1841, and he believes that letter still remains unanswered.

In reference to the case of the *Washington* and those of a similar nature which have formerly occurred, the undersigned cannot but remark upon the impropriety of the conduct of the colonial authorities in undertaking, without directions from her Majesty's government, to set up a new construction of a treaty between the United

---

[a] Appendix, p. 474.

States and England, and in proceeding to act upon it by the forcible seizure of American vessels.[a]

After a lapse of eight months, during which Mr. Everett's note had been referred to the Colonial Office, and by it to the Governor of Nova Scotia, "the result of those references" was communicated to Mr. Everett by Lord Aberdeen in his note of April 15, 1844, from which the following extract is taken:

The words of the treaty of October, 1818, article 1, run thus: "And the United States hereby renounce forever any liberty heretofore enjoyed or claimed by the inhabitants thereof, to take, dry, or cure fish, on or within three marine miles of any of the coasts, bays, creeks or harbors of his Britannic Majesty's dominions in America, not included within the above mentioned limits, (that is, Newfoundland, Labrador, and other parts separate from Nova Scotia;) provided, however, that the American fishermen shall be admitted to enter such bays or harbors for the purpose of shelter," &c.

It is thus clearly provided that American fishermen shall not take fish within three marine miles of any bay of Nova Scotia, &c. If the treaty was intended to stipulate simply that American fishermen should not take fish within three miles of the coast of Nova Scotia, &c., there was no occasion for using the word "bay" at all. But the proviso at the end of the article shows that the word "bay" was used designedly; for it is expressly stated in that proviso, that under certain circumstances the American fishermen may enter *bays*, by which it is evidently meant that they may, under those circumstances, pass the sea-line which forms the entrance of the bay. The undersigned apprehends that this construction will be admitted by Mr. Everett.

That the *Washington* was found fishing within the Bay of Fundy is, the undersigned believes, an admitted fact, and she was seized accordingly.[b]

Mr. Everett replied to Lord Aberdeen on May 25, 1844, stating that, although the immediate occasion of his previous note was the seizure of the *Washington*, it contained a reference to the correspondence between Mr. Stevenson and Lord Palmerston on the subject of former complaints made by the United States against the manner in which the American fishing vessels "had in several ways been interfered with by the provincial authorities in contravention, as is believed, of the treaty of October, 1818", and as no answer had as yet been returned to Mr. Stevenson's note of March 27, 1841, and, as Lord Aberdeen's answer to Mr. Everett's last note was confined exclusively to the case of the *Washington*, it, therefore, became necessary "again to invite his lordship's attention to the correspondence above referred to between Mr. Stevenson and Lord Palmerston and to request that inquiry may be made, without unnecessary delay, into

---

[a] Appendix, p. 475.   [b] Appendix, p. 478.

all the causes of complaint which have been made by the American Government against the improper interference of the British colonial authorities with the fishing vessels of the United States." [a]

Mr. Everett further stated in this note the position of the United States with reference to the case of the *Washington*, and the questions presented thereby as follows:

In reference to the case of the *Washington*, Lord Aberdeen, in his note of the 15th of April, justifies her seizure by an armed provincial vessel, on the assumed fact that, as she was found fishing in the Bay of Fundy, she was within the limits from which the fishing vessels of the United States are excluded by the provisions of the convention between the two countries of October, 1818.

The undersigned had remarked in his note of the 10th of August last, on the impropriety of the conduct of the colonial authorities in proceeding in reference to a question of construction of a treaty pending between the two countries, to decide the question in their own favor, and in virtue of that decision to order the capture of the vessels of a friendly State. A summary exercise of power of this kind, the undersigned is sure would never be resorted to by her Majesty's government, except in an extreme case, while a negotiation was in train on the point at issue. Such a procedure on the part of a local colonial authority is of course highly objectionable, and the undersigned cannot but again invite the attention of Lord Aberdeen to this view of the subject.

With respect to the main question of the right of American vessels to fish within the acknowledged limits of the Bay of Fundy, it is necessary, for a clear understanding of the case, to go back to the treaty of 1783.

By this treaty it was provided that the citizens of the United States should be allowed "to take fish of every kind on such part of the coast of Newfoundland as British fishermen shall use, (but not to dry or cure the same on that island) and also on the coasts, bays and creeks of all other of his Britannic Majesty's dominions in America, and that the American fishermen shall have liberty to dry and cure fish in any of the unsettled bays, harbors and creeks of Nova Scotia, Magdalen Islands and Labrador, so long as the same shall remain unsettled; but so soon as the same or either of them shall be settled, it shall not be lawful for the said fishermen to dry or cure fish at such settlement without previous agreement for that purpose with the inhabitants, proprietors or possessors of that ground."

These privileges and conditions were in reference to a country of which a considerable portion was then unsettled, likely to be attended with differences of opinion as to what should, in the progress of time, be accounted a settlement from which American fishermen might be excluded. These differences in fact arose, and by the year 1818 the state of things was so far changed that her Majesty's government thought it necessary in negotiating the convention of that year, entirely to except the province of Nova Scotia from the number of the places which might be frequented by Americans as

---

being in part unsettled, and to provide that the fishermen of the United States should not pursue their occupation within three miles of the shores, bays, creeks and harbors of that and other parts of her·Majesty's possessions similarly situated. The privilege reserved to American fishermen by the treaty of 1783, of taking fish in all the waters and drying them on all the unsettled portions of the coast of these possessions was accordingly by the convention of 1818 restricted as follows:—

"The United States hereby renounce forever any liberty heretofore enjoyed or claimed by the inhabitants thereof, to take, dry, or cure fish on or within three marine miles of any of the coasts, bays, creeks, or harbors of his Britannic Majesty's dominions in America, not included within the above mentioned limits; provided, however, that the American fishermen shall be admitted to enter such bays or harbors for the purpose of sheltering and repairing damages therein, of purchasing wood, and of obtaining water, and for no other purpose whatever."

The existing doubt as to the construction of the provision arises from the fact that a broad arm of the sea runs up to the northeast between the provinces of New Brunswick and Nova Scotia. This arm of the sea being commonly called the Bay of Fundy, though not in reality possessing all the characters usually implied by the term "bay," has of late years been claimed by the provincial authorities of Nova Scotia to be included among "the coasts, bays, creeks and harbors" forbidden to American fishermen.

An examination of the map is sufficient to show the doubtful nature of this construction. It was notoriously the object of the article of the treaty in question to put an end to the difficulties which had grown out of the operations of the fishermen from the United States along the coasts and upon the shores of the settled portions of the country, and for that purpose to remove their vessels to a distance not exceeding three miles from the same. In estimating this distance, the undersigned admits it to be the intent of the treaty, as it is itself reasonable, to have regard to the general line of the coast; and to consider its bays, creeks and harbors, that is, the indentation usually so accounted, as included within that line. But the undersigned cannot admit it to be reasonable, instead of thus following the general directions of the coast, to draw a line from the southwestern-most point of Nova Scotia to the termination of the northeastern boundary between the United States and New Brunswick, and to consider the arms of the sea which will thus be cut off, and which cannot, on that line be less than sixty miles wide, as one of the bays on the coast from which American vessels are excluded. By this interpretation the fishermen of the United States would be shut out from the waters distant, not three, but thirty miles from any part of the colonial coast. The undersigned cannot perceive that any assignable object of the restriction imposed by the convention of 1818 on the fishing privilege accorded to the citizens of the United States by the treaty of 1783 requires such a latitude of construction.

It is obvious that (by the terms of the treaty) the furthest distance to which fishing vessels of the United States are obliged to hold themselves from the colonial coasts and bays, is three miles. But, owing to the peculiar configuration of these coasts, there is a succession of bays indenting the shores both of New Brunswick and Novia Scotia, within the Bay of Fundy. The vessels of the United States have a general right to approach all the bays in her Majesty's colonial dominions, within any distance not less than three miles—a privilege from the enjoyment of which they will be wholly excluded—in this part of the coast, if the broad arm of the sea which flows up between New Brunswick and Nova Scotia, is itself to be considered one of the forbidden bays.

Lastly—and this consideration seems to put the matter beyond doubt—the construction set up by her Majesty's colonial authorities, would altogether nullify another, and that a most important stipulation of the treaty, about which there is no controversy, viz: the privilege reserved to American fishing vessels of taking shelter and repairing damages in the bays within which they are forbidden to fish. There is, of course, no shelter nor means of repairing damages for a vessel entering the Bay of Fundy, in itself considered. It is necessary, before relief or succor of any kind can be had, to traverse that broad arm of the sea and reach the bays and harbors, properly so called, which indent the coast, and which are no doubt the bays and harbors referred to in the convention of 1818. The privilege of entering the latter in extremity of weather, reserved by the treaty, is of the utmost importance. It enables the fisherman, whose equipage is always very slender (that of the *Washington* was four men all told) to pursue his laborious occupation with comparative safety, in the assurance that in one of the sudden and dangerous changes of weather so frequent and so terrible on this iron bound coast, he can take shelter in a neighboring and friendly port. To forbid him to approach within thirty miles of that port, except for shelter in extremity of weather, is to forbid him to resort there for that purpose. It is keeping him at such a distance at sea as wholly to destroy the value of the privilege expressly reserved.

In fact it would follow, if the construction contended for by the British colonial authorities were sustained, that two entirely different limitations would exist in reference to the right of shelter reserved to American vessels on the shores of her Majesty's colonial possessions. They would be allowed to fish within three miles of the place of shelter along the greater part of the coast; while in reference to the entire extent of shore within the Bay of Fundy, they would be wholly prohibited from fishing along the coast, and would be kept at a distance of twenty or thirty miles from any place of refuge in case of extremity. There are certainly no obvious principles which render such a construction probable.

The undersigned flatters himself that these considerations will go far to satisfy Lord Aberdeen of the correctness of the American understanding of the words "Bay of Fundy," arguing on the terms of the treaties of 1783 and 1818. When it is admitted that, as the undersigned is advised, there has been no attempt till late years to give them any other construction than that for which the American government now contends, the point would seem to be placed beyond doubt.

Meantime Lord Aberdeen will allow that this is a question, however doubtful, to be settled exclusively by her Majesty's government and that of the United States. No disposition has been evinced by the latter to anticipate the decision of the question; and the undersigned must again represent it to the Earl of Aberdeen as a matter of just complaint and surprise on the part of his government, that the opposite course has been pursued by her Majesty's colonial authorities, who have proceeded (the undersigned is confident without instructions from London,) to capture and detain an American vessel on a construction of the treaty which is a matter of discussion between the two governments, and while the undersigned is actually awaiting a communication on the subject promised to his predecessor.[a]

On August 6, 1844, and before a reply had been made by Lord Aberdeen to Mr. Everett's last note, the American fishing schooner *Argus* was seized by the Nova Scotia revenue cutter *Sylph*, while fishing off the coast of Cape Breton at a distance, as reported by the master of the vessel, of not less than fifteen miles from land and "more than three miles to the eastward of a line drawn from the headlands of Cow Bay to Cape North, a distance of fifty miles." [b] The officer making this seizure reported as his reason for making it "that when in command of the *Sylph* on the 6th of August last, then cruizing around the coast of Cape Breton, I discovered the *Argus* some miles off St. Anne's with her crew actually employed fishing; and although more than three miles from any land, still much within the bay that is formed by a straight line drawn from Cape North to the northern head of Cow Bay, and consequently I felt it my duty to take her into Sydney."[c]

Some complaints were made in connection with this seizure of harsh treatment on the part of the captors, which do not require examination here; and, so far as the seizure involved the question of the interpretation of the meaning of the word "bays" in the treaty, Mr. Everett stated, in bringing the case to the attention of Lord Aberdeen in his note of October 9, 1844, that "the undersigned deems it unnecessary, on this occasion, to add anything to the observations contained in his note to Lord Aberdeen, of the 25th, of May on the subject of limitation of the right secured to American fishing vessels by the treaty of 1783 and the convention of 1818 in reply to the note of his lordship of the 15th of April on the same subject."[d]

Lord Aberdeen's reply to Mr. Everett's note of May 25, 1844, is dated March 10, 1845, and makes no reference to any of the questions called to his attention by Mr. Everett, except those presented

---

a Appendix, p. 479.
b Appendix, p. 483.
c Appendix, p. 494.
d Appendix, p. 486.

by the seizure of the *Washington*, with respect to which the position of the British Government is stated as follows:

Her Majesty's government must still maintain, and in this view they are fortified by high legal authority, that the Bay of Fundy is rightfully claimed by Great Britain as a bay within the meaning of the treaty of 1818. And they equally maintain the position which was laid down in the note of the undersigned, dated the 15th of April last, that, with regard to the other bays on the British American coasts, no United States' fisherman has, under that convention, the right to fish within three miles of the entrance of such bays as designated by a line drawn from headland to headland at that entrance.

But while her Majesty's government still feel themselves bound to maintain these positions as a matter of right, they are nevertheless not insensible to the advantages which would accrue to both countries from a relaxation of the exercise of that right; to the United States as conferring a material benefit on their fishing trade; and to Great Britain and the United States, conjointly and equally, by the removal of a fertile source of disagreement between them.

Her Majesty's government are also anxious, at the same time that they uphold the just claims of the British crown, to evince by every reasonable concession their desire to act liberally and amicably towards the United States.

The undersigned has accordingly much pleasure in announcing to Mr. Everett, the determination to which her Majesty's government have come to relax in favor of the United States fishermen that right which Great Britain has hitherto exercised, of excluding those fishermen from the British portion of the Bay of Fundy, and they are prepared to direct their colonial authorities to allow henceforward the United States fishermen to pursue their avocations in any part of the Bay of Fundy, provided they do not approach except in the cases specified in the treaty of 1818, within three miles of the entrance of any bay on the coast of Nova Scotia or New Brunswick.[a]

On the same day Lord Aberdeen also wrote to Mr. Everett in reply to his note of October 9, 1844, on the seizure of the *Argus* in regard to which he says:

As the point of the construction of the convention of 1818 with reference to the rights of fishing on the coasts of the Anglo-American dependencies, by citizens of the United States, is treated in another note of the undersigned of this day's date, relative to the case of the *Washington*, the undersigned abstains from again touching upon that subject, and will confine himself in this note to the point of the harsh treatment of the patron and crew of the *Argus* by the commander of the Nova Scotia revenue cruiser *Sylph*, which is alleged in Mr. Everett's note of the 9th of October and its enclosures.[b]

In acknowledging the receipt of these two notes Mr. Everett says in his note of March 25, 1845, to Lord Aberdeen:

---

[a] Appendix, p. 489. [b] Appendix, p. 490.

While he desires, however, without reserve, to express his sense of the amicable disposition evinced by her Majesty's government on this occasion in relaxing in favor of the United States the exercise of what, after deliberate reconsideration, fortified by high legal authority, is deemed an unquestioned right of her Majesty's government, the undersigned would be unfaithful to his duty did he omit to remark to Lord Aberdeen that no arguments have at any time been adduced to shake the confidence of the government of the United States in their own construction of the treaty. While they have ever been prepared to admit, that in the letter of one expression of that instrument there is some reason for claiming a right to exclude United States fishermen from the Bay of Fundy, (it being difficult to deny to that arm of the sea the name of "bay" which long geographical usage has assigned to it,) they have ever strenuously maintained that it is only on their own construction of the entire article that its known design in reference to the regulation of the fisheries admits of being carried into effect.

The undersigned does not make this observation for the sake of detracting from the liberality evinced by her Majesty's government in relaxing from what they regard as their right; but it would be placing his own government in a false position to accept as mere favor that for which they have so long and strenuously contended as due to them under the convention.

It becomes the more necessary to make this observation, in consequence of some doubts as to the extent of the proposed relaxation.[a]

Mr. Everett then points out the similarity between the *Washington* and the *Argus* cases, and after referring to the paragraph above quoted from Lord Aberdeen's note on the *Argus* case to the effect that the views set forth in his note on the *Washington* case are applicable to the questions presented by the *Argus* case, Mr. Everett goes on to say:

This expression taken by itself would seem to authorize the expectation that the waters where these two vessels respectively were captured would be held subject to the same principles, whether of restriction or relaxation, as indeed all the considerations which occur to the undersigned as having probably led her Majesty's government to the relaxation in reference to the Bay of Fundy, exist in full and even superior in reference to the waters on the northeastern coast of Cape Breton, where the "*Argus*" was seized. But if her Majesty's provincial authorities are permitted to regard as a "bay" any portion of the sea which can be cut off by a direct line connecting two points of the coast, however destitute in other respects of the character usually implied by that name, not only will the waters on the north-eastern coast of Cape Breton, but on many other parts of the shores of the Anglo-American dependencies where such exclusion has not yet been thought of, be prohibited to American fishermen. In fact, the waters which wash the entire south-eastern coast of Nova Scotia, from Cape Sable to Cape Canso, a distance on a straight line

---

[a] Appendix, p. 498.

of rather less than three hundred miles, would in this way constitute a bay from which United States fishermen would be excluded.

The undersigned, however, forbears to dwell on this subject, being far from certain, on a comparison of all that is said in the two notes of Lord Aberdeen of the 10th instant, as to the relaxation proposed by her Majesty's government, that it is not intended to embrace the waters of the northeastern coasts of Cape Breton, as well as the Bay of Fundy.[a]

This correspondence was closed by Lord Aberdeen's note of April 21, 1845, informing Mr. Everett that his note of March 25, 1845, had been brought "under the consideration of Her Majesty's Secretary of State for the Colonies" and that his reply to its contents, therefore, would be postponed "until he shall become acquainted with the results of that reference," but he adds:

In the meantime, however, the undersigned thinks it expedient to guard himself against the assumption of Mr. Everett, that it may have been his intention by his note of the 10th ultimo, to include other bays on the coasts of the British North American provinces, in the relaxation which he therein notified to Mr. Everett, as to be applied henceforward to the Bay of Fundy. That note was intended to refer to the Bay of Fundy alone.[b]

In reporting this correspondence to the Secretary of State Mr. Everett says, in his despatch of April 23, 1845, that Lord Aberdeen's previous note of March 10, 1845, had left some uncertainty as to whether the relaxation referred to was intended to be confined to the Bay of Fundy or to extend to other portions of the coast, and that in answering that note he was careful to point out to Lord Aberdeen that all the reasons for admitting the right of Americans to fish in the Bay of Fundy applied to the waters where the *Argus* was captured and with superior force, inasmuch as they were less land-locked than the Bay of Fundy, and he adds that "the merits of the question are so clear that I cannot but anticipate that the decision of the Colonial Office will be in favor of a liberal construction of the convention."[c]

Mr. Everett's expectation, as expressed in this despatch, that the decision of the Colonial Office would be in favor of a liberal construction of the treaty proved to be well founded, for the Governor of Nova Scotia was officially informed by a letter dated May 19, 1845 that, after mature deliberation, Her Majesty's Government deemed it advisable for the interests of both countries to relax the strict rule

---

[a] Appendix, pp. 499–500. [b] Appendix, p. 505. [c] Appendix, p. 506.

of exclusion exercised by Great Britain over the fishing vessels of the
United States, entering the bays of the sea on the British North
American Coast.[a]

On account of vigorous opposition from Nova Scotia, however,
nothing further was done by the British Government toward relaxation at that time.   The positions taken, as above indicated, by Great
Britain and Nova Scotia on this subject are discussed in the following
extract from a despatch sent on December 4, 1852 by Mr. Everett,
then Secretary of State, to Mr. Ingersoll, the American Minister at
London, with reference to this question, which at that time was again
under consideration:

Nothing is more certain than that this precise question was under
the consideration of Her Majesty's government at this time, in consequence of my complaints. This I shall prove by an authority
which Lord Malmesbury will admit to be decisive.

On the 19th May, 1845, just four weeks after Lord Aberdeen
informed me that my letters of the 25th of March and 2d of April
had been referred to the Colonial Office, Lord Stanley (now the Earl
of Derby, and at that time Secretary of State for the Colonies) wrote
a despatch to Viscount Falkland, governor of Nova Scotia, of which
the following is an extract:

"Her Majesty's government, having frequently had before them
the complaints of the minister of the United States in this country,
on account of the capture of vessels belonging to fishermen of the
United States by the provincial cruisers of Nova Scotia and New
Brunswick, for alleged infractions of the convention of the 20th of
October, 1818, between Great Britain and the United States, I have
to acquaint your lordship that, after mature deliberation, her
Majesty's government deem it advisable, for the interests of both
countries, to relax the strict rule of exclusion over the fishing-vessels
of the United States entering the bays of the sea on the British North
American coasts."

    *   *   *   *   *   *   *

"I have to request that your Lordship will inform me whether you
have any objections to offer, on provincial or other grounds, to the
proposed relaxation of the construction of the treaty of 1818 between
this country and the United States."

The above is all of this important despatch which the colonial
authorities have thought proper to publish. The only cases of capture of our fishermen, of which I had specifically complained, were
those of the "Washington" and "Argus;" and the above letter of
Lord Stanley, of course, demonstrates that I gave the American public no "incorrect view" when I led them, by my letter of 26th
April, 1845, to suppose that on my instance her Majesty's government had under consideration, at that time, the question of extending
to the other outer bays the relaxation which had taken place in
reference to the Bay of Fundy.

---

[a] Appendix, pp. 537–538

Not only so, but it would seem that my representations had been successful; for whereas on the 21st of April Lord Aberdeen informed me that the relaxation announced in his note of the 10th of March was intended to apply to the Bay of Fundy alone, Lord Stanley, four weeks afterwards, as we have just seen, wrote to Lord Falkland that her Majesty's government, after mature deliberation, deemed it advisable, for the interests of both countries to extend the relaxation to the other bays.

The omission of a portion—and that, no doubt, the most important and significant portion—of Lord Stanley's despatch, as published at Halifax, puts it out of my power to quote from it his own words, as to the extent of the proposed relaxation. It appears, however, sufficiently, from the report of Mr. Attorney General Johnston of the 16th June, 1845, that the intention of the imperial government was to admit American fishermen into all bays, creeks, and inlets of which the entrance is more than six miles wide. I cite a passage from the concluding portion of Mr. Attorney General's letter:

"It is hoped, my lord, that if an arrangement such as is contemplated should unhappily be made, its terms may clearly express that the American fishermen are to be excluded from fishing within three miles of the entrance of the bays, creeks, and inlets into which they are not to be permitted to enter.

"Some doubt on this point rests on the language of Lord Stanley's despatch; and the making the criterion of the restricted bays, creeks, and inlets to be the width of the double of the three marine miles would strengthen the doubt, by raising the presumption that the shores of these bays, &c., and the shores of the general coast, were to be considered in the same light, and treated on the same footing."

An extract from another despatch of Lord Stanley, of the 17th of September, will also show that it was intended to admit the American fishermen into all the outer bays of certain dimensions, as it will also unhappily show the cause why that liberal policy was abandoned which had been adopted, as Lord Stanley, in his letter of the 19th of May, 1845, had stated, with great justice, "for the interests of both countries."

"Her Majesty's government have attentively considered the representations contained in your despatches of 17th of June and 2d of July, respecting the policy of granting permission to the fishermen of the United States to fish in the Bay of Chaleurs, and other large bays of a similar character on the coasts of New Brunswick and Nova Scotia, and apprehending from your statements that any such general concession would be injurious to the interests of the British North American provinces, we have abandoned the intention we had entertained on the subject, and shall adhere to the strict letter of the treaties which exist between Great Britain and the United States, relative to the fisheries in North America, except in so far as they may relate to the Bay of Fundy, which has been thrown open to the Americans under certain restrictions."

You will be able to judge from these authorities whether my letter of the 26th of April, 1845, is justly chargeable with having misled the American public as to the fact that the farther relaxation of the exclusion of our fishermen from the great bays had been at my instance referred to the Colonial Office, and to the consideration of her Majesty's government. Should the entire despatch from Lord

Stanley to Lord Falkland, of the 19th May, 1845, ever be published, I apprehend that it will not only still more plainly show this, which is apparent from the fragment of it that has appeared at Halifax, but also that the reasonableness of the American argument had been practically recognised by her Majesty's government.[a]

Great Britain's attempt to harmonize, if possible, the differences between the two Governments on the questions which had arisen up to this time under the treaty, by relaxing the strict construction with respect to bays, so far as the Bay of Fundy was concerned, was supplemented by the suggestion that counter concessions to British trade should be made on the part of the United States, and negotiations subsequently undertaken along the lines of this suggestion ultimately led to the settlement of the fisheries question for the time being by the mutual extension of trade and fisheries concessions under the reciprocity treaty of 1854.

In Lord Aberdeen's note of March 10, 1845, to Mr. Everett, communicating to him the proposed relaxation of the construction adopted by Great Britain with respect to bays, he opens the question of reciprocal concessions as follows:

In thus communicating to Mr. Everett the liberal intentions of her Majesty's government, the undersigned desires to call Mr. Everett's attention to the fact that the produce of the Labor of the British colonial fishermen is at the present moment excluded by prohibitory duties on the part of the United States from the markets of that country; and the undersigned would submit to Mr. Everett that the moment at which the British government are making a liberal concession to United States' trade might well be deemed favorable for a counter concession on the part of the United States to British trade, by the reduction of the duties which operate so prejudicially to the interests of the British colonial fishermen.[b]

Mr. Everett informed Lord Aberdeen in his note of March 25, 1845, that he was "without instructions which enable him to make any definite reply to this suggestion," and the suggestion was not carried further at that time for the reason no doubt that Great Britain's intention of proposing a further relaxation of the strict construction with respect to all the other bays was prevented by the opposition of Nova Scotia.

---

[a] Appendix, pp. 537–539.   [b] Appendix, p. 489.

Conditions immediately preceding the Reciprocity Treaty of 1854.

The questions presented in this Case do not require an examination either of the causes which brought about or the steps which led up to the adoption of the Reciprocity Treaty of 1854. It will be sufficient for the purposes of the present discussion to note that as a result of the repeal by Great Britain of the corn duties in 1846 and of the adoption in that year and in the following years of other free trade legislation, which threw open the British markets to the world, the trade relations between the British North American Colonies and the United States began to develop along new and more important lines. In May, 1846, the Canadian Parliament adopted an address to the Queen, asking that negotiations be undertaken with the United States with a view to arranging for the reciprocal admission into the United States and Canada of the products of those countries upon equal terms, and in December of that year the British Minister, Mr. Pakenham, took up the subject with the United States Government.[a]

The fisheries dispute was not directly involved in these negotiations, but the British colonies urged that the United States should remit the tariff duties on their fish, proposing in exchange for such remission to admit the American fishermen to all the coast fisheries from which they were excluded under the treaty of 1818.

This plan of settlement met with very decided opposition in the United States for several years, and while the subject was still under consideration an incident occurred which led to some further discussion of the British position on the "bays" question, and requires brief attention here.

On July 5, 1852, Mr. Crampton, the British Chargé at Washington, wrote to Mr. Webster, the Secretary of State, referring to complaints which had been made of encroachments by American and French fishing vessels upon the fishing grounds reserved to Great Britain by the treaty of 1818, and informed him that—

Urgent representations having been addressed to her Majesty's government by the governors of the British North American provinces in regard to these encroachments, whereby the colonial fisheries are most seriously prejudiced, directions have been given by the lords of her Majesty's admiralty for stationing off New Brunswick, Nova Scotia, Prince Edward's Island, and in the Gulf of St. Law-

[a] Appendix, pp. 1049–1055.

rence, such a force of small sailing vessels and steamers as shall be deemed sufficient to prevent the infraction of the treaty.[a]

At the same time a circular letter under date of May 26, 1852, addressed by Sir John Packington, Secretary of State for the Colonies, to the Governors of the several North American Colonies, was brought to Mr. Webster's attention, in which letter it was stated—

Her Majesty's Ministers are desirous of removing all grounds of complaint on the part of the colonies, in consequence of the encroachments of the fishing vessels of the United States upon those waters, from which they are excluded by the terms of the Convention of 1818, and they therefore intend to despatch, as soon as possible, a small naval force of steamers or other small vessels, to enforce the observance of that Convention.[b]

This letter also expressed a disinclination on the part of the British Government to prevent the colonies from adopting legislation for promoting the fisheries by means of bounties, and in it occurred the expression "and especially pending the negotiation with the United States of America for the settlement of the principles on which the commerce with the British North American Colonies is hereafter to be carried on."[b]

The information thus received led Mr. Webster to believe that the British Government proposed to change its former policy and attempt to apply the Nova Scotia construction of the meaning of the word "bays" to the Bay of Fundy and to the other bays on the provincial coasts as well. This view was shared by the President and all the members of the Cabinet,[c] and under date of July 6, 1852, Mr. Webster, who had left Washington on the previous day, prepared at his home in Massachusetts a public letter which was given out for publication on July 19th, and appeared in a Boston newspaper on that date. In this letter Mr. Webster states that "with the recent change of Ministry in England has occurred an entire change of policy," and after quoting from the Packington circular, and enumerating the British and Colonial armed vessels which were to compose the fleet to be sent out to seize the American vessels, and reciting and commenting on the provisions of the renunciatory clause of the treaty of 1818, and referring to the construction adopted by the Law Officers of the Crown as to the meaning of the word "bays" as used in that treaty, he concludes the letter as follows:

---

[a] Appendix, p. 506.   [b] Appendix, p. 508.   [c] Appendix, p. 543.

It is this construction of the intent and meaning of the Convention of 1818, for which the colonies have contended since 1841, and which they have desired should be enforced. This, the English Government has now, it would appear, consented to do, and the immediate effect will be, the loss of the valuable fall fishing to American fishermen; a complete interruption of the extensive fishing business of New England, attended by constant collisions of the most unpleasant and exciting character, which may end in the destruction of human life, in the involvement of the Government in questions of a very serious nature, threatening the peace of the two countries. Not agreeing that the construction thus put upon the treaty is conformable to the intentions of the contracting parties, this information is, however, made public to the end that those concerned in the American fisheries may perceive how the case at present stands, and be upon their guard. The whole subject will engage the immediate attention of the Government.[a]

The publication of this letter by Mr. Webster was made the occasion by Lord Malmesbury, then the Secretary of State for Foreign Affairs, for requesting an interview with Mr. Lawrence, the American Minister at London, which interview was held on August 7, 1852, and was reported to Mr. Webster by Mr. Lawrence in his despatch of August 10th of that year. In reporting this interview Mr. Lawrence writes that Lord Malmesbury said, among other things—

That this question was not understood in the United States; that Mr. Webster had sent for Mr. Crampton to come to Boston; that the British government did not intend to assert any new principle, but only to protect the rights of the colonists in the fisheries, which had been neglected by their predecessors; that what had been done, had been done at the urgent request of the colonists themselves; that the concessions made by Lord Aberdeen, of the right to fish in the Bay of Fundy, were fully recognized by the present government, and would not be withdrawn; that an armed force was sent there at this time to keep the American fishermen *three miles from the British shores*, in accordance with the provisions of the convention of 1818; that the orders were the same, both with respect to the French and the American fishermen; and finally, that her Majesty's government did not intend, by sending an armed force into those waters, to give offence either to the government or to the people of the United States; the sole object being to maintain the neglected rights of the colonists.[b]

The following extract from the same despatch will show in part Mr. Lawrence's report of the views expressed by him:

I said that I deeply regretted the course taken by her Majesty's government; that the sending of nineteen armed vessels, without notice, to those waters, (as stated in the provincial journals,) appeared to be a hostile movement, and one that could not but produce

---

unpleasant results; that courtesy demanded that after the right of fishing had been claimed and exercised for thirty years, (whether rightfully or wrongfully,) such notice should be given to the government of the United States as would enable it to seasonably proclaim to all concerned the intentions of the British government. I further stated that this measure taken at this time, when the whole American fishing-fleet was upon the provincial coast, would appear to have been intended (whether really so or not) to coerce the United States into a system of trade which, it is well known, the provinces have long sought for. I further stated that I was personally in favor of a comprehensive and reciprocal system of trade between the United States and the British North American provinces; but that a measure of so much importance, involving so various interests, could not be matured and executed without allowing time. I said that this whole question was at present receiving much attention, not only in the provinces, but in all the States of the Union; that a committee of the House of Representatives had it under consideration, and that I had understood that they were about to report a bill, or at least to make a report. If wisely arranged, I said that I thought the measure would prove conducive to the interests of both countries; and I could not but regret still more that the apparently hostile attitude of her Majesty's ministers would retard its adoption. I said that under all the circumstances I could not but think that this apparent measure of coercion was hastily adopted, and without that deliberation and forethought which had usually characterized the proceedings of British statesmen, and which was becoming a nation acting towards those with whom they were in a state of amicable peace, if not friendship even. I felt, therefore, I added, that under all the circumstances a mistake had been committed in ordering a fleet to those waters, and that I hoped the instructions to the several authorities in the provinces and to the admiral, would be so far modified as to open the way to a final and equitable settlement of the question.

With this the interview of the 7th terminated.[a]

On August 10, 1852, three days after this interview, Lord Malmesbury wrote to Mr. Crampton at Washington, with reference to the publication of Mr. Webster's letter, instructing him to inform Mr. Webster that "Her Majesty's government must necessarily entertain the sincerest regret that such a publication should have been made without what appears to her Majesty's government, sufficient inquiry into the circumstances of the case," and explaining "how greatly this question of the protection of British fisheries has been misunderstood and misinterpreted in the United States," and after reviewing the situation he says, in repetition of what Mr. Lawrence had already reported that he said to him—

Her Majesty's government, so far from having any intention of now excluding American fishermen from the Bay of Fundy, are pre-

---

a Appendix, pp. 517, 518.

pared to maintain that the relaxation granted in 1845 *was reasonable and just, and should be adhered to;* and, in giving orders to strengthen the naval force employed to maintain the exercise of our rights under the treaty of 1818, they could not contemplate that the government of the United States would assume that a relaxation formally granted, as regards the Bay of Fundy, was thereby cancelled, without the equally formal notice which her Majesty's government would undoubtedly feel themselves bound to have given to an ally of the British Crown, had such an act been intended.[a]

He further says that it was not "with any view to disturb arrangements made in good faith with the United States government, that Her Majesty's government issued orders to their officers to put a stop to illicit proceedings—proceedings which are not merely contrary to treaty, but which are mixed up with smuggling transactions damaging to British interests."[a] The following statement made by Lord Malmesbury in this letter is also of interest:

As I propose that this despatch shall merely explain away certain points which have clearly been misunderstood, I shall abstain for the present from entering into a discussion upon the interpretation to be given to the term "bay"; and upon this part of the subject I will only add that her Majesty's government intended to leave the matter precisely where it was left in 1845 by the governments of Great Britain and the United States—namely, that the relaxation as to bays applied, as is stated in Lord Aberdeen's note to Mr. Everett of the 21st of April, 1845, "to the Bay of Fundy alone"—any further discussion of that question being as a matter of negotiation between the two governments.[b]

Three days later, on the 13th of the same month, Lord Malmesbury wrote to Mr. Lawrence on the same subject as follows:

The orders that are to go out to our admiral, and of which I have given Mr. Crampton notice, are—

Not to interfere with the Magdalen islands.

To consider the Bay of Fundy on the same footing as we placed it in 1845.

To capture American fishing vessels only under precisely [the] same circumstances as those which would have been acted upon of late years, and when manifestly infringing the treaty.

To exercise these instructions with the greatest forbearance and moderation.[c]

It appears from Mr. Lawrence's despatch to Mr. Webster, dated August 13, 1852, that at the request of Lord Malmesbury, he had held a further interview with him two days before, and as a result of that interview, Mr. Lawrence reported as follows:

Lord Malmesbury will probably propose to leave that part of the treaty about which we disagree, for the present, just where it has been,

---

[a] Appendix, p. 520.   [b] Appendix, p. 521.   [c] Appendix, p. 522.

and will direct the British authorities to confine their exertions to within three marine miles of the shore, to exercise their power with great leniency, and not to make captures except under flagrant circumstances. He wishes to place the question in position to be adjusted, if possible, when the present excitement has passed away. Whatever may be the views of the colonists, the government here has every desire to settle the whole matter. They have committed an error which I think they wish to repair as soon as possible.[a]

This view was confirmed by the character of the orders which were actually issued, for they proved to be even less stringent than Lord Malmesbury had reported, as will appear from the following incident:

On August 23, 1852, Vice-Admiral Seymour, in command of the British vessels at the North Atlantic station, wrote to the Lieutenant Governor of Nova Scotia, enclosing a copy of statements of American fishermen as to notices given them by the commanders of the provincial vessels employed for the protection of the fisheries, respecting the limits within which they were allowed to fish, which statements were as follows:

1. R. W. Armistead, Master of the United States schooner *Angenora*, of Frankfort, states about the 27th of July, he went on board the *Responsible*, and was informed by her Commander, that if he found him fishing within three marine miles of a line drawn from Cape Gaspé to North Point of Prince Edward's he would seize his vessel.

2. Stephen Morey, master of the U. S. schooner *R. Roster*, of Deer Island, stated that he went on board "*Halifax*" laying in McNair's Cove, Gut of Canso, about the 23rd of July, and was informed by the Commander of that vessel, that his orders were to draw a line from Port Hood to the East Point of P. E. Island, thence to the North Point of P. E. Island, thence to Birch Point on Mission Island, and that he would seize any vessels that he found fishing within three marine miles of that line.

3. William Page, Master of the U. S. schooner *Paragon*, of Newburyport, stated to Mr. Sutton, that on or about the 23rd of July he was informed by the Commander of the Schr. *Responsible* that he should draw a line from headland to headland on any part of the coast of Nova Scotia, and seize any vessel that he found fishing within three marine miles of such a line.

4. Stephen Randall, Master of the U. S. Schr. *Montezuma*, states that on or about 20th July, whilst laying in Pirates Cove, Gut of Canso, he met the Master of the *Halifax*, (James Laybold), who informed him that he was not allowed to fish within three marine miles of a line drawn from the North Cape to Cape Gaspé, and that he would seize his vessel if he found him fishing within that distance of that line.

---

[a] Appendix, p. 523.

Several other Masters of American vessels corroborated these statements, but I did not think it necessary to take the particulars.[a]

Admiral Seymour adds in his letter enclosing these statements:

I am not aware of the lines therein described having been sanctioned by authority.

By direction of the Lieutenant Governor of Nova Scotia, the Provincial Secretary wrote on August 26, 1852, to, Captain Laybold and Captain Dodd of the Provincial Revenue cutters *Halifax* and *Responsible*, calling their attention to these statements and asking them to furnish without delay "such explanation as will enable the Lieutenant Governor to judge how far the conversations which are made matter of complaint, have been accurately reported," and adding: "In the meantime you will take care to detain no vessel which is not found trespassing within *three miles of land*."[b]

Before this official inquiry had reached Captain Dodd of the *Responsible*, it appears that the statements referred to had already been called to his attention by the Admiral, and on August 29, 1852, he wrote to the Provincial Secretary denying the responsibility for any of the statements except that reported to have been made by William Page, with respect to which he says:

The assertion of William Page, Master of the Schooner *Paragon*, may be correct, for I did to several American Captains (and he may have been one of them) say, that I should draw a line from the headlands of the Coast and Bays of Cape Breton, and seize all American Vessels found trespassing within three marine miles of such line; and such are my intentions until further orders, as I consider myself bound to do so by my instructions, in which I am referred to the Convention of 1818; and as it would be great presumption in me to attempt to put any construction on that Treaty, I feel myself bound by the opinions of the Queen's Advocate, and Her Majesty's Attorney General, given in 1841; and also by the result of the trial of the American Schooner *Argus*, which vessel was seized by me within a line drawn from Cow Bay Head to Long Point, near Cape North, Cape Breton, and condemned.[c]

The Provincial Secretary's official communication having subsequently reached him, he again wrote on September 1, 1852, receding from his earlier position and stating in submission to his official instructions, that "the orders not to detain vessels unless found trespassing *within three miles of land* shall be strictly attended to."[d]

The other captain replied on September 1, 1852, denying all responsibility for the statements referred to.

---

[a] Appendix, p. 1078.
[b] Appendix, p. 1080.
[c] Appendix, p. 1081.
[d] Appendix, p. 1082.

No further correspondence seems to have been exchanged with reference to Mr. Webster's misunderstanding of Lord Malmesbury's intentions, but the President in his annual message to Congress, dated December 6, 1852, calls attention to the incident and the situation out of which it arose, and makes the following statement with reference to the settlement of the fisheries question in connection with the pending reciprocity negotiations:

These circumstances, and the incidents above alluded to, have led me to think the moment favorable for a reconsideration of the entire subject of the fisheries on the coasts of the British provinces with a view to place them upon a more liberal footing of reciprocal privilege. A willingness to meet us in some arrangement of this kind is understood to exist, on the part of Great Britain, with a desire on her part to include in one comprehensive settlement as well this subject as the commercial intercourse between the United States and the British provinces. I have thought that, whatever arrangements may be made on these two subjects, it is expedient that they should be embraced in separate conventions. The illness and death of the late Secretary of State prevented the commencement of the contemplated negotiation. Pains have been taken to collect the information required for the details of such an arrangement. The subject is attended with considerable difficulty. If it is found practicable to come to an agreement mutually acceptable to the two parties, conventions may be concluded in the course of the present winter. The control of Congress over all the provisions of such an arrangement, affecting the revenue, will of course be reserved.[a]

Mr. Webster's interpretation of "bays".

Before passing from the consideration of Mr. Webster's public letter of July 6, 1852, a misapprehension, which has arisen on the part of Great Britain with respect to Mr. Webster's interpretation of the meaning of the word "bays" as used in the treaty, requires correction.

This question came up for discussion in the proceedings before the Halifax Commission under the treaty of 1871, and much reliance was placed by Great Britain on the following statement in Mr. Webster's letter as supporting the "headland theory":

It would appear that by a strict and rigid construction of this article, fishing vessels of the United States are precluded from entering into the bays or harbors of the British provinces, except for the purposes of shelter, repairing damages, and obtaining wood and water. A bay, as is usually understood, is an arm or recess of the sea, entering from the ocean between capes or headlands; and the term is applied equally to small and large tracts of water thus situated. It is common to speak of Hudson's Bay, or the Bay of Biscay, although they are very large tracts of water.

---

[a] Appendix, p. 545.

The British authorities insist that England has a right to draw a line from headland to headland, and to capture all American fishermen who may follow their pursuits inside of that line.   It was undoubtedly an oversight in the Convention of 1818, to make so large a concession to England, since the United States had usually considered that those vast inlets or recesses of the ocean ought to be open to American fishermen, as freely as the sea itself, to within three marine miles of the shore.[a]

That this is not a statement of Mr. Webster's opinion of the true intent and meaning of the treaty is evident from his use of the word "oversight" which is clearly intended to apply to the employment of language inaccurately expressing the understanding of the parties, and in fact at the end of the letter, in a paragraph which is generally suppressed when the paragraph above quoted is made use of, he distinctly states his dissent from the "headland theory" interpretation as follows:

Not agreeing that the construction thus put upon the treaty is conformable to the intention of the contracting parties, this information is, however, made public to the end that those concerned in the American fisheries may perceive how the case at present stands and be upon their guard.[a]

Mr. Webster's letter taken as a whole and considered in the light of the surrounding circumstances cannot fairly be understood as expressing an opinion in support of the British contention, and there was certainly no misapprehension on this point on the part of Great Britain at the time the letter was written, for it will be remembered that Lord Malmesbury, in commenting on the publication of the letter, said, in his note of August 10, 1852 to Mr. Crampton, "her Majesty's government must necessarily entertain the sincerest regret that such a publication should have been made" etc.[b]

It may be assumed that if Mr. Webster's letter had been regarded as expressing an opinion in support of the British contention, no regret at its publication would have been entertained by the British Government.

Furthermore the opinion held by Mr. Webster at that time as to the meaning of the word "bays" as used in the treaty, is set forth with great clearness and force in a memorandum prepared by him in July, 1852, to be sent to Mr. Crampton, but which unfortunately was never sent owing to Mr. Webster's failing health and untimely death before it was completed.   This memorandum shows an exhaust-

---

[a] Appendix, p. 510.   [b] Appendix, p. 519.

ive study of the entire history of the fisheries controversy, and in it
Mr. Webster reaches the conclusion that the term "bays" as used in
the renunciatory clause means the inner bays in distinction from
the outer part of the great indentations of the coast.[a]

It will be found that Mr. Webster's views are in accord with those
of Mr. Rush, one of the American Plenipotentiaries who negotiated
the treaty, as will appear from an examination of several statements published by Mr. Rush on the subject, one of which was written on July 18, 1853, to Mr. Marcy, then Secretary of State, in response to a request for his views on the subject, and in this he says,
referring to the treaty of 1818—

> In signing it, we believed that we retained the right of fishing in
> the sea, whether called a bay, gulf, or by whatever other term des-
> ignated, that washed any part of the coast of the British North
> American Provinces, with the simple exception that we did not come
> *within a marine league* of the shore.   We had this right by the law
> of nations.   Its confirmation was in the treaty of :83.   We retained
> it undiminished, unless we gave it up by the first article of the con-
> vention of 1818.   This we did not do.   The article warrants no such
> construction.[b]

Mr. Rush's statements on this subject, coming as they do from
the highest possible authority upon the true intent and meaning of
the renunciatory clause as understood at the time the treaty was
made, are entitled to careful consideration and are printed in full
in the Appendix to this Case.[c]

*The decision of the Claims Commission of 1853 in the Washington and
Argus cases.*

Under the Claims Convention of February 8, 1853, between the
United States and Great Britain, claims for damages for the seizures
of the *Washington* and the *Argus* were submitted for decision to the
Joint Commission established by that convention for the settlement
of claims, and on the disagreement of the commissioners both of these
cases were decided in favor of the claimant by the umpire, Mr. Joshua
Bates, who sustained in all respects the contentions of the United
States as to the true intent and meaning of the word "bays" as used
in the treaty of 1818.   The full text of these decisions is given below:

---

[a] Appendix, pp. 524–533.   [b] Appendix, p. 554.   [c] Appendix, pp. 549–557.

The Washington case—Decision of Bates, Umpire.

The schooner Washington was seized by the revenue schooner Julia, Captain Darby, while fishing in the Bay of Fundy, ten miles from the shore, on the 10th of May, 1843, on the charge of violating the treaty of 1818. She was carried to Yarmouth, Nova Scotia, and there decreed to be forfeited to the crown by the judge of the vice admiralty court, and with her stores ordered to be sold. The owners of the Washington claim for the value of the vessel and appurtenances, outfits and damages, $2,483, and for eleven years interest $1,638, amounted together to $4,121. By the recent reciprocity treaty, happily concluded between the United States and Great Britain, there seems no chance for any future disputes in regard to the fisheries. It is to be regretted, that in that treaty, provision was not made for settling a few small claims of no importance in a pecuniary sense, which were then existing, but as they have not been settled, they are now brought before this commission.

The Washington fishing schooner was seized, as before stated, in the Bay of Fundy, ten miles from the shore, off Annapolis, Nova Scotia.

It will be seen by the treaty of 1783, between Great Britain and the United States, that the citizens of the latter, in common with the subjects of the former, enjoyed the right to *take* and *cure* fish on the shores of all parts of Her Majesty's dominions in America, used by British fishermen; but not to dry fish on the island of Newfoundland, which latter privilege was confined to the shores of Nova Scotia in the following words: "And American fishermen shall have liberty to dry and cure fish on any of the unsettled bays, harbors and creeks of Nova Scotia, but as soon as said shores shall become settled, it shall not be lawful to dry or cure fish at such settlement, without a previous agreement for that purpose with the inhabitants, proprietors, or possessors of the ground."

The treaty of 1818 contains the following stipulations in relation to the fishery: "Whereas, differences have arisen respecting the liberty claimed by the United States to *take, dry,* and *cure fish* on certain *coasts, bays, harbors, and creeks* of his Britannic Majesty's dominions *in America,* it is agreed that the inhabitants of the United States shall have, in common with the subjects of his Britannic Majesty, the liberty to fish on certain portions of the southern, western, and northern coast of Newfoundland; and, also, on the coasts, bays, harbors, and creeks, from Mount Joly, on the southern coast of Labrador, to and through the straits of Belle Isle; and thence northwardly indefinitely along the coast, and that American fishermen shall have liberty to dry and cure fish in any of the unsettled bays, harbors, and creeks of said described coasts, until the same become settled, and the United States renounce the liberty *heretofore enjoyed* or claimed by the inhabitants thereof, to take, dry, or cure fish, *on or within three marine miles* of any of the coasts, bays, creeks, or harbors of his Britannic Majesty's dominions in America, not included in the above mentioned limits: provided, however, that the American fishermen shall be admitted to enter such bays or harbors, for the purpose of shelter, and of repairing damages therein, of purchasing wood, and of obtaining water, and for no other purpose whatever. But they shall be under such restrictions as may be necessary to prevent their taking, drying, or curing fish therein, or in any other manner whatever abusing the privileges hereby reserved to them."

The question turns, so far as relates to the treaty stipulations on the meaning given to the word "bays" in the treaty of 1783. By that treaty the Americans had no right to dry and cure fish on the shores and *bays* of Newfoundland, but they had that right on the coasts, *bays, harbors and creeks* of Nova Scotia; and as they must land to cure fish on the shores, bays, and creeks, they were evidently admitted to the shores of *the bays*, etc. By the treaty of 1818, the same right is granted to cure fish on the coasts, bays, etc. of Newfoundland, but the Americans relinquished that right, *and the right to fish within three miles* of the *coasts, bays, etc. of Nova Scotia.* Taking it for granted that the framers of the treaty intended that the word "bay or bays" should have the same meaning in all cases, and no mention being made of headlands, there appears no doubt that the Washington, in fishing ten miles from the shore, violated no stipulations of the treaty.

It was urged on behalf of the British government, that by coasts, bays, etc., is understood an imaginary line, drawn along the coast from headland to headland, and that the jurisdiction of her Majesty extends three marine miles outside of this line; thus closing all the bays on the coast or shore, and that great body of water called the Bay of Fundy against Americans and others, making the latter a British bay. This doctrine of headlands is new, and has received a proper limit in the convention between France and Great Britain of 2d August, 1839, in which "it is agreed that the distance of three miles fixed as the general limit for the exclusive right of fishery upon the coasts of the two countries shall, with respect to bays, the mouths of which do not exceed ten miles in width, be measured from a straight line drawn from headland to headland."

The Bay of Fundy is from 65 to 75 miles wide, and 130 to 140 miles long, it has several bays on its coasts; thus the word bay, as applied to this great body of water, has the same meaning as that applied to the Bay of Biscay, the Bay of Bengal, over which no nation can have the right to assume the sovereignty. One of the headlands of the Bay of Fundy is in the United States, and ships bound to Passamaquoddy must sail through a large space of it. The island of Grand Menan (British) and Little Menan (American) are situated nearly on a line from headland to headland. These islands, as represented in all Geographies, are situate in the Atlantic Ocean. The conclusion, is, therefore, in my mind irresistible, that the Bay of Fundy is not a British bay, nor a bay within the meaning of the word, as used in the treaties of 1783 and 1818.

The owners of the Washington, or their legal representatives, are therefore entitled to compensation, and are hereby awarded not the amount of their claim, which is excessive, but the sum of three thousand dollars, due on the 15th January, 1855.

The opinion of the American Commissioner in this case is printed in full in the Appendix.[a]

---

[a] Appendix, pp. 1101–1108.

The Argus case—Decision of Bates, Umpire.

The Umpire appointed agreeably to the provisions of the Convention entered into between Great Britain and the United States on the 8th of February 1853 for the Adjustment of Claims by a Mixed Commission having been duly notified by the Commissioners under the said Convenion that they had been unable to agree upon the decision to be given with reference to the Claim of the Owners of the Schooner "Argus" of portland United States Doughty Master against the British Government; And having carefully examined and considered the papers and Evidence produced on the Hearing of the said Claim and having conferred with the said Commissioners thereon hereby reports that the Schooner "Argus" 55 tons burthen was captured on the 4th August 1844 while Fishing on St. Ann's Bank by the Revenue Cruiser Sylph of Lunenburg Nova Scotia commanded by William Carr—Phillip Dod seizing Master—carried to Sidney where she was stripped and everything belonging to her sold at Auction. At the time of the Capture the "Argus" was stated on Oath to have been 28 Miles from the nearest land Cape Smoke there was therefore in this case no violation of the Treaty of 1818. I therefore Award to the Owners of the Argus or their legal Representatives for the loss of their vessel outfits stores and fish the sum of Two thousand Dollars on the 15th January 1855.

JOSHUA BATES, Umpire.

LONDON *23d December 1854.*

PERIOD FROM 1854 TO 1871.

Treaty of June 5, 1854.

The treaty of June 5, 1854, between the United States and Great Britain, commonly called the Reciprocity Treaty, went into operation on September 11, 1854, for a fixed term of ten years from that date and thereafter until the expiration of twelve months after notice given by either party to the other of its wish to terminate. It was terminated on March 11, 1866, by notice from the United States.

So far as it related to the fisheries controversy under the treaty of 1818, its purpose, as recited in the preamble, was to avoid further misunderstandings between the citizens and subjects respectively of the United States and Great Britain in regard to the extent and the right of fishing on the coasts of British North America, secured to each by Article I of the treaty of 1818.

The fisheries provisions of this treaty are printed in full in the Appendix,[a] and the following extract from them will show their rela tion to the fisheries provisions of the treaty of 1818:

It is agreed by the high contracting parties that in addition to the liberty secured to the United States fishermen by the above-mentioned convention of October 20, 1818, of taking, curing and drying fish on certain coasts of the British North American Colonies therein defined, the inhabitants of the United States shall have, in common with the subjects of Her Britannic Majesty, the liberty to take fish of every kind, except shell-fish, on the sea coasts and shores and in the bays, harbors and creeks of Canada, New Brunswick, Nova Scotia, Prince Edward's Island, and of the several islands, thereunto adjacent, without being restricted to any distance from the shore, with permission to land upon the coasts and shores of those colonies, and the islands thereof, and also upon the Magdalen Islands, for the purpose of drying their nets and curing their fish; provided that, in so doing, they do not interfere with the rights of private property, or with British fishermen, in the peaceable use of any part of the said coast in their occupancy for the same purpose.

It is understood that the above-mentioned liberty applies solely to the sea fishery, and that the salmon and shad fisheries, and all fisheries in rivers and the mouths of rivers, are hereby reserved exclusively for British fishermen.[b]

Article II contains reciprocal provisions in similar form, applying to fishing by British subjects on the "eastern sea-coasts and shores of the United States, north of the 36th parallel of north latitude, and on the shores of the several islands thereunto adjacent, and in the bays, harbors, and creeks of the said sea-coast and shores of the United States and of the said islands." [c]

Article VI provided for the extension of the foregoing provisions to Newfoundland so far as they were applicable.

It will be perceived that in so far as these provisions related to the coasts now under consideration, they left undisturbed the liberties to which the American fishermen were entitled under the treaty of 1818, and in addition extended to them the liberty of access to all the waters and coasts from which they were excluded by that treaty, excepting only the mouths of rivers; these new provisions therefore were superadded to the fisheries provisions of the treaty of 1818.

During the entire period that this treaty was in force, no question of dispute involving the fisheries arose between the United States and Great Britain. Subsequently, in 1880, in a dispute which arose under the treaty of 1871, in connection with the Fortune Bay seizures, a

---

[a] Appendix, p. 25.   [b] Appendix, p. 26.   [c] Appendix, p. 27.

circular letter which Secretary of State Marcy had addressed to the American fishermen in 1856 was cited by Lord Salisbury in support of the British contention as to the effect of the words "in common with British subjects" which are found in all of these treaties. The questions thus presented may more conveniently be considered in connection with the circumstances and conditions surrounding them, which are reviewed later.

The situation following the expiration of the Treaty of 1854.

As the date of the expiration of the treaty of 1854 approached, the desire to avoid a renewal of the difficulties under the treaty of 1818, which had been set at rest by the treaty of 1854, directed the attention of both governments to the advisability of entering into some new arrangement on the subject. The steps which were taken in this direction on the part of Great Britain up to the date of the expiration of the treaty, and the British views of the American position at that time, are of interest and will be found stated at some length in a communication written on March 17, 1866, by Lord Clarendon, Secretary of State for Foreign Affairs, to Sir Frederick Bruce, the British Minister at Washington.[a]

On February 16, 1866, a month prior to the expiration of the treaty, Sir Frederick Bruce wrote to Mr. Seward, the Secretary of State, stating that "Her Majesty's Government would be well content to renew the Treaty in its present form" or to reconsider "and so to modify its terms as to render it, if possible, more beneficial to both countries than it has hitherto been," and he further suggested that if the United States should prefer the latter course, an arrangement of a provisional character might be entered into with a view to affording time for fresh negotiations. The reasons which had induced the United States to terminate the treaty made the suggestion of its renewal unacceptable, and Mr. Seward replied to the British Minister on the day following this proposal "that careful inquiry made during the recess of Congress induced the President to believe that there was then no such harmony of public sentiment in favor of the extension of the treaty as would encourage him in directing negotiations to be opened."[b] On the 10th of April, 1866, however, Mr. Seward instructed Mr. Charles Francis Adams, then American Minister at London, to propose to Lord Clarendon an arrangement for the

---

[a] Appendix, p. 562.   [b] Appendix, pp. 560–562.

temporary regulation of the matter in the manner provided in the following draft of a protocol, which he enclosed:

Whereas in the 1st article of the convention between the United States and Great Britain, concluded and signed in London on the 20th of October, 1818, it was declared that "the United States hereby renounce forever any liberty heretofore enjoyed or claimed by the inhabitants thereof to take, dry, or cure fish on or within three marine miles of any of the coasts, bays, creeks, or harbors of his Britannic Majesty's dominions in America not included within certain limits heretofore mentioned;" and whereas differences have arisen in regard to the extent of the above mentioned renunciation, the government of the United States and her Majesty the Queen of Great Britain, being equally desirous of avoiding further misunderstanding, have agreed to appoint, and do hereby authorize the appointment of a mixed commission for the following purposes, namely:

1. To agree upon and define by a series of lines the limits which shall separate the exclusive from the common right of fishing on the coasts and in the seas adjacent of the British North American colonies, in conformity with the 1st article of the convention of 1818; the said lines to be regularly numbered, duly described, and also clearly marked on charts prepared in duplicate for the purpose.

2. To agree upon and establish such regulations as may be necessary and proper to secure to the fishermen of the United States the privilege of entering bays and harbors for the purpose of shelter and of repairing damages therein, of purchasing wood, and of obtaining water, and to agree upon and establish such restrictions as may be necessary to prevent the abuse of the privilege reserved by said convention to the fishermen of the United States.

3. To agree upon and recommend the penalties to be adjudged, and such proceedings and jurisdiction as may be necessary to secure a speedy trial and judgment with as little expense as possible, for the violators of rights and the transgressors of the limits and restrictions which may be hereby adopted:

Provided, however, that the limits, restrictions and regulations which may be agreed upon by the said commission shall not be final, nor have any effect, until so jointly confirmed and declared by the United States and her Majesty the Queen of Great Britain, either by treaty or by laws, mutually acknowledged and accepted by the President of the United States, by and with the consent of the Senate and by her Majesty the Queen of Great Britain.

Pending a definitive arrangement on the subject, the United States government engages to give all proper orders to officers in its employment, and her Britannic Majesty's government engages to instruct the proper colonial or other British officers to abstain from hostile acts against British and United States fishermen respectively.[a]

Pursuant to Mr. Seward's instructions, Mr. Adams promptly submitted the draft of the proposed protocol to Lord Clarendon, and on May 11, 1866, Lord Clarendon wrote to Sir Frederick Bruce, author-

---

[a] Appendix, p. 570.

izing him to accept this proposal on certain conditions, which he stated as follows:

Her Majesty's Government understand that "the southern coast of Newfoundland, which extends from Cape Ray to the Rameau Islands;" "the western and northern coasts of Newfoundland, from the said Cape Ray to the Quirpon Islands;" "the shores of the Magdalen Islands;" "the coasts, bays, harbours, and creeks from Mount Joly, on the southern coast of Labrador, to and through the straits of Belle Isle, and thence northwardly, indefinitely, along the coast;" and also "the unsettled bays, harbours, and creeks of the southern part of the coast of Newfoundland hereabove described, and of the coast of Labrador" will be excluded from the operations of the Commission, whose duty will therefore be confined to ascertaining what is the real extent and meaning of the renunciation, on the part of the United States, "to take, dry, or cure fish on or within three marine miles of any of the coasts, bays, creeks, or harbours of His Britannic Majesty's dominions in America not included within the above-mentioned limits;" and, having ascertained these points, then to lay down regulations under which United States' fishermen may be "admitted to enter such bays or harbours for the purpose of shelter and repairing damages therein, of purchasing wood, and of obtaining water;" and to agree upon a system of police for enforcing the conclusions at which the Commission may arrive.

If I have correctly described the object of the United States in the present proposal, Her Majesty's Government will readily accede to it, and will cordially co-operate in removing a source of much irritation between the subjects and citizens of the two countries.

In any case, however, Her Majesty's Government would reserve, as that of the United States are also prepared for themselves to reserve, the right of considering the recommendations of the Joint Commission, before they can finally be held binding on the two Governments; and Her Majesty's Government would hold themselves entitled to maintain, pending the determination of the questions to be discussed, the principle for which they have heretofore contended, and to enforce all regulations and assert all rights which previously to the conclusions of the Reciprocity Treaty, the British Government asserted and enforced. Therefore, if the purport of the concluding paragraph of Mr. Adams' paper is meant by the United States to involve an obligation on the part of Her Majesty's Government to continue to allow, during the sitting of the Commission, fishermen of the United States to enjoy in British waters the privileges under the Reciprocity Treaty which the Government of the United States have now renounced for their citizens, you will frankly state to Mr. Seward that into such an engagement Her Majesty's Government cannot enter.

Her Majesty's Government are most desirous that the rights of the Colonies should be so enforced as to give the least possible occasion for complaint or discussion. They have cordially approved, and have recommended to the Governments of the other British Provinces, a proposal made by the authorities of Canada, that American fishermen should for the present season be allowed to enjoy, under special licenses, the benefits conferred by the Reciprocity Treaty, and they will be glad to learn that the Lower Provinces have adopted an arrangement intended to prevent the change of circumstances from operating suddenly to the injury of the fishing interests of citizens of the United States; but they cannot engage indefinitely to adhere to this system, though they are perfectly prepared to concert with the United States for substituting for it a more permanent arrangement which, either solely applicable to fisheries, or more generally comprising the common interests of Her Majesty's subjects, and those of the citizens of the United States, shall hold out a promise of mutual interest to both parties, and the strongest assurance of peace and good-will between the two Governments.

You will, of course, freely communicate with Her Majesty's Colonial authorities on the matters referred to in this despatch.[a]

Great Britain's unwillingness "to continue to allow, during the sitting of the Commission, fishermen of the United States to enjoy in British waters the privileges under the reciprocity treaty which the Government of the United States have now renounced for their citizens" left open the whole question of how a recurrence of the hostile treatment of American fishermen by the provincial authorities could be prevented pending the settlement of their differences as to their respective rights under the treaty of 1818.

This difficulty was in part met by carrying out the proposal above referred to by Lord Clarendon, which had been made by the authorities of Canada, "that American fishermen should for the present season be allowed to enjoy, under special licenses, the benefits conferred by the reciprocity treaty." This plan was concurred in by Nova Scotia, New Brunswick, and Prince Edward's Island as Mr. Seward was advised by Sir Frederick Bruce in his notes of June 24, and July 21, 1866,[b] and was continued until 1870.

During this period, however, an attempt was made by the provincial authorities to apply to American fishing vessels found without a special license an even more extreme and severe interpretation of the treaty and the local laws adopted for its enforcement than had been attempted at any time prior to the treaty of 1854. The British North America Act of March 29, 1867, under which the provinces of Nova Scotia, New Brunswick, and Quebec became a part of the Dominion of Canada, gave the Dominion Government authority over their sea-coast fisheries, and on May 22, 1868, that Government adopted an act respecting fishing by foreign vessels on those coasts.[c] The treatment of American vessels under this act and under the

---

[a] Appendix, p. 574.   [b] Appendix, pp. 578, 579.   [c] Appendix, p. 133.

amendment of it adopted on May 12, 1870,[a] led to a report on the subject by the United States Consul at Halifax under date of October 3, 1870, in which he says:

Fishery laws.—The existing laws relating to the fisheries consist of the treaty of 1818, between the United States and Great Britain; the imperial act framed June 14, 1819, for the purpose of carrying the provisions of the treaty into effect; the British North American act framed March 29, 1867, giving authority to the Canadian government over the sea-coast and inland fisheries; and the Dominion acts framed respectively May 22, 1868, and May 12, 1870, relating to fishing by foreign vessels.

All these acts, Canadian as well as imperial, purport to be founded upon the treaty of 1818, and designed to enforce its provisions. Some of the provisions of the colonial acts respecting the fisheries are borrowed from imperial statutes relating to trade and navigation, and although enacted to protect the in-shore fisheries, are not strictly applicable to fishing vessels.

Supplies.—In no act is there any prohibition against fishing vessels visiting colonial ports for supplies. The silence of all the acts upon this point, and the practice of more than half a century under imperial laws, framed expressly for the purpose of carrying into effect the provisions of the treaty, justify the conclusion that no such prohibition was contemplated by it. This view of the subject derives additional support from the fact that at the time of the adoption of the treaty the mackerel fishing, as now carried on, was comparatively unknown.

During the intervening years between 1818 and 1870, throughout all the controversies between the United States and Great Britain on the subject of the fisheries, no question until the present had arisen in reference to supplies. They were always readily procured in colonial ports, and the trade being profitable to the people of the colonies, was facilitated by the local authorities.

The controversies which preceded the adoption of the reciprocity treaty related principally to our right to fish in certain bays, and to the exact limits within which American fishermen, by the convention of 1818, were entitled to fish on the coasts of British North America.

The rights insisted upon by citizens of the United States were practically decided in their favor by the commissioners appointed under the convention of 1853, between the United States and Great Britain, in the case of the schooner *Washington.* That schooner, while fishing in the Bay of Fundy in 1843, ten miles distant from the shore, was seized by the British authorities, taken into Yarmouth, Nova Scotia, and there condemned for a violation of the fishery laws.

In 1853, after the adoption of the reciprocity treaty, the case was brought before the commissioners on a claim of the owners of the schooner for damages; and after a full and careful examination was decided in favor of the claimants, to whom damages were awarded for the illegal seizure and condemnation. Since that time what is termed the "headland" interpretation of the treaty, theretofore at

---

[a] Appendix, p. 136.

different times insisted upon by Great Britain, and uniformly opposed by the United States, if not actually abandoned, has been held in abeyance, and it is not probable that any questions will hereafter arise in relation to it between the two countries.

In regard to fishing supplies, the practice which has so long prevailed of procuring them in colonial ports, with the full knowledge and consent of both governments, whose citizens have mutually shared in the benefits resulting from such practice, must be regarded as a practical construction given to the treaty which concludes all parties.

Transshipment in bond.—Since the abrogation of the reciprocity treaty until within a few weeks past, it has been the practice of the colonial authorities to permit the transshipment in bond of American-caught fish. The practice was founded upon no statutory. enactment, but was adopted as a commercial regulation, mutually beneficial to our fishermen and the people of the provinces. It afforded facilities to the former in the prosecution of a lawful and useful avocation, and increased the trade and contributed to the prosperity of the latter. While its discontinuance, in itself, violates no established commercial usage between friendly nations, as in the case of the prohibition of supplies to our fishermen, yet the *time* of its discontinuance, in the midst of the fishing season, without previous notice, and when much greater and more important bonding privileges were, and still are, extended by the United States to the British colonies, is a just cause of complaint.

Fresh fish.—While fresh fish, the product of the British North American fisheries, is admitted into the United States *duty free*, our fishermen are prohibited from procuring ice for fresh fish caught while fishing side by side with British fishermen on the same banks.

Pilotage.—To subject fishing vessels coming in to colonial ports, as is now the case, to the compulsory regulations respecting pilotage applied to merchant vessels, and at the same time to deny them when in port the ordinary privileges extended to such merchant vessels, is manifestly unjust.

Burden of proof changed.—The Dominion act framed in 1868 reverses, in violation of the principles of common law, the ordinary modes of proof, and declares, in section ten, that "in case a dispute arises as to whether any seizure has or has not been legally made, or as to whether the person seizing was or was not authorized to seize under the act, the burden of proving the illegality of the seizure shall be upon the owner or claimant." Under this section an American fishing vessel coming into port in the exercise of a conceded and unrestricted treaty right, either for the purpose of shelter, of repairing damages therein, of purchasing wood, and obtaining water, and unlawfully seized, instead of being presumed to be in port for a lawful purpose, is presumed by the act of seizure itself, however unauthorized, to be guilty of a violation of the fishery laws. Thus the presumption of guilt, which is to subject a fishing vessel to seizure and confiscation, is made, in the first instance, to depend upon the caprice of the seizing officer, and not upon the conduct of the officers and crew of the captured vessel. It is obvious that such a rule of action must be instrumental in inflicting wrong and injury upon innocent and unoffending parties.

Strait of Canso.   *   *   *   *

Vessels required to leave port.—The manner in which the fishery laws are now construed and attempted to be enforced by the Dominion authorities, if acquiesced in would amount to a practical exclusion of our fishing vessels from colonial ports; for, although their right to enter for the purpose of "shelter, repairing damages, purchasing wood and obtaining water," is guaranteed by solemn treaty, yet, no sooner do they now enter, than, contrary to all former practice, they are required to depart even before it is ascertained for what purpose and under what circumstances they resort thither.

While authority is given to certain officers, both imperial and Canadian, to seize any American fishing vessel "found within three marine miles of any of the coasts, bays, creeks, or harbors in Canada," which, after examination, "has been found fishing or preparing to fish, or to have been fishing in British waters," yet nothing in any of the acts respecting the fisheries warrants this summary exclusion of such vessel from port, or prohibits any vessel from entering as well for the purpose of procuring supplies, as for shelter, repairs, wood and water. On the contrary, the fishery laws themselves, as well as the regulations respecting pilotage, recognize the right of foreign fishing vessels freely to enter the ports of the British North American provinces.

The rigorous measures now for the first time adopted, which materially affect the interests of a large class of American citizens engaged in the prosecution of an important branch of industry, while deriving no sanction from the treaty of 1818, or the usages of nations, are rendered still more objectionable from having been undertaken without notice previously given, either by the Canadian minister of marine and fisheries, by the collectors of colonial customs, or by the vice-admiral in command of her Majesty's fleet in the British North American waters.[a]

On the 29th of the same month Mr. Fish, then Secretary of State, wrote to the United States Consul General in Canada, calling for information on another branch of the same question, and stating the position of the United States as follows:

The present embarrassment is, that while we have reports of several seizures upon grounds as stated by the interested parties, which seem to be in contravention of international law and special treaties relating to the fisheries, these alleged causes of seizure are regarded as pretensions of over-zealous officers of the British navy and the colonial vessels, which will, as we hope and are bound in courtesy to expect, be repudiated by the courts before which our vessels are to be brought for adjudication. It is the desire of this Government, nevertheless, that our consular officers should watch the course of proceeding in these cases, and give prompt and authentic information of any decision which may be made in them. In particular if the charge against any American fishing vessel is only that she has been preparing to fish, without actual fishing in the prohibited limits, it is to be made known to the counsel of the owners of

---

[a] Appendix, p. 625–628.

the vessel that this Government is not disposed to regard such mere preparation as an infraction of the obligations of our citizens engaged in the outfit and employment of fishing vessels, and it is desirous of having the point distinctly presented and adjudicated, if possible, without being complicated with other questions, so that if adversely decided, a case presenting that single issue may be made for appeal to the British tribunal of last resort. It is understood that the instructions of the imperial government of Great Britain do not authorize the capture of an American vessel found fishing within three miles of the coasts from which they are prohibited, or of a line drawn across the mouths of bays whose mouths do not exceed six geographical miles in width. In any case of condemnation it is desirable to have it appear with precision as well whether the vessel condemned was fishing within the prohibited distance, as whether the actual capture was made within that distance or beyond it, so as to be upon the high seas, in the sense which this Government is disposed to attach to these words, for the purpose of questions arising out of the operations of our fishing vessels on the northeastern coast.[a]

In reply to this communication the United States Consul General wrote on November 3, 1870, to the Secretary of State as follows:

It seems to me that the unfriendly construction given by the Dominion government of the treaty of 1818 was intensified in its harshness by the almost covert manner in which it was sought to be enforced. It was with the greatest difficulty that our consuls could ascertain from the commanders of the various armed vessels what they would consider cause for seizure and condemnation.

No adequate or suitable notice was given to the captains of American fishing vessels, and they were seized for acts which they had been permitted to do from time immemorial, as well before as subsequently to the above-mentioned treaty.

Information has come to me from so many sources of declarations made by the various ministers of the Dominion government, that I cannot doubt, and it is openly proclaimed here and believed to be true, that the enforcement of the above mentioned treaty, in the manner it has been enforced, has two objects, viz: one of which is to create a Canadian sentiment in antagonism to the United States, with a view to check the spread of American sentiment here looking to ultimate annexation; the other object is, by the close control of the fishing interests to compel the United States, through her interests, to make a treaty of reciprocity of trade between the United States and the British provinces in North America.[b]

The contrast between the attitude of the Canadian and British Governments.

In contrast with the provincial attitude thus disclosed on the questions in dispute, attention is called to the action taken by Great Britain at this time on the subject of seizures. In his note of May 26, 1870, the British Minister at Washington communicated to Mr.

---

a Appendix, p. 630.   b Appendix, p. 632.

Fish copies of certain letters addressed by the Admiralty to Vice-Admiral Wellesley, Commanding Her Majesty's Naval Forces on the North Atlantic Station, and of a letter from the Colonial Department to the Foreign Office "from which you will see the nature of the instructions to be given to her Majesty's and the Canadian officers who will be employed in maintaining order at the fisheries in the neighborhood of the coasts of Canada." Among these enclosures is a copy of a letter from the Foreign Office to the Secretary of the Admiralty, April 30, 1870, from which is taken the following extract:

The Canadian Government has recently determined, with the concurrence of H. M. Ministers to increase the stringency of the existing practice by dispensing with the warnings hitherto given and seizing at once any vessel detected in violating the law.

In view of this change and of the questions to which it may give rise, I am directed by Lord Granville to request that you will move their Lordships to instruct the officers of Her Majesty's ships employed in the protection of the Fisheries that they are not to seize any vessel unless it is evident and can be clearly proved that the offense of fishing has been committed, and the vessel itself is captured, within three miles of land.[a]

In the letter from the Lords of Admiralty to Vice-Admiral Wellesley, written on May 5, 1870, pursuant to the foregoing request from the Foreign Office, and transmitting the letter above quoted from, the following language occurs:

My Lords desire me to remind you of the extreme importance of commanding officers of the ships selected to protect the fisheries, exercising the utmost discretion in carrying out their instructions, paying special attention to Lord Granville's observation that no vessel should be seized unless it is evident and can be clearly proved that the offence of fishing has been committed and that the vessel is captured within three miles of land.[a]

In Lord Granville's letter of April 30, 1870, to Sir John Young, then Governor General of Canada, transmitting a copy of his letter to the Admiralty respecting these instructions, he says:

H. M.'s Government do not doubt that your Ministers will agree with them as to the propriety of these instructions and will give corresponding instructions to the vessels employed by them.[b]

It subsequently appeared that before these instructions were received the vice-admiral had already issued instructions to the commanders on the coast in which was expressed

the opinion of her Majesty's government, that the United States have renounced the right of fishing within three miles of a line drawn across

---

[a] Appendix, p. 591.   [b] Appendix, p. 592.

the mouth of any British bay or creek, and also that American fishermen should not be interfered with, either by notice or otherwise, unless they are found within three miles of a line drawn across the mouth of a bay or creek which is less than ten geographical miles in width, in conformity with the arrangement made with France in 1839, and that American vessels found within these limits should be warned that by engaging or preparing to engage in fishing they will be liable to forfeiture, and should receive notice to depart.[a]

This was called to the attention of the British Minister by Mr. Fish in his note of June 8, 1870, and Mr. Thornton replied on the 11th of the same month, informing Mr. Fish that the vice-admiral had received instructions on the subject and that the instructions issued by him had already been so modified as to bring them into conformity with the views of the Admiralty, as expressed in the instructions previously referred to.[a]

The same point of difference also arose directly between the British and Canadian Governments in reference to the form of instructions to be issued by the Canadian Government to officers in command of vessels engaged as marine police in protecting the inshore fisheries of Canada.   These instructions as originally prepared under date of May 14, 1870, were in part as follows:

POWERS.—The capacity in which you are vested with magisterial powers is that of Fishery Officer for the Provinces forming the Dominion of Canada.   Your power and authority as a Fishery Officer are derived from the following Statutes: "The Fisheries Act" (31 Vict., cap. 60.)

"An Act respecting Fishing by Foreign Vessels" (31 Vict. cap. 61) and the subsequent Statute, entitled "An Act to amend the Act respecting Fishing by Foreign Vessels" made and passed in the present Session of the Parliament of Canada;

"Chapter 94 of the Revised Statutes (third series) of Nova Scotia" (Of the Coast and Deep-sea fisheries);

The Act entitled "An Act to amend cap. 94 of the Revised Statutes of Nova Scotia," (29 Vict., cap. 35.)

An Act passed by the Legislature of the Province of New Brunswick, entitled "An Act relating to the Coast Fisheries, and for the Prevention of Illicit Trade" (16 Vict., cap. 69;)

Also from such Regulations as have been passed or may be passed by the Governor General in Council, or from Instructions from the Department of Marine and Fisheries, under The Fisheries Act hereinbefore cited.

In such capacity, your jurisdiction must be strictly confined within the limit of "three marine miles of any of the coasts, bays, creeks, or harbors," of Canada, with respect to any action you may take against American fishing vessels and United States citizens engaged in fishing.   Where any of the bays, creeks, or harbors shall not exceed *ten*

---

[a] Appendix, p. 610.

geographical miles in width, you will consider that the line of demarcation extends from headland to headland, either at the entrance to such bay, creek or harbor, or from and between given points on both sides thereof, at any place nearest the mouth where the shores are less than *ten* miles apart; and may exclude foreign fishermen and fishing vessels therefrom, or seize if found within three marine miles of the coast.

Jurisdiction.—The limits within which you will, if necessary exercise the power to exclude United States fishermen, or to detain American fishing vessels or boats, are for the present to be exceptional. Difficulties have arisen in former times with respect to the question, whether the exclusive limits should be measured on lines drawn parallel everywhere to the coast and describing its sinuosities, or on lines produced from headland to headland across the entrances of bays, creeks or harbors.   Her Majesty's Government are clearly of opinion, that by the Convention of 1818, the United States have renounced the right of fishing not only within three miles of the Colonial shores, but within three miles of a line drawn across the mouth of any British bay or creek.   It is, however, the wish of Her Majesty's Government neither to concede, nor for the present to enforce any rights in this respect, which are in their nature open to any serious question.   Until further instructed, therefore, you will not interfere with any American fishermen unless found within three miles of the shore, or within three miles of a line drawn across the mouth of a bay or creek (which is less than *ten* geographical miles in width.)   *In case of any other bay, as Bay de Chaleurs, for example, you will not admit any United States fishing vessel or boat, or any American fishermen, inside of a line drawn across at that part of such bay where its width does not exceed ten miles.*

Action.—You will accost every United States vessel or boat actually within three marine miles of the shore, along any other part of the coast except Labrador and around the Magdalen Islands, or within three marine miles of the entrance of any bay, harbor or creek, which is less than *ten* geographical miles in width, or inside of a line drawn across any part of such bay, harbor or creek, at points nearest to the mouth thereof, not wider apart than *ten* geographical miles, and if either fishing, preparing to fish, or having obviously fished within the exclusive limits, you will, in accordance with the above recited Acts, seize at once any vessel detected in violating the law, and send or take her into port for condemnation.   *It must be evident and susceptible of the clearest proof that the offence has been committed, and the capture effected within the prohibited limits.* [a]

Lord Granville, knowing that even this modified application of the "headlands" theory would raise an issue with the United States Government, promptly telegraphed on June 6, 1870, to the Governor General of Canada as follows:

Her Majesty's Government hope that the United States fishermen will not be for the present prevented from fishing except within

---

[a] Appendix, pp. 583–585.

three miles of land or in bays, which are less than six miles broad at the mouth.[a]

In deference to the wishes thus expressed, a new set of instructions was issued by the Canadian Government under date of June 27, 1870, in which the width of the bays, or portions thereof, from which the American fishermen were to be excluded, was changed throughout from ten geographical miles to six geographical miles, and the other provisions printed in *italics* in the above extract were amended so as to read—

In the case of any other bay, as Bay des Chaleurs, for example, you will *not interfere* with any United States fishing vessel or boat, or any American fishermen, unless they are found within three miles of the shore.

And——

But you are not to do so unless it is evident, and can be clearly proved, that the *offence of fishing* has been committed, and that the vessel is captured within the prohibited limits.[b]

It will be observed that in both circulars alike the reason for limiting the application of the headland theory is frankly admitted to be that in its nature it is open to serious question, as appears from the above quoted phrase: "It is, however, the wish of Her Majesty's Government neither to concede, nor for the present to enforce any rights in this respect which are in their nature open to any serious question."

These later instructions were re-issued in 1871 without change.

While this feature of the question was still under discussion between Canada and Great Britain, the Canadian Minister of Marine and Fisheries took occasion, in a report made by him on May 31, 1870, "to urge that her Majesty's Government may be requested to bring it [the fishery question] to a speedy settlement in the manner proposed by Lord Clarendon in 1866 on the suggestion of the American Minister at London,"[c] and on July 1, 1870, a report was adopted by the Canadian Privy Council, in connection with the mission to England of a Mr. Campbell as the Canadian representative in the matter, recommending—

That the instructions which may be addressed to Mr. Campbell, with reference to bringing to an early settlement all matters that have been admitted into dispute between the British and American Governments, affecting the fisheries, should embrace the following principal points:

---

[a] Appendix, p. 609.   [b] Appendix, p. 614.   [c] Appendix, p. 596.

1. That fishing rights in British American waters shall be in future enforced, as they existed and were maintained, under the Treaty of 1818, anterior to the Reciprocity Treaty of 1854, in accordance with the Laws of Nations.

2. That failing such positive enforcement of these undoubted rights, the question arising out of the said Treaty, as to the definition of certain limits of exclusion, by headland lines, be referred to a mixed commission, to be named by the British and American Governments, and to be composed of one Imperial, one United States, and one Canadian Commissioner, providing some independent reference in case of need; the principle on which such commission shall be chosen and act, to be as provided in the Earl of Clarendon's Despatch of 11th May, 1866.

3. That such mixed Commission shall be formed during the current year, and shall, in order to facilitate speedy reference, hold its sittings either at Halifax, Washington, or Ottawa; the negotiations and preliminary arrangements for the same to be carried out between the Governor General of Canada and the United States Government, through the British Minister at the American Capital. [a]

On the 27th of the same month, Lord Kimberly, referring to this proposal, informed Sir John Young, Governor General of Canada, that he concurred with the Canadian Government "that it would be desirable that the questions which have been so long in dispute with the United States, as to the geographical limits of the exclusive fishing rights of Canada under the treaty of 1818, should be settled by a joint British and American Commission, on which the Dominion should be represented," and that "Her Majesty's Government will propose to the United States Government the appointment of such a Commission." [b] Such proposal, however, was never officially communicated to the United States Government, but it appears that while the subject was under consideration between Great Britain and Canada, a Foreign Office memorandum was prepared, and that in October, 1870, Lord Kimberly wrote to Lord Granville requesting him to transmit a copy of it to Sir Edward Thornton, then British Minister at Washington, with instructions to communicate with the Governor General of Canada "before addressing himself to the Government of the United States on the subject to which the memorandum relates." [c] The memorandum referred to is as follows:

---

[a] Appendix, p. 617.   [b] Appendix, p. 620.   [c] Appendix, p. 628.

Memorandum for Foreign Office respecting a Commission to settle limits of the right of exclusive Fishery on the Coast of British North America.

A convention made between Great Britain and the United States, on the 20th October, 1818, after securing to American fishermen certain rights to be exercised on part of the coasts of Newfoundland and Labrador, proceeded as follows:—

"And the United States hereby renounce, for ever, any liberty heretofore enjoyed or claimed by the inhabitants thereof, to take, dry, or cure fish on or within three miles of any of the coasts, bays, creeks, or harbors of His Brittanic Majesty's Dominions in America, not included within the above limits."

The right of Great Britain to exclude American fishermen from waters within three miles of the coast is unambiguous, and it is believed, uncontested. But there appears to be some doubt what are the waters described as within three miles of bays, creeks, and harbors. When a bay is less than six miles broad, its waters are within the three miles limit, and therefore clearly within the meaning of the Treaty; but when it is more than that breadth, the question arises whether it is a bay of Her Britannic Majesty's Dominions.

This is a question which has to be considered in each particular case with regard to International Law and usage. When such a bay, etc., is not a bay of Her Majesty's Dominions, the American fishermen will be entitled to fish in it, except within three miles of the "coast"; "when it is a bay of Her Majesty's Dominions" they will not be entitled to fish within three miles of it, that is to say, (it is presumed), within three miles of a line drawn from headland to headland.

It is desirable that the British and American Governments should come to a clear understanding in the case of each bay, creek, or harbor, what are the precise limits of the exclusive rights of Great Britain, and should define those limits in such a way as to be incapable of dispute, either by reference to the bearings of certain headlands, or other objects on shore, or by laying the lines down in a map or chart.[a]

The Canadian "treaty coasts."

One other question arose during this period which requires brief attention. On April 14, 1870, Mr. Thornton, the British Minister at Washington, transmitted to Mr. Fish, the Secretary of State, a copy of an order in council of the Dominion of Canada adopted January 8, 1870, providing "that the system of granting fishing licenses to foreign vessels, under the act 31 Vic., cap. 61, be discontinued, and that henceforth all foreign fishermen be prevented from fishing in the waters of Canada."[b] On the 21st of the same month Mr. Fish replied, calling attention to the words "and that henceforth all foreign fishermen be prevented from fishing in the waters of

---

[a] Appendix, p. 629.   [b] Appendix, p. 580.

Canada" which he said "seem to contemplate an interference with rights guaranteed to the United States under the first article of the treaty of 1818, which secures to American fishermen the right of fishing in certain waters which are understood to be claimed at present as belonging to Canada."[a]

In the correspondence which ensued on this subject, it became necessary for Mr. Fish to renew his objection to the provision of the order in council above quoted, which he did in his note of May 31, 1870, to Mr. Thornton, from which the following extract is taken:

The question arose, What are the waters of Canada?

At the date of the treaty of 1818 the boundary of Canada, as understood, was defined by the 27 chap. 49 George III., entitled "An act for establishing courts of jurisdiction in the island of Newfoundland and the islands adjacent, and for reannexing part of the coast of Labrador and the islands lying on said coast to the government of Newfoundland," (March 30, 1809,) by the 14th section of which it was enacted "that such parts of the coast of Labrador from the river Saint John to Hudson's Streights, and the said island of Anticosti, and all other smaller islands so annexed to the government of Newfoundland by the said proclamation of the seventh day of October, one thousand seven hundred and sixty-three (except the said islands of Madelaine,) shall be separated from the said government of Lower Canada, and be again re-annexed to the government of Newfoundland."

The mouth of the river Saint John, referred to in this act, is understood to be between the 64th and 65th meridian of longitude west from Greenwich.

We further understood that in June, 1825, by the 9th section of cap. 59, 6 Geo. IV., entitled "An act to provide for the extinction of federal and seigniorial rights and burthens in lands held *a titre de tief* and *a titre de cens*, in the province of Lower Canada, and for the gradual conversion of those tenures into the tenure of free and common socage, and for other purposes relating to said province," it was enacted that so much of the said coast as lies to the westward of a line to be drawn due north and south from the bay or harbor of Ance Sablon, inclusive, as far as the 52d degree of north latitude, with the island of Anticosti, and all other islands adjacent to such part as last aforesaid of the coast of Labrador, shall be, and the same are hereby, reannexed to and made a part of the said province of Lower Canada, and shall henceforward be subject to the laws of the said province, and to none other.

The bay or harbor of Ance Sablon is understood to be in the longitude of about 57° 8', at or near the entrance of the Straits of Belle Isle.

The treaty of 1818 secures to the inhabitants of the United States, in common with the subjects of her Britannic Majesty, the liberty to take fish of any kind on the shores of the Magdalen Islands, and also on the coasts, bays, harbors, and creeks from Mount Joly, on the southern coast of Labrador, to and through the Straits of Belle Isle, and thence northwardly, &c.

---

[a] Appendix, p. 581.

Mount Joly, thus fixed by treaty as the westernmost limit on the coast of Labrador of the liberty of fishing for the inhabitants of the United States, is understood to be in the longitude of about 61° 40′. From that point eastward and northward, on the shores of what was then called Labrador, the fishermen of the United States have the liberty to take fish.

The act last above recited seems to establish the boundaries and the jurisdiction of Canada as extending to the bay of Ance Sablon, about four and a half degrees of longitude to the east of Mount Joly, and to include the Magdalen Islands.

It was under the impression that this act establishes the jurisdiction and the boundary of Canada, as extending to a line drawn due north and south from the bay or harbor of Ance Sablon, and including the Magdalen Islands, that on the 21st of April last I invited your attention to the first paragraph of the order in council of the Dominion of Canada on the 8th January last, declaring "that henceforth all foreign fishermen be prevented from fishing in the waters of Canada," as contemplating a possible interference with the rights guaranteed to the United States under the treaty of 1818. The minister of the privy council and the report of the minister of marine and fisheries, of which you have given me copies, give assurance of the intent of the authorities of the Dominion government not to abridge those rights; but the order in council may be interpreted by those to whom its execution is intrusted to authorize their interference with fishermen of the United States while in the exercise of their guaranteed liberty. If our understanding that the boundary and jurisdiction of Canada extend to the bay or harbor of Ance Sablon, and include the Magdalen Islands, be correct, "the waters of Canada" embrace the coast of Labrador from Mount Joly to the Bay of Ance Sablon, and include also the Magdalen Islands. Desirous to avoid the possibility of any misapprehension on the part of those who may be charged with the execution of the order in council, I beg to call your attention to the acts to which I have referred, and to request, in case I am in error with regard to the eastern boundary and the extent of jurisdiction in Canada, that you will advise me of the real boundary and jurisdiction. If I am correct in this respect, and if that part of the coast of what in 1818 was known as Labrador included between Mount Joly and the bay or harbor of Ance Sablon, or the Magdalen Islands, be in "the waters of Canada," I do not doubt that the authorities of the Dominion will recognize the necessity of such modification of the order in council of the 8th of January last, or of such additional instructions to be given as will secure the fishermen of the United States from interference while in the exercise of the liberty guaranteed to them by the treaty of 1818.[a]

Mr. Thornton informed Mr. Fish in reply, on June 2, 1870, that his note had been referred to the Canadian Government, and that he was inclined to think that Mr. Fish was right in supposing that the limit of Canada extends as far east as Ance Sablon on the coast of Labrador and that the Magdalen Islands are comprised within it.

---

[a] Appendix, p. 593.

Mr. Thornton had previously informed Mr. Fish that the Canadian Government had not the slightest intention in issuing the above-mentioned order "to abridge citizens of the United States of any of the rights to which they are entitled by the treaty of October 20, 1818, and which are tacitly acknowledged in the Canadian law of May 22, 1868,"[a] and this was confirmed by Mr. Thornton's note of July 11, 1870, to Mr. Fish enclosing a copy of a letter on the subject from the Governor General of Canada forwarding a memorandum from the Canadian Minister of Marine from which the following extract is taken: .

A further despatch from Mr. Thornton of 1st. instant, inclosing Mr. Fish's correspondence at length, now explains the full meaning of Mr. Fish's objection to the phraseology of the Order in Council of 8 January last, and states the argument on which Mr. Thornton acquiesces in Mr. Fish's request that the order should be modified as far as U. S. fishermen are concerned.

Mr. Fish takes exception to the terms of this Order in Council because of the words "Waters of Canada" which have since 1825 included part of the Southern coast of Labrador and Islands in the Gulf of St. Lawrence, and which at the time of the Treaty of 1818 were subject to the municipal jurisdiction of Newfoundland.

The Act of 6 Geo. IV by which this ancient change of Provincial boundaries was effected in an Imperial Statute, and necessarily reserves by implication all existing Treaty arrangements of an unconditional nature between the Empire and foreign Powers. Such also would be the necessary effect of legislative or executive action, regarding any matter of local jurisdiction.

The territory and waters affected would not cease to be British because of changes of inter colonial boundaries established by the Imperial Parliament.

Mr. Fish seems to desire a modification of this Order in Council chiefly with a view to providing against any misapprehension in respect of the Treaty rights of U. S. citizens on the part of those who may be charged with its execution, and suggests that additional instructions should issue.

The undersigned considers that the subsequent Order in Council of 10th ulto. is sufficiently explicit and ought to be quite satisfactory.

If anything were really wanting to assure Mr. Thornton & remove Mr. Fish's apprehensions, reference might be made to the Canadian Statutes relating to fishing by foreign vessels (copy herewith) and to the following extract from the Special Instructions (dated 14 ultimo) which govern officers engaged in the fisheries protection service.

1. "U. S. fishermen may exercise the liberty of fishing in common with British subjects along that part of the Coast of Canada extending from Mount Joy near the River Grande Natashquhan, to the easterly limit of Canada, at Blanc Sablon Bay, and around the

---

[a] Appendix, p. 581.

Magdalen Islands; and enjoy freedom also to land and cure fish on certain of the unsettled shores of the Labrador Coast.

"Wherever any settlement exists within those limits, the privilege of landing and curing fish may be enjoyed by previous agreement with the settlers or proprietors of the ground."[a]

The Order in Council of May 10, 1870, referred to in this report concurs with the statement of the Minister of Marine and Fisheries "that the Canadian Government never contemplated any interference with rights secured to United States citizens by the treaty in question between the British and American Governments," and that "Mr. Thornton was therefore quite right in assuring Mr. Fish, in general terms, that there could be no intention to abridge any rights to which citizens of the United States are entitled by treaty."[b]

Questions of treaty interpretation rest with the British and not the Colonial Governments.

Before passing from this period, attention must be called to one peculiarly significant feature of the situation in connection with the differences which arose between the British and Colonial Governments in regard to the interpretation and enforcement of the provisions of the treaty of 1818. It will be remembered that frequently, during the course of the diplomatic correspondence previously reviewed, the United States had occasion to insist that the interpretation of the provisions of this treaty rested with the United States and Great Britain rather than with the British Colonies, and it will be found upon an examination of the correspondence between the British and Colonial Governments with reference to these differences during this period, that the British Government not only fully concurred with the view of the United States on this point, but took occasion to impress it upon the Colonial Governments in no uncertain terms.

When the proposal for issuing special licenses to American vessels for the purpose of continuing to them the privileges in the inshore fisheries under the reciprocity treaty was being considered by the several provinces in 1866, the Government of Nova Scotia expressed an unwillingness to join with the other provinces in adopting this proposal, preferring to insist upon the enforcement of the rights asserted by them under their interpretation of the treaty of 1818.

---

[a] Appendix, p. 619.   [b] Appendix, 588.

On being informed of these views of the Provincial Government, Mr. Cardwell, Secretary of State for the Colonies, promptly wrote on May 26, 1866, to the Lieutenant Governor of Nova Scotia expressing regret at the attitude of that Government with respect to which he says:

I must distinctly inform you that on a matter so intimately connected with the international relations of this country, her Majesty's government will not be disposed to *yield their own opinion* of what it is reasonable to insist on, nor to *enforce* the strict rights of her Majesty's subjects beyond what appears to them to be required by the reason and justice of the case.[a]

So also when the negotiations which resulted in the treaty of 1871 were being undertaken, Lord Kimberley wrote on February 16, 1871, to Lord Lisgar, the Governor General of Canada, stating generally the British attitude on these questions as follows:

You have already been informed by telegram of the views of Her Majesty's Government upon the Fishery Questions, but I think it will be convenient, with reference to the pending negotiations, that a somewhat fuller statement of those views should now be placed on record.

It would not be possible for Her Majesty's Government to pledge themselves to any foregone conclusion upon any particular point connected with these negotiations, but they have anxiously considered the questions which concern Canada; and they feel confident that the Canadian Government, will agree with them that a satisfactory termination of the difficulties which have arisen with the United States, can only be attained by taking as broad and liberal a view as is consistent with the just rights and real interests of the Dominion.

As at present advised, Her Majesty's Government are of opinion that the right of Canada to exclude Americans from fishing in the waters within the limits of three marine miles of the coast, is beyond dispute, and can only be ceded for an adequate consideration.

Should this consideration take the form of a money payment, it appears to Her Majesty's Government, that such an arrangement would be more likely to work well than if any conditions were annexed to the exercise of the privilege of fishing within the Canadian waters.

The presence of a considerable number of cruisers would always be necessary to secure the performance of such conditions and the enforcement of penalties for the non-observance of them would be certain to lead to disputes with the United States.

With respect to the question, what is a Bay or Creek, within the meaning of the first Article of the Treaty of 1818, Her Majesty's Government adhere to the interpretation which they have hitherto maintained of that Article, but they consider that the difference which has arisen with the United States on this point, might be a fit subject for compromise.

The exclusion of American fishermen from resorting to Canadian Ports, "except for the purpose of shelter, and of repairing damages therein, of purchasing wood and of obtaining water," might be

---

[a] Appendix, p. 577.

warranted by the letter of the Treaty of 1818, and by the terms of the Imperial Act, 59, Geo. III, chap. 38, but Her Majesty's Government feel bound to state that it seems to them an extreme measure—inconsistent with the general policy of the Empire, and they are disposed to concede this point to the United States Government, under such restrictions as may be necessary to prevent smuggling, and to guard against any substantial invasion of the exclusive rights of fishing which may be reserved to British subjects.[a]

Again on March 17, 1871, Lord Kimberly took occasion to write to the Governor General of Canada—

I think it right however to add that the responsibility of determining what is the true construction of a Treaty made by Her Majesty with any foreign power, must remain with Her Majesty's Government, and that the degree to which this Country would make itself a party to the strict enforcement of Treaty Rights may depend not only on the liberal construction of the Treaty, but on the moderation and reasonableness with which those rights are asserted.[b]

Seizures for " preparing to fish."

It will be remembered that in Mr. Fish's note, above quoted, of May 29, 1870, to the United States Consul-General in Canada, he said, in instructing him with respect to the position of the United States Government on the subject of seizures for "preparing to fish":

In particular if the charge against any American fishing vessel is only that she has been preparing to fish, without actually fishing in the prohibited limits, it is to be made known to the counsel of the owner of the vessel that this Government is not disposed to regard such mere preparation as an infraction of the obligations of our citizens engaged in the outfitting and employment of fishing vessels, and it is desirous of having the point distinctly presented and adjudicated without being complicated with other questions, so if adversely decided, the case presenting that single issue may be made for appeal to the British tribunal of last resort.[c]

An adjudication on the point thus referred to by Mr. Fish was soon afterwards rendered in the case of the American fishing vessel *White Fawn*, which was seized on November 25, 1870, at Head Harbor, New Brunswick, charged with having obtained there a quantity of herring to be used as bait for fishing. In the proceedings subsequently taken for her condemnation in the Vice-Admiralty Court at St. John, the determination of the legality of the seizure turned upon the question of the meaning and effect of the words "preparing to fish" in the Canadian statute under which the seizure was made. This question is discussed at considerable length in the opinion of

[a] Appendix, p. 636.   [b] Appendix, p. 637.   [c] *Supra*, p. 141.

the Court, in which it was held that the facts presented did not make out a *prima facie* case for condemnation. The opinion of the Court is printed in full in the Appendix, and the portions of it relating to this feature of the case are covered by the following extract:

By the Imperial Statute, 59 George III., cap. 38, it is declared that if any foreign vessel, or person on board thereof, "shall be found to be fishing, or to have been fishing, or preparing to fish within such distance (three marine miles) of the coast, such vessel and cargo shall be forfeited."

The Dominion Statute, 31 Vic., Cap. 61, as amended by 33 Vic., Cap. 15, enacts: "If such foreign vessel is found fishing, or preparing to fish, or to have been fishing in British waters, within three marine miles of the coast, such vessel, her tackle, etc., and cargo, shall be forfeited."

The *White Fawn* was a foreign vessel in British waters; in fact, within one of the Counties of this Province when she was seized. It is not alleged that she is subject to forfeiture for having entered Head Harbour for other purposes than shelter or obtaining wood and water. Under Section III, of the Imperial Act, no forfeiture but a penalty can be inflicted for such entry. Nor is it alleged that she committed any infraction of the Customs or Revenue Laws. It is not stated that she had fished within the prescribed limits, or had been found fishing, but that she was "preparing to fish," having bought bait (an article no doubt very material if not necessary for successful fishing) from the inhabitants of Campobello. Assuming that the fact of such purchase establishes a "preparing to fish" under the Statutes (which I do not admit), I think, before a forfeiture could be incurred, it must be shown that the preparations were for an illegal fishing in British waters: hence, for aught which appears, the intention of the Master may have been to prosecuting his fishing outside of the three-mile limit, in conformity with the Statutes; and it is not for the court to impute fraud or an intention to infringe the provisions of our statutes to any person, British or foreign, in the absence of evidence of such fraud. He had a right, in common with all other persons, to pass with his vessel through the three miles, from our coast to the fishing grounds outside, which he might lawfully use, and, as I have already stated, there is no evidence of any intention to fish before he reached such grounds.

The construction sought to be put upon the statutes by the Crown officers would appear to be thus:—"A foreign vessel, being in British waters and purchasing from a British subject any article which may be used in prosecuting the fisheries, without its being shown that such article is to be used in illegal fishing in British waters, is liable to forfeiture as preparing to fish in British waters."

I cannot adopt such a construction. I think it harsh and unreasonable, and not warranted by the words of the statutes. It would subject a foreign vessel, which might be of great value, as in the present case, to forfeiture, with her cargo and outfits, for purchasing (while she was pursuing her voyage in British waters, as she lawfully might do, within three miles of our coast) of a British subject any article, however small in value (a cod-line or net for instance) without its being shown that there was any intention of using such articles in illegal fishing in British waters before she reached the fishing ground to which she might legally resort for fishing under the terms of the Statutes.

I construe the Statutes simply thus:—If a foreign vessel is found— 1st, having taken fish; 2nd, fishing, although no fish have been taken; 3rd, "preparing to fish," (i. e.), with her crew arranging her nets, lines, and fishing tackle for fishing, though not actually applied to fishing, in British waters, in either of those cases specified in the statutes the forfeiture attaches.

I think the words "preparing to fish" were introduced for the purpose of preventing the escape of a foreign vessel which, though with intent of illegal fishing in British waters, had not taken fish or engaged in fishing by setting nets and lines, but was seized in the very act of putting out her lines, nets, etc., into the water, and so preparing to fish. Without these a vessel so situated would escape seizure, inasmuch as the crew had neither caught fish nor been found fishing.

Taking this view of the Statutes, I am of the opinion that the facts disclosed by the affidavits do not furnish legal grounds for the seizure of the American schooner *White Fawn*, by Captain Betts, the commander of the Dominion vessel *Water Lily*, and do not make out a *prima facie* case for condemnation in this Court, of the schooner, her tackle, &c., and cargo.

I may add that as the construction I have put upon the Statutes differs from that adopted by the Crown Officers of the Dominion, it is satisfactory to know that the judgement of the Supreme Court may be obtained by information, filed there, as the Imperial Act 59, George III., Cap. 38, gave concurrent jurisdiction to that Court in cases of this nature.[a]

It does not appear that any further action in the case was taken.

A further statement of the position of the United States on the question of "preparing to fish" as well as on the several other questions under consideration at that time relating to the fisheries, will be found in the following extract from President Grant's Annual Message of December 5, 1870:

The course pursued by the Canadian authorities toward the fishermen of the United States during the past season has not been marked by a friendly feeling. By the first article of the convention of 1818 between Great Britain and the United States it was agreed that the inhabitants of the United States should have forever, in common with British subjects, the right of taking fish in certain waters therein defined. In the waters not included in the limits named in the convention (within 3 miles of parts of the British coast) it has been the custom for many years to give to intruding fishermen of the United States a reasonable warning of their violation of the technical rights of Great Britain. The Imperial Government is understood to have delegated the whole or a share of its jurisdiction or control of these inshore fishing grounds to the colonial authority known as the Dominion of Canada, and this semi-independent but irresponsible agent has exercised its delegated powers in an unfriendly way. Vessels have been seized without notice or warning, in violation of the

_____

[a] Appendix, p. 1099.

custom previously prevailing, and have been taken into the colonial ports, their voyages broken up, and the vessels condemned. There is reason to believe that this unfriendly and vexatious treatment was designed to bear harshly upon the hardy fishermen of the United States, with a view to political effect upon this Government. The statutes of the Dominion of Canada assume a still broader and more untenable jurisdiction over the vessels of the United States. They authorize officers or persons to bring vessels hovering within 3 marine miles of any of the coasts, bays, creeks, or harbors of Canada into port, to search the cargo, to examine the master on oath touching the cargo and voyage, and to inflict upon him a heavy pecuniary penalty if true answers are not given; and if such vessel is found "preparing to fish" within 3 marine miles of any of such coasts, bays, creeks, or harbors without a license, or after the expiration of the period named in the last license granted to it, they provide that the vessel, with her tackle, etc., shall be forfeited. It is not known that any condemnations have been made under this statute. Should the authorities of Canada attempt to enforce it, it will become my duty to take such steps as may be necessary to protect the rights of the citizens of the United States.

It has been claimed by Her Majesty's officers that the fishing vessels of the United States have no right to enter the open ports of the British possessions in North America, except for the purposes of shelter and repairing damages, of purchasing wood and obtaining water; that they have no right to enter at the British custom-houses or to trade there except in the purchase of wood and water, and that they must depart within twenty-four hours after notice to leave. It is not known that any seizure of a fishing vessel carrying the flag of the United States has been made under this claim. So far as the claim is founded on an alleged construction of the convention of 1818, it can not be acquiesced in by the United States. It is hoped that it will not be insisted on by Her Majesty's Government.

During the conferences which preceded the negotiation of the convention of 1818 the British commissioners proposed to expressly exclude the fishermen of the United States from "the privilege of carrying on trade with any of His Britannic Majesty's subjects residing within the limits assigned for their use;" and also that it should not be "lawful for the vessels of the United States engaged in said fishery to have on board any goods, wares, or merchandise whatever, except such as may be necessary for the prosecution of their voyages to and from the said fishing grounds; and any vessel of the United States which shall contravene this regulation may be seized, condemned, and confiscated, with her cargo."

This proposition, which is identical with the construction now put upon the language of the convention, was emphatically rejected by the American commissioners, and thereupon was abandoned by the British plenipotentiaries, and Article I, as it stands in the convention, was substituted.

If, however, it be said that this claim is founded on provincial or colonial statutes, and not upon the convention, this Government can not but regard them as unfriendly, and in contravention of the spirit, if not of the letter, of the treaty, for the faithful execution of which the Imperial Government is alone responsible.

Anticipating that an attempt may possibly be made by the Canadian authorities in the coming season to repeat their unneighborly acts toward our fishermen, I recommend you to confer upon the Executive the power to suspend by proclamation the operation of the laws authorizing the transit of goods, wares, and merchandise in bond across the territory of the United States to Canada, and, further, should such an extreme measure become necessary, to suspend the operations of any laws whereby the vessels of the Dominion of Canada are permitted to enter the waters of the United States.

No question involving the fishery rights of American fishermen on the Newfoundland coasts arose during this period.

PERIOD FROM 1871 TO 1888.

Treaty of May 8, 1871.

The fisheries provisions of the treaty of May 8, 1871, between the United States and Great Britain,[a] although differing slightly from the fisheries provisions of the treaty of 1854, are in effect a repetition of those provisions, in so far as they apply to the fisheries under consideration in this Case. In the later treaty, however, the provisions of the earlier treaty for reciprocal trade concessions were omitted with the exception of a provision for free entry into each country of fish oil and fish of all kinds being the produce of the fisheries of the other country, and it was provided in Article XXII of the treaty that—

Inasmuch as it is asserted by the Government of Her Britannic Majesty that the privileges accorded to the citizens of the United States under Article XVIII. of this Treaty are of greater value than those accorded by Articles XIX. and XXI. of this Treaty to the subjects of Her Britannic Majesty, and this assertion is not admitted by the Government of the United States, it is further agreed that Commissioners shall be appointed to determine, having regard to the privileges accorded by the United States to the subjects of Her Britannic Majesty, as stated in Articles XIX and XXI. of this Treaty, the amount of any compensation which, in their opinion, ought to be paid by the Government of the United States to the Government of Her Britannic Majesty in return for the privi-

---

[a] Appendix, p. 28.

leges accorded to the citizens of the United States under Article XVIII. of this Treaty.[a]

The fisheries provisions of this treaty came into force on July 1, 1873, although they did not become applicable to Newfoundland until May 29, 1874, and by the terms of the treaty they remained in force for a fixed term of ten years from the date on which they came into operation, and further until the expiration of two years after notice given by either party to the other of its wish to terminate the same, which notice was given by the United States to Great Britain on July 2, 1883, and in consequence of which the fisheries provisions of the treaty terminated on July 1, 1885.[b]   It was mutually agreed, however, by the *modus vivendi* of 1885, entered into prior to the termination of the fisheries articles, that the fishing privileges secured by the treaty of 1871 should be continued throughout the season of 1885; so that actually the fishing privileges under this treaty continued until the 1st of January, 1886.[c]

By the terms of the treaty the assent of the Parliament of Canada and the Legislature of Prince Edward's Island was required to carry the fisheries provisions into operation, and on June 17, 1871, the Earl of Kimberly wrote to Lord Lisgar, the Governor General of Canada, for the purpose of informing the Canadian Government of the conclusion of the treaty and recommending the adoption of appropriate legislation to give it effect.   The following extract from this letter will be of interest as showing the British view of the situation at the time this treaty was entered into:

The Canadian Government itself took the initiative in suggesting that a Joint British and American Commission should be appointed, with a view to settle the disputes which had arisen as to the interpretation of the Treaty of 1818, but it was certain that however desirable it might be, in default of any complete settlement, to appoint such a Commission, the causes of the difficulty lay deeper than any question of interpretation, and the mere discussion of such points as the correct definition of bays could not lead to a really friendly agreement with the United States.   It was necessary, therefore, to endeavor to find an equivalent which the United States might be willing to give in return for the fishery privileges, and which Great Britain, having regard both to Imperial and Colonial interests, could properly accept.   Her Majesty's Government are well aware that the arrangement which would have been most agreeable to Canada was the conclusion of a Treaty similar to the Reciprocity Treaty of 1854, and a proposal to this effect was pressed upon the United States Commissioners, as you will find in the 36th Protocol of the Confer-

---

[a] Appendix, p. 30.   [b] Appendix, p. 749.   [c] Appendix, p. 33.

ences. This proposal was, however, declined, the United States Commissioners stating "that they could hold out no hope that the Congress of the United States would give its consent to such a tariff arrangement as was proposed, or to any extended plan of reciprocal free admission of the products of the two countries." The United States Commissioners did indeed propose that coal, salt and fish, should be reciprocally admitted free, and lumber after the 1st of July 1874; but it is evident that looked at as a tariff arrangement this was a most inadequate offer, as will be seen at once when it is compared with the long list of articles admitted free under the Reciprocity Treaty. Moreover, it is obvious from the frank avowal of the United States Commissioners, that they only made this offer because one branch of Congress had recently more than once expressed itself in favor of the abolition of duties on coal and salt, and because Congress had partially removed the duty from lumber, and the tendency of legislation in the United States was towards the reduction of taxation and of duties, so that to have ceded the Fishery rights in return for these concessions would have been to exchange them for commercial arrangements, which there is reason to believe may before long be made without any such cession, to the mutual advantage of both the Dominion and the United States; and Her Majesty's Government are bound to add that whilst in deference to the strong wishes of the Dominion Government they used their best efforts to obtain a renewal in principle of the Reciprocity Treaty, they are convinced that the establishment of free trade between the Dominion and the United States is not likely to be promoted by making admission to the fisheries dependent upon the conclusion of such a Treaty; and that the repeal by Congress of duties upon Canadian produce on the ground that a Protective Tariff is injurious to the country which imposes it, would place the commercial relations of the two countries on a far more secure and lasting basis than the stipulations of a Convention framed upon a system of reciprocity. Looking, therefore, to all the circumstances, Her Majesty's Government found it their duty to deal separately with the Fisheries, and to endeavor to find some other equivalent; and the reciprocal concession of free fishery with free import of fish and fish oil, together with the payment of such a sum of money as may fairly represent the excess of value of the Colonial over the American concessions, seems to them to be an equitable solution of the difficulty. It is perfectly true that the right of fishery on the United States coasts, conceded under Article XIX, is far less valuable than the right of fishery in Colonial waters, conceded under Article XVIII, to the United States, but on the other hand, it cannot be denied that it is most important to the Colonial fishermen to obtain free access to the American market for their fish and for fish oil, and the balance of advantage on the side of the United States will be duly redressed by the Arbitrators under Article XXII. In some respects a direct money payment is perhaps a more distinct recognition of the rights of the Colonies than a tariff concession, and there does not seem to be any difference in principle between the admission of American fishermen for a term of years in consideration of the payment of a sum of money in gross, and their admission under the system of Licenses, calculated at so many dollars per ton, which was adopted by the Colonial Government for several years after the termination of the Reciprocity Treaty. In the latter case, it must be observed, the use of the Fisheries was granted without any tariff concession whatever on the part of the United States, even as to the importation of fish.

Canada could not reasonably expect that this country should, for an indefinite period, incur the constant risk of serious misunderstanding with the United States; imperilling, perhaps, the peace of the whole Empire, in order to endeavor to force the American Government to change its commercial policy; and Her Majesty's Government are confident that, when the Treaty is considered as a whole, the Canadian people will see that their interests have been carefully borne in mind, and that the advantages, which they will derive from its provisions, are commensurate with the concessions which they are called upon to make.[a]

The Halifax Award.

The Fisheries Commission referred to in Article XXII. of the treaty of 1871 met at Halifax on June 15, 1877, for the purpose of determining under the provisions of that treaty, how much, if any, greater was the value of the privileges accorded to the citizens of the United States under Article XVIII. than those accorded by Articles XIX. and XXI. to the subjects of Her Britannic Majesty; and on the 23rd day of November of that year the British commissioner and the umpire rendered a decision, the American commissioner dissenting, by which they awarded "the sum of $5,500,000. in gold to be paid by the Government of the United States to the Government of Her Britannic Majesty" as compensation for the excess value of the privileges accorded to the citizens of the United States over those accorded to the subjects of Great Britain in accordance with the provisions of the treaty.

In the proceedings before the Halifax Commission it was contended on the part of Great Britain that among the privileges secured to the inhabitants of the United States under the treaty, "*the entire freedom of the inshore fisheries on the coast of Newfoundland*," apart from the freedom of the fisheries on the treaty coasts under the treaty of 1818, was of immense value. As this privilege was described in the treaty of 1871 as a liberty "in common with the subjects of Her Britannic Majesty," which is the same expression used in the treaty of 1818 with respect to the fishing liberty of the inhabitants of the United States on the treaty coasts under that treaty, the British contention with respect to the extent and value of the liberty thus

---

[a] Appendix, p. 640.

described and the award of $5,500,000, based in part upon the value of such liberty is of particular importance in the present Case.[a]

The bearing of that question upon the questions presented in this Case will more fully appear in the discussion which arose between the United States and Great Britain with respect to the Fortune Bay case in the year 1878, which is reviewed below.

The Fortune Bay Case.

On January 6, 1878, barely a month and a half after the date of the Halifax award, a number of American fishermen, who were engaged in taking fish with seines in Fortune Bay on the coast of Newfoundland, "were compelled, by a large and violent mob of the inhabitants of Newfoundland, to take up their seines, discharge the fish already inclosed, and abandon their fishery, and in one case at least the seine was absolutely destroyed."[b] As appeared in the subsequent investigation of the circumstances surrounding this incident, the fishermen using the seines were acting in the interests of all the American fishing vessels in the harbor at that time, twenty-two in number, and if they had been undisturbed the catch would have been sufficient to load all of them with profitable cargoes.   It further appeared that the American vessels had been waiting at Fortune Bay for several weeks for the expected arrival of schools of herring in that Bay; and it so happened that the day of the arrival of these schools was Sunday, on which, under the laws of Newfoundland, the Newfoundland fishermen were prohibited from fishing.[c]

The action of the Newfoundland fishermen in preventing the American fishermen from taking advantage of their long awaited opportunity could hardly have been inspired by a respect for law and order.   Great Britain, however, in resisting the resulting claims for damages, which were demanded by the United States on behalf of the American fishing vessels, advanced the argument that the Newfoundland law prohibiting Sunday fishing applied to the American as well as to the British fishermen in those waters, and that the American fishermen were violating not only that law but another law as well which prohibited the use of seines at the season of the year when this incident occurred.[d] As bearing upon the intention with which the laws referred to were adopted, it may be noted in

---

[a] Appendix, p. 1109.
[b] Appendix, p. 666.
[c] Appendix, pp. 651, 666.
[d] Appendix, pp. 651, 667.

passing that they both contained the express provision that nothing therein should "affect the rights and privileges granted by treaty to the subjects of any state or power in amity with Her Majesty," which provision is common to all of the laws of Newfoundland relating to the fisheries.[a]

The position thus taken by Great Britain led to a discussion between the two Governments with reference to the validity of British or Colonial legislation as applied to American fishermen when the effect of such legislation was to limit or restrain the exercise by American fishermen of the fishing liberty secured to them by treaty. Although Fortune Bay is not on the treaty coast covered by the treaty of 1818, and the discussion related to the fishing liberty under the treaty of 1871, yet in both treaties alike such liberty is described as a liberty in common with British subjects, and therefore the discussion is of interest in connection with the questions at issue in the present case.

The following extract from a letter of instructions written on August 1, 1879, by Mr. Evarts, then Secretary of State, to Mr. Welsh, the American Minister at London, and communicated by him to Lord Salisbury, then Secretary of State for Foreign Affairs, reviews the course of the discussion up to that time and states the position of the United States on the questions involved:

As soon as the violence to which citizens of the United States had been subjected in Newfoundland was brought to the attention of this department, I instructed you, on 2d March, 1878, to represent the matter to Her Britannic Majesty's Government, and upon such representation you were informed that a prompt investigation would be ordered for the information of that government.

On August 23, 1878, Lord Salisbury conveyed to you, to be transmitted to your Government, the result of that investigation, in the shape of a report from Captain Sulivan, of Her Majesty's ship *Sirius*. In furnishing you with this report, Lord Salisbury, on behalf of Her Britannic Majesty's Government, said:

"You will perceive that the report in question appears to demonstrate conclusively that the United States fishermen on this occasion had committed three distinct breaches of the law, and that no violence was used by the Newfoundland fishermen, except in the case of one vessel, whose master refused to comply with the request which was made to him that he should desist from fishing on Sunday in violation of the law of the colony and of the local custom, and who threatened the Newfoundland fishermen with a revolver, as detailed in paragraphs 5 and 6 of Captain Sulivan's report."

---

[a] Appendix, p. 665.

The three breaches of the law thus reported by Captain Sulivan and assumed by Lord Salisbury as conclusively established, were: 1. The use of seines and the use of them also at a time prohibited by a colonial statute. 2. Fishing upon a day—Sunday—forbidden by the same local law; and 3. Barring fish in violation of the same local legislation. In addition Captain Sulivan reported that the United States fishermen were, contrary to the terms of the treaty of Washington—

"Fishing illegally, interfering with the rights of British fishermen and their peaceable use of that part of the coast then occupied by them and of which they were actually in possession—their seines and boats, their huts and gardens and land granted by government being situated thereon."

Yours, containing this dispatch and the accompanying report, was received on 4th September, 1878, and on the 28th of the same month you were instructed that it was impossible for this government duly to appreciate the value of Captain Sulivan's report, until it was permitted to see the testimony upon which the conclusions of that report professed to rest. And you were further directed to say that, putting aside for after examination the variations of fact, it seemed to this government that the assumption of the report was, that the United States fishermen were fishing illegally, because their fishing was being conducted at a time and by methods forbidden by certain colonial statutes; that the language of Lord Salisbury, in communicating the report with his approval, indicated the intention of Her Britannic Majesty's Government to maintain the position, that the treaty privileges secured to United States fishermen by the treaty of 1871 were held subject to such limitations as might be imposed upon their exercise by colonial legislation; and "that so grave a question, in its bearing upon the obligations of this government under the treaty, makes it necessary that the President should ask from Her Majesty's Government a frank avowal or disavowal of the paramount authority of provincial legislation to regulate the enjoyment by our people of the inshore fishery, which seems to be intimated, if not asserted, in Lord Salisbury's note."

In reply to this communication, Lord Salisbury, 7th November, 1878, transmitted to you the depositions which accompanied Captain Sulivan's report, and said:

"In pointing out that the American fishermen had broken the law within the territorial limits of Her Majesty's domains, I had no intention of inferentially laying down any principles of international law, and no advantage would, I think, be gained by doing so to a greater extent than the facts in question absolutely require. * * * Her Majesty's Government will readily admit—what is, indeed, self-evident—that British sovereignty, as regards those waters, is limited in its scope by the engagements of the Treaty of Washington, which can not be modified or affected by any municipal legislation."

It is with the greatest pleasure that the United States Government receives this language as "the frank disavowal" which it asked "of the paramount authority of provincial legislation to regulate the enjoyment by our people of the inshore fishery."

Removing, as this explicit language does, the only serious difficulty which threatened to embarrass this discussion, I am now at liberty to resume the consideration of these differences in the same spirit and with the same hopes so fully and properly expressed in the concluding paragraph of Lord Salisbury's dispatch. He says:

"It is not explicitly stated in Mr. Evarts' dispatch that he considers any recent acts of the colonial legislature to be inconsistent with the rights acquired by the United States under the Treaty of Washington. But if that is the case, Her Majesty's Government will, in a friendly spirit, consider any representations he may think it right to make upon the subject, with the hope of coming to a satisfactory understanding."

It is the purpose, therefore, of the present dispatch to convey to you, in order that they may be submitted to Her Brittanic Majesty's Government, the conclusions which have been reached by the Government of the United States as to the rights secured to its citizens under the treaty of 1871 in the herring fishery upon the Newfoundland coast, and the extent to which those rights have been infringed by the transactions in Fortune Bay on January 6, 1878.

Before doing so, however, I deem it proper, in order to clear the argument of all unnecessary issues, to correct what I consider certain misapprehensions of the views of this Government contained in Lord Salisbury's dispatch of 7th of November, 1878. The secretary for foreign affairs of Her Brittanic Majesty says:

"If, however, it be admitted that the Newfoundland legislature have the right of binding Americans who fish within their waters by any laws which do not contravene existing treaties, it must be further conceded that the duty of determining the existence of such contravention must be undertaken by the governments, and can not be remitted to the discretion of each individual fisherman. For such discretion, if exercised on one side, can hardly be refused on the other. If any American fisherman may violently break a law which he believes to be contrary to a treaty, a Newfoundland fisherman may violently maintain it if he believes it to be in accordance with treaty."

His lordship can scarcely have intended this last proposition to be taken in its literal significance. An infraction of law may be accompanied by violence which affects the person or property of an individual, and that individual may be warranted in resisting such illegal violence, so far as it directly affects him, without reference to the relation of the act of violence to the law which it infringes, but simply as a forcible invasion of his rights of person or property. But that the infraction of a general municipal law, with or without violence, can be corrected and punished by a mob, without official character or direction, and who assume both to interpret and administer the law in controversy, is a proposition which does not require the reply of elaborate argument between two governments whose daily life depends upon the steady application of the sound and safe principles of English jurisprudence. However this may be, the Government of the United States can not for a moment admit that the conduct of the United States fishermen in Fortune Bay was in any—the remotest—degree a violent breach of the law.

Granting any and all the force which may be claimed for the colonial legislation, the action of the United States fishermen was the peaceable prosecution of an innocent industry, to which they thought they were entitled. Its pursuit invaded no man's rights, committed violence upon no man's person, and if trespassing beyond its lawful limits could have been promptly and quietly stopped by the interference and representations of the lawfully constituted authorities. They were acting under the provisions of the very statute which they are alleged to have violated, for it seems to have escaped the attention of Lord Salisbury that section 28 of the title of the consolidated acts referred to contains the provision that "Nothing in this chapter shall affect the rights and privileges granted by treaty to the subjects of any state or power in amity with Her Majesty." They were engaged, as I shall hereafter demonstrate, in a lawful industry, guaranteed by the treaty of 1871, in a method which was recognized as legitimate by the award of the Halifax Commission, the privilege to exercise which their government had agreed to pay for. They were forcibly stopped, not by legal authority, but by mob violence. They made no resistance, withdrew from the fishing grounds, and represented the outrage to their Government, thus acting in entire conformity with the principle as justly stated by Lord Salisbury himself, that—

"If it be admitted, however, that the Newfoundland legislature have the right of binding Americans who fish within their waters by any laws which do not contravene existing treaties, it must be further conceded that the duty of determining the existence of such contravention must be undertaken by the governments, and can not be remitted to the judgment of each individual fisherman."

There is another passage of Lord Salisbury's dispatch to which I should call your attention. Lord Salisbury says:

"I hardly believe, however, that Mr. Evarts would in discussion adhere to the broad doctrine, which some portion of his language would appear to convey, that no British authority has a right to pass any kind of laws binding Americans who are fishing in British waters; for if that contention be just the same disability applies *a fortiori* to any other powers, and the waters must be delivered over to anarchy."

I certainly can not recall any language of mine in this correspondence which is capable of so extraordinary a construction. I have nowhere taken any position larger or broader than that which Lord Salisbury says:

"Her Majesty's Government will readily admit, what is, indeed, self-evident, that British sovereignty, as regards these waters, is limited in its scope by the engagements of the Treaty of Washington, which can not be affected or modified by any municipal legislature."

I have never denied the full authority and jurisdiction, either of the imperial or colonial governments, over their territorial waters, except so far as by treaty that authority and jurisdiction have been deliberately limited by these governments themselves. Under no claim or authority suggested or advocated by me could any other government demand exemption from the provisions of British or colonial law, unless that exemption was secured by treaty; and if these waters must be delivered over to anarchy, it will not be in consequence of any pretensions of the United States Government, but because the British Government has, by its own treaties, to use Lord Salisbury's phrase, limited the scope of British sovereignty. I am not aware of any such treaty engagements with other powers, but if there are, it would be neither my privilege nor duty to consider or criticise their consequences where the interests of the United States are not concerned.[a]

After setting forth the undisputed facts in the case, which have already been stated above, Mr. Evarts continues as follows:

The provisions of the treaty of Washington (1871), by which the right to prosecute this fishery was secured to the citizens of the United States, are very simple and very explicit.

The language of the treaty is as follows:

"XVIII. It is agreed by the high contracting parties that in addition to the liberties secured to the United States fishermen by the convention between the United States and Great Britain, signed at London on the 20th day of October, 1818, of taking, curing, and drying fish on certain coasts of the British North American colonies, therein defined, the inhabitants of the United States shall have, in common with the subjects of Her Britannic Majesty, the liberty for the term of years mentioned in Article XXXIII of this treaty to take fish of every kind, except shell-fish, on the sea coast and shores and in the bays, harbors, and creeks of the provinces of Quebec, &c.

"XXXII. It is further agreed that the provisions and stipulations of Articles XVIII to XXV of this treaty, inclusive, shall extend to the colony of Newfoundland, so far as they are applicable."

Title XXVII, chapter 102, of the consolidated acts of Newfoundland, provides:

"SECTION 1. That no person shall take herring on the coast of Newfoundland by a seine or other such contrivance, at any time between the 20th day of October and the 12th day of April, in any year, or at any time use a seine except by way of shooting and forthwith hauling the same.

"SEC. 2. That no person shall, at any time, between the 20th day of December and the 1st day of April, in any year, catch or take herring with seines of less than 2¾ inches mesh, &c.

"SEC. 4. No person shall, between the 20th day of April and the 20th day of October, in any year, haul, catch, or take herring or other bait for exportation within one mile, measured by the shore across the water, of any settlement situated between Cape Chapeau Rouge and Point Emajer, near Cape Ray."

The act of 1876 provides that "No person shall, between the hours of twelve o'clock on Saturday night and twelve o'clock on Sunday night, haul or take any herring, capelin, or squid, with net, seine, bunts, or any such contrivance for the purpose of such hauling or taking."

It seemed scarcely necessary to do more than place the provisions of the treaty and the provisions of these laws in contrast, and apply the principle so precisely and justly announced by Lord Salisbury as self-evident, "that British sovereignty, as regards those waters, is limited in its scope by the engagements of the Treaty of Washington, which can not be modified or affected by any municipal legislation." For it will not be denied that the treaty privilege of "taking fish of every kind, except shell-fish, on the sea coast and shores, and in the bays, harbors, and creeks" of Newfoundland, is both seriously "modified" and injuriously affected by municipal legislation, which closes such

---

[a] Appendix, p. 662.

fishery absolutely for seven months of the year, prescribes a special method of exercise, forbids exportation for five months, and, in certain localities, absolutely limits the three-mile area, which it was the express purpose of the treaty to open.

But this is not all. When the treaty of 1871 was negotiated, the British Government contended that the privilege extended to United States fishermen of free fishing within the three-mile territorial limit was so much more valuable than the equivalent offered in the treaty that a money compensation should be added to equalize the exchange. The Halifax Commission was appointed for the special purpose of determining that compensation, and, in order to do so, instituted an exhaustive examination of the history and value of the colonial fisheries, including the herring fishery of Newfoundland.

Before that commission, the United States Government contended that the frozen-herring fishery in Fortune Bay, Newfoundland, the very fishery now under discussion, was not a fishery, but a traffic; that the United States vessels which went there for herring always took out trading permits from the United States custom-house, which no other fishermen did; that the herring were caught by the natives in their nets and sold to the vessels, the captains of which froze the herring after purchase, and transported them to market, and that consequently this was a trade, a commerce beneficial to the Newfoundlanders, and not to be debited to the United States account of advantages gained by the treaty. To this the British Government replied, that whatever the character of the business had been, the treaty now gave the United States fishermen the right to catch as well as purchase herring; that the superior character of the United States vessels, the larger capacity and more efficient instrumentality of the seines used by the United States fishermen, together with their enterprise and energy, would all induce the United States fishermen to catch herring for themselves, and thus the treaty gave certain privileges to the United States fishermen, which inflicted upon the original proprietor a certain amount of loss and damage, from this dangerous competition, which, in justice to their interests, required compensation. The exercise of these privileges, therefore, as stated in the British case, as evidenced in the British testimony, as maintained in the British argument, for which the British Government demanded and received compensation, is the British construction of the extent of the liberty to fish in common, guaranteed by the treaty.

Mr. Whiteway, then attorney-general of Newfoundland, and one of the British counsel before the commission, said in his argument:

"And now one word with regard to the winter herring-fishery in Fortune Bay. It appears that from 40 to 50 United States vessels proceed there between the months of November and February, taking from thence cargoes of frozen herring of from 500 to 800 or 1,000 barrels. According to the evidence, these herrings have hitherto generally been obtained by purchase. It is hardly possible, then, to conceive that the Americans will continue to buy, possessing as they now do the right to catch."

The British case states the argument as to the Newfoundland fisheries in the following language:

"It is asserted on the part of Her Majesty's Government, that the actual use which may be made of this privilege at the present moment is not so much in question as the actual value of it to those who may, if they will, use it.   It is possible, and even probable, that the United States fishermen may at any moment avail themselves of the privilege of fishing in Newfoundland inshore waters to a much larger extent than they do at present; but even if they should not do so, it would not relieve them from the obligation of making the just payment for a right which they have acquired subject to the condition of making that payment.   The case may be not inaptly illustrated by the somewhat analogous one of a tenancy of shooting or fishing privileges; it is not because the tenant fails to exercise the rights which he has acquired by virtue of his lease that the proprietor should be debarred from the recovery of his rent.

"There is a marked contrast to the advantage of the United States citizens between the privilege of access to fisheries the most valuable and productive in the world and the barren right accorded to the inhabitants of Newfoundland, of fishing in the exhausted and preoccupied waters of the United States, north of the 39th parallel of north latitude, in which there is no field for lucrative operations, even if British subjects desired to resort to them; and there are strong grounds for believing that year by year, as United States fishermen resort in greater numbers to the coasts of Newfoundland, for the purpose of procuring bait and supplies, they will become more intimately acquainted with the resources of the inshore fisheries and their unlimited capacity for extension and development.   As a matter of fact United States vessels have, since the Washington Treaty came into operation, been successfully engaged in these fisheries; and it is but reasonable to anticipate that as the advantages to be derived from them become more widely known larger numbers of United States fishermen will engage in them.

"A participation by fishermen of the United States in the freedom of these waters, must, notwithstanding their wonderfully reproductive capacity, tell materially on the local catch, and, while affording to the United States fishermen a profitable employment, must seriously interfere with local success.   The extra amount of bait also which is required for the supply of the United States demand for the bank fishery must have the effect of diminishing the supply of cod for the inshores, as it is well known that the presence of that fish is caused by the attraction offered by a large quantity of bait fishes, and as this quantity diminishes the cod will resort in fewer numbers to the coast·

• "The effect of this diminution may not in all probability be apparent for some years to come, and whilst United States fishermen will have the liberty of enjoying the fisheries for several years in their present teeming and remunerative state, the effects of overfishing may, after their right to participate in them has lapsed, become seriously prejudicial to the interests of the local fishermen.

II. The privilege of procuring bait and supplies, refitting, drying, transshipping, &c.

"Apart from the immense value to United States fishermen of participation in the Newfoundland inshore fisheries, must be estimated the important privilege of procuring bait for the prosecution of the bank and deep-sea fisheries, which are capable of unlimited expansion.   With Newfoundland as a basis of operations, the right of procuring bait, refitting their vessels, drying and curing fish, procuring ice in abundance for the preservation of bait, liberty of trans-shipping their cargoes, &c., an almost continuous prosecution of the bank fishery is secured to them.   By means of these advantages, United States fishermen have acquired by the Treaty of Washington all the requisite facilities for increasing their fishing operations to such an extent as to enable them to supply the demand for fish food in the United States markets, and largely to furnish the other fish markets of the world, and thereby exercise a competition which must inevitably prejudice Newfoundland exporters.   It must be remem-bered, in contrast with the foregoing, that United States fishing craft, before the conclusion of the treaty of Washington, could only avail themselves of the coast of Newfoundland for obtaining a supply of wood and water, for shelter, and for necessary repairs in case of ac-cident, and for no other purpose whatever.   They therefore pros-ecuted the bank fishery under great disadvantages, notwithstanding which, owing to the failure of the United States local fisheries, and the consequent necessity of providing new fishing grounds, the bank fisheries have developed into a lucrative source of employment to the fishermen of the United States.

"That this position is appreciated by those actively engaged in the bank fishery is attested by the statement of competent witnesses, whose evidence will be laid before the Commission."

And in the reply of the British Government, referring to the same Newfoundland fisheries, is the following declaration:

"As regards the herring fishery on the coast of Newfoundland, it is availed of to a considerable extent by the United States fishermen, and evidence will be adduced of large exportations by them in Ameri-can vessels, particularly from Fortune Bay and the neighborhood, both to European and their own markets.

"The presence of United States fishermen upon the coast of New-foundland, so far from being an advantage, as is assumed in the answer, operates most prejudicially to Newfoundland fishermen. Bait is not thrown overboard to attract the fish, as asserted, but the United States bank fishing vessels, visiting the coast in such large numbers as they do for the purpose of obtaining bait, sweep the coast, creeks, and inlets, thereby diminishing the supply of bait for local catch and scaring it from the grounds, where it would otherwise be an attraction for cod."

In support of these views, the most abundant testimony was pro-duced by the British Government showing the extent of the United States herring fishery, the character and construction of the seines used, the time when the vessels came and left, and the employment of the native fishermen by the United States vessels.   And it follows unanswerably that upon the existence of that fishery between the months of October and April (the very time prohibited by the colonial law), and upon the use of just such seines as were used by the complainants in this case (the very seines forbidden by the colonial law), and because the increasing direct fishery of the United States vessels was interfering with native methods and native profits, the British Government demanded and received compensation for the damages thus alleged to proceed from "the liberty to take fish of every kind" secured by the treaty.

This Government cannot anticipate that the British Government will now contend that the time and method for which it asked and received compensation are forbidden by the terms of the very treaty under which it made the claim and received the payment. Indeed, the language of Lord Salisbury justifies the Government of the United States in drawing the conclusion that between itself and Her Britannic Majesty's Government there is no substantial difference in the construction of the privileges of the treaty of 1871, and that in the future the colonial regulation of the fisheries with which, as far as their own interests are concerned, we have neither right nor desire to intermeddle, will not be allowed to modify or affect the rights which have been guaranteed to citizens of the United States.

You will therefore say to Lord Salisbury that the Government of the United States considers the engagements of the treaty of 1871 contravened by the local legislation of Newfoundland, by the prohibition of the use of seines, by the closing of the fishery with seines between October and April, by the forbidding of fishing for the purpose of exportation between December and April, by the prohibition to fish on Sunday, by the allowance of nets of only of a specified mesh, and by the limitation of the area of fishing between Cape Ray and Cape Chapeau Rouge. Of course, this is only upon the supposition that such laws are considered as applying to United States fishermen; as local regulations for native fishermen we have no concern with them. The contravention consists in excluding United States fishermen during the very times in which they have been used to pursue this industry, and forbidding the methods by which alone it can be profitably carried on. The exclusion of the time from October to April covers the only season in which frozen herring can be procured, while the prohibition of the seines would interfere with the vessels, who, occupied in codfishing during the summer, go to Fortune Bay in the winter, and would consequently have to make a complete change in their fishing gear, or depend entirely upon purchase from the natives for their supply. The prohibition of work on Sunday is impossible under the conditions of the fishery. The vessels must be at Fortune Bay at a certain time, and leave for market at a certain time. The entrance of the schools of herring is uncertain, and the time they stay equally so. Whenever they come they must be caught, and the evidence in this very case shows that after Sunday, the 6th of January, there was no other influx of these fish, and that prohibition on that day would have been equivalent to shutting out the fishermen for the season.[a]

The concluding paragraph of Mr. Evarts' letter is as follows:

In conclusion I would not be doing justice to the wishes and opinions of the United States Government if I did not express its profound regret at the apparent conflict of interests which the exercise of its treaty privileges appears to have developed. There is no intention on the part of this Government that these privileges should be abused, and no desire that their full and free enjoyment should harm the Colonial fishermen. While the differing interests and methods of the shore fishery and the vessel fishery make it impossible that the regulations of the one should be entirely given to the other, yet if the mutual obligations of the treaty of 1871 are to be maintained, the United States Government would gladly co-operate with the Government of Her Britannic Majesty in any effort to make those regulations a matter of reciprocal convenience and right; a means of

---

[a] Appendix, p. 667.

preserving the fisheries at their highest point of production, and of conciliating a community of interests by a just proportion of advantages and profits.[a]

A further statement of the position of the United States on the question above considered will be found in a letter written by Mr. Evarts on August 5, 1879, to Mr. Babson, who had been selected by the Department of State to examine and report upon certain features of the fisheries question, in the course of which letter Mr. Evarts says:

> It is quite possible that some of our fishermen may wish to be advised as to the course which the government thinks them justified in taking should the local authorities assume to interfere with them in the peaceable pursuit within the three-miles line of their fishing methods and the use of their seines and fishing-tackle. This interference, if attempted, will doubtless be based upon the local legislation of the provinces regulating the fisheries on their coast within the three-miles line. In the view of this government, these local regulations are incompetent to curtail or control the participation of our fishermen, as accorded by the Treaty of Washington, in their inshore fisheries. So long as our fishermen use methods and apparatus in their judgment adapted to catching the fish in the most efficient and most profitable manner to the industry they are pursuing, to wit, fishing from vessels manned and fitted from our ports, and seeking profit therefrom, and so long as they do not molest the provincial fishermen, pursuing their own methods in their equal right, this government regards our fishermen as within the treaty right and under no necessity of conforming, either in regard to days or seasons, or apparatus, to the prescriptions of the local regulations of the provinces.[b]

After much delay, which was explained on the ground that owing to the great importance of the points involved, it had been necessary to consult Newfoundland and to prepare a case upon them for submission to the Law Officers of the Crown, Lord Salisbury finally informed the American Chargé at London on March 2, 1880, "that the report of the Law Officers of the Crown upon the case has now been received, and that therefore the reply of Her Majesty's Government will be sent with the least possible delay having regard to the question under consideration."[c] The report of the Law Officers of the Crown was not communicated by Lord Salisbury to the United States Government, but the position of the British Government on the questions discussed by Mr. Evarts, was stated by Lord Salisbury

---

[a] Appendix, p. 672.   [b] Appendix, p. 673.   [c] Appendix, p. 683.

in his note of April 3, 1880, to the American Chargé at London, as follows, so far as it relates to the questions now under consideration:

Such being the facts, the following two questions arise:

1. Have United States fishermen the right to use the strand for purposes of actual fishing?

2. Have they the right to take herrings with a seine at the season of the year in question, or to use a seine at any season of the year for the purpose of barring herrings on the coast of Newfoundland?

The answers to the above questions depend on the interpretation of the treaties.

* * * * * * *

Further, they used seines for the purpose of in-barring herrings, and this leads me to the consideration of the second question, namely, whether United States fishermen have the right to take herrings with a seine at the season of the year in question, or to use a seine at any season of the year for the purpose of barring herrings on the coast of Newfoundland.

The in-barring of herrings is a practice most injurious, and, if continued, calculated in time to destroy the fishery; consequently it has been prohibited by statute since 1862.

In my note to Mr. Welsh, of the 7th of November, 1878, I stated "that British sovereignty, as regards these waters, is limited in its scope by the engagements of the Treaty of Washington, which *cannot* be modified or affected by any municipal legislation," and Her Majesty's Government fully admit that United States fishermen have the right of participation on the Newfoundland *inshore fisheries, in common* with British subjects, as specified in Article XVIII of that treaty. But it can not be claimed, consistently with this right of participation in common with the British fishermen, that the United States fishermen have any *other*, and still less that they have *greater* rights than the British fishermen had at the *date* of the treaty.

If, then, at the *date* of the signature of the Treaty of Washington, certain restraints were, by the municipal law, imposed upon the *British fishermen*, the United States fishermen were, by the *express terms* of the treaty, equally subjected to those restraints, and the obligation to observe in common with the British the then existing local laws and regulations, which is implied by the words *"in common,"* attached to the United States citizens as *soon* as they claimed the benefit of the treaty. That such was the view entertained by the Government of the United States during the existence of the reciprocity treaty, under which United States fishermen enjoyed precisely the same rights of fishing as they do now under the Treaty of Washington, is proved conclusively by the circular issued on the 28th of March, 1856, to the collector of customs at Boston, which so thoroughly expressed the views of Her Majesty's Government on this point that I quote it here *in extenso.*

"DEPARTMENT OF STATE,
" *Washington, March 28, 1856.*

"SIR: It is understood that there are certain acts of the British North American colonial legislatures, and also, perhaps, executive regulations intended to prevent the wanton destruction of the fish which frequent the coasts of the colonies, and injurious to the fishing thereon.   It is deemed reasonable and desirable that both the United States and British fishermen should pay a like respect to such laws and regulations which are designed to preserve and increase the productiveness of the fisheries on those coasts.   Such being the object of these laws and regulations, the observance of them is enforced upon the citizens of the United States in the like manner as they are observed by British subjects.   By granting the mutual use of the inshore fisheries, neither party has yielded its right to civic jurisdiction over a marine league along its coasts.

"Its laws are as obligatory upon the citizens or subjects of the other as upon its own.   The laws of the British provinces, not in conflict with the provisions of the reciprocity treaty, would be as binding upon the citizens of the United States within that jurisdiction as upon British subjects.   Should they be so framed or executed as to make any discrimination in favor of British fishermen, or to impair the rights secured to American fishermen by that treaty, those injuriously affected by them will appeal to this government for redress.

"In presenting complaints of this kind, should there be cause for doing so, they are requested to furnish the Department of State with a copy of the law or regulation which is alleged injuriously to affect their rights or to make an unfair discrimination between the fishermen of the respective countries, or with a statement of any supposed grievance in the execution of such law or regulation, in order that the matter may be arranged by the two governments.

"You will make this direction known to the masters of such fishing vessels as belong to your port in such manner as you may deem most advisable.

(Signed)   "W. L. MARCY.

"COLLECTOR OF THE CUSTOMS, Boston."

I have the honor to inclose a copy of an act passed by the colonial legislature of Newfoundland, on the 27th March, 1862, for the protection of the herring and salmon fisheries on the coast, and a copy of cap. 102 of the consolidated statutes of Newfoundland, passed in 1872. The first section of the act of 1862, prohibiting the taking of herrings with a seine between the 20th day of October and the 12th day of April, and, further, prohibited the use of seines at any time for the purpose of barring herrings.   These regulations, which were in force at the date of the Treaty of Washington, were not abolished, but con firmed by the subsequent statutes, and are binding under the treaty upon the citizens of the United States in common with British subjects.

The United States fishermen, therefore, in landing for the purpose of fishing at Tickle Beach, in using a seine at a prohibited time, and in barring herrings with seines from the shore exceeded their treaty privileges, and were engaged in unlawful acts.

Her Majesty's Government have no wish to insist on any illiberal construction of the language of the treaty, and would not consider it necessary to make any formal complaint on the subject of a casual infringement of the letter of its stipulations which did not involve any substantial detriment to British interests and to the fishery in general.

An excess on the part of the United States fishermen of the precise limit of the rights secured to them might proceed as much from ignorance as from wilfulness; but the present claim for compensation is based on losses resulting from a collision which was the direct consequence of such excess, and Her Majesty's Government feel bound to point to the fact that the United States fishermen were the first and real cause of the mischief, by overstepping the limits of the privileges secured to them in a manner gravely prejudicial to the rights of other fishermen.

For the reasons above stated, Her Majesty's Government are of opinion that, under the circumstances of the case as at present within their knowledge, the claim advanced by the United States fishermen for compensation on account of the losses stated to have been sustained by them on the occasion in question is one which should not be entertained.

Mr. Evarts will not require to be assured that Her Majesty's Government, while unable to admit the contention of the United States Government on the present occasion, are fully sensible of the evils arising from any difference of opinion between the two governments in regard to the fishery rights of their respective subjects. They have always admitted the incompetence of the colonial or the imperial legislature to limit by subsequent legislation the advantages secured by treaty to the subjects of another power. If it should be the opinion of the Government of the United States that any act of the colonial legislature subsequent in date to the Treaty of Washington has trenched upon the rights enjoyed by the citizens of the United States in virtue of that instrument, Her Majesty's Government will consider any communication addressed to them in that view with a cordial and anxious desire to remove all just grounds of complaint.[a]

No reply was made by the Secretary of State to Lord Salisbury's note, but upon its receipt the President sent on May 17, 1880, a special message to Congress transmitting and concurring in a report by Mr. Evarts on the subject, in which he expressed the opinion that the import duties upon fish and fish oil which had been removed under the provisions of the treaty of 1871, should be reimposed by Congress as measures proper to be taken by the United States in maintenance of the rights accorded to American fishermen under that treaty.

The British Minister reported that the reason assigned for the action thus taken was that in the opinion of the Government of the United States "Her Majesty's Government had not sufficiently considered the gravity of the case; had paid but little attention to it, and had unnecessarily delayed replying to the representations of the United States' Government."[b]

Soon afterwards the British Government took occasion to reopen the negotiations for a settlement of the Fortune Bay claims, and on October 27, 1880, Lord Granville, who had succeeded Lord Salis-

---

[a] Appendix, p. 684.   [b] Appendix, p. 709.

bury as Secretary of State for Foreign Affairs, wrote to Mr. Lowell, the American Minister at London:

As regards the claim of the United States fishermen to compensation for the injuries and losses which they are alleged to have sustained in consequence of the violent obstruction which they encountered from British fishermen at Fortune Bay on the occasion referred to, I have to state that Her Majesty's Government are quite willing that they should be indemnified for any injuries and losses which, upon a joint inquiry, may be found to have been sustained by them, and in respect of which they are reasonably entitled to compensation; but on this point I have to observe that a claim is put forward by them for the loss of fish which had been caught, or which, but for the interference of the British fishermen, might have been caught by means of strand fishing, a mode of fishing to which, under the treaty of Washington, they were not entitled to resort.[a]

After some further discussion as to the amount of compensation to be paid in settlement of these claims, it was finally agreed, as stated in notes exchanged on May 28, 1881, between Sir Edward Thornton, British Minister at Washington, and Mr. Blaine, the Secretary of State, that fifteen thousand pounds sterling should be paid by Great Britain to the United States in full satisfaction of all claims for disturbance of American fishing vessels in their fishing operations on the coasts of Newfoundland and its dependencies up to March 4, 1881, and including two additional claims arising from occurrences on the coasts of Nova Scotia and Canada, it being mutually understood, however, "that the above mentioned payment will be made without prejudice to any question of the rights of either of the two Governments under Articles XVIII. to XXV., both inclusive, and Article XXXII. of the treaty of May 8, 1871, between the United States and Great Britain."[b]

Joint Regulations.

In the course of the discussion which grew out of the Fortune Bay case, the question of the joint regulation of the fisheries came up for consideration, and the views expressed by the two Governments on this subject at that time are of interest in connection with similar questions which have arisen under the treaty of 1818. It will be remembered that Mr. Evarts in the portion of his letter above quoted made the following statement with respect to joint regulations:

---

[a] Appendix, p. 713.   [b] Appendix, p. 736.

While the differing interests and methods of the shore fishery and the vessel fishery make it impossible that the regulations of the one should be entirely given to the other, yet if the mutual obligations of the treaty of 1871 are to be maintained, the United States Government would gladly co-operate with the Government of Her Britannic Majesty in any effort to make those regulations a matter of reciprocal convenience and right; a means of preserving the fisheries at their highest point of production, and of conciliating a community of interests by a just proportion of advantages and profits.[a]

In Lord Granville's reply to Mr. Evarts, dated October 27, 1880, from which an extract is quoted above, he stated the position of his Government in regard to Mr. Evarts' suggestion as follows:

Her Majesty's Government entirely concur in Mr. Marcy's circular of the 28th of March, 1856.   The principle therein laid down appears to them perfectly sound, and as applicable to the fishery provisions of the treaty of Washington as those of the treaty which Mr. Marcy had in view.   They cannot, therefore, admit the accuracy of the opinion expressed in Mr. Evarts's letter to Mr. Welsh, of the 28th of September, 1878, "that the fishery rights of the United States conceded by the treaty of Washington are to be exercised wholly free from the restraints and regulations of the statutes of Newfoundland," if by that opinion anything inconsistent with Mr. Marcy's principle is really intended.   Her Majesty's Government, however, fully admit that if any such local statutes could be shown to be inconsistant with the express stipulations, or even with the spirit of the treaty, they would not be within the category of those reasonable regulations by which American (in common with British) fishermen ought to be bound, and they observe, on the other hand, with much satisfaction, that Mr. Evarts, at the close of his letter to Mr. Welsh, of the 1st of August, 1879, after expressing regret at "the conflict of interests which the exercise of the treaty privileges enjoyed by the United States appears to have developed," expressed himself as follows:

"There is no intention on the part of this [the United States] government that these privileges should be abused, and no desire that their full and free enjoyment should harm the colonial fishermen.

"While the differing interests and methods of the shore fishery and the vessel fishery make it impossible that the regulation of the one should be entirely given to the other, yet if the mutual obligations of the treaty of 1871 are to be maintained, the United States Government would gladly co-operate with the Government of Her Britannic Majesty in any effort to make those regulations a matter of reciprocal convenience and right, a means of preserving the fisheries at their highest point of production, and of conciliating a community of interest by a just proportion of advantages and profits."

Her Majesty's Government do not interpret these expressions in any sense derogatory to the sovereign authority of Great Britain in the territorial waters of Newfoundland, by which only regulations having the force of law within those waters can be made.   So regarding the proposal, they are pleased not only to recognize in it an indi-

---

[a] *Supra*, p. 171.

cation that the desire of Her Majesty's Government to arrive at a friendly and speedy settlement of this question is fully reciprocated by the Government of the United States, but also to discern in it the basis of a practical settlement of the difficulty, and I have the honor to request that you will inform Mr. Evarts that Her Majesty's Government, with a view to avoiding further discussion and future misunderstandings, are quite willing to confer with the Government of the United States respecting the establishment of regulations under which the subjects of both parties to the treaty of Washington shall have the full and equal enjoyment of any fishery which, under that treaty, is to be used in common. The duty of enacting and enforcing such regulations, when agreed upon, would of course rest with the power having the sovereignty of the shore and waters in each case.[a]

Subsequently, in the course of the discussion, the attention of Lord Granville was called to the plan then under consideration by the President of "sending a ship to protect the American fishermen on the coast of Newfoundland," and in commenting upon this proposed action Lord Granville said in his letter of February 24, 1881, to Sir Edward Thornton that he had at first been taken by surprise at the idea "but that on consideration it appeared to me that such a course might be taken which might be of great advantage, if each Government sent vessels with commanders who receive identic and conciliatory instructions for the purpose of keeping the peace among the fishermen of their respective countries."[b] Lord Granville evidently informed Mr. Lowell of this view for Mr. Lowell stated in his telegram of March 9, 1881, to Mr. Blaine, as a result of an interview with Lord Granville, that "if cruisers be sent as intimated in 109[c] he would be glad to know your opinion of joint cruisers with joint instructions."[d] Again in Mr. Lowell's despatch of March 12, 1881, he said on the same subject "I omitted to mention in my former despatch that Lord Granville at one of our earlier interviews, wished me to inquire whether my Government, in case it should become necessary, as suggested in your No. 109, to take measures for the protection of our fishermen, would have any objection to the sending of joint cruisers with joint orders."[e] In reply to this inquiry Mr. Blaine telegraphed to Mr. Lowell on March 14, 1881, instructing him to inform Lord Granville that "the subject of joint cruisers may be postponed, or, if desired, may also be referred to Sir Edward and myself, to be taken up afterwards, with power to agree upon a series of regulations under which treaty rights may be mutually secured."[e]

---

[a] Appendix, p. 712.
[b] Appendix, p. 726.
[c] Appendix, p. 714.
[d] Appendix, p. 730.
[e] Appendix, p. 731.

Mr. Blaine's instructions on this point were promptly communicated to Lord Granville by Mr. Lowell in his note bearing date the following day.[a] With reference to the same subject, Sir Edward Thornton wrote to Lord Granville on March 14, 1881, as a result of an interview with Mr. Blaine, stating that "upon my inquiring what steps it was proposed to take with a view to an agreement as to the rules and regulations which are to prevail hereafter respecting the fisheries, Mr. Blaine replied that this question would meet the early consideration of the United States' Government, and that he thought it was very desirable that a decision should be arrived at as soon as possible." [b]

In reply Lord Granville wrote to Sir Edward Thornton on April 2, 1881, stating that he need not remind him how desirable it was in view of the approach of the fishing season that an understanding should be arrived at with regard to the regulations to be framed for the fisheries with a view to the prevention of future misunderstandings.[c]

While this question of joint regulations was still under consideration, the negotiations for the settlement of the Fortune Bay cases were concluded, leaving the question of joint regulations still unsettled, but it was held open for further consideration, as appears from the following extract from Mr. Blaine's note of May 6, 1881, to Sir Edward Thornton:

In accepting Lord Granville's offer in this matter, I desire to state that at your convenience I will discuss the subject of the joint cruisers on the fishing grounds, and the code of instructions under which they should sail.[d]

The proposal that a joint agreement should be arrived at as to the regulations which should govern the fisheries, was renewed a year later by Mr. West, the British Minister at Washington, who submitted to Mr. Frelinghuysen, the Secretary of State, on May 3, 1882, the following memorandum:

British Memorandum.

With reference to correspondence which has passed between Her Majesty's Legation and the State Department respecting the Newfoundland Fisheries question, it is sought to determine what Regulations it would be expedient to enforce for the protection of the

---

a Appendix, p. 732.
b Appendix, p. 732.
c Appendix, p. 733.
d Appendix, p. 736.

fisheries, and to this end attention is called to the following Acts, viz.
Cap: 102 Consolidated Statutes Newfoundland,

38. Vict:	Cap:	7
39 "	"	6
40 "	"	13
42 "	"	2

which Documents were appended to the message from President
Hayes to the House of Representatives. The United States Government is invited to examine these Statutes, and to state whether
they find in them anything open to objection or have any suggestions
to make with regard to them.

Any Communication which the United States Government may
make upon this subject will receive careful consideration on the part
of Her Majesty, and when an agreement has been arrived at as to the
regulations which should govern the fisheries the Legislature of Newfoundland will be invited to make the necessary changes in the law
if any such should be found to be necessary.[a]

In reply to this proposal the following paper was handed by the
Secretary of State to the British Minister on May 9, 1882:

United States Memorandum.

Referring to the British Memorandum relating to the Newfoundland Statutes restricting the fisheries, viz:

Cap. 102 Consolidated Statutes of Newfoundland.
38 Vic. cap. 7.
39 Vic. cap. 6.
40 Vic. cap. 13.
42 Vic. cap. 2.

the Government of the United States makes the following observations on these Acts:

Section 2 of cap. 102, which is as follows:

"No person shall at any time between the 20th day of December
"and the 1st day of April in any year, use any net to haul, catch
"or take herrings on or near the coasts of this colony or of its depend-
"encies, or in any bays, harbors or other places therein, having the
"mokes, meshes or scales of such net less than two inches and three
"eighths of an inch at least or having any false or double bottom
"of any description; nor shall any person put any net, though of
"legal size mesh, upon or behind any other net not of such size mesh
"for the purpose of catching or taking such herring or herring fry
"passing a single net of legal size mesh;"

and Section 4 of the same Act:

"No person shall between the 20th day of May and the 20th day
"October in any year, haul, catch or take herrings or other bait for
"exportation, within one mile measured by the shore or across the
"water of any settlement situate between Cape Chapeau Rouge and
"Point Enragee, near Cape Ray; and any person so hauling, catching
"or taking, within the said limits, may be examined on oath by a
"justice, officer of customs or person commissioned for the purpose,
"as to whether the herrings or other bait are intended for exporta-

---

[a] Appendix, p. 742.

"tion or otherwise, and on refusal to answer or answering untruly,
"such person shall, on conviction, be subject to the provisions of the
"twelfth section of this chapter,"
are both considered to be in their provisions restrictive of the rights,
guaranteed to American fishermen by the XVIII Article of the
Treaty of 1871, and the amendment to section 4, by the 39th Victoria,
cap. 6 which substitutes the tenth day of May for the twentieth day
of April while it modifies the hardship does not remove it.

Section 4 of the latter Act 39 Victoria, cap. 6: "No person shall,
"between the hours of twelve o'clock on Saturday night and twelve
"o'clock on Sunday night, haul or take any herring, caplin or
"squids, with nets, seines, bunts, or any such contrivance or set or
"put out any such net, seine, bunt or contrivance for the purpose of
"such hauling or taking,"
is in itself objectionable, and as amended by the 40th Victoria, cap. 13
which provides: "That the fourth section of the said recited Act
"shall be held to include and apply to the jigging of squids, and to
"the use of any contrivance whatever, and to any mode of taking
"and obtaining fish for bait,"
becomes if possible still more restrictive, and the 1st section of 42nd
Victoria, cap. 2 is conceived by this Government to be clearly in contravention of the right of American fishermen under the stipulations
of the Treaty. That section is in these words:

"No person shall haul, catch or take herrings by or in a seine or
"other such contrivance on or near any part of the coast of this
"colony or its dependencies or in any of the bays, harbors or other
"places therein, at any time between the twentieth day of October
"in any year and the eighteenth day of April in the following year
"or at any time use a seine or other contrivance for the catching and
"taking of herrings, except by way of shooting and forthwith hauling
"the same:

"Provided, that nothing herein contained shall prevent the taking
"of herrings by nets set in the usual and customary manner, and not
"used for in barring or enclosing herrings in a cove, inlet or other
"place."

It is true that by the 18th section of cap. 102 Consolidated Statutes
of Newfoundland which say that "Nothing in this chapter shall
"affect the rights and privileges granted by treaty to the subjects of
"any state or power in amity with Her Majesty," the intention of the
Legislature of Newfoundland to hold in due regard the rights of
American fishermen under the Treaty is manifested, but the complaint of citizens of the U. S., engaged in the herring fisheries on the
coast of Newfoundland, is that this provision has been wholly disre-
garded by the local ministerial and executive officers, and that while
the prohibitory provisions of the Consolidated Statutes were rigidly
enforced against American fishermen, the native fishermen were
allowed complete immunity in the constant violation of the statutes.

Section 5 of the 42nd Victoria cap. 2, provides a summary mode
for the execution of the statutes and the enforcement of penalties,
namely:

"Any justice of the peace, sub-collector of customs, preventive
"officer, fishery warden or constable, may board any vessel suspected
"of carrying herrings in bulk between the twentieth day of October
"in any year, and the eighteenth day of April in the following year;

"and in case any such justice, sub-collector, preventive officer, fishery
"warden or constable shall make signal to any vessel suspected as
"aforesaid, from any vessel employed by the government, by dipping
"the ensign at the main peak three times and firing a gun, it shall be
"the duty of the owner, master or person managing or controlling
"such vessel so signalled, to heave to such vessel until such justice,
"sub-collector, preventive officer, fishery warden or constable, shall
"have boarded and examined such last named vessel; and in case of
"such master, owner or person managing or controlling as aforesaid
"such last named vessel omitting so to heave her to, or to afford facilities
"for such justice, sub-collector, preventive officer, fishery warden or
"constable, boarding such vessel or obstructing such justice, sub-
"collector, preventive officer, fishery warden or constable, boarding
"or examining any such vessel, he shall be subject to a penalty of five
"hundred dollars, to be recovered with costs in a summary manner
"before a justice of the peace, and in case default shall be made in
"the payment of such penalty, such justice shall issue his warrant
"and cause such offender to be imprisoned for a period not exceeding
"thirty days."

Americans have been constantly subjected to the surveillance contemplated by that section while Newfoundland fishermen have been
not only exempted from its provisions but have been called on by the
local officials to aid them in enforcing the statute against American
fishing vessels.

The views entertained by the Government of the U. S. on the subject were thus expressed to H. M.'s Government in 1878 by Mr.
Evarts who then said:

"This Government conceives that the fishery rights of the United
"States conceded by the Treaty of Washington are to be exercised
"wholly free from the restraints and regulations of the statutes of
"Newfoundland, now set up as authority over our fishermen, and
"from every other regulation of fishing now in force or that may
"hereafter be enacted by that government."

The President adheres to the interpretation thus given to the
Treaty, and it is evident that so long as these several provisions remain on the statute books of Newfoundland and the disposition of
the local officers to discriminate against American fishermen in their
enforcement continues, the treaty rights become a nullity and the
American fishermen have no security in the pursuit of this great
industry.

If the Legislature of Newfoundland cannot dispense with these provisions altogether then this Government conceives that an Act should
be passed by it expressly declaring that the provisions enumerated
shall have no application to citizens of the U. S. who are now or who
may hereafter be engaged in fishing in the waters of Newfoundland
under the stipulations of the Treaty of the 8th of May 1871, between
the United States and Great Britain.[a]

This reply memorandum was transmitted by Mr. West to his Government and on July 15, 1882, Lord Granville wrote to Mr. West on
the subject as follows:

---

[a] Appendix, p. 743.

I have to acknowledge the receipt of your despatch of the 9th May last, transmitting a Memo drawn up by the State Dept of the U. S. Govt upon certain Acts of the Legislature of Newfoundland for the regulation of the fisheries in the waters of that Colony.

This Memo was communicated to you by Mr Frelinghuysen in answer to the request of H. M's Govt to be favored with any suggestions which the U. S. Govt might be prepared to offer with a view to the friendly consideration by the two Govts of such amendments of the Fishery Regulations as might be reasonably called for in the interests of both countries.

H. M's Govt regrets to find that the Memo contains no suggestion of any kind tending to that object, but that it reopens a discussion on the construction of the Treaty of Washington which it was hoped had been exhausted in the previous correspondence.

The Memo cites the following extract from a dispatch written by Mr Evarts in 1878, as representing the views of the U. S. Govt:—

"This Govt conceives that the fishery rights of the U. S. con-
"ceded by the Treaty of Washington are to be exercised wholly
"free from the restraints and regulations of the Statutes of New-
"foundland, now set up as authority over our fishermen, and from
"every other Regulation now in force, or that may hereafter be
"enacted by that Government."

H. M.'s Govt however, have never accepted that construction of the Treaty and on this point I have nothing to add to the views expressed in the Note which I had the honour to address to Mr Lowell on the 27th of October 1880.

In that Note I used the following language:—

"Without entering into lengthy discussion on this point, I feel
"bound to state that, in the opinion of H. M.'s Govt, the clause in
"the Treaty of Washington which provides that the citizens of the
"U. S. shall be entitled 'in common with British subjects,' to fish
"in Newfoundland waters within the limits of British Sovereignty,
"means that the American and the British fishermen shall fish in
"these waters upon terms of equality and not that there shall be
"an exemption of American fishermen from any reasonable regula-
"tions to which British fishermen are subject.

"H. M.'s Govt entirely concur in Mr Marcy's Circular of the 28th
"of March 1856. The principle therein laid down appears to them
"perfectly sound, and as applicable to the fishery provisions of the
"Treaty of Washington as to those of the Treaty which Mr Marcy
"had in view; they can not, therefore, admit the accuracy in Mr
"Evarts' letter to Mr Welsh of the 28th Septr 1878, 'that the fishery
"'rights of the U. S. conceded by the Treaty of Washington are to
"'be exercised wholly free from the restraints and regulations of
"'the Statutes of Newfoundland,' if by that opinion anything
"inconsistent with Mr Marcy's principle is really intended. H. M.'s
"Govt, however, fully admit that, if any such local statutes could
"be shewn to be inconsistent with the express stipulations, or even
"with the spirit of the Treaty, they would not be within the category
"of those reasonable regulations by which American (in common
"with British) fishermen ought to be bound; and they observe, on
"the other hand, with much satisfaction that Mr. Evarts, at the close
"of his letter to Mr Welsh of the 1st of August, 1879, after expressing
"regret at 'the conflict of interests which the exercise of the Treaty

" 'privileges enjoyed by the U. S. appears to have developed,'
"expressed himself as follows:—
" ' There is no intention on the part of this (the U. S.) Gov^t that
" 'these privileges should be abused; and no desire that their full
" 'and free enjoyment should harm the colonial fishermen.
" 'While the differing interests and methods of the shore fishery
" 'and the vessel fishery make it impossible that the regulation of the
" 'one should be entirely given to the other, yet if the mutual
" 'obligations of the Treaty of 1871 are to be maintained, the U. S.
" 'Gov^t would gladly cooperate with the Gov^t of Her Britannic
" 'Majesty in any effort to make those regulations a matter of recip-
" 'rocal convenience and right, a means of preserving the fisheries
" 'at their highest point of production, and of conciliating a com-
" 'munity of interest by a just proportion of advantages and profits.' "
I expressed the satisfaction with which H. M.'s Gov^t not only
recognized in Mr Evarts' proposal above referred to, an indication
that their desire to arrive at a friendly and speedy settlement of the
controversy was fully reciprocated by the Gov^t of the U. S., but also
discerned in it the basis of a practical solution of the difficulty; and
I assured Mr Lowell of the readiness of H. M.'s Gov^t to confer with
the Gov^t of the U. S. respecting the establishment of regulations under
which the subjects of both parties to the Treaty of Washington
should have the full and equal enjoyment of any fishery which, under
the Treaty is to be used in common.
The Memo of the U. S. Gov^t after reviewing certain provisions of
the Newfoundland Acts, complains of partiality in their enforcement
by the Magistrates and other officials of the Colony (a complaint
which H. M.'s Gov^t cannot admit to be well founded, and in support
of which no facts are adduced) and concludes with a suggestion that
if the Legislature of Newfoundland cannot dispense with those provisions altogether, it should pass an act expressly declaring that they
shall have no application to the citizens of the U. S.
I can only renew the expression of the regret and disappointment
which is felt by H. M.'s Gov^t at the apparent disinclination on the
part of the Gov^t of the U. S. to carry out Mr Evarts' proposal; and I
have to instruct you to read this dispatch to Mr Frelinghuysen, and
to leave a copy of it with him should he desire it, conveying to him
at the same time the hope of H. M.'s Gov^t that, upon further consideration, the Gov^t of the U. S. will agree to let the disputed question
of Treaty rights remain in abeyance, and will unite with H. M.'s
Gov^t in carrying out the revision of the fishery regulations in the
spirit and with the object indicated by Mr Evarts.[a]

This letter from Lord Granville was handed by Mr. West to Mr.
Frelinghuysen, then Secretary of State, on August 3, 1882, as appears
from the following letter, and no reply having been made to it by
Mr. Frelinghuysen, Mr. West again wrote to him on October 9, 1883
on the subject as follows:

Referring to a communication from Earl Granville conveyed to
me in a despatch copy of which I had the honor to place in your
hands on the 3rd of August of last year respecting the revision of

_____
[a] Appendix, p. 744.

the Fishery regulations, I have the honor to inform you that His Lordship has requested me again to bring this matter before the United States Government.

Although notice has been given by the United States Government of their intention to terminate the fishery Articles of the Treaty of Washington in two years time from the 1st of July last no further communication has been as yet received by Her Majesty's Government relative to the proposed revision of the regulations for the protection of the fisheries in Newfoundland waters, and Her Majesty's Government are anxious that in the interval no cause of difference should arise between the fishermen of Newfoundland and those of the United States who may resort to those waters.

They would be glad, therefore, to know the views of the Government of the United States on the proposed revision. At the same time Her Majesty's Government hope that in the interval before the termination of the Fishery Articles in question, the Government of the United States will agree to let the disputed question of Treaty rights remain in abeyance and will unite with Her Majesty's Government in carrying out the revision of the Fishery regulations in the spirit and with the object indicated by Mr. Evarts in his letter to Mr. Welsh of the 1st of August, 1879, in which it is said that "there "is no intention on the part of the United States Government that "privileges should be abused and no desire that their full and free "enjoyment should harm the Colonial fishermen. While the differ- "ent interests and methods of the shore fishery and the vessel fishery "make it impossible that the regulation of the one should be entirely "given to the other, yet if the mutual obligations of the Treaty of "1871 are to be maintained, the United States Government would "gladly cooperate with the Government of Her Britannic Majesty "in any effort to make those regulations a matter of reciprocal con- "venience and right, a means of preserving the Fisheries at their "highest point of production and of conciliating a community of "interest by a just proportion of advantages and profits."

In expressing therefore the hope on the part of Her Majesty's Government that this matter may receive the early consideration of the Government of the United States I have the honor to be with the highest consideration, etc.[a]

No further communications on this subject seem to have been exchanged at that time, and the termination of the fisheries articles of the treaty of 1871 on July 1, 1885, less than two years later, made further discussion of American fishing rights under that treaty unnecessary.

Situation following the termination of the Fisheries Articles of the Treaty of 1871.

After the final termination of the fisheries privileges under the treaty of 1871, which, as above stated, were temporarily extended until January 1, 1886, by the *modus vivendi* of 1885, a series of special

---

[a] Appendix, p. 751.

instructions were issued by the Canadian Government under date of March 16, 1886, to fishery officers in command of government steamers and vessels engaged as fisheries police vessels in protecting the inshore fisheries of Canada.   In forwarding a copy of these instructions to the British Government, the Governor General of Canada, Lord Lansdowne, stated in his letter of March 25, 1886, to Lord Granville, that they were substantially the same as those which were issued under similar circumstances in 1870 upon the expiration of the treaty of 1854; and, although these instructions differ somewhat in form from the earlier instructions, yet it will be found that so far as they relate to the "bays" question they carefully observe the requirement, insisted upon by Great Britain with respect to the instructions of 1870, that American fishing vessels should not be interfered with beyond the distance of three miles from the land, and it is specifically provided that the fisheries officers should "omit no precaution to establish on the spot that the trespass was or is being committed *within three miles of land."* [a]

With respect also to the Magdalen Islands, the following provisions are found both in the 1886 and 1870 instructions:

With regard to the Magdalen Islands, although the liberty to land and to dry, and cure fish there, is not expressly given by the terms of the Convention to United States fishermen, it is not at present intended to exclude them.[b]

It will be perceived that this provision leaves undisturbed the liberty of using the shores of those islands for strand fishing, to which the United States has always insisted that the American fishermen were entitled under the customary and accepted interpretation of the words "on the shores of the Magdalen Islands" in the treaty of 1818.

With respect generally to the use of unsettled bays by American fishermen, both instructions alike provide that it is not desired that a narrow construction should be put on the term "unsettled," and that—

Places containing a few isolated houses might not, in some instances, be susceptible of being considered as "settled" within the meaning and purpose of the Convention.   Something would, however, depend upon the facts of the situation, and the circumstances of the settlement.   Private and proprietary rights form an element in the consideration of this point.   The generally conciliatory spirit in which it is desirable that you should carry out these instructions, and the desire of Her Majesty's Government that rights of exclusion should

---

[a] Appendix, p. 760.   [b] Appendix, pp. 583, 757.

not be strained, must influence you in making as fair and liberal an application of the term as shall consist with the just claims of all parties.[a]

With respect to American fishing vessels on the portion of the Canadian coast not covered by the renunciatory clause, that is on the shores of the Magdalen Islands and on the Canadian portion of the Labrador coast, the following provision is found in the same form in the 1886 and 1870 instructions:

Should you have occasion to compel any American fishing vessels or fishermen to conform to the requirements of the "Fisheries Act and Regulations," as regards the modes and incidents of fishing, at those places to which they are admitted under the Convention of 1818, particularly in relation to ballast, fish offals, setting of nets, and hauling of seines, and use of "trawls," or "bultows," more especially at and around the Magdalen Islands, your power and authority over such cases will be similar to that of any other Fishery Officer appointed to enforce the Fishery Laws in Canadian waters. (Vide "Fisheries Act.")[b]

As no attempt was ever made by the colonial authorities to enforce this provision against American fishermen, it never became the subject of discussion between the United States and Great Britain.

With respect, however, to the right of American fishermen to enter bays and harbors on the portion of the coast covered by the renunciatory clause of the treaty of 1818 for the four purposes of shelter, repairs, wood, and water, a marked difference is found in the provisions of the instructions of 1870 and 1886. The earlier instructions provide—

American vessels may, however, enter into all bays and harbors for certain specified purposes.

These purposes are:—for shelter, repairing damages, purchasing wood, and obtaining water. They are to be admitted for no other purpose whatever. And during such admission they may be subjected to any restrictions necessary to prevent them from taking, drying, or curing fish therein, or in any other manner abusing the privileges thus accorded to them. You will be careful to observe that such qualified admission to the ports and harbors of Canada, be not made a pretext or cloak for transferring cargoes, or transacting any other business connected with their fishing operations.[c]

These provisions are replaced by the following in the later instructions:

In all other parts the exclusion of foreign vessels and boats is absolute, so far as fishing is concerned, and is to be enforced within the limits laid down by the Convention of 1818, they being allowed

_____

[a]Appendix, pp. 583, 758.   [b]Appendix, pp. 584, 759.   [c]Appendix, p. 582.

to enter bays and harbours for four purposes only, viz.,—for shelter, the repairing of damages, the purchasing of wood, and to obtain water.

You are to compel, if necessary, the maintenance of peace and good order by foreign fishermen pursuing their calling and enjoying concurrent privileges of fishing or curing fish with British fishermen, in those parts to which they are admitted by the Treaty of 1818.

You are to see that they obey the laws of the country, that they do not molest British fishermen in the pursuit of their calling and that they observe the regulations of the fishery laws in every respect.

You are to prevent foreign fishing vessels and boats which enter bays and harbors for the four legal purposes above mentioned, from taking advantage thereof, to take, dry or cure fish therein, to purchase bait, ice, or supplies, or to transship cargoes, or from transacting any business in connection with their fishing operations.[a]

Soon after the adoption of these instructions, the Canadian authorities proceeded under the provisions last above quoted to seize American fishing vessels on the coasts covered by the renunciatory clause of the treaty, and it at once became evident that the purpose of these provisions was to interrupt and put an end to the trade privileges which had been extended to American fishermen on those coasts for many years under concurrent and reciprocal laws and mercantile regulations of the respective countries, independently of any treaty whatever.[b]

It was also made evident by the action of the provincial authorities that in addition to the denial of commercial privileges to American fishing vessels exercising their treaty right of entering the bays and harbors on the coasts covered by the renunciatory clause for the four purposes of shelter, repairs, wood, and water, such vessels were to be subjected to the same conditions and exactions imposed upon the American vessels enjoying commercial privileges.

The position of the provincial authorities, as indicated by these instructions and the seizures made under them, was at once called to the attention of the British Government by the Government of the United States, and made the subject of vigorous protest and objection.

The diplomatic correspondence which ensued is printed in full in the Appendix, but so far as it relates to the question of commercial privileges on the coasts covered by the renunciatory clause it does not call for special comment in this Case inasmuch as the only question with respect to commercial privileges submitted to the Tribunal for

---

[a] Appendix, p. 758.   [b] Appendix, pp. 765–766.

decision under the Special Agreement of January 27, 1909, relates to the exercise of such privileges on the so-called treaty coasts in distinction from the coasts covered by the renunciatory clause. It should be noted in passing, however, that the United States did not claim that commercial privileges on the Canadian coasts depended upon the treaty of 1818, the contention of the United States on that point being stated by Secretary of State Bayard in his note of May 10, 1886, to Sir Lionel Sackville-West, the British Minister at Washington at that time, as follows:

But since the date of the treaty of 1818, a series of laws and regulations importantly affecting the trade between the North American Provinces of Great Britain and the United States have been, respectively, adopted by the two countries, and have led to amicable and mutually beneficial relations between their respective inhabitants.

This independent and yet concurrent action by the two Governments has effected a gradual extension, from time to time, of the provisions of Article I of the convention of July 3, 1815, providing for reciprocal liberty of commerce between the United States and the territories of Great Britain in Europe, so as gradually to include the colonial possessions of Great Britain in North America and the West Indies within the results of that treaty.

President Jackson's proclamation of October 5, 1830, created a reciprocal commercial intercourse, on terms of perfect equality of flag, between this country and the British American dependencies, by repealing the navigation acts of April 18, 1818, May 15, 1820, and March 1, 1823, and admitting British vessels and their cargoes "to an entry in the ports of the United States from the islands, provinces, and colonies of Great Britain on or near the American continent, and north or east of the United States." These commercial privileges have since received a large extension in the interests of propinquity, and in some cases favors have been granted by the United States without equivalent concession. Of the latter class is the exemption granted by the shipping act of June 26, 1884, amounting to one-half of the regular tonnage-dues on all vessels from the British North American and West Indian possessions entering ports of the United States. Of the reciprocal class are the arrangements for transit of goods, and the remission, by proclamation, as to certain British ports and places of the remainder of the tonnage-tax, on evidence of equal treatment being shown to our vessels.

On the other side, British and colonial legislation, as notably in the case of the imperial shipping and navigation act of June 26, 1849, has contributed its share toward building up an intimate intercourse and beneficial traffic between the two countries founded on mutual interest and convenience.[a]

The British position on the other hand, as stated in the course of the correspondence, was that under the renunciatory clause of the treaty it had been agreed that the American fishermen were to

---

[a] Appendix, p. 764.

be admitted to the bays and harbors of that coast for four specified purposes and for no other purpose whatever, and, therefore, fishing vessels as such were not entitled to claim the commercial privileges which had been extended to other vessels since the treaty of 1818. It will be observed, however, that the only renunciation contained in the renunciatory clause relates not to commerce but to fishing on the coasts referred to, which renunciation is made with the express proviso that fishermen shall nevertheless be permitted to enter the bays and harbors on such coast for four specified purposes.   There is nothing in the renunciation, therefore, which applies to commercial privileges extended generally to American vessels after the date of the treaty; and as fishing vessels were not expressly exempted from the commercial privileges subsequently extended to American vessels, the provisions of the treaty would seem to have no bearing on either side of the question.   That question, however, as above stated, is not submitted for decision in this Case and it is unnecessary to pursue the discussion of it further, for obviously it has no bearing whatsoever on the question of commercial privileges on the treaty coasts, which question also arose in connection with some of the seizures made during this period, and is considered below in reviewing the resulting diplomatic correspondence.

Commercial Privileges on the Treaty Coasts.

In connection with Question 7 of the Special Agreement of January 27, 1909, relating to commercial privileges on the treaty coasts, attention is called to the interference by the colonial authorities with the American fishing vessels *Thomas F. Bayard* and the *Mascot* on the west coast of Newfoundland and on the coast of the Magdalen Islands respectively, with reference to which Mr. Bayard, wrote to the British Minister at Washington, on July 30, 1886, as follows:

By the provisions of Article I of that convention [1818] the liberty to take fish of every kind, forever, in common with the subjects of His Britannic Majesty is secured to the inhabitants of the United States ''on that part of the southern coast of Newfoundland, which extends from Cape Ray to the Rameau Islands, on the western and northern coast of Newfoundland, from the said Cape Ray to the Quirpon Islands, on the shores of the Magdalen Islands,'' and on the other coasts and shores in the said article set forth.

Notwithstanding these plain provisions, I regret to be obliged to inform you that by the affidavit of the master of the American fishing vessel *Thomas F. Bayard*, that being at Bonne Bay, which is on the western coast of Newfoundland within the limits specified in Article I of the convention referred to, the master of the said vessel was formally notified by one N. N. Taylor, the officer of customs at that point, that his vessel would be seized if he attempted to obtain a supply of fish for bait or for any other transaction in connection with fishing operations within three marine miles of that coast.

To avoid the seizure of his vessel the master broke up his voyage and returned home.

I am also in possession of the affidavit of Alexander T. Eachern, master of the American fishing schooner *Mascot*, who entered Port Amherst, Magdalen Islands, and was there threatened by the customs official with seizure of his vessel if he attempted to obtain bait for fishing or to take a pilot.

These are flagrant violations of treaty rights of their citizens for which the United States expect prompt remedial action by Her Majesty's Government; and I have to ask that such instructions may be issued forthwith to the provincial officials of Newfoundland and of the Magdalen Islands as will cause the treaty rights of citizens of the United States to be duly respected.[a]

On the same day Mr. Bayard also wrote to Mr. Phelps, the American Minister at London, in regard to the interference with these vessels, instructing him to bring the matter to the attention of the British Government, and in the course of this letter he said:

Previous attempts or suggestions have been made by the local authorities of Newfoundland to inhibit the purchase or sale of fresh fish for use as bait, and the same have been distinctly disapproved by Her Majesty's Government, notably by the Duke of Newcastle, when secretary of state for the colonies, in his dispatch of August 3, 1863, to the governor of Newfoundland, Sir A. Bannerman, a copy of which you will find at page 111 in the public document (Ex. Doc. No. 84, House of Representatives, Forty-sixth Congress, second session) sent you by this mail.[b]

The letter, referred to by Mr. Bayard, from the Duke of Newcastle to the Governor of Newfoundland was written in response to a request for observations on a proposed bill framed by the Newfoundland Government with a view to the regulation of the Newfoundland fisheries, in regard to which the Duke of Newcastle expresses himself in that letter as follows:

The observations which suggest themselves to me, however, on the perusal of the draft bill are—

1st. That if any misconception exists in Newfoundland respecting the limits of the colonial jurisdiction, it would be desirable that it should be put at rest by embodying in the act a distinct settlement

---

[a] Appendix, p. 805.　　　　　[b] Appendix, p. 806.

that the regulations contained in it are of no force except within three miles of the shore of the colony.

2nd. That no act can be allowed which prohibits expressly, or is calculated by a circuitous method to prevent, the sale of bait.

3rd. That all fishing acts shall expressly declare that their provisions do not extend or interfere with any existing treaties with any foreign nation in amity with Great Britain.

4th. That, in any part of the colonial waters, it would be highly unjust and inconvenient to impose upon British fishermen restrictions which could not, without violating existing treaties, be imposed upon foreigners using the same fisheries. On this point, however, I would refer you to my despatch, marked "confidential", of the 2nd of February.[a]

Mr. Bayard also enclosed in his letter of July 30, 1886, to Mr. Phelps, a copy of a notice served by the Newfoundland customs officer on the captain of the schooner *Thomas F. Bayard* at Bonne Bay under date of July 12, 1886, which was as follows:

I am instructed to give you notice that the presence of your vessel in this port is in violation of the articles of the international convention of 1818 between Great Britain and the United States, in relation to fishery rights on the coast of Newfoundland, and of the laws in force in this country for the enforcement of the articles of the convention and that the purchase of bait or ice, or other transaction in connection with fishery operations, within 3 miles of the coasts of this colony, will be in further violation of the terms of said convention and laws.[b]

The facts out of which these cases arose and the position of the United States with respect thereto, will appear from the following extract from the note written by Mr. Phelps, pursuant to Mr. Bayard's instructions, on September 11, 1886, to Lord Iddesleigh, Secretary of State for Foreign Affairs, with reference to these cases and others which were then pending:

To two recent instances of interference by Canadian officers with American fishermen, of a somewhat different character, I am specially instructed by my Government to ask your lordship's attention; those of the schooners *Thomas F. Bayard* and *Mascot*.

These vessels were proposing to fish in waters in which the right to fish is expressly secured to Americans by the terms of the treaty of 1818; the former in Bonne Bay, on the northwest coast of Newfoundland, and the latter near the shores of the Magdalen Islands.

For this purpose the *Bayard* attempted to purchase bait in the port of Bonne Bay, having reported at the custom-house and announced its object. The *Mascot* made a similar attempt at Port Amherst in the Magdalen Islands, and also desired to take on board a pilot. Both vessels were refused permission by the authorities to purchase bait, and the *Mascot* to take a pilot, and were notified to leave the

---

[a] Appendix, p. 1082.   [b] Appendix, p. 807.

ports within twenty-four hours on penalty of seizure. They were therefore compelled to depart, to break up their voyages, and to return home, to their very great loss. I append copies of the affidavits of the masters of these vessels, stating the facts.

Your lordship will observe, upon reference to the treaty, not only that the right to fish in these waters is conferred by it, but that the clause prohibiting entry by American fishermen into Canadian ports, except for certain specified purposes, which is relied on by the Canadian Government in the cases of the *Adams* and of some other vessels, has no application whatever to the ports from which the *Bayard* and the *Mascot* were excluded.[a]

Lord Iddesleigh replied to Mr. Phelps on November 30, 1886, stating in regard to these cases:

The privileges manifestly secured to United States fishermen by the convention of 1818 in Newfoundland, Labrador, and the Magdalen Islands are not contested by Her Majesty's Government, who, whilst determined to uphold the rights of Her Majesty's North American subjects, as defined in the convention, are no less anxious and resolved to maintain in their full integrity the facilities for prosecuting the fishing industry on certain limited portions of the coast which are expressly granted to citizens of the United States. The communications on the subject of these two schooners, which I have requested Her Majesty's minister at Washington to address to Mr. Bayard, can not, I think, have failed to afford to your Government satisfactory assurances in this respect.[b]

The communications referred to by Lord Iddesleigh will be found in the following extract from Sir Lionel Sackville West's note of September 17, 1886, to Mr. Bayard:

On the arrival of your note in London, Her Majesty's secretary of state for the colonies telegraphed to the officers administering the Governments of Canada and Newfoundland calling attention to the cases, and explaining that under the treaty of 1818 United States fishermen have the right to fish off the coasts of the Magdalen Islands and off certain coasts of Newfoundland, and stating that it was presumed that the customs officials in those places had not been instructed in the same way as on other parts of the coast.

On the 25th ultimo the Governments of Canada and Newfoundland were further instructed by dispatches from the colonial office to make full reports on the subject of the complaints in question, and *it was recommended that special instructions should be issued to the authorities at these places where the inshore fishery has been granted by the convention of 1818 to the United States fishermen*, calling their attention to the provisions of that convention, and warning them that no action contrary thereto may be taken in regard to United States fishing vessels.

I may add that information has been received that the warning notices referred to by you were discontinued in the beginning of August.[c]

---

[a] Appendix, p. 837.   [b] Appendix, p. 870.   [c] Appendix, p. 839.

In connection with the question of commercial privileges on the treaty coasts, presented by the above cases, attention is also called to a statement made by the Canadian Minister of Marine and Fisheries in his report approved by the Canadian Privy Council on June 14, 1886. In this report he discusses the question of commercial privileges on the coasts covered by the renunciatory clause and he draws a distinction between the exercise of such privileges on those coasts and on the treaty coasts as follows:

Mr. Bayard states that in the proceedings prior to the treaty of 1818 the British commissioners proposed that United States fishing vessels should be excluded "from carrying also merchandise," but that this proposition "being resisted by the American negotiators, was abandoned," and goes on to say, "this fact would seem clearly to indicate that the business of fishing did not then, and does not now, disqualify vessels from also trading in the regular ports of entry. A reference to the proceedings alluded to will show that the proposition mentioned related only to United States vessels visiting those portions of the coast of Labrador and Newfoundland on which the United States fishermen had been granted the right to fish, and to land for drying and curing fish, and the rejection of the proposal can, at the utmost, be supposed only to indicate that the liberty to carry merchandise might exist without objection in relation to those coasts, and is no ground for supposing that the right extends to the regular ports of entry, against the express words of the treaty.[a]

It must also be noted that the renunciatory clause, which was the basis for denying commercial privileges to American fishermen on the coasts covered by it, does not apply to the treaty coasts, and, therefore, on those coasts the American fishermen are not limited by the treaty to the use of the bays and harbors for the four purposes of shelter, repairs, wood, and water, and the "no other purposes whatever" provision has no application to them there.

Customs Entry and Harbor Dues on Coasts Covered by Renunciatory Clause.

Several seizures or threatened seizures of American vessels occurred in 1886 and 1887 resulting in some diplomatic correspondence of interest in connection with Question 4, submitted for decision in this Case, which asks whether under the provisions of the renunciatory clause of the treaty it is permissible to impose restrictions making the exercise of the four privileges referred to in that clause conditional upon the payment of light, or harbor, or other dues, or entry, or reporting at custom-houses, or any similar conditions.

---

[a] Appendix, p. 818.

Two or three of the interferences referred to will sufficiently illustrate the questions discussed, and for that purpose attention is called to the cases of the *Rattler*, the *Julia Ellen*, and the *Shiloh*.

The circumstances of the seizure of the *Rattler* were stated in a note from Mr. Bayard to the British Chargé at Washington, under date of August 9, 1886, as follows:

I regret that it has become my duty to draw the attention of Her Majesty's Government to the unwarrantable and unfriendly treatment, reported to me this day by the United States consul-general at Halifax, experienced by the American fishing schooner *Rattler*, of Gloucester, Mass., on the 3d instant, upon the occasion of her being driven by stress of weather to find shelter in the harbor of Shelburne, Nova Scotia.

She was deeply laden and was off the harbor of Shelburne when she sought shelter in a storm and cast anchor just inside the harbor's entrance.

She was at once boarded by an officer of the Canadian cutter *Terror*, who placed two men on board.

When the storm ceased the *Rattler* weighed anchor to proceed on her way home, when the two men placed on board by the *Terror* discharged their pistols as a signal, and an officer from the *Terror* again boarded the *Rattler* and threatened to seize the vessel unless the captain reported at the custom-house.

The vessel was then detained until the captain reported at the custom-house, after which she was permitted to sail.

The hospitality which all civilized nations prescribe has thus been violated and the stipulations of a treaty grossly infracted.

A fishing vessel, denied all the usual commercial privileges in a port, has been compelled strictly to perform commercial obligations.[a]

In the cases of the *Julia Ellen* and the *Shiloh* the circumstances complained of were stated by Mr. Bayard in his note of August 18, 1886, to the British Minister at Washington as follows:

Grave cause of complaint is alleged by the masters of several American fishing vessels, among which can be named the schooners *Shiloh* and *Julia Ellen*, against the hostile and outrageous misbehavior of Captain Quigley, of the Canadian cruiser *Terror*, who, upon the entrance of these vessels into the harbor of Liverpool, Nova Scotia, fired a gun across their bows to hasten their coming to, and placed a guard of two armed men on board each vessel, who remained on board until the vessels left the harbor.

In my note to your legation of the 9th instant I made earnest remonstrance against another unfriendly act of Captain Quigley, against the schooner *Rattler*, of Gloucester, Mass., which, being fully laden and on her homeward voyage, sought shelter from stress of weather in Shelburne Harbor, Nova Scotia, and was then compelled to report at the custom-house, and have a guard of armed men kept on board.

---

[a] Appendix, p. 824.

Such conduct cannot be defended on any just ground, and I draw your attention to it in order that Her Britannic Majesty's Government may reprimand Captain Quigley for his unwarranted and rude act.

It was simply impossible for this officer to suppose that any invasion of the fishing privileges of Canada was intended by these vessels under the circumstances.

The firing of a gun across their bows was a most unusual and wholly uncalled for exhibition of hostility, and equally so was the placing of armed men on board the peaceful and lawful craft of a friendly nation. [a]

The facts as reported by the Canadian authorities were in substantial agreement with Mr. Bayard's statement of these cases, and the following additional information is found in the report of the seizing officer:

In the case of the *Julia and Ellen*, she came into the harbor of Liverpool on the 9th of August, about 5 p. m. Being some distance from me, I fired a blank musket shot to round her to. When she anchored I boarded her, and the captain reported that he came in for water. I told him to report his vessel in the morning, as it was then after customs hours, and that he must not let his men ashore, and that I would leave two men on his vessel to see that my instructions were carried out, and to see that he did not otherwise break the law.

In the morning, at 8 o'clock, I called for the captain to go to the custom-house and told him his men could go on and take water while he was reporting, so that he would be all ready to sail when he returned, which they did, and he sailed at noon.

In the case of the *Shiloh*, she came into the harbor about 6 p. m. on the 9th of August, at Liverpool, and a signal was fired in her case the same as the others.

When she anchored I boarded her, and the captain reported she was in for water. I told him it was then too late to report at the customs till morning, and that he must not allow his crew on shore; also that I would leave two men on board to see that he did not otherwise break the law, and that my instructions were carried out. [b]

In the course of the discussion which followed these and other similar interferences with American fishing vessels, the position of the United States on this subject was stated by Mr. Phelps, then American Minister at London in his note of January 26, 1887, to Lord Salisbury, Secretary of State for Foreign Affairs, as follows:

Aside from the question as to the right of American vessels to purchase bait in Canadian ports, such a construction has been given to the treaty between the United States and Great Britain as amounts virtually to a declaration of almost complete non-intercourse with American vessels. The usual comity between friendly nations has been refused in their case, and in one instance, at least, the ordinary offices of humanity. The treaty of friendship and amity which, in return for very important concessions by the United States to Great Britain, reserved to the American vessels certain specified privileges

---

[a] Appendix, p. 830.   [b] Appendix, p. 884.

has been construed to exclude them from all other intercourse common to civilized life and to universal maritime usage among nations not at war, as well as from the right to touch and trade accorded to all other vessels.

And quite aside from any question arising upon construction of the treaty, the provisions of the custom-house acts and regulations have been systematically enforced against American ships for alleged petty and technical violations of legal requirements in a manner so unreasonable, unfriendly, and unjust as to render the privileges accorded by the treaty practically nugatory.

It is not for a moment contended by the United States Government that American vessels should be exempt from those reasonable port or custom-house regulations which are in force in countries which such vessels have occasion to visit. If they choose to violate such requirements, their Government will not attempt to screen them from the just legal consequences.[a]

It appears, therefore, that no objection was raised by the United States to the imposition of harbor dues or the requirement of customs entry in the case of American vessels permitted to enjoy commercial privileges on these coasts, and that the objection on the part of the United States was directed particularly to the imposition of such conditions and exactions upon American fishing vessels exercising their treaty right of entering the bays and harbors on these coasts for the purposes specified in the treaty, when at the same time such vessels were not permitted to enjoy commercial privileges. The position of the Canadian Government on the other hand will appear from the following extracts from two reports of the Canadian Privy Council, approved respectively on January 15, and March 31, 1887:

United States fishing vessels are cheerfully accorded the right to enter Canadian ports for the purpose of obtaining shelter, repairs, and procuring wood and water; but in exercising this right they are not, and can not be, independent of the customs laws. They have the right to enter for the purposes set forth, but there is only one legal way in which to enter, and that is by conformity to the customs regulations.[b]

With reference to Mr. Bayard's reiteration of Captain Jacobs's complaint that in different harbors he was obliged to pay a different scale of dues, the minister of marine submits that in Canada there are distinct classes of harbors. Some are under the control of a commission appointed wholly or in part by the Government, under whose management improvements are made and which regulates, subject to

---

[a] Appendix, p. 899.   [b] Appendix, p. 919.

the approval of Government, the harbor dues which are to be paid by all vessels entering such ports and enjoying the advantages therein provided.

Others are natural harbors in great part unimproved, whose limits are generally defined by order in council and for which a harbor-master is appointed by Government, to whom all vessels entering pay certain nominal harbor-master's fees, which are regulated by a general act of parliament, and which constitute a fund out of which the harbor-master is paid a small salary for his services in maintaining order within the harbor. The port of St. John, New Brunswick, is entirely under municipal control and has its own stated and uniform scale of charges.

Harbor dues are paid whenever a vessel enters a port which is under a commission, and harbor-master's fees are paid only twice per calendar year by vessels entering ports not under a commission.[a]

It is understood that on the Canadian coasts no light-house dues are exacted.

It does not appear what communications passed between the British and the Canadian Governments as a result of the protest by the United States on the subject of requiring American vessels to report at custom houses and pay harbor dues when, on account of the denial of commercial privileges, their only purpose in entering the Canadian harbors was to exercise their treaty right of resorting to those harbors for shelter, repairs, wood or water.

It does appear, however, from a report adopted by the Canadian Privy Council on March 23, 1887, that before the opening of the 1887 fishing season, the Canadian position was considerably modified with respect to the requirement of reporting at custom houses. Referring to the report above mentioned, Lord Lansdowne, then Governor General of Canada, wrote on April 2, 1887, to Sir Henry Holland, the Secretary of State for the Colonies, as follows:

I have much pleasure in calling your attention to the penultimate paragraph of that report, from which you will observe that it will, in the opinion of my Government, be possible, in cases like that of the *Jennie Seaverns*, where a foreign fishing vessel has entered a Canadian harbor for a lawful purpose and in the pursuance of her treaty rights, to exercise, the necessary supervision over the conduct of her master and crew, and to guard against infractions of the customs law and other statutes binding upon foreign vessels while in Canadian waters, without placing an armed guard on board or preventing reasonable communication with the shore.

---

[a]Appendix, p. 928.

My advisers are, in regard to such matters, fully prepared to recognize that a difference should be made between the treatment of vessels *bona fide* entering a Canadian harbor for shelter or repair, or to obtain wood and water, and that of other vessels of the same class entering such harbors ostensibly for a lawful purpose, but really with the intention of breaking the law.[a]

The penultimate paragraph of the report of the Privy Council to which he makes reference, is as follows:

The minister, however, while assured that the vessel in question suffered no deprivation of or interference with its rights as defined by the convention of 1818, is of opinion that, in pursuance of the spirit of uniform kindly interpretation of the law, which it has been the constant aim of the government of Canada to exemplify in its dealings with United States fishermen, it is possible for the officers in charge of the cruisers to efficiently guard the rights of Canadian citizens and enforce the provisions of the law without in such cases as the above finding it necessary to place an armed guard on board the fishing vessel, or preventing what may be deemed reasonable communication with the shore.

The committee, concurring, in the report of the minister of marine and fisheries, recommend that your excellency be moved to transmit a copy of this minute to the right honorable the secretary of state for the colonies for the purpose of communication to the Government of the United States.[b]

Following the adoption of this report, the Canadian Minister of Marine and Fisheries issued, under date of April 16, 1887, some special instructions to fisheries officers in command of fisheries protection vessels, from which instructions the following extract is taken:

I have every reason for believing that these have been executed with efficiency and firmness, as well as with discretion, and a due regard to the rights secured by Treaty to foreign fishing vessels resorting to Canadian waters.

I desire, however, to impress upon you that, in carrying out these instructions and protecting Canadian inshore fisheries, you should be most careful not to strain the interpretation of the law in the direction of interference with the rights and privileges remaining to United States' fishermen in Canadian waters under the Convention of 1818. To this end, the largest liberty compatible with the full protection of Canadian interests is to be granted United States' fishing vessels in obtaining in our waters, shelter, repairs, wood and water. Care should be taken that while availing themselves of these privileges, such vessels do not engage in any illegal practices, and all proper supervision necessary to accomplish this object is to be exercised, but it is not deemed necessary that in order to effect this an armed guard should be placed on board, or that any reasonable communication with the shore should be prohibited, after the vessel has duly entered, unless sufficient reasons appear for the exercise of such precautions.

In places where United States' fishing vessels are accustomed to come into Canadian *waters for shelter only*, the Captain of the Cruiser

---

[a] Appendix, p. 934.   [b] Appendix, p. 935.

which may be there is authorized to *take entry from and grant clearance* to the masters of such fishing *vessels without requiring them to go on shore for that purpose.* Blank forms of entry and clearance are furnished to the Captains of Cruisers; these, after being filled in, are to be forwarded by the Captain of the Cruiser to the Customs Officer of the ports within whose jurisdiction they have been used. In cases of distress, disaster, need of provisions for the homeward voyage, of sickness or death on board a foreign fishing vessel, all needful facilities are to be granted for relief, and both you and your officers will be carrying out the wishes of the Department in courteously and freely giving assistance in such instances.[a]

Protective Measures by the United States.

In view of the attitude of the Canadian authorities toward American fishermen during this period, it was deemed necessary by the United States that some protective measures should be taken in their behalf, and for that purpose the Act of Congress approved March 3, 1887, was passed. This Act is entitled—

An Act to Authorize the President of the United States to protect and defend the rights of American fishing vessels, American fishermen, American trading and other vessels, in certain cases, and for other purposes.

It provided, in part, that, whenever the President of the United States shall be satisfied that American fishing vessels or fishermen, visiting waters or at any ports of the British Dominions of North America, are denied or abridged in the enjoyment of any rights secured to them by treaty or law, or are unjustly vexed or harassed in said waters or ports in the enjoyment of such rights, or subjected to unreasonable restrictions, regulations or requirements in respect of such rights, &c., &c., it shall be the duty of the President of the United States in his discretion, by proclamation to that effect, to deny vessels of the British Dominions of North America any entrance into the waters or ports of the United States; and also to deny entry into any port or place of the United States of fresh fish or salt fish or any other product of said Dominions or other goods coming from said Dominions to the United States. The President has never exercised the retaliatory power thus conferred upon him.

The text of this act will be found printed in full in the Appendix.[b]

---

[a] Appendix, p. 921. [b] Appendix, p. 96.

Ineffectual attempt to revive the Headland Theory.

An attempt was made, during this period, by a Canadian official to revive the headland theory, but without success, owing to the prompt action of the British Government, as will appear from the following extracts taken from the correspondence on the subject between the United States and Great Britain, and between Great Britain and Canada.

On June 14, 1886, Mr. Bayard wrote to the British Minister at Washington as follows:

I have also to inform you that the masters of the four American fishing vessels of Gloucester, Mass., *Martha A. Bradley, Rattler, Eliza Boynton,* and *Pioneer,* have severally reported to the consul-general at Halifax that the subcollector of customs at Canso had warned them to keep outside an imaginary line drawn from a point three miles outside Canso Head to a point three miles outside St. Esprit, on the Cape Breton coast, a distance of 40 miles. This line for nearly its entire continuance is distant 12 to 25 miles from the coast.

The same masters also report that they were warned against going inside an imaginary line drawn from a point three miles outside North Cape, on Prince Edward Island, to a point three miles outside of East Point, on the same island, a distance of over 100 miles, and that this last-named line was for nearly that entire distance about 30 miles from the shore.

The same authority informed the masters of the vessels referred to that they would not be permitted to enter Bay Chaleur.

Such warnings are, as you must be well aware, wholly unwarranted pretensions of extraterritorial authority and usurpations of jurisdiction by the provincial officials.

It becomes my duty, in bringing this information to your notice, to request that if any such orders for interference with the unquestionable rights of the American fishermen to pursue their business without molestation at any point not within three marine miles of the shores, and within the defined limits as to which renunciation of the liberty to fish was expressed in the treaty of 1818, may have been issued, the same may at once be revoked as violative of the rights of citizens of the United States under convention with Great Britain.[a]

This note was forwarded by the British Minister to his Government on the following day, and on July 12, 1886, in response to a request from the Foreign Office for a report on the incident, Lord Lansdowne, the Governor General of Canada, telegraphed to the British Government, as the collector's explanation of the incident, that "in conversation with the master of a fishing vessel, the Collector expressed his opinion that the headland line ran from Cranberry Island to St. Esprit," and Lord Lansdowne added "but this was not authorized by my Government in any manner."[b]

---

a Appendix, p. 787. b Appendix, p. 800.

Lord Rosebery, then Secretary of State for Foreign Affairs, promptly wrote to the British Minister at Washington on July 23, 1886, instructing him to inform Mr. Bayard of this explanation of the occurrence, which was done by the British Chargé at Washington in his note of August 2, 1886, to Mr. Bayard, thus closing the incident.[a]

Negotiations for a new fisheries arrangement resulting in the proposed Treaty of 1888.

During this period many expressions are found in the diplomatic correspondence on both sides indicating a desire to settle the entire controversy by entering into some arrangement for adjusting the fisheries question on some new basis mutually acceptable to both sides. In recognition of this situation, Mr. Bayard forwarded in his letter of November 15, 1886, to Mr. Phelps, a draft agreement which he had caused to be prepared, with instructions to propose it to Lord Iddesleigh in the hope that it would be found "to contain a satisfactory basis for the solution of existing difficulties and assist in securing an assured, just, honorable, and, therefore, mutually satisfactory settlement of the long-vexed question of the North Atlantic Fisheries." [b]

To this proposal Lord Salisbury replied in his note of March 24, 1887, to the American Chargé at London, commenting at some length upon Mr. Bayard's draft,[c] and enclosing a memorandum of observations; and Mr. Bayard in turn sent on July 12, 1887, to Mr. Phelps for transmission to Lord Salisbury, a series of observations in reply to the British observations.[d]

It is unnecessary to examine the terms of Mr. Bayard's proposal or the observations exchanged with reference thereto, inasmuch as they were intended rather as a basis of compromise than as an expression of opinion or interpretation of the true intent and meaning of the fisheries provisions of the treaty of 1818, and the main feature of Mr. Bayard's proposal was the appointment of a mixed commission for the purpose of agreeing upon the meaning of some of the disputed provisions of the treaty of 1818, subject to certain conditions and directions limiting the scope of the commissioners' powers.

While these negotiations were proceeding, it was proposed and agreed that a joint commission should be appointed to negotiate a

---

a Appendix, pp. 809–823.   c Appendix, pp. 908–912.
b Appendix, pp. 863, 865.   d Appendix, pp. 945, 948.

new treaty, with the result that plenipotentiaries were appointed and negotiations undertaken for that purpose. In these negotiations the plenipotentiaries on the part of the United States were Thomas F. Bayard, William L. Putnam and James B. Angell; and the plenipotentiaries on the part of Great Britain were Joseph Chamberlain, Sir L. S. West and Sir Charles Tupper.

These plenipotentiaries reached an agreement for a treaty on February 15, 1888, but the proposed treaty, on which they agreed, when submitted to the Senate of the United States for its advice and consent, failed to secure its approval; and, as under the Constitution of the United States a treaty cannot be made without the advice and consent of the United States Senate, this proposed treaty never became effective.

Under this proposed treaty, Article I. of the treaty of 1818 was left undisturbed, but the questions of difference which had arisen with respect to it were dealt with by the new provisions. It was proposed that a mixed commission should be appointed to delimit, in the manner prescribed, the British waters, bays, creeks, and harbors on the coasts of Canada and of Newfoundland as to which the United States by Article I. of the treaty of 1818 renounced the liberty to take, dry or cure fish. It was provided that in this delimitation the three marine miles mentioned in the earlier treaty should be measured seaward from low water mark; or, in the case of bays, creeks, and harbors, from a straight line drawn across the bay, creek, or harbor in the part nearest the entrance at the first point where the width does not exceed ten marine miles, except in the following cases:

At or near the following bays the limits of exclusion under Article I. of the Convention of October 20, 1818, at points more than three marine miles from low water mark, shall be established by the following lines, namely:

At the Baie des Chaleurs the line from the Light at Birch Point on Miscou Island to Macquereau Point Light; at the Bay of Miramichi, the line from the light at Point Escuminac to the Light on the Eastern Point of Tabisintac Gully; at Egmont Bay, in Prince Edward Island, the line from the Light at Cape Egmont to the Light at West Point; and off St. Ann's Bay, in the Province of Nova Scotia, the line from Cape Smoke to the Light at Point Aconi.

At Fortune Bay, in Newfoundland, the line from Connaigre Head to the Light on the South-easterly end of Brunet Island, thence to Fortune Head; at Sir Charles Hamilton Sound, the line from the South-east point of Cape Fogo to White Island, thence to the North end of Peckford Island, and from the South end of Peckford Island to the East Headland of Ragged Harbor.

At or near the following bays the limits of exclusion shall be three marine miles seaward from the following lines, namely:

At or near Barrington Bay, in Nova Scotia, the line from the Light on Stoddard Island to the Light on the south point of Cape Sable, thence to the Light at Baccaro Point; at Chedabucto and St. Peter's Bays, the line from Cranberry Island Light to Green Island Light, thence to Point Rouge; at Mira Bay, the line from the Light on the East Point of Scatari Island to the North-easterly Point of Cape Morien; and at Placentia Bay, in Newfoundland, the line from Latine Point, on the Eastern mainland shore, to the most Southerly Point of Red Island, thence by the most Southerly Point of Merasheen Island to the mainland.

Long Island and Bryer Island, at St. Mary's Bay, in Nova Scotia, shall, for the purpose of delimitation, be taken as the coasts of such bay.

It was further provided that—

United States fishing vessels entering the bays or harbors referred to in Article I. of this Treaty shall conform to harbor regulations common to them and to fishing vessels of Canada or of Newfoundland.

They need not report, enter, or clear, when putting into such bays or harbors for shelter or repairing damages, nor when putting into the same, outside the limits of established ports of entry, for the purpose of purchasing wood or of obtaining water; except that any such vessel remaining more than twenty-four hours, exclusive of Sundays and legal holidays, within any such port, or communicating with the shore therein, may be required to report, enter, or clear; and no vessel shall be excused hereby from giving due information to boarding officers.

They shall not be liable in any such bays or harbors for compulsory pilotage; nor, when therein for the purpose of shelter, of repairing damages, of purchasing wood, or of obtaining water, shall they be liable for harbor dues, tonnage dues, buoy dues, light dues, or other similar dues; but this enumeration shall not permit other charges inconsistent with the enjoyment of the liberties reserved or secured by the Convention of October 20, 1818.

And also that—

United States fishing vessels entering the ports, bays, and harbors of the Eastern and Northeastern coasts of Canada or of the coasts of Newfoundland under stress of weather or other casualty may unload, reload, tranship, or sell, subject to customs laws and regulations, all fish on board, when such unloading, transshipment, or sale is made necessary as incidental to repairs, and may replenish outfits, provisions and supplies damaged or lost by disaster; and in case of death or sickness shall be allowed all needful facilities, including the shipping of crews.

Licenses to purchase in established ports of entry of the aforesaid coasts of Canada or of Newfoundland, for the homeward voyage, such provisions and supplies as are ordinarily sold to trading vessels, shall be granted to United States fishing vessels in such ports promptly upon application and without charge; and such vessels having obtained licenses in the manner aforesaid, shall also be accorded upon all occasions such facilities for the purchase of casual or needful provisions and supplies as are ordinarily granted to trading vessels;

but such provisions or supplies shall not be obtained by barter, nor purchased for re-sale or traffic.

Provision was also made regulating the penalties to be imposed and the procedure to be taken in case of the violation of the provisions agreed upon.

The proposed treaty also contemplated reciprocal trade arrangements for which provision was made.

The text of this unratified treaty will be found printed in full in the Appendix.[a]

Modus Vivendi of 1888.

At the close of the negotiations for the unratified treaty of 1888, the British plenipotentiaries offered to make "a temporary arrangement for a period not exceeding two years in order to afford a *modus vivendi* pending the ratification of the treaty."

The *modus vivendi* thus proposed was established by the protocol of February 15, 1888, of those negotiations and was in terms as follows:

1. For a period not exceeding two years from the present date, the privilege of entering the bays and harbors of the Atlantic coasts of Canada and Newfoundland shall be granted to United States fishing vessels by annual Licenses at a fee of $1½ per ton—for the following purposes:

The purchase of bait, ice, seines, lines and all other supplies and outfits.

Transshipment of catch and shipping of crews.

2. If during the continuance of this arrangement, the United States should remove the duties on fish, fish oil, whale and seal oil (and their coverings, packages, &c.), the said Licenses shall be issued free of charge.

3. United States fishing vessels entering the bays and harbors of the Atlantic coasts of Canada or of Newfoundland for any of the four purposes mentioned in Article I. of the Convention of October 20, 1818, and not remaining therein more than twenty-four hours, shall not be required to enter or clear at the custom house, providing that they do not communicate with the shore.

4. Forfeiture to be exacted only for the offences of fishing or preparing to fish in territorial waters.

5. This arrangement to take effect as soon as the necessary measures can be completed by the Colonial Authorities.[b]

---

[a] Appendix, p. 39.   [b] Appendix, p. 44.

PERIOD FROM 1888 TO 1909.

During this period no new question involving the interpretation of the fisheries article of the treaty of 1818 in its relation to the Canadian coasts came up for discussion between the United States and Great Britain, and no question involving its interpretation in relation to the Newfoundland coasts arose until 1905.

Although the *modus vivendi* of February 15, 1888, was entered into for a period not exceeding two years in order to afford a temporary arrangement pending the ratification of the proposed treaty of 1888, and the United States Senate refused its consent to the proposed treaty in August of that year, nevertheless the *modus vivendi* has been regarded as continuing in force for the period of two years following its date. So far as Canada is concerned this *modus vivendi* has been continued in practical effect down to the present time by action of the Canadian Government without formal extension, and during this period no change has taken place in the attitude either of the United States or British Governments on the questions of difference which had previously arisen in the fisheries controversy with reference either to the so-called treaty coasts or other coasts of Canada. So far as Newfoundland is concerned, the laws of that colony in force during this period down to 1905 authorized the granting of licenses to foreign fishing vessels, permitting such vessels, within the jurisdiction of that colony, to purchase bait and ice and fishing supplies and outfits generally, and to ship fishing crews for such vessels. These laws provided for the seizure and forfeiture of such vessels for purchasing bait or other supplies, or engaging members of the crew without first obtaining a license therefor; and although no distinction is made in the acts referred to between the treaty coasts and those covered by the renunciatory clause, except that entering within the three mile limit on the latter coasts for any purposes not permitted by treaty is made a ground for seizure, nevertheless the acts referred to contained the usual provision, found in all Newfoundland fishery legislation, that nothing therein should affect "the rights and privileges granted by treaty to subjects of any state or power in amity with Her Majesty." It does not appear that any questions involving the interpretation of the fisheries provisions of the treaty of 1818 arose between the United States and Great Britain in connection with such legislation.

The Newfoundland controversy.

In 1905, however, the Newfoundland Government completely reversed its former attitude toward American fishing interests and undertook by legislative and administrative action to terminate all the commercial privileges, which for many years prior to that time had been extended to American fishing vessels both on the treaty coasts and on the other coasts of Newfoundland. The admitted purpose of this new policy of the Newfoundland Government was to compel the American Government to open the American markets to Newfoundland fish and fish products free of duty in exchange for more extensive fishing and commercial privileges; and it soon became evident that in furtherance of this plan the Newfoundland Government was likely to attempt to impose certain limitations and restraints upon the American fishermen in the enjoyment of the fishing liberties secured to them under the treaty of 1818 upon the treaty coasts of Newfoundland.

As a result of this situation the Government of the United States at once proceeded to take up with Great Britain the question of protecting the rights of American fishermen on the treaty coasts of Newfoundland under the treaty of 1818, which were threatened by the attitude of the Newfoundland Government.

In October, 1905, it was reported to the Secretary of State that the Newfoundland Minister of Marine and Fisheries "has forbidden all vessels on American registry to fish on treaty coast, where they now are, and where they have fished unmolested since 1818." Mr. Root, the Secretary of State, promptly called this report to the attention of the British Ambassador at Washington, Sir H. M. Durand, in his note of October 12, 1905[a]; and in reply the British Ambassador, by note of October 19, 1905[b], informed the Secretary of State that the report was without foundation and that the Newfoundland Minister had exercised no interference whatever with such vessels. Meanwhile, however, it having been reported, as a result of inquiries as to the precise difficulty on the Newfoundland coast, that the captain of one American vessel had been informed by an inspector of the Revenue Protection Service of Newfoundland that he could not fish there, and that several others had been ordered not

---

[a] Appendix, p. 964.　　　　　　[b] Appendix, p. 965.

to take herring by the Collector of Customs at Bonne Bay, New-foundland, the Secretary of State wrote again to the British Ambassador on October 19, 1905, as follows:

It would seem that the Newfoundland officials are making a distinction between two classes of American vessels. We have vessels which are registered, and vessels which are licensed to fish and not registered. The licence carries a narrow and restricted authority; the registry carries the broadest and most unrestricted authority. The vessel with a licence can fish, but cannot trade; the registered vessels can lawfully both fish and trade. The distinction between the two classes in the action of the Newfoundland authorities would seem to have been implied in the despatch from Senator Lodge which I quoted in my letter of the 12th, and the imputation of the prohibition of the Minister of Marine and Fisheries may perhaps have come from the port officers, in conversation with the masters of American vessels, giving him as their authority for their prohibitions.

As the buying of herring and bait fish, which until recently has been permitted for a good many years in Newfoundland, is trading, the American fishing fleet have come very generally to take an American registry, instead of confining themselves to the narrower fishing licence, and far the greater part of the fleet now in northern waters consists of registered vessels. The prohibition against fishing under an American register substantially bars the fleet from fishing. American vessels have also apparently been in the habit of entering at the Newfoundland custom-houses and applying for a Newfoundland licence to buy or take bait, and I gather from all the information I have been able to get that both the American masters and the Customs officials have failed to clearly appreciate the different conditions created by the practical withdrawal of all privileges on the part of Newfoundland and the throwing of the American fishermen back upon the bare rights which belong to them under the Treaty of 1818.

I am confident that we can reach a clear understanding regarding those rights and the essential conditions of their exercise, and that a statement of this understanding to the Newfoundland Government, for the guidance of its officials on the one hand, and to our American fishermen for their guidance on the other, will prevent causeless injury and possible disturbances, such as have been cause for regret in the past history of the north-eastern fisheries.

I will try to state our view upon the matters involved in the situation, which now appears to exist upon the Treaty Coast. We consider that—

1. Any American vessel is entitled to go into the waters of the Treaty Coast and take fish of any kind.

She derives this right from the Treaty (or from the conditions existing prior to the Treaty and recognized by it) and not from any permission or authority proceeding from the Government of Newfoundland.

2. An American vessel seeking to exercise the Treaty right is not bound to obtain a licence from the Government of Newfoundland, and, if she does not purpose to trade as well as fish, she is not bound to enter at any Newfoundland custom-house.

3. The only concern of the Government of Newfoundland with such a vessel is to call for proper evidence that she is an American vessel, and, therefore, entitled to exercise the Treaty right, and to have her refrain from violating any laws of Newfoundland not inconsistent with the Treaty.

4. The proper evidence that a vessel is an American vessel and entitled to exercise the Treaty right is the production of the ship's papers of the kind generally recognized in the maritime world as evidence of a vessel's national character.

5. When a vessel has produced papers showing that she is an American vessel, the officials of Newfoundland have no concern with the character or extent of the privileges accorded to such a vessel by the Government of the United States. No question as between a registry and licence is a proper subject for their consideration. They are not charged with enforcing any laws or regulations of the United States. As to them, if the vessel is American she has the Treaty right, and they are not at liberty to deny it.

6. If any such matter were a proper subject for the consideration of the officials of Newfoundland, the statement of this Department that vessels bearing an American registry are entitled to exercise the Treaty right should be taken by such officials as conclusive.

If your Government sees no cause to dissent from these propositions, I am inclined to think a statement of them as agreed upon would resolve the immediate difficulty now existing on the Treaty Coast.[a]

In the same note from which the above extract is taken, Mr. Root also brought up for consideration the question of the possible interference with the rights of American fishermen on the treaty coast of Newfoundland by the application to that coast of certain provisions of the new foreign fishing vessels act of June 15, 1905, which had then recently been assented to by the British Government, with respect to which act Mr. Root said:

I have, however, to call your attention to a further subject, which I apprehend may lead to further misunderstanding in the near future if it is not dealt with now. That is, the purposes of the Government of Newfoundland in respect of the treatment of American fishing-vessels as exhibited in a Law enacted during the past summer by the Legislature of that Colony, under the title "An Act respecting Foreign Fishing-Vessels."

This Act appears to be designed for the enforcement of laws previously enacted by Newfoundland, which prohibited the sale to foreign fishing-vessels of herring, caplin, squid, or other bait fishes, lines, seines, or other outfits or supplies for the fishery or the shipment by a foreign fishing-vessel of crews within the jurisdiction of Newfoundland.

The Act of last summer respecting foreign fishing-vessels provides:—

"Section 1. Any Justice of the Peace, sub-collector, preventive officers, fishery warden, or constable, may go on board any foreign

---

[a] Appendix p. 966.

fishing-vessel being within any port of the coasts of this island, or hovering within British waters within 3 marine miles of any of the coasts, bays, creeks, or harbours in this island, and may bring such foreign fishing-vessel into port, may search her cargo and may examine the master upon oath touching the cargo and voyage, and the master or person in command, shall answer truly such questions as shall be put to him under a penalty not exceeding 500 dollars. And if such foreign fishing-vessel has on board any herring, caplin, squid, or other bait fishes, ice, lines, seines, or other outfits or supplies for the fishery purchased within any port on the coast of this island, or within the distance of 3 marine miles from any coasts, bays, creeks, or harbours of this island, or if the master of the said vessel shall have engaged or attempted to engage any person to form part of the crew of the said vessel in any port or on any part of the coasts of this island, or has entered such waters for any purpose not permitted by Treaty or Convention for the time being in force such vessel and the tackle, rigging, apparel, furniture, stores, and cargo thereof shall be forfeited.

"Section 3. In any prosecution under this Act the presence on board any foreign fishing-vessel in any port of this island, or within British waters aforesaid of any caplin, squid, or other bait fishes, of ice, lines, seines, or other outfits or supplies for the fishery shall be *primâ facie* evidence of the purchase of the said bait, fishes, and supplies and outfits within such port or waters."

It seems plain that the provisions above quoted constitute a warrant to the officers named to interfere with and violate the rights of American fishing-vessels under the Treaty of 1818.

The 1st section authorizes any of the officers named to stop an American vessel while fishing upon the Treaty Coast and compel it to leave the fishing grounds, to prevent it from going to the places where the fish may be, to prevent it departing with the fish which it may have taken, and to detain it for an indefinite period during a search of the cargo and an examination of the master under oath under a heavy penalty.

It is to be observed that this section does not require that the vessel shall have been charged with any violation of the laws of Newfoundland, or even that she shall have been suspected of having violated the laws of Newfoundland as a condition precedent to compelling it to desist from the exercise of its Treaty rights, and virtually seizing it and taking it into port. In the consideration of this provision, it is unnecessary to discuss any question as to the extent to which American vessels may be interfered with in the exercise of their Treaty rights pursuant to judicial proceedings based upon a charge of violation of law, or even upon reasonable ground to belive that any law has been violated, for the authority of the Acts authorized appears to be part of no such proceeding.

When we consider that the minor officials named in the Act, invested with this extraordinary and summary power, are presumptively members of the fishing communities, in competition with which the American fishermen are following their calling, it is plain that in denying the right of the Government of Newfoundland to do what this section provides for we are not merely dealing with a theoretical question, but with the probability of serious injustice.

The 3rd section of the Act, above quoted in full, makes the presence on board of an American vessel of the fish, gear—the implements necessary to the exercise of the Treaty right—*primâ facie* evidence of a criminal offence against the laws of Newfoundland, and it also makes the presence on board the vessel of the fish which the vessel has a right to take under Treaty *primâ facie* evidence of a criminal offence under the laws of Newfoundland. This certainly cannot be justified. It is, in effect, providing that the exercise of the Treaty right shall be *primâ facie* evidence of a crime.

I need not argue with the Government of Great Britain that the 1st section of this Act purports to authorize the very kind of official conduct which led to the establishment in England of the rule against unreasonable searches and seizures, now firmly embedded in the jurisprudence of both nations. Nor need I argue that American vessels are of right entitled to have on them in the waters of the Treaty Coast both fish of every kind, and the gear for the taking of fish, and that a law undertaking to make that possession *primâ facie* proof of crime deprives them of that presumption of innocence to which all citizens of Great Britain and America are entitled. When the Legislature of Newfoundland denies these rights to American fishing-vessels, it imposes upon them a heavy penalty for the exercise of their rights under the Treaty, and we may reasonably apprehend that this penalty will be so severe in its practical effect as to be an effectual bar to the exercise of the Treaty right.

I feel bound to urge that the Government of Great Britain shall advise the Newfoundland Government that the provisions of law which I have quoted are inconsistent with the rights of the United States under the Treaty of 1818, and ought to be repealed; and that, in the meantime, and without any avoidable delay, the Governor in Council shall be requested by a Proclamation which he is authorized to issue under the 8th section of the Act respecting Foreign Fishing-Vessels, to suspend the operation of the Act.[a]

Mr. Root also took occasion to bring up for consideration, as requiring the careful attention of the British Government, another possible source of trouble, arising from the attitude of the Newfoundland Government at that time, as follows:

There is still another phase of this subject to which I must ask your attention. I am advised that there is a very strong feeling among the Newfoundland fishermen on the Treaty Coast against the enforcement of the Newfoundland Act prohibiting the sale of bait, and that at a recent mass meeting of fishermen at the Bay of Islands, Resolutions were adopted urging the repeal or suspension of that Act, and containing the following clauses:—

"If our requests are not granted immediately we shall be compelled, in justice to ourselves and families, to seek other ways and means to engage with the Americans.

"We would also direct the attention of his Excellency the Governor in Council to what took place in Fortune Bay a few years ago when Captain Solomon Jacobs seined herring against the wishes of the

---

[a] Appendix, p. 967.

people, and the result. If a similar occurrence should take place here, who will be responsible?"

This resolution indicates the existence of still another source from which, if not controlled, may come most unfortunate results when the American fishermen proceed to the exercise of their Treaty rights, that is, the Newfoundland fishermen themselves acting independently of their Government.

You are aware that for a considerable period American fishing-vessels, instead of themselves taking herring, caplin, and squid upon the Treaty Coast, have been in the habit of buying those fish from the Newfoundland fishermen. For many of the Newfoundland fishermen this trade has been a principal means of support. That has been especially so in and about the Bay of Islands. It has been profitable to the local fishermen, and it has been for the Americans a satisfactory substitute for the exercise of their Treaty right to catch the fish themselves. It is, indeed, not unnatural that these fishermen should struggle in every way open to them to prevent the loss of their means of support, and that if they cannot control their own Government so as to secure permission to sell herring and bait, they should seek to prevent the Americans from taking the bait, in the hope that as the result of that prevention, their profitable trade may be restored.

The Resolution which I have quoted referring to the Fortune Bay case is a clear threat of violence to prevent the exercise of the Treaty right. If the threat should be carried out it is too much to expect that some at least of the American fishermen will not refuse to yield to lawless force which seeks to deprive them of their rights and of their means of livelihood.

We shall do everything in our power to prevent such a collision, and we should indeed deeply deplore it, but the true and effective method of prevention plainly must be the exercise of proper control by the Government of Newfoundland over the fishermen of Newfoundland, and it seems to me that the danger is sufficiently real and imminent to justify me in asking that the Government of Great Britain shall take speedy steps to bring about the exercise of such control.[a]

On February 2, 1906, Sir Edward Grey, the Secretary of State for Foreign Affairs, replying to Mr. Root's note to the British Ambassador at Washington above quoted, wrote to Mr. Reid, the American Ambassador at London, enclosing "a memorandum dealing *seriatim* with the six propositions formulated by Mr. Root, and with his observations with regard to some of provisions of the recent Newfoundland legislation for the regulation of the fisheries", and referring to the last portion of Mr. Root's note, he said that—

As, owing to the prompt measures adopted and to the conciliatory spirit displayed by both Governments, the fishing season has now closed without any collision between the British and American fishermen, or the development of any such friction as was at one time

[a] Appendix, p. 969.

anticipated, it is unnecessary to deal more particularly with the latter portion of Mr. Root's note, which was devoted to that side of the question.[a]

The memorandum enclosed in Sir Edward Grey's note is quoted in full below:

Memorandum.

Mr. Root's note to Sir M. Durand of the 19th October, 1905, on the subject of the United States' fishery in the waters of Newfoundland under the Convention of the 20th October, 1818, may be divided into three parts:

The first deals with complaints which had reached the United States' Government to the effect that vessels of United States' registry had been forbidden by the Colonial authorities to fish on the Treaty Coast, the second with the provisions of "The Newfoundland Foreign Fishing-Vessels Act, 1905," and the third with the possibility of a lawless and violent interruption of the United States' fishery by the inhabitants of the Bay of Islands.

The complaints referred to in the first part of Mr. Root's note were at once brought to the notice of the Government of Newfoundland, and they replied that there had been no attempt to prevent American fishermen from taking fish. The complaints in question appear to have been based on some misunderstanding, and the subsequent course of the fishery proved that the apprehensions on the part of the United States' Government to which they gave rise were, fortunately, not well founded.

His Majesty's Government, however, agree with the United States' Government in thinking that inasmuch as the privileges which citizens of the United States have for many years enjoyed of purchasing bait and supplies and engaging men in Newfoundland waters have recently been withdrawn and American fishermen have consequently, in Mr. Root's words, been thrown back upon their rights under the Convention of 1818, it is desirable that a clear understanding should be reached regarding those rights and the essential conditions of their exercise, and they have accordingly given the most careful consideration to the six propositions advanced in Mr. Root's note as embodying the views of the United States' Government on the subject.

They regret, however, that they are unable to record their assent to these propositions without some important qualifications.

Proposition 1 states:—

"Any American vessel is entitled to go into the waters of the Treaty Coast and take fish of any kind. She derives this right from the Treaty (or from the conditions existing prior to the Treaty and recognized by it) and not from any permission or authority proceeding from the Government of Newfoundland."

The privilege of fishing conceded by Article I of the Convention of 1818 is conceded, not to American vessels, but to inhabitants of the United States and to American fishermen.

His Majesty's Government are unable to agree to this or any of the subsequent propositions if they are meant to assert any right of American vessels to prosecute the fishery under the Convention of

---
[a] Appendix p. 971.

1818 except when the fishery is carried on by inhabitants of the United States. The Convention confers no rights on American vessels as such. It enures for the benefit only of inhabitants of the United States.

Proposition 2 states:—

"An American vessel seeking to exercise the Treaty right is not bound to obtain a licence from the Government of Newfoundland, and, if she does not purpose to trade as well as fish, she is not bound to enter at any Newfoundland custom-house."

His Majesty's Government agree that the Government of Newfoundland could not require that American fishermen seeking to exercise the Treaty right should take out a licence from the Colonial Government. No licence is required for what is a matter of right, and no such licence has, His Majesty's Government are informed, been, in fact, required.

With the last part of the proposition it will be more convenient to deal in conjunction with proposition 3.

Proposition 3 states:—

"The only concern of the Government of Newfoundland with such a vessel is to call for proper evidence that she is an American vessel, and therefore entitled to exercise the Treaty right, and to have her refrain from violating any laws of Newfoundland not inconsistent with the Treaty."

It has already been pointed out that the Convention of 1818 confers no rights on American vessels as such, and that the exercise of the right of fishing under the Convention is subject to the condition that the fishing is carried on by inhabitants of the United States. His Majesty's Government, however, agree that no law of Newfoundland should be enforced on American fishermen which is inconsistent with their rights under the Convention.

Mr. Root's note does not give any indication of what laws of the Colony would be regarded by the United States' Government as inconsistent with the Convention if applied to American fishermen. The opinion of His Majesty's Government on this point is as follows:—

The American fishery, under Article I of the Convention of 1818, is one carried on within the British jurisdiction and 'in common with" British subjects. The two Governments hold different views as to the nature of this Article. The British Government consider that the war of 1812 abrogated that part of Article III of the Treaty of Peace of 1783 which continued to inhabitants of the United States "the liberty" (in the words used by Mr. Adams to Earl Bathurst in his note of the 25th September, 1815) "of fishing and drying, and curing their fish within the exclusive jurisdiction on the North American coasts to which they had been accustomed while themselves forming a part of the British nation," and that consequently Article I of the Convention of 1818 was a new grant to inhabitants of the United States of fishing privileges within the British jurisdiction. The United States' Government, on the other hand, contend that the war of 1812 had not the effect attributed to it by the British Government, and that Article I of the Convention of 1818 was not a new grant, but merely a recognition (though limited in extent) of privileges enjoyed by inhabitants of the United States prior, not only to the war, but to the Treaty of 1783. Whichever of these views be adopted, it is certain that inhabitants of the United States would not now be entitled to fish in British North American waters but for the fact that they were entitled to do so when they were British subjects. American fishermen cannot therefore rightly claim to exercise their right of fishery under the Convention of 1818 on a footing of greater freedom than if they had never ceased to be British subjects. Nor consistently with the terms of the Convention can they claim to exercise it on a footing of greater freedom than the British subjects "in common with" whom they exercise it under the Convention. In other words, the American fishery under the Convention is not a free but a regulated fishery, and, in the opinion of His Majesty's Government, American fishermen are bound to comply with all Colonial Laws and Regulations, including any touching the conduct of the fishery, so long as these are not in their nature unreasonable, and are applicable to all fishermen alike. One of these Regulations prohibits fishing on Sundays. His Majesty's Government have received information that several breaches of this Regulation were committed by American fishermen during the past fishing season. This Regulation has been in force for many years, and looking to the insignificant extent to which American fishermen have exercised their right of fishery on the Treaty Coast in the past, it cannot be regarded as having been made with the object of restricting the enjoyment of that right. Both its reasonableness and its *bona fides* appear to His Majesty's Government to be beyond question, and they trust that the United States' Government will take steps to secure its observance in the future.

As regards the treatment of American vessels from which American fishermen exercise the Treaty right of fishery, His Majesty's Government are prepared to admit that, although the Convention confers no rights on American vessels as such, yet since the American fishery is essentially a ship fishery, no law of Newfoundland should be enforced on American fishing-vessels which would unreasonably interfere with the exercise by the American fishermen on board of their rights under the Convention. The United States' Government, on their part, admit, in Mr. Root's note, that the Colonial Government are entitled to have an American vessel engaged in the fishery refrain from violating any laws of Newfoundland not inconsistent with the Convention, but maintain that if she does not purpose to trade, but only to fish, she is not bound to enter at any Newfoundland custom-house.

Mr. Root's note refers only to the question of entry inwards, but it is presumed that the United States' Government entertain the same views on the question of clearing outwards. At all events, American vessels have not only passed to the fishing grounds in the inner waters of the Bay of Islands without reporting at a Colonial custom-house, but have also omitted to clear on returning to the United States. In both respects they have committed breaches of the Colonial Customs Law, which, as regards the obligations to enter and to clear, makes no distinction between fishing- and trading-vessels.

His Majesty's Government regret not to be able to share the view of the United States' Government that the provisions of the Colonial Law which impose those obligations are inconsistent with the Convention of 1818, if applied to American vessels which do not purpose to trade, but only to fish. They hold that the only ground on which the application of any provisions of the Colonial Law to American vessels engaged in the fishery can be objected to is that it unreasonably interferes with the exercise of the American right of fishery.

It is admitted that the majority of the American vessels lately engaged in the fishery on the western coast of the Colony were registered vessels, as opposed to licensed fishing-vessels, and as such were at liberty both to trade and to fish. The production of evidence of the United States' registration is therefore not sufficient to establish that a vessel, in Mr. Root's words, "does not purpose to trade as well as fish," and something more would seem clearly to be necessary. The United States' Government would undoubtedly be entitled to complain if the fishery of inhabitants of the United States were seriously interfered with by a vexatious and arbitrary enforcement of the Colonial Customs laws, but it must be remembered that, in proceeding to the waters in which the winter fishery is conducted, American vessels must pass in close proximity to several custom-houses, and that in order to reach or leave the grounds in the arms of the Bay of Islands, on which the fishery has been principally carried on during the past season, they have sailed by no less than three custom-houses on the shores of the bay itself. So that the obligation to report and clear need not in any way have interfered with a vessel's operations. It must also be remembered that a fishery conducted in the midst of practically the only centres of population on the west coast of the Colony affords ample opportunities for illicit trade, and consequently calls for careful supervision in the interests of the Colonial revenue.

The provisions in question are clearly necessary for the prevention of smuggling, and His Majesty's Government are of opinion that exception cannot be taken to their application to American vessels as an unreasonable interference with the American fishery, and they entertain the strong hope that the United States' Government will, on reconsideration, perceive the correctness of this view, and issue instructions accordingly for the future guidance of those in charge of American vessels.

It is, moreover, to the advantage of the American vessels engaged in the winter fishery in the Bay of Islands that they should report at a Colonial custom-house. Owing to the extent and peculiar configuration of that bay, and owing to the prevalence of fogs, vessels that enter its inner waters may remain for days without the local officers becoming aware that they are on the coast unless they so report. In such circumstances it is difficult for the Colonial Government to insure to American fishermen that protection against lawless interference for which Mr. Root calls in the concluding part of his note.

His Majesty's Government desire further to invite the attention of the United States' Government to the fact that certain United States' vessels engaged in the fishery refused to pay light dues. This is the first time, His Majesty's Government are informed, that American vessels have refused to pay these dues, and it is presumed that the refusal is based on the denial by the Colonial Government of the trading privileges allowed in past years. His Majesty's Government, however, cannot admit that such denial entitles American vessels to exemption from light dues in the ports in which they fish. As already stated, American fishing-vessels engaged in the fishery under the Convention of 1818 have no Treaty status as such, and the only ground on which, in the opinion of His Majesty's Government, the application of any Colonial law to such vessels can be objected to is that such application involves an unreasonable interference with the exercise of the Treaty rights of the American fishermen on board. The payment of light dues by a vessel on entering a port of the Colony clearly involves no such interference. These dues are payable by all vessels of whatever description and nationality other than coasting- and fishing-vessels owned and registered in the Colony (which are, on certain conditions, exempt either wholly or in part). His Majesty's Government trust that in these circumstances such directions will be issued as will prevent further refusals in the future, and they would point out generally that it is the duty of all foreigners sojourning in the limits of the British jurisdiction to obey that law, and that, if it is considered that the local jurisdiction is being exercised in a manner not consistent with the enjoyment of any Treaty rights, the proper course to pursue is not to ignore the law, but to obey it, and to refer the question of any alleged infringement of their Treaty rights to be settled diplomatically between their Government and that of His Majesty.

Propositions 4, 5, and 6 state:—

Proposition 4. "The proper evidence that a vessel is an American vessel, and entitled to exercise the Treaty right, is the production of the ship's papers of the kind generally recognized in the maritime world as evidence of a vessel's national character."

Proposition 5. "When a vessel has produced papers showing that she is an American vessel, the officials of Newfoundland have no concern with the character or extent of the privileges accorded to such a vessel by the Government of the United States. No question as between a registry and licence is a proper subject for their considera- tion. They are not charged with enforcing any Laws or Regulations of the United States, As to them, if the vessel is American she has the Treaty right, and they are not at liberty to deny it."

Proposition 6. "If any such matter were a proper subject for the consideration of the officials of Newfoundland, the statement of this Department that vessels bearing an American registry are entitled to exercise the Treaty right should be taken by such officials as con- clusive."

His Majesty's Government are unable to agree to these propositions, except with the reservations as to the status of American vessels under the Convention already indicated, and with reference to proposition 6, they would submit that the assurance to be given by the Department of State of the United States should be that the persons by whom the fishery is to be exercised from the American vessels are inhabitants of the United States.

In point of fact the Colonial Government have informed His Majesty's Government that they do not require an American vessel to produce a United States' fishing licence. The distinction between United States' registration and the possession of a United States' fishing licence is, however, of some importance, inasmuch as a vessel which, so far as the United States' Government are concerned, is at liberty both to trade and to fish naturally calls for a greater measure of supervision by the Colonial Government than a vessel fitted out only for fishing and debarred by the United States' Government from trading; and information has been furnished to His Majesty's Govern- ment by the Colonial Government which shows that the proceedings of American fishing-vessels in Newfoundland waters have in the past been of such a character as to make it impossible, from the point of view of the protection of the Colonial revenue, to exempt such vessels from the supervision authorized by the Colonial Customs Law.

His Majesty's Government now turn to that part of Mr. Root's note which deals with "The Foreign Fishing-Vessels Act, 1905."

His Majesty's Government would have viewed with the strongest disapproval any disposition on the part of the Colonial authorities to administer this Act in a manner not consistent with His Majesty's Treaty obligations, but they are confident that the United States' Government will readily admit that the fears expressed on this head in Mr. Root's note have not been realized.

They desire, however, to point out that, though the Act in question was passed to give effect to the decision of the Colonial Government to withdraw from American fishing-vessels the privileges which they had been allowed to enjoy for many years previously of purchasing bait and supplies and of engaging crews in the ports of the Colony, the provisions objectionable to the United States' Government which it embodies are in no sense new. They will be found in "The Foreign Fishing-Vessels Act, 1893." The present Act differs from the earlier Act in that it takes away, by omission, from the Colonial Government the power conferred upon them by the earlier Act of authorizing the issue of licences to foreign fishing-vessels for the enjoyment of the privileges mentioned. Allowing for this change, the provisions of the two Acts are in all essential respects identical. The provisions as to boarding, bringing into port, and searching appear in both Acts, and also the provisions as to the possession of bait, outfits, and supplies being *primâ facie* evidence of the purchase of the same in the Colonial jurisdiction, except that in the earlier Act there was a further provision, consequential on the authority which it conferred on the Colonial Government to issue licences, directing that the failure or refusal to produce a license should be *primâ facie* evidence of the purchase of such articles without a licence. The position of any American fishing-vessel choosing to fish for herself on the Treaty Coast has consequently been since 1893 the same as it is to-day. His Majesty's Government do not advance these considerations with the object of suggesting that the objections which the United States' Government have taken to sections 1 and 3 of the Foreign Fishing-Vessels Act are impaired by the fact that these provisions have been on the Statute Book of the Colony since 1893 without protest, and they are ready to assume that no such protest has been lodged merely because the privileges accorded to American vessels in the ports of the Colony up to the present have been such as to render it unnecessary for inhabitants of the United States to avail themselves of their right of fishing under the Convention of 1818. The object of His Majesty's Government is simply to remove any impression which may have formed itself in the mind of the United States' Government that the language of the Act of 1905 was selected with any special view of prejudicing the exercise of the American Treaty right of fishery, and to point out that, on the contrary, it dates back to 1893, that is, to a time when it was the policy of the Colonial Government to treat American vessels on a favoured footing.

A new Act was not necessary to give effect to the present policy of the Colonial Government. Effect to it could have been given under the Act of 1893 by the mere suspension of the issue of licences to American vessels, and the only object of the new Act, as His Majesty's Government understand the position, was to secure the express and formal approval of the Colonial Legislature for the carrying out of the policy of the Colonial Government.

Having offered these general remarks, His Majesty's Government desire to point out that, in discussing the general effects of "The Foreign Fishing-Vessels Act, 1905," on the American fishery under the Convention of 1818, the United States' Government confine themselves to sections 1 and 3 and make no reference to section 7, which preserves "the rights and privileges granted by Treaty to the subjects of any State in amity with His Majesty." In view of this provision, His Majesty's Government are unable to agree with the United States' Government in regarding the provisions of sections 1 and 3 as "constituting a warrant to the officers named to interfere with and violate" American rights under the Convention of 1818. On the contrary, they consider section 7 as, in effect, a prohibition of any vexatious interference with the exercise of the Treaty rights whether of American or of French fishermen. As regards section 3, they admit that the possession by inhabitants of the United States of any fish and gear which they may lawfully take or use in the exercise of their rights under the Convention of 1818 cannot properly be made *primâ facie* evidence of the commission of an offence, and, bearing in mind the provisions of section 7, they cannot believe that a Court of Law would take a different view.

They do not, however, contend that the Act is as clear and explicit as, in the circumstances, it is desirable that it should be, and they propose to confer with the Government of Newfoundland with the object of removing any doubts which the Act in its present form may suggest as to the power of His Majesty to fulfil his obligations under the Convention of 1818.

On the concluding part of Mr. Root's note it is happily not necessary for His Majesty's Government to offer any remarks, since the fishing season has come to an end without any attempt on the part of British fishermen to interfere with the peaceful exercise of the American Treaty right of fishery.[a]

In reply to the memorandum received from Sir Edward Grey, Mr. Root wrote a letter of instructions under date of June 30, 1906, to the American Ambassador at London, a copy of which letter was transmitted to Sir Edward Grey by the American Ambassador in his note of July 20, 1906.[b] In this letter of instructions, Mr. Root sets forth the position of the United States on the various questions under consideration and gives the reasons which prevented his agreement with many of the views stated in the memorandum referred to, as follows:

The memorandum inclosed in the note from Sir Edward Grey to you of the 2nd February, 1906, and transmitted by you on the 6th February, has received careful consideration.

---

[a] Appendix, p. 972.   [b] Appendix, pp. 978, 985.

The letter which I had the honour to address to the British Ambassador in Washington on the 19th October last stated with greater detail the complaint in my letter to him of the 12th October, 1905, to the effect that the local officers of Newfoundland had attempted to treat American ships as such, without reference to the rights of their American owners and officers, refusing to allow such ships sailing under register to take part in the fishing on the Treaty coast, although owned and commanded by Americans, and limiting the exercise of the right to fish to ships having a fishing licence.

In my communications the Government of the United States objected to this treatment of ships as such—that is, as trading-vessels or fishing-vessels, and laid down a series of propositions regarding the treatment due to American vessels on the Treaty coast, based on the view that such treatment should depend, not upon the character of the ship as a registered or licensed vessel, but upon its being American; that is, owned and officered by Americans, and, therefore, entitled to exercise the rights assured by the Treaty of 1818 to the inhabitants of the United States.

It is a cause of gratification to the Government of the United States that the prohibitions interposed by the local officials of Newfoundland were promptly withdrawn upon the communication of the facts to His Majesty's Government, and that the Memorandum now under consideration emphatically condemns the view upon which the action of the local officers was based, even to the extent of refusing assent to the ordinary forms of expression which ascribe to ships the rights and liabilities of owners and masters in respect of them.

It is true that the Memorandum itself uses the same form of expression when asserting that American ships have committed breaches of the Colonial Customs Law, and ascribing to them duties, obligations, omissions, and purposes which the Memorandum describes. Yet we may agree that ships, strictly speaking, can have no rights or duties, and that whenever the Memorandum, or the letter upon which it comments, speaks of a ship's rights and duties, it but uses a convenient and customary form of describing the owner's or master's right and duties in respect of the ship. As this is conceded to be essentially "a ship fishing," and as neither in 1818 nor since could there be an American ship not owned and officered by Americans, it is probably quite unimportant which form of expression is used.

I find in the Memorandum no substantial dissent from the first proposition of my note to Sir Mortimer Durand of the 19th October, 1905, that any American vessel is entitled to go into waters of the Treaty coast and take fish of any kind, and that she derives this right from the Treaty and not from any authority proceeding from the Government of Newfoundland.

Nor do I find any substantial dissent from the fourth, fifth, and sixth propositions, which relate to the method of establishing the nationality of the vessel entering the Treaty waters for the purpose of fishing, unless it be intended, by the comments on those propositions, to assert that the British Government is entitled to claim that, when an American goes with his vessel upon the Treaty coast for the purpose of fishing, or with his vessel enters the bays or harbours of the coast for the purpose of shelter and of repairing damages therein, or of purchasing wood, or of obtaining water, he is bound to furnish evidence that all the members of his crew are inhabitants of the

United States. We cannot for a moment admit the existence of any such limitation upon our Treaty rights. The liberty assured to us by the Treaty plainly includes the right to use all the means customary or appropriate for fishing upon the sea, not only ships and nets and boats, but crews to handle the ships and the nets and the boats. No right to control or limit the means which Americans shall use in fishing can be admitted unless it is provided in the terms of the Treaty, and no right to question the nationality of the crews employed is contained in the terms of the Treaty. In 1818, and ever since, it has been customary for the owners and masters of fishing-vessels to employ crews of various nationalities. During all that period I am not able to discover that any suggestion has ever been made of a right to scrutinize the nationality of the crews employed in the vessels through which the Treaty right has been exercised.

The language of the Treaty of 1818 was taken from the IIIrd Article of the Treaty of 1783. The Treaty made at the same time between Great Britain and France, the previous Treaty of the 10th February, 1763, between Great Britain and France, and the Treaty of Utrecht of the 11th April, 1713, in like manner contained a general grant to "the subjects of France" to take fish on the Treaty coast. During all that period no suggestion, so far as I can learn, was ever made that Great Britain had a right to inquire into the nationality of the members of the crew employed upon a French vessel.

Nearly two hundred years have passed during which the subjects of the French King and the inhabitants of the United States have exercised fishing rights under these grants made to them in these general terms, and during all that time there has been an almost continuous discussion in which Great Britain and her Colonies have endeavoured to restrict the right to the narrowest possible limits, without a suggestion that the crews of vessels enjoying the right, or whose owners were enjoying the right, might not be employed in the customary way without regard to nationality. I cannot suppose that it is now intended to raise such a question.

I observe with satisfaction that the Memorandum assents to that part of my second proposition to the effect that "an American vessel seeking to exercise the Treaty right is not bound to obtain a licence from the Government of Newfoundland," and that His Majesty's Government agree that "no law of Newfoundland should be enforced on American fishermen which is inconsistent with their rights under the Convention."

The views of His Majesty's Government, however, as to what laws of the Colony of Newfoundland would be inconsistent with the Convention if applied to American fishermen, differ radically from the view entertained by the Government of the United States. According to the Memorandum, the inhabitants of the United States going in their vessels upon the Treaty coast to exercise the Treaty right of fishing are bound to enter and clear in the Newfoundland custom-houses, to pay light dues, even the dues from which coasting and fishing-vessels owned and registered in the Colony are exempt, to refrain altogether from fishing except at the time and in the manner prescribed by the Regulations of Newfoundland. The Colonial prohibition of fishing on Sundays is mentioned by the Memorandum as one of the Regulations binding upon the American fishermen. We are told that His Majesty's Government "hold that the only ground on which the application of any provisions of Colonial law to American vessels engaged in the fishery can be objected to is that it unreasonably interferes with the American right of fishery."

The Government of the United States fails to find in the Treaty any grant of right to the makers of Colonial law to interfere at all, whether reasonably or unreasonably, with the exercise of the American rights of fishery, or any right to determine what would be a reasonable interference with the exercise of that American right if there could be any interference. The argument upon which the Memorandum claims that the Colonial Government is entitled to interfere with and limit the exercise of the American right of fishery, in accordance with its own ideas of what is reasonable, is based first, upon the fact that, under the terms of the Treaty the right of the inhabitants of the United States to fish upon the Treaty coast is possessed by them "in common with the subjects of His Britannic Majesty;" and, second, upon the proposition that "the inhabitants of the United States would not now be entitled to fish in British North American waters but for the fact that they were entitled to do so when they were British subjects," and that "American fishermen cannot therefore rightfully claim any other right to exercise the right of fishery under the Treaty of 1818 than if they had never ceased to be British subjects."

Upon neither of these grounds can the inferences of the Memorandum be sustained. The qualification that the liberty assured to American fishermen by the Treaty of 1818 they were to have "in common with the subjects of Great Britain" merely negatives an exclusive right. Under the Treaties of Utrecht, of 1763 and 1783, between Great Britain and France, the French had constantly maintained that they enjoyed an exclusive right of fishery on that portion of the coast of Newfoundland between Cape St. John and Cape Raye, passing around by the north of the island. The British, on the other hand, had maintained that British subjects had a right to fish along with the French, so long as they did not interrupt them.

The dissension arising from these conflicting views had been serious and annoying, and the provision that the liberty of the inhabitants of the United States to take fish should be in common with the liberty of the subjects of His Britannic Majesty to take fish was precisely appropriate to exclude the French construction and leave no doubt that the British construction of such a general grant should apply under the new Treaty. The words used have no greater or other effect. The provision is that the *liberty* to take fish shall be held in common, not that the *exercise* of that liberty by one people shall be the limit of the exercise of that liberty by the other. It is a matter of no concern to the American fishermen whether the people of Newfoundland choose to exercise their right or not, or to what extent they choose to exercise it. The statutes of Great Britain and its Colonies limiting the exercise of the British right are mere voluntary and temporary self-denying ordinances. They may be repealed to-morrow. Whether they are repealed, or whether they stand, the British right remains the same, and the American right remains the same. Neither right can be increased nor diminished by the determination of the other nation that it will or will not exercise its right, or that it will exercise its right under any particular limitations of time or manner.

The proposition that "the inhabitants of the United States would not now be entitled to fish in British North American waters but for the fact that they were entitled to do so when they were British subjects," may be accepted as a correct statement of one of the series of facts which led to the making of the Treaty of 1818. Were it not for that fact there would have been no fisheries Article in the Treaty of 1783, no controversy between Great Britain and the United States as to whether that Article was terminated by the war of 1812, and no settlement of that controversy by the Treaty of 1818. The Memorandum, however, expressly excludes the supposition that the British Government now intends to concede that the present rights of American fishermen upon the Treaty coast are a continuance of the right possessed by the inhabitants of the American Colonies as British subjects, and declares that this present American right is a new grant by the Treaty of 1818. How then can it be maintained that the limitations upon the former right continued although the right did not, and are to be regarded as imposed upon the new grant, although not expressed in the instrument making the grant? On the contrary, the failure to express in the terms of the new Treaty the former limitations, if any there had been, must be deemed to evidence an intent not to attach them to the newly created right.

Nor would the acceptance by Great Britain of the American view that the Treaty of 1783 was in the nature of a partition of Empire, that the fishing rights formerly enjoyed by the people of the Colonies and described in the instrument of partition continued notwithstanding the war of 1812, and were in part declared and in part abandoned by the Treaty of 1818, lead to any different conclusion. It may be that under this view the rights thus allotted to the Colonies in 1783 were subject to such Regulations as Great Britain had already imposed upon their exercise before the partition, but the partition itself and the recognition of the independence of the Colonies in the Treaty of partition was a plain abandonment by Great Britain of the authority to further regulate the rights of the citizens of the new and independent nation.

The Memorandum says: "The American fishermen cannot rightly claim to exercise their right of fishery under the Convention of 1818 on a footing different than if they had never ceased to be British subjects." What then was the meaning of independence? What was it that continued the power of the British Crown over this particular right of Americans formerly exercised by them as British subjects, although the power of the British Crown over all other rights formerly exercised by them as British subjects was ended? No answer to this question is suggested by the Memorandum.

In previous correspondence regarding the construction of the Treaty of 1818, the Government of Great Britain has asserted, and the Memorandum under consideration perhaps implies, a claim of right to regulate the action of American fishermen in the Treaty waters, upon the ground that those waters are within the territorial jurisdiction of the Colony of Newfoundland. This Government is constrained to repeat emphatically its dissent from any such view. The Treaty of 1818 either declared or granted a perpetual right to the inhabitants of the United States which is beyond the sovereign power of England to destroy or change. It is conceded that this right is, and for ever must be, superior to any inconsistent exercise of sovereignty within that territory. The existence of this right is a qualification of British sovereignty within that territory. The limits of the right are not to be tested by referring to the general jurisdictional powers of Great Britain in that territory, but the limits of those powers are to be tested by reference to the right as defined in the instrument created or declaring it. The Earl of Derby in a letter to the Governor of Newfoundland, dated the 12th June, 1884, said: "The peculiar fisheries rights granted by Treaties to the French in Newfoundland invest those waters during the months of the year when fishing is carried on in them, both by English and French fishermen, with a character somewhat analogous to that of a common sea for the purpose of fishery." And the same observation is applicable to the situation created by the existence of American fishing rights under the Treaty of 1818. An appeal to the general jurisdiction of Great Britain over the territory is, therefore, a complete begging of the question, which always must be, not whether the jurisdiction of the Colony authorizes a law limiting the exercise of the Treaty right, but whether the terms of the grant authorize it.

The distinguished writer just quoted observes in the same letter:—

"The Government of France each year during the fishing season employs ships of war to superintend the fishery exercised by their countrymen, and, in consequence of the divergent views entertained by the two Governments respectively as to the interpretation to be placed upon the Treaties, questions of jurisdiction which might at any moment have become serious have repeatedly arisen."

The practice thus described, and which continued certainly until as late as the modification of the French fishing rights in the year 1904, might well have been followed by the United States, and probably would have been, were it not that the desire to avoid such questions of jurisdiction as were frequently arising between the French and the English has made this Government unwilling to have recourse to such a practice so long as the rights of its fishermen can be protected in any other way.

The Government of the United States regrets to find that His Majesty's Government has now taken a much more extreme position than that taken in the last active correspondence upon the same question arising under the provisions of the Treaty of Washington. In his letter of the 3rd April, 1880, to the American Minister in London, Lord Salisbury said:—

"In my note to Mr. Welsh of the 7th November, 1878, I stated 'that British sovereignty as regards these waters, is limited in scope by the engagements of the Treaty of Washington, which *cannot* be modified or affected by any municipal legislation,' and Her Majesty's Government fully admit that United States' fishermen have the right of participation on the Newfoundland *inshore fisheries, in common* with British subjects, as specified in Article XVIII of that Treaty. But it cannot be claimed, consistently with this right of participation in common with the British fishermen, that the United States' fishermen have any *other*, and still less that they have any *greater*, rights than the British fishermen had at the date of the Treaty.

"If, then, at the *date* of the signature of the Treaty of Washington certain restraints were, by the municipal law, imposed upon the *British fishermen*, the United States' fishermen were, by the *express terms* of the Treaty, equally subjected to those restraints, and the obligation to observe *in common* with the British the then existing local laws and regulations, which is implied by the words 'in common,' attached to the United States' citizens *as soon as* they claimed the benefit of the Treaty."

Under the view thus forcibly expressed, the British Government would be consistent in claiming that all regulations and limitations upon the exercise of the right of fishing upon the Newfoundland coast, which were in existence at the time when the Treaty of 1818 was made, are now binding upon American fishermen.

Farther than this, His Majesty's Government cannot consistently go, and, farther than this, the Government of the United States cannot go.

For the claim now asserted that the Colony of Newfoundland is entitled at will to regulate the exercise of the American Treaty right is equivalent to a claim of power to completely destroy that right. This Government is far from desiring that the Newfoundland fisheries shall go unregulated. It is willing and ready now, as it has always been, to join with the Government of Great Britain in agreeing upon all reasonable and suitable regulations for the due control of the fishermen of both countries in the exercise of their rights, but this Government cannot permit the exercise of these rights to be subject to the will of the Colony of Newfoundland. The Government of the United States cannot recognize the authority of Great Britain or of its Colony to determine whether American citizens shall fish on Sunday. The Government of Newfoundland cannot be permitted to make entry and clearance at a Newfoundland custom-house and the payment of a tax for the support of Newfoundland lighthouses conditions to the exercise of the American right of fishing. If it be shown that these things are reasonable the Government of the United States will agree to them, but it cannot submit to have them imposed upon it without its consent. This position is not a matter of theory. It is of vital and present importance, for the plain object of recent legislation of the Colony of Newfoundland has been practically to destroy the value of American rights under the Treaty of 1818. Those rights are exercised in competition with the fishermen and merchants of Newfoundland. The situation of the Newfoundland fishermen residing upon the shore and making the shore their base of operations, and of the American fishermen coming long distances with expensive outfits, devoting long periods to the voyage to the fishing grounds and back to the market, obliged to fish rapidly in order to make up for that loss of time, and making ships their base of operations, are so different that it is easy to frame regulations which will offer slight inconvenience to the dwellers on shore and be practically prohibitory to the fishermen from the coasts of Maine and Massachusetts; and, if the grant of this competitive right is to be subject to such laws as our competitors choose to make, it is a worthless right. The Premier of Newfoundland in his speech in the Newfoundland Parliament, delivered on the 12th April, 1905, in support of the Foreign Fishing Bill, made the following declaration:—

"This Bill is framed specially to prevent the American fishermen from coming into the bays, harbours, and creeks of the coast of

Newfoundland for the purpose of obtaining ·herring, caplin, and squid for fishing purposes."

And this further declaration:—

"This communication is important evidence as to the value of the position we occupy as mistress of the northern seas so far as the fisheries are concerned. Herein was evidence that it is within the power of the Legislature of this Colony to make or mar our competitors to the North Atlantic fisheries. Here was evidence that by refusing or restricting the necessary bait supply, we can bring our foreign competitors to realize their dependency. upon us. One of the objects of this legislation is to bring the fishing interests of Gloucester and New England to a realization of their dependence upon the bait supplies of this Colony. No measure could have been devised having more clearly for its object the conserving, safeguarding, and protecting of the interests of those concerned in the fisheries of the Colony."

It will be observed that there is here the very frankest possible disavowal of any intention to so regulate the fisheries as to be fair to the American fishermen. The purpose is, under cover of the exercise of the power of regulation, to exclude the American fishermen. The Government of the United States surely cannot be expected to see with complacency the rights of its citizens subjected to this kind of regulation.

The Government of the United States finds assurance of the desire of His Majesty's Government to give reasonable and friendly treatment to American fishing rights on the Newfoundland coast in the statement of the Memorandum that the Newfoundland Foreign Fishing-Vessels Act is not as clear and explicit as, in the circumstances, it is desirable that it should be, and in the expressed purpose of His Majesty's Government to confer with the Government of Newfoundland with the object of removing any doubts which the Act, in its present form, may suggest as to the power of His Majesty to fulfil his obligation under the Convention of 1818. It is hoped that, upon this Conference, His Majesty's Government will have come to the conclusion, not merely that the seventh section of the Act, which seeks to preserve "the rights and privileges granted by Treaty to the subjects of any State in amity with His Majesty," amounts to a prohibition of any "vexatious interference" with the exercise of the Treaty rights of American fishermen, but that this clause ought to receive the effect of entirely excluding American vessels from the operation of the first and third clauses of the Act relating to searches and seizures and *primâ facie* evidence. Such a construction by His Majesty's Government would wholly meet the difficulty pointed out in my letter of the 19th October, as arising under the first and third sections of the Act. A mere limitation, however, to interference which is not "vexatious," leaving the question as to what is "vexatious interference" to be determined by the local officers of Newfoundland, would be very far from meeting the difficulty.

You will inform His Majesty's Government of these views, and ask for such action as shall prevent any interference upon any ground by the officers of the Newfoundland Government with American fishermen when they go to exercise their Treaty rights upon the Newfoundland coast during the approaching fishing season.[a]

The following extract from a telegram sent by Lord Elgin, Secretary of State for the Colonies, to the Governor of Newfoundland on August 8, 1906, soon after the receipt of Mr. Root's reply to the Foreign Office memorandum, is of interest in connection with the questions discussed by Mr. Root:

Copies went to you by last mail of communication from United States' Government in which they contend that Convention of 1818 justifies no interference, reasonable or unreasonable, with exercise of American rights of fishery, and request His Majesty's Government to prevent any interference upon any ground by officers of Newfoundland Government with American fishermen when they go to exercise their Treaty rights upon the coast of Newfoundland during approaching fishing season. They disclaim desire that Newfoundland fisheries shall go unregulated, and express their readiness to join with His Majesty's Government in agreeing upon all reasonable and suitable regulations for due control of fishermen of both countries in exercise of their rights, but state that they cannot permit exercise of these rights to be subject to will of Newfoundland. Pending such an agreement, the furthest they are prepared to go is to accept such limitations as were in existence at time Convention of 1818 was concluded, and in support of this position appeal to Lord Salisbury's note to United States' Minister of the 3rd April, 1880, in connection with disturbances at Fortune Bay. Light dues were presumably not levied in 1818, seines were apparently in use, the prohibition of Sunday fishing had been abolished in 1776 (see 15 George III, cap. 31), and fishing-ships were exempted from entry at Custom-house, and required only to make a report on first arrival and on clearing (see same Act). United States' vessels could, on the basis of the *status quo* in 1818, only be asked to make report at custom-house on arrival and on clearing.[b]

The Modus Vivendi of 1906.

In communicating Mr. Root's reply to Sir Edward Grey, the American Ambassador stated in his note of July 20, 1906, that he was instructed ''to ask for such action as shall prevent any interference upon any ground by the officers of the Newfoundland Government with American fishermen, when they go to exercise their treaty rights upon the Newfoundland coast during the approaching fishing season.'' In reply to the American Ambassador's note Sir Edward Grey wrote to him on August 14, 1906, stating that Mr. Root's letter was receiving the careful consideration of His Majesty's Government and that

[a] Appendix, p. 978.   [b] Appendix p. 986.

"they have observed with much regret that the wide divergence of view between the two Governments, which is disclosed by the correspondence, makes it hopeless to expect an immediate settlement of the various questions at issue." He expressed his willingness, however, to enter into a temporary arrangement in the nature of a *modus vivendi*, with respect to which he said in this note—

Pending the further discussion of these questions, however, and without prejudice to it, His Majesty's Government are prepared, in accordance with the suggestion made in Mr. Root's letter, to confer with the United States' Government, with a view to some arrangement which will secure the peaceable and orderly conduct of the forthcoming fishery, and they hope very shortly to be able to submit proposals with this object. I may add that such an arrangement would be merely in the nature of a *modus vivendi*, applicable only to the ensuing season, and would not in any way affect any of the rights and claims of either party.[a]

In pursuance of Sir Edward Grey's statement above quoted, that His Majesty's Government hoped very shortly to be able to submit proposals for a *modus vivendi*, Sir Edward Grey again wrote to Mr. Reid on September 3, 1906, submitting such proposals, which were as follows:

In my note of the 14th August I stated that His Majesty's Government hoped shortly to be able to submit to the Government of the United States proposals for a provisional Arrangement, which would secure the peaceable and orderly conduct of the forthcoming herring fishery on the coast of Newfoundland. I have now the honour, on the understanding mentioned in my note, viz., that the Arrangement would be in the nature of a *modus vivendi* to be applicable only to the ensuing season, and not in any way to affect the rights and claims of either party to the Convention of 1818, to submit the following proposals, viz.:—

(1.) His Majesty's Government will not bring into force "The Newfoundland Foreign Fishing Vessels Act, 1906," [b] which imposes on United States' fishing-vessels certain restrictions in addition to those imposed by the Act of 1905.

(2.) The provisions of the first part of section 1 of the Act of 1905 as to boarding and bringing into port, and the whole of section 3 of the same Act will not be regarded as applying to the United States' fishing-vessels.

(3.) The United States' Government will in return direct their fishermen to comply with the Colonial Fishery Regulations, as was in fact done last year, with the exception of certain breaches of the prohibition of Sunday fishing.

(4.) The demand for payment of light dues will be waived by His Majesty's Government.

---

[a] Appendix p. 987.   -   [b] Appendix p. 199.

(5.) The United States' Government will direct the masters of United States' fishing-vessels to comply with the provisions of the Colonial Customs Law as to reporting at a customs-house, on arrival in and departure from colonial waters.

2. As regards head (3) of this Arrangement, I would point out that of the three restrictions which the Colonial Fishery Regulations impose on the herring fishery in the waters open to United States' fishermen, the first, viz., the prohibition of "purse" seines, is in force in all the waters of the Colony. It is also in force in all the waters of Canada. The second, the prohibition of herring traps, is also in force in Placentia, St. Mary's and Fortunes Bays, and in the district of Twillingate. The third, the prohibition of "herring" seines, is in force also subject to some reservations as to baiting purposes in the inner waters of Placentia Bay, and in certain waters on the north-east coast. The application of these three restrictions to the herring bays of the west coast is, of course, prior to and not in any way connected with the present policy of the Colonial Government, and His Majesty's Government have the testimony of the naval officers who have been employed on the Treaty Coast as to the destructive results of the use of seines. His Majesty's Government therefore hope that the United States' Government will recognize that His Majesty's Government are, apart from any question of right, acting in the interests of the continuation of the common fishery in proposing as a part of the provisional Arrangement compliance with the three restrictions mentioned.

The fourth restriction, viz., the prohibition of Sunday fishing, is of general application throughout the Colony, and is also in force in Canada. Having regard to the duration of the fishing season and to other circumstances, His Majesty's Government do not feel that compliance with this prohibition involves any material inconvenience to United States' fishermen. On the other hand, in view of the strong feeling against Sunday fishing which prevails in the Colony, the disregard of it is fraught with possibilities of serious disorder. It is therefore hoped that the United States' Government will assist His Majesty's Government in the maintenance of peaceable relations between the two sets of fishermen by not countenancing any breach of the prohibition during the ensuing season.

3. As regards head (5), as explained in the Memorandum communicated to your Excellency on the 2nd February, a call at a customs-house, whether on entering or on leaving the waters of the Colony, need involve no interference with a vessel's fishing operations, and is in itself a requirement which may be reasonably made in the interests not only of the colonial revenue but of the United States' fishermen.

4. I trust that you will be able to inform me at an early date that the Arrangement outlined above is agreed to by your Government.[a]

The views of the United States Government on the proposals for a *modus vivendi*, submitted by Sir Edward Grey, are set forth in the

---

[a] Appendix, p. 989.

following memorandum presented by the American Ambassador to the Foreign Office under date of September 12, 1906:

My Government hears with the greatest concern and regret that in the opinion of His Majesty's Government there is so wide a divergence of views with regard to the Newfoundland Fisheries that an immediate settlement is hopeless.

But it is much gratified with His Majesty's Government's desire to reach a *modus vivendi* for this season, and appreciates the readiness to waive the Foreign Fishing Vessels Act of 1906. This and other restrictive legislation had compelled our fishermen to use purse seines or abandon their treaty rights.

My Government sees in the offer not to apply Section 3, Act of 1905 and that part of Section 1 relating to boarding fishing vessels and bringing them into port fresh proof of a cordial disposition not to press unduly this kind of regulation.

Our fishermen will also gladly pay light dues, if not hindered in their right to fish. They are not unwilling either, to comply with the regulation to report at Custom Houses, when possible. It is sometimes physically impossible, however, to break through the ice for that purpose.

Most unfortunately the remaining proposals, those as to purse-seining and Sunday fishing, present very grave difficulties.

We appreciate perfectly the desire of His Majesty's Government to prevent Sunday fishing. But if both this and purse-seine fishing are taken away, as things stand there might be no opportunity for profitable fishing left under our treaty rights. We are convinced that purse seines are no more injurious to the common fishery than the gill nets commonly used—are not in fact so destructive and do not tend to change the migratory course of the herring as gill nets do, through the death of a large percentage of the catch and consequent pollution of the water.

The small amount of purse-seining this season could not of course materially affect the common fishery anyway. Besides many of our fishermen have already sailed, with purse seines as usual, and the others are already provided with them. This use of the purse seine was not the free choice of our fishermen. They have been driven to it by local regulations and the continued use of it at this late date this year seems vital.

But we will renounce Sunday fishing for this season if His Majesty's Government will consent to the use of purse seines, and we cannot too strongly urge an acceptance of this solution.[a]

The views of the British Government in reply were presented in a Foreign Office memorandum under date of September 25, 1906, as follows:

His Majesty's Government have considered, after consultation with the Government of Newfoundland, the proposals put forward in the Memorandum communicated by the United States Ambassador on the

---

[a] Appendix, p. 46.

12th instant, respecting the suggested "modus vivendi" in regard to the Newfoundland Fishery question.

They are glad to be able to state that they accept the arrangement set out in the above Memorandum and consent accordingly to the use of purse seines by United States fishermen during the ensuing season, subject, of course, to due regard being paid, in the use of such implements, to other modes of fishery.

His Majesty's Government trust that the United States Government will raise no objection to such a stipulation, which is only intended to secure that there shall be the same spirit of give and take and of respect of common rights between the users of purse seines and the users of stationary nets as would be expected to exist if both sets of fishermen employed the same gear.

They further hope that, in view of this temporary authorization of the purse seines, the United States Government will see their way to arranging that the practice of engaging Newfoundland fishermen just outside the three mile limit which to some extent prevailed last year should not be resorted to this year.

An arrangement to this effect would save both His Majesty's Government and the Newfoundland Government from embarrassment which it is conceived, having regard to the circumstances in which the "modus vivendi" is being settled, the United States Government would not willingly impose upon them: Moreover it is not in itself unreasonable, seeing that the unwillingness of the United States Government to forego the use of purse seines appears to be largely based upon the inability of their fishermen to engage local men to work the form of net recognized by the Colonial fishery regulations.

The United States Government assured His Majesty's late Government in November last that they would not countenance a specified evasion of the Newfoundland Foreign Fishing Vessels Act 1905, and the proposed arrangement would appear to be in accordance with the spirit which prompted that assurance.[a]

The agreement thus indicated by the concurrence of views exchanged in these negotiations was given effect by an exchange of diplomatic notes between the American Ambassador and the British Foreign Office, setting forth the terms of the agreement. The note from the American Ambassador under date of October 6, 1906, was as follows:

I am authorized by my Government to ratify a *modus vivendi* in regard to the Newfoundland Fishery Question on the basis of the Foreign Office Memorandum, dated the 25th of September, 1906, in which you accept the arrangement set out in my Memorandum of the 12th of September and consent accordingly to the use of purse seines by American fishermen during the ensuing season, subject of course to due regard being paid in the use of such implements to other modes of fishery, which, as you state, is only intended to secure that there shall be the same spirit of give and take and of respect for common rights

---

[a] Appendix, p. 47.

between the users of purse seines and the users of stationary nets as would be expected to exist if both sets of fishermen employed the same gear.

My Government understand by this that the use of purse seines by American fishermen is not to be interfered with, and that the shipment of Newfoundlanders by American fishermen outside the 3 mile limit is not to be made the basis of interference or to be penalized; at the same time they are glad to assure His Majesty's Government, should such shipments be found necessary, that they will be made far enough from the exact 3 mile limit to avoid any reasonable doubt.

On the other hand it is also understood that our fishermen are to be advised by my Government, and to agree, not to fish on Sunday.

It is further understood that His Majesty's Government will not bring into force the Newfoundland Foreign Fishing Vessels Act of 1906 which imposes on American fishing vessels certain restrictions in addition to those imposed by the Act of 1905, and also that the provisions of the first part of Section I of the Act of 1905, as to boarding and bringing into port, and also the whole of Section 3 of the same Act, will not be regarded as applying to American fishing vessels.

It also being understood that our fishermen will gladly pay light dues if they are not deprived of their rights to fish, and that our fishermen are not unwilling to comply with the provisions of the Colonial Customs Law as to reporting at a custom house when physically possible to do so.

I need not add that my Government are most anxious that the provisions of the *modus vivendi* should be made effective at the earliest possible moment. I am glad to be assured by you that this note will be considered as sufficient ratification of the *modus vivendi*, on the part of my Government.[a]

The note from the Foreign Office under date of October 8, 1906, was as follows:

I have received with satisfaction the note of the 6th instant in which Your Excellency states that you have been authorized by your Government to ratify a *modus vivendi* in regard to the Newfoundland Fishery Question on the basis of the Memorandum which I had the honour to communicate to you on the 25th ultimo, and I am glad to assure Your Excellency that the note in question will be considered by His Majesty's Government as a sufficient ratification of that arrangement on the part of the United States Government.

His Majesty's Government fully share the desire of your Government that the provisions of the *modus vivendi* should be made effective at the earliest moment possible and the necessary instructions for its observance were accordingly sent to the Government of Newfoundland immediately on receipt of Your Excellency's communication.[b]

Soon after the *modus vivendi* of 1906 went into effect the United States Government was informed that the members of an American fishing vessel's crew who, in accordance with the provisions of the

a Appendix p. 45.   b Appendix, p. 46.

modus vivendi, had enlisted outside of the three mile limit had been summoned by the Newfoundland authorities to appear in court on the charge that such enlistment was a violation of the local laws. It was known to the United States Government that the Newfoundland Government had questioned the legality of some of the provisions of the *modus vivendi* and the authority of the British Government to enter into it, and it was supposed by the United States Government that the action of the Newfoundland Government was taken for the purpose of making a test case on that question between the New-foundland and the British Governments.

On this supposition the Secretary of State instructed the American Ambassador at London to bring informally and unofficially to the attention of the British Government the views of the United States in regard to this occurrence, which was done at an interview between the American Ambassador and Sir Edward Grey held on November 14, 1906, when the following points of fact were presented by the American Ambassador:

United States Fishery Agent in Newfoundland reported that on 12th November Colonial authorities summoned crew to appear at Court, Birchy Cove, for enlisting outside three-mile limit. Captain was inclined to ignore summons.

In answer to Agent's request for instructions, State Department said that penal proceedings under such circumstances against men shipped outside three-mile limit appeared plain violation of *modus vivendi*, but Department could not believe Newfoundland Government intended wholesale punishment of their own fishermen for seeking means of livelihood with clear permission from British Government. Department supposed whole purpose was to make a test case, and instructed Agent to ascertain. If so, to avoid conflict or disturbance, was willing, without waiving rights, to facilitate raising and disposition of the question in an orderly way, for which appearance of one or two men in Court would be sufficient. If, on contrary, wholesale arrests were intended, effect would be either to break up or seriously interfere with fishing under the *modus vivendi*, and the Department should be promptly informed.

Department explains desire to avoid any conflict that might excite Colonial feeling or cause embarrassment in dealing with Colony. But if Newfoundland Government really trying to break up fishing under *modus vivendi*, United States could not permit men to be taken from its ships. No doubt of Great Britain's full intention to enforce respect for its agreement, but prompt action seemed necessary.[a]

As the understanding of the United States Government, thus set forth, in regard to the purpose of the Newfoundland Government in

---

[a] Appendix p. 1002.

taking the action referred to was subsequently confirmed, the incident closed without the necessity for further action on the part of the United States.

Renewal of the discussion.

The reasons for the delay of the British Government in replying to the arguments contained in Mr. Root's letter of June 30, 1906, and the views of that Government on the questions discussed by Mr. Root are stated by Sir Edward Grey in his note of June 20, 1907, to Mr. Reid as follows:

On the 20th of July last, Your Excellency communicated to me a letter addressed to you by Mr. Root in which he gave reasons which prevented his agreement with the views of His Majesty's Government as to the rights of American fishing vessels in the waters of Newfoundland under the Convention of 1818.

No reply was returned at the time to the arguments contained in this letter, as the divergence of views between the two Governments made it hopeless to expect an immediate and definitive settlement of the various questions at issue and it was essential to arrive at some arrangement immediately which would secure the peaceable and orderly conduct of the impending fishery season.

Upon the conclusion of the *Modus Vivendi*, His Majesty's Government further deferred any additional observations on the questions at issue until the arrival in this country of the Premier of Newfoundland to attend the Imperial Conference.

They have now had the advantage of a full discussion with Sir R. Bond, and although His Majesty's Government are unable to modify the views to which they have on various occasions given expression, of the proper interpretation of the Convention of 1818 in its bearing on the rights of American fishermen, they are not without hope, having regard to the willingness of the United States Government from a practical point of view to discuss reasonable and suitable regulations for the due control of the fishermen of both countries, that an arrangement may be arrived at which will be satisfactory to both countries.

I desire at the outset to place on record my appreciation of the moderation and fairness with which Mr. Root has stated the American side of the question and I shall in my turn endeavour to avoid anything of a nature to embitter this long-standing controversy.

It will be convenient to recapitulate the main grounds of divergence between the two Governments on the question of principle.

His Majesty's Government, on the one hand, claim that the Treaty gave no fishing rights to American vessels as such, but only to inhabitants of the United States and that the latter are bound to conform to such Newfoundland laws and regulations as are reasonable and not inconsistent with the exercise of their Treaty rights. The United States Government, on the other hand, assert that American rights may be exercised irrespectively of any laws or regulations which the Newfoundland Government may impose, and agree that as ships strictly speaking can have no rights or duties, whenever the term is used, it is but a convenient or customary form of describing the owners' or masters' rights. As the Newfoundland fishery, however, is essentially a ship fishery, they consider that it is probably quite unimportant which form of expression is used.

By way of qualification Mr. Root goes on to say that if it is intended to assert that the British Government is entitled to claim that, when an American goes with his vessel upon the Treaty Coast for the purpose of fishing, or with his vessel enters the bays or harbours of the coast for the purpose of obtaining shelter, and of repairing damages therein, or of purchasing wood, or of obtaining water, he is bound to furnish evidence that all the members of the crew are inhabitants of the United States, he is obliged entirely to dissent from any such proposition.

The views of His Majesty's Government are quite clear upon this point. The Convention of 1818 laid down that the inhabitants of the United States should have for ever in common with the subjects of His Britannic Majesty the liberty to take fish of every kind on the coasts of Newfoundland within the limits which it proceeds to define.

This right is not given to American vessels, and the distinction is an important one from the point of view of His Majesty's Government, as it is upon the actual words of the Convention that they base their claim to deny any right under the Treaty to American masters to employ other than American fishermen for the taking of fish in Newfoundland Treaty waters.

Mr. Root's language, however, appears to imply that the condition which His Majesty's Government seek to impose on the right of fishing is a condition upon the entry of an American vessel into the Treaty waters for the purpose of fishing. This is not the case. His Majesty's Government do not contend that every person on board an American vessel fishing in the Treaty waters must be an inhabitant of the United States, but merely that no such person is entitled to take fish unless he is an inhabitant of the United States. This appears to meet Mr. Root's argument that the contention of His Majesty's Government involves as a corollary that no American vessel would be entitled to enter the waters of British North America (in which inhabitants of the United States are debarred from fishing by the Convention of 1818) for any of the four specified purposes, unless all the members of the crew are inhabitants of the United States.

Whatever may be the correct interpretation of the Treaty as to the employment of foreigners generally on board American vessels, His Majesty's Government do not suppose that the United States Government lay claim to withdraw Newfoundlanders from the jurisdiction of their own Government so as to entitle them to fish in the employment of Americans in violation of Newfoundland laws. The United States Government do not, His Majesty's Government understand, put their claim higher than that of a "common" fishery, and such an arrangement cannot override the power of the Colonial Legislature to enact laws binding on the inhabitants of the Colony.

It can hardly be contended that His Majesty's Government have lost their jurisdiction not only over American fishermen fishing in territorial waters of Newfoundland, but also over the British subjects working with them.

It may be as well to mention incidentally in regard to Mr. Root's contention that no claim to place any such restriction on the French right of fishery was ever put forward by Great Britain; that there was never any occasion to advance it, for the reason that foreigners other than Frenchmen were never employed by French fishing vessels.

The main question at issue is, however, that of the application of the Newfoundland regulations to American fishermen.   In this connection the United States Government admit the justice of the view that all regulations and limitations upon the exercise of the right of fishing upon the Newfoundland Coast, which were in existence at the time of the Convention of 1818, would now be binding upon American fishermen.   Although Mr. Root considers that to be the extreme view which His Majesty's Government could logically assert, and states that it is the utmost to which the United States Government could agree, His Majesty's Government feel that they cannot admit any such contention, as it would involve a complete departure from the position which they have always been advised to adopt as to the real intention and scope of the treaties upon which the American fishing rights depend.   On this vital point of principle there does not seem to be any immediate prospect of agreement with United States views, and it would, therefore, seem better to endeavour to find some temporary solution of the difficulty as to the regulations under which the Americans are to fish.

His Majesty's Government note with satisfaction Mr. Root's statement that the American Government are far from desiring that the fishery should go unregulated, and believing as they do that the Newfoundland regulations have been framed with the intention of preserving and maintaining the fishery in the most efficient and productive condition, and for the prevention of practices that must be detrimental to the common interests they propose to communicate a copy of all the regulations that are now in force, and if there is anything in these regulations which the United States Government feel to bear hardly upon the American fishermen, His Majesty's Government will gladly pay the utmost consideration to any American representations on the subject with a view to the amendment of the regulations in the sense desired, provided that such be consistent, with the due preservation of the fishery.

Pending this examination of the regulations, His Majesty's Government would propose the following arrangements as to the provisions in the Newfoundland enactments that have been most discussed.

These are the obligation to report at a Custom House and to pay light dues, and the prohibition to use purse seines, and to fish on Sundays.   Other regulations, such as the prohibition to throw ballast or rubbish into the water frequented by herring, and to throw overboard on the fishing ground fish offal, heads and bones, have occasionally come in question, but are clearly reasonable, and are not, it is believed, objected to by the United States Government. Fishing at night is another question which has been discussed, although it is not forbidden by the regulations.   His Majesty's Government understand that by tacit consent among the fishermen themselves fishing is not pursued at night, and with this arrangement there seems no reason to interfere.

With regard to the entry and clearance of American vessels at Newfoundland ports, I would remind Your Excellency that the American vessels engaged in the winter fishery in the Bay of Islands must pass in close proximity to several Custom Houses, and that it cannot be said that the obligation to report and clear unduly interferes with the operations of the vessels. On this point, however, His Majesty's Government would, in order to secure an arrangement for the next fishing season, be prepared to defer discussion of the question of right; but they would urge, on the other hand, that it would be most advisable that American vessels should comply with the regulation on the ground that unless the vessels enter at the Custom Houses, the British authorities have no cognizance that they are in Newfoundland waters, and that, as His Majesty's Government are responsible for keeping the peace, it is important that they should know exactly what American vessels are on the fishing grounds. Moreover, the provision in question is clearly necessary for the prevention of smuggling, and unless American vessels have made proper entry at a Custom House, there is no means, short of searching the vessels, of ascertaining whether they are really fishing vessels, and not smugglers.

The next point in dispute is the prohibition of purse seines. His Majesty's Government have the independent testimony of British naval officers who have been employed on the Treaty Coast as to the destructive results of their use; and they would, therefore, point out that there is complete justification for the Colonial regulation.

I would, moreover, remind Your Excellency that the regulation is in force in all the waters of the Colony of Newfoundland and of the Dominion of Canada, and applies equally to all fishermen whether they be Newfoundlanders or not. His Majesty's Government, therefore, feel that they cannot interfere with the enforcement of the regulation which prohibits purse seines in the waters of Newfoundland. They would also point out that fishing on Sundays is always liable to lead to regrettable breaches of the peace, and they would propose that the American fishermen should agree to abstain from this practice.

Finally, His Majesty's Government feel that the payment of light dues by an American vessel entering a port of the Colony clearly does not involve an unreasonable interference with the exercise of the treaty rights of the American fishermen on board. These dues are payable by all vessels of whatever description and nationality, other than coasting and fishing vessels owned and registered in the Colony. As, however, vessels of the latter class are under certain conditions exempt either wholly or in part from payment, His Majesty's Government consider that it would be unfair to introduce any discrimination against American vessels in this respect, and it is proposed that the demand for light dues should be waived under the same conditions as in the case of the Newfoundland vessels.

I venture to express the hope that the temporary arrangement outlined above will be agreed to by the United States Government.[a]

---

[a]Appendix, p. 1003.

Proposal for arbitration and Modus Vivendi of 1907.

The propositions advanced by Sir Edward Grey in his note of June 20, 1907, above quoted, were so much in conflict with the views of the United States Government on the subject that the impossibility of finding a basis for an agreement for the permanent adjustment of the dispute at once became evident, and, under instructions from his Government, Mr. Reid wrote to that effect on July 12, 1907, to Sir Edward Grey, and at the same time proposed that the questions of difference should be submitted to The Hague Court for arbitration, out of which suggestion, it is of interest to note, grew the negotiations which resulted in the present arbitration, and Mr. Reid further proposed a renewal of the *modus vivendi* of the preceding year pending such arbitration.   Mr. Reid's note is in full as follows:

Referring to your letter of June 20th, in relation to the Newfoundland Fisheries, I beg to say that while its propositions seemed so much in conflict with our views on the subject that my previous instructions would have enabled me to make an immediate reply, I hastened to lay them before my Government.

Before communicating the result I desire to acknowledge and reciprocate to the full the kindly expressions you have been good enough to use as to the moderation and fairness with which Mr. Root has stated the American side of the case.   We have had the same appreciation of your conduct of the discussion, and we share your wish to bring the long-standing controversy on the subject to a satisfactory conclusion without having added anything tending in the slightest degree to embitter it.

But with the utmost desire to find in your last letter some practical basis for an agreement, we are unable to perceive it.   Acquiescence in your present proposals would seem to us equivalent to yielding all the vital questions in dispute, and abandoning our fishing rights on the coast of Newfoundland under the Treaty of 1818.

Without dwelling on minor points, on which we would certainly make every effort to meet your views, I may briefly say that in our opinion, sustained by the observations of those best qualified to judge, the surrender of the right to hire local fishermen, who eagerly seek to have us employ them, and the surrender at the same time of the use of purse seines and of fishing on Sunday would, under existing circumstances, render the Treaty stipulation worthless to us.

My Government holds this opinion so strongly that the task of reconciling it with the positions maintained in your letter of June 20th seems hopeless.

In this conviction my Government authorises me, and I now have the honour, to propose a reference of the pending questions under the Treaty of 1818 to arbitration before the Hague Tribunal.

We have the greater reason to hope that this solution may be agreeable to you since your Ambassador to the United States recently suggested some form of arbitration, with a temporary *modus vivendi* pending the decision, as the best way of reaching a settlement. We hope also that the reference of such a long-standing question between two such nations at such a time to the Hague Tribunal might prove an important step in promoting the spread of this peaceful and friendly method of adjusting differences among all civilised countries of the world.

If this proposition should be agreeable to you we should trust that the conclusion might be reached in so short a period that the continuation in force meantime of the *modus vivendi* I had the honour of arranging with you last year could work no real hardship to any British or Colonial interests. In its practical operation last year it resulted in voluntary arrangements by which our fishermen gave up purse seines. They did, however, employ Newfoundland fishermen. We do not think the continued employment of men so eager for the work, and the consequent influx of their wages into the Colony could, for the short time involved, work the Colony any harm. But if for any reason you should find it unsuitable or inconvenient to renew for so short a time this feature of the *modus vivendi*, we should be compelled to insist on the use of purse seines for the reason already stated. To give that up too we should consider under existing circumstances as giving up altogether our Treaty rights of fishing on that coast.

Hoping that in these proposals we have made an offer not only indicating our earnest desire to reach a mutually satisfactory arrangement, but an honourable and agreeable means of doing so, etc.[a]

The *modus vivendi* agreed upon in 1907 differs slightly from that of the preceding year, as will be found from an examination of the notes exchanged between the American Ambassador and the British Foreign Office, setting forth the terms of such agreement. The note from the American Ambassador to the Foreign Office, under date of September 4, 1907, was as follows:

I am authorized by my Government to ratify a *Modus Vivendi* in regard to the Newfoundland fishery question, as follows:

It is agreed that the fisheries shall be carried on during the present year substantially as they were actually carried on for the most of the time by mutual agreement, under the *Modus Vivendi* of 1906.

(1) It is understood that His Majesty's Government will not bring into force the Newfoundland foreign fishing vessels act of 1906, which imposes on American fishing vessels certain restrictions in addition to those imposed by the act of 1905, and also that the provisions of the first part of Section One of the act of 1905, as to boarding and bringing into port, and also the whole of Section three of the same act, will not be regarded as applying to American fishing vessels.

(2) In consideration of the fact that the shipment of Newfoundlanders by American fishermen outside the three-mile limit is not to be made the basis of interference or to be penalized, my Government

---

[a] Appendix p. 1007.

waives the use of purse seines by American fishermen during the term governed by this agreement, and also waives the right to fish on Sundays.

(3) It is understood that American fishing vessels will make their shipment of Newfoundlanders, as fishermen, sufficiently far from the exact three-mile limit to avoid reasonable doubt.

(4) It is further understood that American fishermen will pay light dues when not deprived of their rights to fish, and will comply with the provisions of the colonial customs law as to reporting at a custom house when physically possible to do so.

I need not add that my Government is most anxious that the provisions of this *Modus Vivendi* should be made effective at the earliest possible moment, and that, in view of this, and of the actual presence of our fishing fleet on the treaty shore, we do not feel that an exchange of ratifications should be longer delayed. But my Government has every desire to make the arrangement, pending arbitration, as agreeable as possible to the Newfoundland authorities consistent with the due safeguarding of treaty rights which we have enjoyed for nearly a century. If, therefore, the proposals you have recently shown me from the Premier of Newfoundland or any other changes in the above *Modus Vivendi* should be proposed by mutual agreement between the Newfoundland authorities and our fishermen, having due regard to the losses that might be incurred by a change of plans so long after preparations for the season's fishing had been made and the voyage begun, my Government will be ready to consider such changes with you in the most friendly spirit, and if found not to compromise our rights, to unite with you in ratifying them at once.

I am glad to be assured by you that this note will be considered as a sufficient ratification of the *Modus Vivendi* on the part of my Government.[a]

The note from the Foreign Office to the American Ambassador, under date of September 6, 1907, was as follows:

I have the honour to acknowledge the receipt of Your Excellency's note of the 4th instant, containing the terms of the *Modus Vivendi* with regard to the Newfoundland fisheries,—which you are authorized by your Government to ratify.

I am glad to assure your Excellency that His Majesty's Government agrees to the terms of the *Modus Vivendi* and that your Excellency's note will be considered by His Majesty's Government as a sufficient ratification of that arrangement on the part of His Majesty's Government.

His Majesty's Government fully shares the desire of your Government that the provisions of the *Modus Vivendi* should be made effective at the earliest possible moment, and the necessary steps will be taken by His Majesty's Government to secure its observance.

His Majesty's Government takes note of the conciliatory offer of the United States Government to consider in a most friendly spirit any changes in the *Modus Vivendi* which may be agreed upon locally between the Newfoundland authorities and the United States fishermen and which may be acceptable both to the United States Government and to His Majesty's Government.[b]

[a] Appendix, p. 48.   [b] Appendix, p. 49.

Modus Vivendi of 1908.

In 1908 a renewal of the *modus vivendi* of 1907 was arranged by an exchange of notes for that purpose between the British Foreign Office and the American Ambassador. The note from the Foreign Office, under date of July 15, 1908, was as follows:

On the 18th ultimo Your Excellency proposed on behalf of the United States Government that, as arbitration in regard to the Newfoundland fisheries question could not be arranged before the forthcoming fishery season, the "modus vivendi" of last year should be renewed with the same elasticity as before for the parties concerned to make local arrangements satisfactory to both sides.

I have the honor to inform Your Excellency that the Newfoundland government, having been consulted on the subject, have expressed the desire that the herring fishery during the ensuing season should be conducted on the same principles as in the season of 1907, and formally undertake to permit during this year the conduct of the herring fishery as last year.

As the arrangements for last year were admittedly satisfactory to all concerned in the fishing, His Majesty's Government hope that the United States Government will see their way to accept this formal assurance on the part of the Newfoundland government as a satisfactory arrangement for the season of 1908. If this course be adopted it would seem unnecessary to enter into any further formal arrangements, seeing that the communication of this assurance to the United States Government and its acceptance by them would be tantamount to a modus vivendi.[a]

The note of the American Ambassador, under date of July 23, 1908, was as follows:

The reply, in your letter of July 15, 1908, to my proposal of June 18th, for a renewal of last year's modus vivendi for the approaching Newfoundland fisheries season, with the same elasticity as before for local arrangements, has been duly considered.

I am gratified to learn that the Newfoundland Government was so well satisfied with the result of these arrangements under the modus vivendi for last year that it offers a formal undertaking that the American fishermen shall be permitted to conduct the herring fisheries this year in the same way.

It is proper to observe that our fishermen would have preferred last year, and would prefer now to work the fisheries with purse seines, as heretofore, as provided in the modus vivendi. But they yielded last year to the strong wishes of the Newfoundland Government in this matter, and joined in the arrangement under the elastic clause at the close of the modus vivendi by which, with the approval of the British and American Governments, they gave up the use of purse seines in return for certain concessions. I must reserve their right to this use, as heretofore enjoyed, as not now abandoned, and

---

a Appendix, p. 49.

therefore to be duly considered in the pending arbitration before the Hague Tribunal.

But with this reservation and with the approval of my Government, I now have pleasure in accepting the offer that the herring fishery during the ensuing season shall be conducted on the same principles as in the season of 1907, and the formal undertaking against interference with this by the Newfoundland Government, as a substantial agreement on my proposal of June 18th.

We unite also with you in regarding this exchange of letters as constituting in itself a satisfactory agreement for the season of 1908, without the necessity for any further formal correspondence.

I am glad to add that Mr. Alexander of the United States Fish Commission, will be sent again this year to the treaty shore, and that my Government feels sure that, through his influence, there will be general willingness to carry out the spirit of the understanding, and work on the lines of least resistance.[a]

The purpose of the Order in Council of September 9, 1907.

It appears that after the *modus vivendi* of 1907 had been agreed upon between Great Britain and the United States some opposition to certain features of it developed in Newfoundland, and the Newfoundland Government finally refused to accept the *modus vivendi* and declined to put it into effect or be bound by its terms. In order, therefore, to give effect to this *modus vivendi* the British Government determined to pass an order in council for that purpose under section I of the act of 59 Geo. III., ch. 38, the position of the Government in the matter being stated in a telegram of September 9, 1907, from Lord Elgin to the Governor of Newfoundland as follows:

With reference to my telegram of 7th September, His Majesty's Government have had under their careful consideration the measures necessary to fulfil the undertaking given to the American Government in connection with *modus vivendi* that the shipping of Newfoundland fishermen by American vessels shall not be penalised. In doing so they are most anxious in no way to detract from your Government's control over Newfoundland fishermen, and they have, therefore, decided that it would be most satisfactory to pass an Order in Council under the Act 59, Geo. III., ch. 38, Section 1, which will forbid the serving of process on board any American vessel or arrest of any vessel or of its gear, &c. They consider that this Order, while ensuring to the Americans the undisturbed enjoyment of the fishery in accordance with the *modus vivendi*, will cause the least inconvenience to the Government of Newfoundland, as it merely gives legal sanction to the arrangement in force last year under which the fishery was conducted without serious disturbance or breach of the peace.

---

[a] Appendix p. 50.

His Majesty's Government invite the co-operation of your Government in carrying out the Order and have instructed the Senior Naval Officer on the station to render them every assistance in maintaining the law of the Colony as modified by the Order. They will be prepared to revoke or modify its provisions immediately a satisfactory arrangement is made by the Colonial Government with the American fishermen as contemplated in the *modus vivendi*, or the *modus vivendi* is accepted by your Government.

His Majesty's Government feel compelled, however, to place on record their deep regret that they should have had no alternative in consequence of the action of your Ministers but to avail themselves of the legal powers conferred on them by the Act 59 Geo. III.

His Majesty's Government recognise to the full the inconvenience caused to the Government of Newfoundland by the treaty obligations binding upon it, but these obligations were not created by His Majesty's Government, and in 1904 this country made no inconsiderable sacrifice of territory and money in order to reduce the pressure of French treaty rights. I may remind your Ministers that in this case the Government of Canada have, in order to meet their wishes, consented to share in the arbitration, although they have already obtained a friendly understanding with the United States. His Majesty's Government consider, therefore, that they were entitled to expect your Government's co-operation in arranging a new temporary *modus vivendi* pending the decision of the Arbitral Tribunal to which, in deference to your Government's wishes, the whole question is shortly to be referred.[a]

The order in council referred to in the above telegram is the same order which is discussed at page 74 of this Case, where it is shown that the act, under which it was made, authorizes the adoption of such orders "as shall or may be from time to time deemed proper and necessary for carrying into effect the purpose of said Convention [1818] with relation to the taking, drying and curing of fish by the inhabitants of the United States of America, in common with British subjects, within the limits set forth in the said Article of the said Convention and heretofore recited."

The promulgation of this order in council seems to have been temporarily postponed at the request of the Newfoundland Government, and on September 21, 1907, the Governor of Newfoundland telegraphed to Lord Elgin a *resumé* of a minute from his ministers, from which the following extract is taken:

Promulgation of Order in Council would practically destroy case of this Colony before the Hague Tribunal as furnishing argument that the law of Newfoundland is not binding on Americans. My responsible advisers refuse to accept any responsibility for Order in

---

[a] Appendix, p. 1018.

Council which cannot be with justice put on them. To assist His Majesty's Government ameliorate embarrassing position they proposed reference to Hague Tribunal, and also a temporary working arrangement to lawfully give Americans the privileges they had before this dispute. My responsible advisers cannot be parties to the *modus vivendi*, and they protest against the promulgation of the Order in Council. They are advised by Attorney-General and English Counsel that Order in Council is not operative against the law of the Colony. Order in Council cannot grant any new right or immunity. His Majesty's Government appear to overlook that my responsible advisers undertake to place Americans in precisely the same position as they occupied in 1905, thus making the *modus vivendi* and Order in Council unnecessary. Whether Order in Council is published or revoked, my responsible advisers will issue lawful authority to the local fishermen on the Treaty Coast to sell fish to Americans and others as heretofore, thus removing any possible grounds of complaint so far as Americans are concerned and at the same time upholding the law of this Colony.[a]

In reply to this telegram Lord Elgin telegraphed to the Governor of Newfoundland on September 23, 1907, as follows:

Your telegram 20th September. His Majesty's Government have received with great regret the refusal of your Ministers to cooperate in carrying out the *modus vivendi*, which leaves His Majesty's Government no alternative but definitely to instruct you to publish the Order in Council. This step should, therefore, be taken at once.

The points raised by your Ministers will be dealt with by despatch, but I think it right to warn them that His Majesty's Government cannot support them in any attempt to enforce the service of process on American vessels, and that the Senior Naval Officer on the Station has been so instructed.

While taking the necessary steps to promulgate and legalize the *modus vivendi*, you will understand that His Majesty's Government will gladly welcome any friendly arrangement which can be made to facilitate the fishery as between your Government and the American fishermen provided the pledges given by His Majesty's Government to the United States Government are fully safeguarded. Indeed, you may be able to suggest such an arrangement yourself, and your good offices would, no doubt, be greatly appreciated.[b]

Newfoundland's proposed new construction of the Treaty.

Although Great Britain has never by word or act, throughout the entire history of this controversy, questioned the right of the inhabitants of the United States under the treaty of 1818 to take fish in the bays and harbors on the southern and western coasts of Newfoundland, which form part of the so-called treaty coasts, and although such question has never been raised or even mentioned in any of the dis-

---

[a] Appendix, p. 1021.　　　　[b] Appendix, p. 1022.

cussions between the two Governments with respect to the interpretation of this treaty, which discussions, as shown by the foregoing review of this controversy, would seem to have covered every conceivable aspect of the case, and although the United States has always asserted the right of the American fishermen to take fish in the waters referred to, and American fishermen have ever since the treaty was made, openly exercised their right to take fish in these waters without objection or interference by the Newfoundland Government up to the present time, yet it appears that in 1907, when the arbitration of the fisheries controversy was under consideration between the Newfoundland and British Governments, the Government of Newfoundland proposed for the treaty a new interpretation which raises this question, and insisted that it should be included among the questions to be submitted for decision.[a] This question was first suggested by Sir Robert Bond, the premier of Newfoundland, in his speech delivered April 7, 1905, in the Legislative Assembly on the second reading of the Foreign Fishing-vessels Bill of 1905, from which speech the following extract is taken:

I desire to emphasize the statement that, in my opinion, the fishermen of the United States of America have no right, under the Treaty of 1818, either to take for themselves or to purchase bait fishes in the harbours, creeks, or coves between Cape Ray and Rameau Islands, on the southern coast of Newfoundland, or in the harbours, creeks, or coves between Cape Ray and Quirpon Islands, on the northern and western coast; and that the liberty extended to them under the Treaty of 1818 to take fish in the harbours, bays, and creeks of this Colony is limited to that portion of our dependency from Mount Joli, on the southern coast of Labrador, to and through the Straits of Belle Isle, and thence northwardly indefinitely. This is a point of vast importance to the people of this country. I believe I am correct in saying that it is the first time that this position has been taken, and, if I am correct in my interpretation of the Treaty of 1818, the whole winter herring fishery of the West Coast has been carried on for years by the Americans simply at the sufference of the Government of this Colony.[b]

This question was not called to the attention of the United States Government at that time, and no official notice of it was ever given to this Government until the negotiations for the Special Agreement, under which this arbitration is held, were actually undertaken, when this question, which afterwards became Question 6 of

---

[a] Appendix, p. 1013.
[b] British Blue Book, United States, No. 1 (1906), p. 54.

the questions submitted for decision, was proposed on the part of Great Britain.   The right to submit such question being secured to Great Britain under the general arbitration treaty of April 4, 1908, between Great Britain and the United States, pursuant to which the Special Agreement of January 27, 1909, was entered into, Great Britain introduced among the questions to be submitted Question 6 which arises out of this belated interpretation proposed by Newfoundland.

In the circumstances above set forth, the United States must reserve further discussion of Question 6 until it has been informed, as presumably will be done by the British Case, of the grounds upon which Great Britain supports its contention on that question.

STATEMENT IN CONCLUSION.

The United States, on the evidence herewith presented in the Case and Appendix thereto, and on the facts established thereby, claims that the questions referred for decision to the Tribunal, as set forth in Article I of the Special Agreement of January 27, 1909, should be answered and decided in accordance with the position taken by the United States with respect to the true intent and meaning of Article I of the treaty of 1818; and in order that such position may be clearly defined, it is stated below in the form of an answer to each of the questions submitted, and the United States requests that such questions be answered accordingly.

1. The position of the United States with reference to Question 1 is, as stated therein, that the exercise of the liberty to take fish, referred to in Article I of the treaty of 1818, which the inhabitants of the United States have forever in common with the subjects of His Britannic Majesty, is not subject to limitations or restraints by Great Britain, Canada, or Newfoundland in the form of municipal laws, ordinances, or regulations in respect of (1) the hours, days, or seasons when the inhabitants of the United States may take fish on the treaty coasts, or (2) the method, means, and implements used by them in taking fish or in carrying on fishing operations on such coasts, or (3) any other limitations or restraints of similar character—

(a) Unless they are appropriate and necessary for the protection and preservation of the common rights in such fisheries and the exercise thereof; and

(b) Unless they are reasonable in themselves and fair as between local fishermen and fishermen coming from the United States, and not so framed as to give an advantage to the former over the latter class; and

(c) Unless their appropriateness, necessity, reasonableness and fairness be determined by the United States and Great Britain by common accord and the United States concurs in their enforcement.

The United States requests the Tribunal to answer and decide that this contention on the part of the United States is wholly justified, and that the contention of Great Britain, stated in this Question, is without justification in so far as it is inconsistent with the contention of the United States.

2. The position of the United States on Question 2 is that the inhabitants of the United States have, while exercising the liberties referred to in the said Article, a right to employ as members of the fishing crews of their vessels, persons not inhabitants of the United States; and the United States requests the Tribunal to answer and decide this Question accordingly.

3. The position of the United States on Question 3 is that the exercise by the inhabitants of the United States of the liberties referred to in the said Article cannot be subjected, without the consent of the United States, to the requirements of entry or report at custom-houses or the payment of light or harbor or other dues, or to any other similar requirement or condition or exaction; and the United States requests the Tribunal to answer and decide this Question accordingly.

4. The position of the United States with reference to Question 4 is that under the provision of the said Article that the American fishermen shall be admitted to enter certain bays or harbors for shelter, repairs, wood, or water, and for no other purpose whatever, but that they shall be under such restrictions as may be necessary to prevent their taking, drying, or curing fish therein or in any other manner whatever abusing the privileges thereby reserved to them, it is not permissible to impose restrictions making the exercise of such privileges conditional upon the payment of light or harbor or other dues, or entering or reporting at custom-houses or any similar conditions; and the United States requests the Tribunal to answer and decide this Question accordingly.

5. The position of the United States with reference to Question 5 is that the distance of "three marine miles of any of the coasts, bays, creeks, or harbors" referred to in the said Article, must be measured from low water mark following the indentations of the coast; and the United States requests the Tribunal to answer and decide this Question accordingly.

6. The position of the United States with reference to Question 6 is that the inhabitants of the United States have the liberty under the said Article and otherwise, to take fish in the bays, harbors, and creeks

on that part of the southern coast of Newfoundland which extends from Cape Ray to Rameau Islands, and on the western and northern coasts of Newfoundland. from Cape Ray to Quirpon Islands, and on the Magdalen Islands; and the United States requests the Tribunal to answer and decide this Question accordingly.

7. The position of the United States with reference to Question 7 is that it is raised only in relation to the provisions of Article I of the treaty of 1818, which this Tribunal is called upon to interpret, and that, so far as such provisions bear upon the question, the inhabitants of the United States, whose vessels resort to the treaty coasts for the purpose of exercising the liberties referred to in Article I aforesaid, are entitled to have for those vessels, when duly authorized by the United States in that behalf, the commercial privileges on the treaty coasts accorded by agreement or otherwise to United States trading vessels generally; and the United States requests the Tribunal to answer and decide this Question accordingly.

CHANDLER P. ANDERSON,
Agent of the United States in the
North Atlantic Coast Fisheries Arbitration.

O

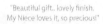

CPSIA information can be obtained
at www.ICGtesting.com
Printed in the USA
BVHW090054280819
556849BV00017B/2691/P